# America in Historical Fiction

# AMERICA IN HISTORICAL FICTION

*A Bibliographic Guide*

### Vandelia L. VanMeter
*Library Director*
*Professor*
*Spalding University*
*Louisville, Kentucky*

1997
LIBRARIES UNLIMITED, INC.
Englewood, Colorado

*For the Grandchildren*

———————

LIBRARIES UNLIMITED, INC.
P.O. Box 6633
Englewood, CO 80155-6633
1-800-237-6124

*Production Editor:* Kevin W. Perizzolo
*Copy Editor:* D. Aviva Rothschild
*Proofreader:* Susie Sigman
*Design and Layout:* Pamela J. Getchell

**Library of Congress Cataloging-in-Publication Data**

VanMeter, Vandelia.
    America in historical fiction : a bibliographic guide / Vandelia
L. VanMeter.
    xvi, 280 p. 17x25 cm.
    Includes indexes.
    ISBN 1-56308-496-1
    1. Historical fiction, American--Bibliography.   2. United States--
In literature--Bibliography.   3. America--In literature--
Bibliography.    I. Title.
    Z1231.F4V36
    [PS374.H5] 2998  1997
    016.813'081093273--DC20                               96-34745
                                                          CIP

# CONTENTS

Acknowledgments . . . . . . . . . . . . . . . . . . . . . . . . . ix

Introduction . . . . . . . . . . . . . . . . . . . . . . . . . . xiii

1 ♦ **The Age of Exploration and the Colonization of America,**
   **1492-1775** . . . . . . . . . . . . . . . . . . . . . . . . . . 1
   Exploration . . . . . . . . . . . . . . . . . . . . . . . . . . 1
   Colonial America . . . . . . . . . . . . . . . . . . . . . . . . 3

2 ♦ **The American Revolution: The War and Its Causes,**
   **1776-1783** . . . . . . . . . . . . . . . . . . . . . . . . . 13
   Events in the East . . . . . . . . . . . . . . . . . . . . . . . 13
   Events Along the Frontier . . . . . . . . . . . . . . . . . . . 21

3 ♦ **The Age of Expansion, 1783-1860** . . . . . . . . . . . . . 25
   Inclusive Titles . . . . . . . . . . . . . . . . . . . . . . . . 25
   Life in the Young Nation . . . . . . . . . . . . . . . . . . . . 27
      Eastern and Southern Living . . . . . . . . . . . . . . . . . 27
      The Midwest . . . . . . . . . . . . . . . . . . . . . . . . . 40
      The Plains and Mountain States . . . . . . . . . . . . . . . 44
      California and the Pacific Northwest . . . . . . . . . . . . 54

4 ♦ **The Civil War, 1861-1865** . . . . . . . . . . . . . . . . . 57

5 ♦ **The Expanding Frontier, 1866-1899** . . . . . . . . . . . . 73
   Eastern and Southern States . . . . . . . . . . . . . . . . . . 73
   The Plains, West, Southwest, and Pacific Northwest . . . . . . . 82

6 ♦ **Progressive Era, Twenties, and Depression, 1900-1939** . . . 101
   Inclusive Titles . . . . . . . . . . . . . . . . . . . . . . . 101
   Early Twentieth Century . . . . . . . . . . . . . . . . . . . . 103
   World War I . . . . . . . . . . . . . . . . . . . . . . . . . . 109
   The Twenties . . . . . . . . . . . . . . . . . . . . . . . . . 111
   The Thirties . . . . . . . . . . . . . . . . . . . . . . . . . 117

**7 ◆ World War II, 1939-1945** . . . . . . . . . . . . . . . . . . . . 127
  Inclusive Titles . . . . . . . . . . . . . . . . . . . . . . 127
  At Home . . . . . . . . . . . . . . . . . . . . . . . . . 128
  Military Personnel Stateside . . . . . . . . . . . . . . . . . . 131
  European Theater . . . . . . . . . . . . . . . . . . . . . . . 132
  Pacific Theater . . . . . . . . . . . . . . . . . . . . . . . 135

**8 ◆ The Late Twentieth Century, 1945-1995** . . . . . . . . . . . 141
  1945-1962 (Including the Korean War) . . . . . . . . . . . . . . . 141
  1963-1995 (Including the Vietnam War) . . . . . . . . . . . . . . 149

**9 ◆ Epic Novels** . . . . . . . . . . . . . . . . . . . . . . . . . . 159

**10 ◆ Additional Titles** . . . . . . . . . . . . . . . . . . . . . . 171
  Alabama . . . . . . . . . . . . . . . . . . . . . . . . . . 171
  Alaska . . . . . . . . . . . . . . . . . . . . . . . . . . . 171
  Arizona . . . . . . . . . . . . . . . . . . . . . . . . . . . 172
  Arkansas . . . . . . . . . . . . . . . . . . . . . . . . . . 173
  California . . . . . . . . . . . . . . . . . . . . . . . . . . 173
  Colorado . . . . . . . . . . . . . . . . . . . . . . . . . . 174
  Connecticut . . . . . . . . . . . . . . . . . . . . . . . . . 174
  Florida . . . . . . . . . . . . . . . . . . . . . . . . . . . 175
  Georgia . . . . . . . . . . . . . . . . . . . . . . . . . . . 175
  Hawaii . . . . . . . . . . . . . . . . . . . . . . . . . . . 175
  Idaho . . . . . . . . . . . . . . . . . . . . . . . . . . . . 176
  Illinois . . . . . . . . . . . . . . . . . . . . . . . . . . . 176
  Indiana . . . . . . . . . . . . . . . . . . . . . . . . . . . 177
  Iowa . . . . . . . . . . . . . . . . . . . . . . . . . . . . 177
  Kansas . . . . . . . . . . . . . . . . . . . . . . . . . . . 178
  Kentucky . . . . . . . . . . . . . . . . . . . . . . . . . . 178
  Louisiana . . . . . . . . . . . . . . . . . . . . . . . . . . 179
  Maine . . . . . . . . . . . . . . . . . . . . . . . . . . . 180
  Massachusetts . . . . . . . . . . . . . . . . . . . . . . . . 180
  Michigan . . . . . . . . . . . . . . . . . . . . . . . . . . 180
  Minnesota . . . . . . . . . . . . . . . . . . . . . . . . . 182
  Mississippi . . . . . . . . . . . . . . . . . . . . . . . . . 182
  Missouri . . . . . . . . . . . . . . . . . . . . . . . . . . 182
  Montana . . . . . . . . . . . . . . . . . . . . . . . . . . 183
  Nebraska . . . . . . . . . . . . . . . . . . . . . . . . . . 183
  Nevada . . . . . . . . . . . . . . . . . . . . . . . . . . . 184
  New Hampshire . . . . . . . . . . . . . . . . . . . . . . . 184
  New Mexico . . . . . . . . . . . . . . . . . . . . . . . . . 185
  New York . . . . . . . . . . . . . . . . . . . . . . . . . . 187
  North Carolina . . . . . . . . . . . . . . . . . . . . . . . . 188
  North Dakota . . . . . . . . . . . . . . . . . . . . . . . . 188
  Ohio . . . . . . . . . . . . . . . . . . . . . . . . . . . . 188

Oklahoma . . . . . . . . . . . . . . . . . . . . . . . . . . . . . . . . . . . 189
Oregon . . . . . . . . . . . . . . . . . . . . . . . . . . . . . . . . . . . . . 189
Pennsylvania . . . . . . . . . . . . . . . . . . . . . . . . . . . . . . . . 189
South Carolina . . . . . . . . . . . . . . . . . . . . . . . . . . . . . . 190
South Dakota . . . . . . . . . . . . . . . . . . . . . . . . . . . . . . . 190
Tennessee . . . . . . . . . . . . . . . . . . . . . . . . . . . . . . . . . . 191
Texas . . . . . . . . . . . . . . . . . . . . . . . . . . . . . . . . . . . . . . 192
Utah . . . . . . . . . . . . . . . . . . . . . . . . . . . . . . . . . . . . . . 193
Vermont . . . . . . . . . . . . . . . . . . . . . . . . . . . . . . . . . . . 193
Virginia . . . . . . . . . . . . . . . . . . . . . . . . . . . . . . . . . . . 193
Washington . . . . . . . . . . . . . . . . . . . . . . . . . . . . . . . . . 194
West Virginia . . . . . . . . . . . . . . . . . . . . . . . . . . . . . . . 194
Wisconsin . . . . . . . . . . . . . . . . . . . . . . . . . . . . . . . . . . 194
Wyoming . . . . . . . . . . . . . . . . . . . . . . . . . . . . . . . . . . 195

**Author Index** . . . . . . . . . . . . . . . . . . . . . . . . . . . . . 197
**Title Index** . . . . . . . . . . . . . . . . . . . . . . . . . . . . . . . 219
**Subject Index** . . . . . . . . . . . . . . . . . . . . . . . . . . . . 237

# ACKNOWLEDGMENTS

Many persons responded with great generosity to letters asking for information concerning books appropriate for this work, and I am pleased to thank them publicly for their assistance.

Barry L. Buford, of the Alabama State Department of Education, suggested titles and sent the State-Adopted Textbook List. The Alaska Department of Education sent a fine work titled *Common Ground 1989: Suggested Literature for Alaskan Schools Grades 7-12*. Bob Razer of the Central Arkansas Library System sent a helpful list (based on his book review column) that concerns materials about Arkansas. Maxine Lewis of the Arkansas State Department of Education sent a list of recommended textbooks and information about publishers of books on Arkansas; Sharon Murray at Dover, Perry Lewis at Alma High School, and D'Anne Easton at Conway also suggested Arkansas titles.

Californians who were particularly helpful are Rodney Atkinson at the California Department of Education, R. A. Reinstedt of Ghost Town Publications, and Janis Schuett at the Sacramento Public Library. Judith D. King of the Hartford (Connecticut) Public Library and Maureen K. Crocker of the Colorado Department of Education were generous in sending useful suggestions.

Ideas for books about Delaware were sent by Jack G. Nichols from the Department of Public Instruction and Sue Gooden of the Concord High School Library. Edith Belden of the Georgia Department of Education, William J. Wilson and Diane Osgood Broome of the Boise (Idaho) Public Library, A. M. Hubbs of the Illinois State Library, and Ann M. Hobbs of the Lincoln Library in Springfield, Illinois all responded with beneficial lists.

Suggestions concerning materials about Indiana were received from Roberta Adamson at North Posey High School, Elizabeth Crawford of the Indianapolis-Marion County Public Library, and Jacqueline G. Morris of the Indiana Department of Education. Joyce Misner of the Allen County Public Library in Fort Wayne, Indiana also sent suggestions. Mary Jo Bruett of the Iowa Department of Education and Jan Leise of Lincoln High School in Des Moines provided titles of books about Iowa.

Kansas titles were suggested by Thomas F. Averill of Washburn University and Warren E. Taylor of the Topeka and Shawnee County Public Library. In addition to the many helpful suggestions about Kentucky books that I received from my colleagues and friends, Thomas H. Appleton, Jr. of the Kentucky Historical Society, James Gifford of the Jesse Stuart Foundation, and Sandy Barts of the University Press of Kentucky were generous with their assistance. Responses were also received from Virginia R. Smith of the State Library of Louisiana, Catherine Clancy of the Boston (Massachusetts) Public Library, Barbara C. Danielson of the Lansing (Michigan) Public Library, and Judy Hood of the Michigan Department of Education. The *Checklist of Michigan Authors and Poets* proved to be very serviceable.

Ideas for titles about Minnesota came from Helen Fleming of the City of Saint Paul Public Library and Mary S. Pfeifer of the Minnesota Department of Education. Otis Baker of the Missouri Department of Elementary & Secondary Education sent a list, and suggestions came from Cheri Bergeron of the Montana Office of Public Instruction. Rex L. Filmer of the Nebraska Department of Education and Laura Lacy of the Bennett Martin Public Library in Lincoln sent Nebraska information. Generous assistance in identifying works about Nevada was supplied by Jane Brookey of the Pershing County School District in Lovelock, Marilyn Grosshans of the Las Vegas High School Library, and Pat Ferraro Klos, another Nevada high school librarian. I am ashamed to admit that I have misplaced Pat's location, for the list that she sent was extraordinarily thorough.

Ideas concerning fiction about New Hampshire came from Sandi Jarmak at the City of Concord Library and Diane Suite at Memorial High School Library, Manchester. Special thanks go to Joseph D. Baca of Santa Fe, who called several times and sent a multipage annotated list and a computer disk for my use. His courtesy, enthusiasm, and encouragement were much appreciated.

Susan Pahlmeyer of the North Dakota State Library sent a list, as did Cheryl Chernis of the Ohioana Library Association, Columbus. A very thorough list was received from the Oklahoma State Department of Education, and suggestions about Rhode Island books were received from Elizabeth Fitzgerald of the Providence Public Library and L. Wood of the South Kingstown High School Library. Pennsylvania was represented by Melba Tomeo of Slippery Rock. Jennifer F. Walker of the Richland County (South Carolina) Public Library sent title suggestions. Two excellent bibliographies about South Dakota were received from Donna Gilliland of the South Dakota Department of Education and Cultural Affairs. Katharine Bruner of Brown Middle School in Harrison, Mary Glenn Hearne of the Ben West Library in Nashville, and Edna Major from Murfreesboro sent suggestions about Tennessee books. Lawrence L. Richard of the Texas Education Agency sent a number of items that proved beneficial, and Linda Gentry of Highland High School in Salt Lake City sent a list of books about Utah and U.S. historical fiction that are enjoyed by her students.

Leda Schubert of the Vermont Department of Education sent *Green Mountain Sampler*, an extended bibliography. Information about Virginia was received from Harry L. Smith of the Department of Education, Catherine Mishler of the Virginia State Library and Archives, and the Richmond Public Library. Vince Kueter of the Washington State Library outdid himself by sending a three-inch thick packet of bibliographies concerning Washington and the Northwest. Thanks, Vince. Also received was a fine bibliography compiled by Eileen Andersen of the Sehome (Washington) High School Library.

Information concerning titles about Washington, D.C. was received from Cornelia R. Stokes of the Historical Society of Washington, D.C. and from Shelia G. Handy of the District of Columbia School District. Susan H. Harper, of the Kanawha County Public Libraries in Charleston, prepared a bibliography of West Virginia titles at my request, even checking to be certain the titles were in print. Assistance about Wisconsin books was received from Marianne Scheele of the Wisconsin Department of Public Instruction, Jerry Minnich of Prairie Oak Press, Mary Knapp of the Madison Public Library, and Jack Holzhueter of the State Historical Society. And finally, thanks go to Esther Rickelton of the King County (Washington) Library System for answering an Internet query about a troublesome title.

Thanks to everyone for your generous assistance and helpful suggestions. This project is more complete than it ever could have been without your kindness.

Also, it must be admitted that, without the generous support, tactful suggestions, and able editorial eye of my secretary, Gloria Edwards, this work might never have been completed. She is due much appreciation, and I am happy to acknowledge her valuable contribution.

Experience shows that even with the utmost effort and most excellent assistance, errors creep into a work of this type. For those, I accept full responsibility, and I apologize to the reader for any inconvenience.

# INTRODUCTION

Any reference work designed to serve the needs of secondary history classes should support the National Standards for United States History, which are explained in *National Standards for United States History: Exploring the American Experience: Grades 5-12 Expanded Edition*, developed by the National Council for History. The value of *America in Historical Fiction* is that it directly meets a need expressed in Chapter 1 of the *National Standards*:

> Through social history, students come to deeper understandings of society: of what it means to be human, of different and changing views of family structures, of men's and women's role, of childhood and of children's roles, of various groups and classes in society, and of relationships among all these individuals and groups. This sphere considers how economic, religious, cultural, and political changes have affected social life, and it incorporates developments shaping the destiny of millions: the history of slavery; of class conflict; of mass migration and immigration; the human consequences of plague, war, and famine; and the longer life expectancy and rising living standards following upon medical, technological and economic advances. (*National Standards for United States History: Exploring the American Experience: Grades 5-12 Expanded Edition*, p. 5)

The *Standards* continue with discussions of the importance of understanding political history, the history of science and technology, economic history, and cultural history. The section concludes by emphasizing the critical need to consider these topics in context, both in historical time and in geographic place, and to understand how these ideas are interwoven—how religious, philosophical, or political ideas may support (or be in competition with) the economic interests or social values of an individual or group.

Throughout *National Standards* are examples of student achievement for each Standard. Reading through these, one notes how many of these examples are related to social life and customs; gender, racial, and ethnic concerns; and respect for individualism. In examining titles to be included in *America in Historical Fiction*, these issues received particular attention and careful indexing. Of the 1,168 titles annotated in *America in Historical Fiction*, more than 500 received Social Life and Customs as a subject heading, subdivided according to geographic region or time period. More than 75 are indexed that relate to slaves and slavery or post-Civil War African Americans, more than 100 to women, more than 80 to immigrants and immigration (subdivided by home nation) or ethnic groups, and more than 100 to Native Americans. Other topics, such as medicine, racism, laborers and labor unions, witchcraft, and frontier and pioneer life, are also indexed.

Anyone interested in the role of historical fiction in developing an understanding of our nation's past will ask whether that fiction is adequately based upon research according to the National Council's Standards, and whether it encourages the integration of historical understanding—chronological thinking, historical comprehension, research, analysis, and interpretation. This author contends that well-written and well-researched fiction can not only support a study of history, but can enhance it as well. Insofar as possible, information related to the research base of the titles included in *America in Historical Fiction* is indicated in the annotation. Books that use a historic setting as incidental to the story are not included.

*America in Historical Fiction* is intended to serve secondary students and adults who seek either classic or contemporary fiction dealing with the history of the United States. The chapters are arranged to reflect the major chronological divisions of U.S. history. In addition to the chronological chapters, a chapter is included that provides annotations for epic novels and a chapter of additional titles arranged by state name.

Each entry within the chronologically arranged chapters and the chapter of epic novels includes normal bibliographic information: author, title, original publisher and date, current publisher and date, ISBN, and cost. If the title has three or more editions in print, the notation "several editions available" is included. If one publisher has two editions of a title available, the dates, ISBNs, and prices for both are given; the name of the publisher is not repeated if the "publisher identification" portion of the ISBN is the same for both. All titles included were listed as in-print in either the 1993-1994 or 1994-1995 editions of *Books in Print*, or in *Forthcoming Books* of 1994-1995 or 1995-1996.

Also included in each entry is the time period of the setting and an annotation that indicates the subject matter, location, research base (if known), and, where suitable, whether the title is appropriate for mature students or younger secondary students. Items designated for younger students generally have a lower reading level and a simpler-than-usual story line. Items designated for mature students are apt to be so designated because of their complexity rather than because of concerns about language or questionable content, although these issues may also be characteristic of that work. Reviews of these books are widely available; interested readers who have concerns about suitability should check those reviews or examine the books themselves. Where the information was available, prequels and sequels are identified, even if those are out-of-print. If an annotation states that a title is lengthy, that novel exceeds 600 pages.

Within the Additional Titles chapter, all basic bibliographic information is included, along with the time of setting and enough subject headings to give the user a general sense of the book topic.

## CRITERIA FOR SELECTION

To select the titles included in this work, many sources were examined, including:

Abrahamson, Richard F., Betty Carter, and the Committee on the Senior High School Booklist. *Books for You: A Booklist for Senior High Students*. 10th ed. National Council of Teachers of English, 1988.

Applebee, Arthur N. *A Study of Book-Length Works Taught in High School English Courses*. State University of New York, 1989.

*Fiction Catalog.* H. W. Wilson, 1941. 12th ed., 1991.

Gerhardstein, Virginia B. *Dickinson's American Historical Fiction.* 5th ed. Scarecrow Press, 1986.

Gillespie, John T. *The Senior High School Paperback Collection.* American Library Association, 1986.

Howard, Elizabeth F. *America as Story: Historical Fiction for Secondary Schools.* American Library Association, 1988.

Kirk, Ersye. *The Black Experience in Books for Children and Young Adults.* Positive Impact, 1993.

*Masterplots II: Juvenile and Young Adult Fiction Series.* Salem Press, 1991.

National Council of Teachers of English. Committee on Women in the Profession. *Guidelines for a Gender-Balanced Curriculum in English Grades 7-12,* n.d.

*National Standards for United States History: Exploring the American Experience: Grades 5-12 Expanded Edition.* National Center for History in the Schools, 1994.

*Senior High School Library Catalog.* 14th ed. H. W. Wilson, 1992.

Stotsky, Sandra, and Philip Anderson. *Variety and Individualism in the English Class: Teacher-Recommended Lists of Reading for Grades 7-12.* New England Association of Teachers of English, n.d.

VanMeter, Vandelia. *American History for Children and Young Adults.* Englewood, CO: Libraries Unlimited, 1990.

Titles too recent to appear in bibliographies such as these were identified, and annotations were verified, by examination of the books themselves and through reviews in such publications as *Book Report, Booklist, Library Journal, New York Times Book Reviews, Publishers Weekly, School Library Journal,* and *Voice of Youth Advocates.*

To identify titles of interest concerning the history of a particular state, queries were sent to the state department of education and to the state library in every state. Public libraries of many major cities were also asked for suggestions. To assist in the selection, I wrote to librarians in two school libraries (one small and one large, randomly chosen) in every state, asking them to suggest books about their state, and for recommendations of U.S. historical fiction in general. Many of these individuals responded graciously and sent excellent ideas that were incorporated within this work. Finally, an appeal was sent through LM_Net on the Internet for assistance in identifying titles about several states that seemed to be underrepresented.

All books included have been recommended in at least one, and usually in several, normal review sources. Attention was paid to comments concerning the success of the author in providing authentic period detail. No short story collections are included.

Items cover the history of the nation from 1492 to 1995. Items about historic events that predate Columbus's voyage are not included; items of this nature, as well as works specifically about Native American culture, fall within the scope of books that focus on those topics.

In correspondence with librarians in the various states, there were several suggestions that out-of-print items should be included. The decision to focus only on items that are in-print at the time this work was being compiled was made with the understanding that many excellent out-of-print titles are available in libraries, and that any list of in-print items will soon need updating. The reason for using "in-print" as a selection criteria was simply to have an objective way to limit what is included. Any attempt to include all the recommended books on U.S. history that have been published would result in a work of many volumes, and is outside the scope of this work. Rather, two factors enter into the selection of those included: either an older book has proven to be of such value that it remains in print, or the title is relatively current.

# *ARRANGEMENT*

In the primary portion of this work, entries are arranged under broad chronological headings that are compatible with those used in *Sears List of Subject Headings*. Subdivisions within those broad headings were determined according to the prime thrust of events within that time period, and are explained at the beginning of each chapter.

All items are indexed by author and title. Where action takes place primarily within a state, that state is indexed; action taking place within a territory that later became a state is identified by the state name; where necessary, regional names are used to allow further access (e.g., Mississippi River). Additional indexing is by names of persons, events, and broad subjects addressed in the books (e.g., Esther Forbes's *Johnny Tremain* may be located in the index under Revere, Paul; Massachusetts; Apprentices; and Politics and Government—1776-1783). Such thorough indexing is intended to help users access items in many ways.

The terms "Native Americans" and "Indians" are used interchangeably in annotations; the term "Indians of North America" is used in the index, with subdivisions by specific Native American nations wherever possible. The terms "Black" and "African American" are used interchangeably in annotations; the term "African Americans" is used in the index.

# Chapter 1

# The Age of Exploration and the Colonization of America, 1492-1775

For the convenience of the reader, entries in this chapter are divided into the following categories:

♦ Exploration

♦ Colonial America

## EXPLORATION

1.   Barreiro, Jose. **The Indian Chronicles**. Arte Publico Press, 1993. (1-55885-067- M&U
8) text ed. $19.95. « Time: ca. 1490s.
     The author tells of the Native American reaction to the early days of Columbus's exploration in the New World, as the natives came to understand the acquisitive nature of the newcomers. This serious work is based upon a script purportedly written by Diego Colon, a Taino Indian who became Columbus's adopted son and interpreted for him. *Indian Chronicles*, written by a published historian of Taino descent, will appeal to mature readers.

2.   Costain, Thomas B. **High Towers**. Doubleday, 1949. (0-385-04194-2) $6.95. « CC
Time: 1697- .
     The LeMoyne family is noted for their attempts at establishing a French empire in America. Costain's novel of high adventure follows their life in Montreal, their exploration of the Mississippi, and the founding of New Orleans and Mobile.

3.   Cross, Ruth. **Soldier of Good Fortune**. Banks Upshaw, 1936. Pelican, 1936. (0-88289-287-8) $12.50. « Time: 1715.
     French cavalier and explorer Louis Juchereau de St. Denis went on a trading expedition into Texas and Mexico for the French colony at Mobile. This appealing tale is based on his adventures.

1

4. DiPerna, Paula. **The Discoveries of Mrs. Christopher Columbus: His Wife's Version**. Permanent Press, 1994. (1-877946-48-6) $22.00. « Time: ca. early 1490s.

Rich with historical detail, DiPerna's romantic adventure is based on the idea that Felipa, Columbus's wife, was responsible for the idea to sail west. The tale, which traces the difficulties of promoting the idea, assembling the ships and crew, and the actual voyage, is told by Felipa.

*cc*

5. Forester, C. S. **To the Indies**. Little, Brown, 1940. Repr. Amereon, n.d. (0-88411-926-2) Lib Bdg $17.95. « Time: 1498-1499.

This engrossing swashbuckler features Narciso Rich, a successful attorney who is sent by King Ferdinand to accompany Columbus on his third voyage to investigate the Viceroy's administration of the new lands. Fights with natives and a crocodile, a shipwreck, and a kidnapping are part of the action in a novel that presents a good view of the time, place, and values of the people.

6. Frohlich, Newton. **1492**. St. Martin's Press, 1990. (0-312-05041-0) $19.95. Dorchester, 1991. (0-8439-3196-5) Pb $4.99. « Time: 1475-1492.

This well-researched account spans the 15 years before the first Columbus voyage. It reveals the social and political climate in Spain at the time, including the wars between the Spaniards and the Arabs, and the cruel efforts of the Inquisition to remove all Jews from Spain.

7. Garland, Sherry. **Indio**. Harcourt Brace, 1995. (0-15-238631-9) $11.00. (0-15-200021-6) Pb $5.00. « Time: Late 1500s.

When the Spanish conquistadors attack, Ipa-tah-chi and the other members of the Jumanos village must adjust to a new reality that includes slavery, forced labor in silver mines, and devastating disease brought by the invaders. Garland set this revealing story in the region that became Texas and provides a fine view of life under an occupying force. Suitable for younger secondary students, this story is filled with many realistic details about daily life.

8. Lytle, Andrew. **At the Moon's Inn: A Novel About the De Soto Expedition**. Bobbs-Merrill, 1941. Univ. of Alabama Press, 1990. (0-8173-0511-4) Pb $18.95. « Time: ca. 1540.

Hernando De Soto was a Spanish conquistador and explorer who discovered the Mississippi River in 1541 after he played a prominent part in the conquest of Peru. Lytle's colorful novel portrays his life well, with a fine feeling for time and place, and clearly shows the courage, ambition, religious conviction, and greed of the conquistadors.

9. O'Dell, Scott. **King's Fifth**. Houghton Mifflin, 1966. (0-395-06963-7) $14.45. « Time: ca. 1540.

Esteban, a map maker, accompanies six members of Coronado's army who are looking for the legendary Seven Cities of Gold in the area between Mexico and the Grand Canyon. In a well-researched, well-written, believable, and dramatic story, O'Dell pits white men against red and Spaniard against Spaniard. Suitable for younger secondary students.

10. Roberts, Kenneth L. **Northwest Passage**. Doubleday, 1937. Fawcett, 1986. (0-449-21383-8) Pb $4.95. « Time: 1759-1780.

The central figure of this novel is American ranger and Indian fighter Major Robert Rogers, whose dream was to find an overland passage to the Pacific. His expeditions range over most of the American frontier, but northern New York and Michigan see most of the action. The narrator is Langdon Towne, whose ambition was to paint the Indians as they really looked. The author's account of Rogers's life and adventures has become a classic.

# COLONIAL AMERICA

11. Barth, John. **The Sot-Weed Factor**. Doubleday, 1960, 1987. (0-385-24088-0) Pb $11.95. « Time: Late 1600s.

Written in the style of eighteenth-century novelists, this lengthy tale satirizes other historical fiction as it examines life in colonial Maryland and England through the adventures of would-be scholar and poet Ebenezer Cooke, his twin sister, and their tutor. The book also provides a different version of the John Smith/Pocahontas story. Suitable for mature readers who appreciate complex irony.

12. Bernhard, Virginia. **A Durable Fire**. Morrow, 1990. (0-688-08900-3) $22.95. Avon, 1991. (0-380-70873-6) Pb $4.95. « Time: 1602.

Based on the writings of John Smith and other Jamestown settlers, this is a realistic account of the cold, hunger, disease, boredom, and poor management that the newcomers faced, along with the threat of massacre. Bernhard tells the Jamestown story through the struggles of Temperance Yardley.

13. Bigsby, Christopher. **Hester**. Viking, 1994. (0-670-85588-X) $21.95. « Time: Mid-1600s.

Nathaniel Hawthorne's *Scarlet Letter* concerns the life of Hester Prynne, condemned to wear a scarlet letter because of her adultery. Bigsby's *Hester* tells her story before the events in Hawthorne's novel. The reader sees her husband's eccentric behavior before the fateful voyage and the tragic chain of events that led to the birth of Hester's child. Bigsby explores the inner battles of the characters in an appropriate gothic style.

14. Cannon, LeGrand. **Look to the Mountain**. Holt, 1942. Countryman, 1991. (0-88150-215-4) Pb $5.95. « Time: 1769-1777.

This lengthy novel centers around a young bride and groom who leave the settlements to make their home on the New Hampshire frontier just before the American Revolution. The book was highly acclaimed when it was first published for the vividness of its characters, the richness of its story, and the quality of the research upon which it was based.

15. Clapp, Patricia. **Witches' Children: A Story of Salem**. Lothrop, 1982. Peter Smith, 1992. (0-8446-6572-X) $17.00. Puffin, 1987. (0-14-032407-0) Pb $4.99. « Time: 1692.

Using a first-person narrative, Clapp presents a compelling account of how superstition, boredom, and hysteria combined to create a massive witch hunt in Salem, Massachusetts, that resulted in the deaths of 19 persons. Recommended for younger secondary students.

16. Coldsmith, Don. **Return of the Spanish**. Doubleday, 1991. (0-385-26302-3) $15.00. « Time: 1720.

To limit the influence of the French along the Mississippi river, the Spanish send out an expedition to capture Indians allied with the French. The result is a massacre by the Pawnee. A young Spanish captive is a slave at first, but later marries into the Pawnee tribe. This is the eighteenth novel in the popular Spanish Bit series that chronicles early contact between Native Americans and white settlers and explorers.

17. Conde, Maryse. **I, Tituba, Black Witch of Salem**. University Press of Virginia, 1992. (0-8139-1398-5) $19.95. « Time: 1680s-1690s.

Tituba is born a slave on Barbados. After seeing her mother executed, she is raised by a woman who teaches her the African arts, including communicating with spirits and healing. When her Puritan master moves to Massachusetts, Tituba uses her powers to help her owners, but finds herself misunderstood and feared.

18. Cooper, James Fenimore. **The Deerslayer**. Scribner, 1841. Several editions available. « Time: 1744.

Natty Bumppo is a young hunter brought up among the Delaware Indians. This lengthy story of his adventures is set around New York's Lake Oswego during King George's War; it concerns warfare between the Iroquois Indians and white settlers. This is the first of the Leatherstocking tales; it is followed by *The Pathfinder*.

19. Cooper, James Fenimore. **The Last of the Mohicans**. Scribner, 1826. Several editions available. « Time: ca. 1760.

Two sisters trying to reach their father, the commander at Fort William Henry, travel through rugged terrain. They are led astray by a treacherous Huron Indian but are befriended by Hawkeye Bumppo and his Mohican friend. The wilderness area around Lake George, New York, is the setting for this story of the French and Indian Wars. Followed by *The Pioneers*.

20. Cooper, James Fenimore. **The Pathfinder**. Dodd, 1840. Several editions available. « Time: ca. 1760.

Natty Bumppo is now middle-aged. A small outpost near Lake Ontario is under attack, but, in a story of high adventure and romance, Pathfinder (Bumppo) and his friends save the day. Followed by *The Last of the Mohicans*.

21. Cooper, James Fenimore. **The Red Rover**. Putnam, 1827. Several editions available. « Time: 1759.

Impressive seamanship and daring adventure provide lively reading in Cooper's tale of a pirate who dreams of American independence and eventually fights for his country during the Revolution. The subplot about Henry Wilder, the long-lost son of the pirate's estranged sister, provides romance and mystery.

22. Donnell, Susan. **Pocahontas**. Berkeley, 1991. (0-425-12617-X). Pb $8.95. « Time: ca. 1616.

A descendant of Pocahontas tells, from the Native American point of view, an action-filled adventure filled with information about Powhatan culture and ways in which the Native Americans helped Jamestown settlers survive.

23. Elliott, Edward E. **The Devil and the Mathers**. Strawberry Hill, 1989. (0-89407-142-4) $16.95. (0-89407-095-9) Pb $9.95. « Time: 1692.

When a group of girls accuse a West Indian servant of sorcery, overzealous religious leaders fuel the fires of superstition that lead to the Salem witchcraft trials. Careful research underlies Elliott's account of events that occurred because there was no place for any but the most orthodox religious thought.

24. Fletcher, Inglis. **Bennet's Welcome**. Bobbs, 1950. Repr. Queens House, 1976. (0-89244-001-5) Lib Bdg $21.95. Repr. Buccaneer Books, 1990. (0-89968-503-X) Lib Bdg $25.95. « Time: Early 1650s.

Richard Monington, who supported Charles I in a losing cause, is sent to Virginia and indentured to a tobacco planter, but within a year he takes his place as a gentleman among the colonists, loyal to the king. This well-researched and dramatic story of the first permanent English settlement in North Carolina shows the author's grasp of complex historical events.

25. Fletcher, Inglis. **Cormorant's Brood**. Lippincott, 1959. Repr. Queens House, 1976. (0-89244-002-3) Lib Bdg $21.95. « Time: 1725-1729.

Fletcher tells of the struggle of colonists to wrest political power from George Burrington, an unscrupulous royal governor (cormorant) in the Albemarle region of North Carolina. A parallel story is of the romance of the governess of the Burrington children. Thus, both political and cultural events of the time and place are included.

26. Fletcher, Inglis. **Lusty Wind for Carolina**. Bobbs, 1944. Several editions available. « Time: 1718-1725.

Among the Huguenots founding a settlement on the Cape Fear River after the Peace of Utrecht (1713) are the daughter of a weaver, a king's officer in disguise, and a beautiful woman pirate. High adventure and romance are woven together in this carefully researched novel that shows the dangers threatening early plantation owners in North Carolina.

27. Fletcher, Inglis. **Men of Albemarle**. Bobbs, 1942. Bantam, 1986. (0-553-25670-X) Pb $4.50. Repr. Buccaneer Books, 1990. (0-89968-505-6) Lib Bdg $27.95. « Time: 1710-1712.

The significance of this novel is its presentation of the struggles of the new colonists to develop the principles of justice and freedom upon which later American society was built. Among the chief characters in this story of settlers in colonial North Carolina are Lady Mary Tower, with her worn Stuart tartan; her ward, the lovely Marita; and Roger Mainwaring, lord of the estate called Queen's Gift.

28. Fletcher, Inglis. **Roanoke Hundred**. Bobbs, 1948. Repr. Queens House, 1976. (0-89244-007-4) Lib Bdg $21.95. Repr. Buccaneer Books, 1990. (0-89968-507-2) Lib Bdg $26.95. « Time ca. 1585-1586.

Roanoke Island was the site of the first British settlement in America. Sir Richard Grenville, Sir Walter Raleigh, and other settlers appear in this first part of the author's series on North Carolina history, which also pictures English life in the court of Queen Elizabeth and in the countryside.

29.  Follett, Ken. **A Place Called Freedom**. Random/Crown, 1995. (0-517-70176-6) $25.00. Random, 1995. (0-679-76509-3) Pb large print ed. $24.00. « Time: 1767-1773.

Mack McAsh is a coal miner in Scotland, where living and working conditions are abysmal. Yearning to be free, he becomes troublesome to his employer and is publicly humiliated. He flees to London and then to the American colonies. His story presents a fine view of eighteenth-century living conditions for working people and the struggles of new immigrants.

30.  Forbes, Esther. **A Mirror for Witches**. Houghton, 1928. Amereon, n.d. (0-8488-0050-8) $18.95. Academy Chicago Publishing, 1985. (0-89733-154-0) Pb $9.00. « Time: 1690s.

In England, Doll witnesses the execution of her parents, who were accused of witchcraft. Rescued by a sea captain, she is then taken to Massachusetts. Hated by a foster mother determined to brand her as a witch, and driven by her own fears, Doll's actions result in her trial for witchcraft. This highly acclaimed work retains the flavor of the seventeenth century.

31.  Gear, Kathleen O'Neal. **This Widowed Land**. Tor, 1991. (0-8125-8307-8) Pb $4.99. Tor Books, 1993. (0-312-85464-1) $21.95. « Time: 1636.

When three Jesuit priests arrive in New France charged with converting the Hurons, they follow the Jesuit practice of grafting Christian belief onto native customs. Disease, power struggles, and strongly conflicting cultural norms set the stage for turmoil among the priests and between them and the Hurons. The tale is well researched and realistically told from the perspectives of both the Huron and the missionaries. For mature readers.

32.  Gilman, Dorothy Butters. **Girl in Buckskin**. Macrae Smith, 1957. Fawcett, 1990. (0-449-70380-0) Pb $3.50. « Time: 1703.

Sixteen-year-old indentured servant Rebecca Pumroy, an orphan, is afraid that marriage to an older man will be forced upon her. She and her brother Eseck, who knows the way of the wilderness, flee into Indian territory. Becky expects that the natives will be her enemy, but Eseck teaches her how to live as an Indian. Suited for younger secondary students.

33.  Hawthorne, Nathaniel. **The Scarlet Letter**. Tichnor, 1850. Several editions available. « Time: Mid-1600s.

For the sin of committing adultery, Hester Prynne is forced by her community to wear a scarlet "A" and is shunned by most of the townspeople. When her cuckolded husband unexpectedly returns, he sets out to ruin the life of the adulterer. Hester's life is constrained by the necessity of raising her daughter alone and wearing the scarlet "A" required by local custom. Life in Massachusetts under rigid, unmerciful, Puritan standards is clearly shown in this classic work.

34.  Heidish, Marcy. **Witnesses**. Houghton, 1980. Ballantine, 1983. (0-345-29742-3) Pb $2.50. « Time: 1630s.

Religious freedom is not to be found in the Massachusetts Bay Colony. Anne Hutchinson is tried there twice for heresy before she finds freedom in Rhode Island. Based on primary sources.

35.  Johnston, Mary. **To Have and To Hold**. Houghton, 1900. Several editions available. « Time: 1621.

A beautiful ward of the king flees an unwanted suitor by traveling to Virginia with a cargo of brides sent by the London Company. She marries a rough settler, and they have many adventures.

36.  Jordan, Mildred A. **One Red Rose Forever**. Knopf, 1941. Repr. Buccaneer Books, 1990. (0-89966-723-6) Lib Bdg $35.95. « Time: 1750-1785.

Henry William Stiegel was a famous German-born American iron and glass manufacturer, noted for the beauty of his glass. Jordan's fictionalized biography shows his ambition and artistic leanings that led to the manufacture of products still highly regarded today. Of Stiegel's personal life, little is known, but Jordan weaves an interesting romance and informs the reader about the customs of colonial Philadelphia and early manufacturing methods.

37.  Keehn, Sally M. **I Am Regina**. Putnam, 1991. (0-399-21797-5) $15.95. Dell, 1993. (0-440-40754-0) Pb $3.50. « Time: 1755-1764.

When Regina Leininger is 10, her brother and father are killed in an Indian raid and she and many other children are kidnapped and raised by the Indians. By the time she is rescued, nine years later, she has assimilated into the tribe. The simply told story is based on true events and is very informative concerning the Native American way of life and brutality and betrayal by both whites and Native Americans. Suitable for younger secondary students.

38.  Koller, Jackie French. **The Primrose Way**. Harcourt Brace, 1992. (0-15-256745-3) $15.95. « Time: Late 1600s.

Sixteen-year-old Rebecca befriends the nearby Indians to relieve the tedium and difficulty of life in a Puritan village. She becomes friends with the niece of the Pawtucket chief to learn the language, and soon begins to question Puritan religious beliefs and social values. Her behavior shocks the Puritans, who believe that she is headed "down the primrose way" to hellfire. This carefully researched work is suitable for younger secondary students.

39.  L'Amour, Louis. **Sackett's Land**. Saturday Review Press, 1974. Bantam, 1984. (0-553-25271-2) Pb $2.95. (0-553-27686-7) Pb $3.99. « Time: Early 1600s.

Action-adventure in Elizabethan England and colonial America as Barnabas Sackett, a small English landowner with noble ancestors, sails for America. He trades and fights with Indians and returns to England with a load of furs, knowing that his future lies in America. Followed by *To the Far Blue Mountains*.

40.  L'Amour, Louis. **To the Far Blue Mountains**. Saturday Review Press, 1976. Bantam, 1984. (0-553-27688-3) Pb $3.99. « Time: Early 1600s.

After returning to England from the American colonies, Barnabas Sackett is accused of a crime against the crown and thrown into prison. He escapes and makes his way to Virginia, where he leads other pioneers on a journey to find rich farmland in the Blue Mountains. Sequel to *Sackett's Land*.

41.  Lasky, Kathryn. **Beyond the Burning Time**. Scholastic, 1994. (0-590-47331-X). $13.95. « Time: 1692.

When accusations of witchcraft surface in her small New England village, 12-year-old Mary Chase fights to save her mother from execution. Based on extensive research, this work maintains the dynamics of the witch trials at a time when the absence of a legal system allowed hysteria to prevail.

42.  Lederer, Paul Joseph. **Manitou's Daughter**. NAL-Dutton, 1982. (0-451-15429-0) Pb $3.95. « Time: ca. 1760.

After Crenna, an Oneida headwoman, saves the life of a Dutch captive, the two individuals seek peace in the Hudson River Valley (New York) while the British and French struggle for supremacy in the New World. The culture of the Oneida Indians, and their eventual destruction, is well portrayed. Followed by *Shawnee Dawn, Seminole Skies,* and *Cheyenne Dreams.*

43.  Meyers, Maan. **The Dutchman**. Doubleday, 1992. (0-385-42603-8) $18.50. Bantam, 1993. (0-553-56285-1) Pb $4.99. « Time: 1664.

Authentic details of life in New Amsterdam underlie a suspense-filled mystery in which Pieter Tonneman, the local sheriff, tries to solve a series of murders before the British take over the city. Projected to be the first of a series on members of the Tonneman family.

44.  Moss, Robert. **The Firekeeper: A Narrative of the Eastern Frontier**. Forge/Tor; distributed by St. Martin's Press, 1995. (0-312-85738-1) $24.95. « Time: 1760s.

Through the eyes of a Mohawk woman and two immigrants, Moss tells the story of the escalation of the bitter rivalry between the French and the English and the ways in which Native American nations were drawn into the conflict. Moss provides an accurate picture of the time based on careful research.

45.  O'Dell, Scott. **The Serpent Never Sleeps: A Novel of Jamestown and Pocahontas**. Houghton Mifflin, 1987. (0-395-44242-7) $16.95. Fawcett, 1989. (0-449-70328-2) Pb $3.99. « Time: Early 1600s.

From an English castle, across the stormy Atlantic, and finally to Jamestown, the maid Serena Lynn follows nobleman Anthony Foxcroft. After his death, she considers returning to England, but finally decides that Jamestown will be her home. Many real characters, including Pocahontas, appear in this novel, which provides a strong sense of time and place. Suitable for younger secondary students.

46.  Petry, Ann. **Tituba of Salem Village**. Crowell, 1965. Harper, 1988. (0-690-04766-5) Pb Lib Bdg $14.89. Harper, 1991. (0-06-44043-X) Pb $3.95. « Time: 1692.

This is a somewhat fictionalized biography that chronicles real events. Tituba and her husband John are slaves on the island of Barbados. After being sold to a minister, they move to Salem Village, where Tituba cares for the minister's family. Tituba's background does not prepare her for Massachusetts culture, and she soon finds herself accused of being a witch.

47.   Pye, Michael. **The Drowning Room**. Viking, 1996. (0-670-86598-2) $22.95. «
Time: 1642.

Drawing from a few historic facts about a real woman named Gretje Reyniers,
Pye has created a strong character who defies social convention to make an inde-
pendent life for herself. During a harsh winter, when food is scarce, she opens her
home to a young boy. Through their conversations, the story of her life is revealed.
The story provides many details of daily life and a strong sense of time and place.
Suitable for mature readers.

48.   Richter, Conrad. **The Light in the Forest**. Knopf, 1953. Several editions
available. « Time: 1765.

Pennsylvania and Ohio are the settings for Richter's account of Bouquet's
expedition to free those who have been Indian captives. John Butler is rescued at the
age of 15 after spending 11 years with the Delaware Indians, but he wishes to rejoin
the tribe, which causes many complications for everyone. Richter's sensitive characterization of persons in both cultures makes this a classic work suitable for a wide
range of readers. Followed by *A Country of Strangers*.

49.   Riefe, Barbara. **For Love of Two Eagles**. Tor, 1995. (0-312-85703-9) $22.95.
Forge, 1996. (0-614-05509-1) Pb $5.99. « Time: 1700s.

Margaret Addison is married to Two Eagles, an Oneida warrior. Margaret has adopted
Oneida customs and plans to raise her son to follow his father, but her family in England
intends to force her return to their home. The story has details of daily life among the
Oneida, reveals the rivalries within the Oneida nation and with other tribes, and provides
a vivid and realistic picture of warfare. The complexity of the plot makes this exciting
work suitable for mature readers. Sequel to *The Woman Who Fell from the Sky*.

50.   Riefe, Barbara. **The Woman Who Fell from the Sky**. Tor/Forge; distributed
by St. Martin's Press, 1994. (0-312-85446-3) $22.95. Forge, 1995. (0-8125-2377-6)
Pb $5.99. « Time: Late 1600s.

During a lull in the war between France and Britain over control of the Hudson
Valley, Margaret Addison travels toward Quebec to meet the husband she has married
by proxy. Following a Mohawk raid that leaves the other members of her traveling party
dead, Margaret is rescued by a group of Oneida Indians. Riefe's well-developed characters, lively action, and knowledge of Indian culture enrich this fast-paced romance.
There is an exceptional amount of period detail. Prequel to *For Love of Two Eagles*.

51.   Rinaldi, Ann. **A Break with Charity: A Story About the Salem Witch Trials**.
Harcourt Brace, 1992. (0-15-200353-3) $16.95. « Time: 1692.

Teenager Susanna English is the daughter of a freethinking Salem family. When
girls in the circle led by Ann Putnam begin naming various townspeople as witches,
Susanna knows they are lying just to create excitement and relieve the tedium of
Puritan life. But when things go too far, the girls threaten to accuse Susanna's family
unless she keeps quiet. Rinaldi includes an enlightening discussion of her research.
This detailed account of the Salem trials is suitable for younger secondary students.

52.   Roberts, Kenneth L. **Boon Island**. Doubleday, 1956. Fawcett, 1981. (0-449-
24408-3) Pb $2.50. « Time: 1710.

Somber and unforgettable, this fact-based novel concerns shipwreck survivors
who cling to life on a rocky island near Portsmouth, New Hampshire.

53.   Robson, Lucia St. Clair. **Mary's Land**. Ballantine, 1995. (0-345-37196-8) $24.00. « Time: 1638.

Using a mix of historical and fictional characters, Robson tells an exciting story of life in early Maryland. The action centers around Margaret, an upper-class Catholic who came in search of personal and religious freedom, and Anicah, an orphan who works as an indentured servant. Through their experiences, the reader learns the details of everyday life during that period.

54.   Seifert, Shirley. **Never No More**. Lippincott, 1964. Repr. Amereon, 1976. (0-89190-137-X) Lib Bdg $14.95. « Time: 1770s.

Life on the Virginia and Kentucky frontiers is presented in this account of the life of Rebecca Boone, who endures Indian raids and the death of her oldest son before she and her husband Daniel move to Kentucky.

55.   Seton, Anya. **Devil Water**. Houghton, 1962. Ulverscroft, 1977. (0-85456-554-X) Large type ed. $16.95. « Time: ca. 1715-1745.

As a result of the Jacobite uprising, Charles Radcliffe and his daughter Jenny find their lives profoundly changed. Jenny escapes to America, eventually marries, and lives a frontier life in western Virginia. Detailed and colorful, this fictionalized true story is well researched. Genealogical charts are included.

56.   Simms, William Gilmore. **The Yemassee**. American Book, 1835. North Carolina University Press, 1964. (0-8084-0337-0) Pb $15.95. « Time: Early 1700s.

Using the viewpoints of the original inhabitants, Simms recounts the events that led to the Yemassee War in South Carolina between white settlers and Indians under the leadership of Sanutee, who foresaw the destruction of his race by the newcomers.

57.   Thom, James Alexander. **Follow the River**. Ballantine, 1984, 1986. (0-345-33854-5) Pb $5.95. « Time: 1755.

Mary Ingles is kidnapped from her home on the Virginia frontier by the Shawnee. Her captivity and 1,000-mile-long winter escape along the Ohio and its tributaries (western Pennsylvania, eastern Ohio, and Kentucky) are told in this realistic, fictionalized account of a true story suitable for mature readers. A map and source material are included.

58.   Unsworth, Barry. **Sacred Hunger**. Doubleday, 1992. (0-385-26530-1) $25.00. Norton, 1993. (0-393-31114-7) Pb $11.95. « Time: 1750s-1760s.

The mid-1700s is a time of economic growth, and the slave trade is an important part of the economy. In this serious novel, which focuses upon the Black and white passengers of the *Liverpool Merchant*, Unsworth reveals the results of the "sacred hunger" for profits. When a plague spreads illness aboard the *Merchant*, the slaves are able to revolt. The survivors, both slaves and crew, including the ship's doctor, land in an uninhabited part of Florida and attempt to establish an egalitarian society. The political and character developments seen in this isolated community will be appreciated by mature readers.

59.   Van Wyck Mason, F. **Rascals Heaven**. Doubleday, 1964. Repr. Amereon, 1976. (0-89190-351-8) Lib Bdg $28.95. « Time: ca. 1733.

The Spanish and the natives both resist the settling of Georgia by General James Oglethorpe, who championed prison reform by establishing a refuge for the poor and persecuted.

60. Van Wyck Mason, F. **The Sea Venture**. Doubleday, 1961. Repr. Amereon, 1976. (0-89190-353-4) Lib Bdg $22.95. « Time: ca. 1620.

A ship sets out from England with supplies for the new colony at Jamestown, but is blown by a hurricane onto an island in the Bermudas. There the survivors endure hardship and conflict while building a small vessel to carry them to Virginia. *The Sea Venture* presents a fresh account of the hardships of living at this time.

61. Van Wyck Mason, F. **The Young Titan**. Doubleday, 1959. Repr. Amereon, 1976. (0-89190-355-0) Lib Bdg $31.95. « Time: 1754.

Through this fast-paced and well-researched adventure, the author realistically shows the dangers of frontier living in Maine and the New England area during the French and Indian Wars. The author believes that it was due to the battles of the wars that the colonists first felt their collective strength and their love for independence. The title refers to this initial flexing of the strength of a giant in the making.

# Chapter 2

# The American Revolution: The War and Its Causes, 1776-1783

For the convenience of readers, entries in this chapter have been divided into the following categories:

♦ Events in the East

♦ Events Along the Frontier

## EVENTS IN THE EAST

62.  Armstrong, Jennifer. **Ann of the Wild Rose Inn**. Bantam, 1994. (0-553-29867-4) Pb $3.99. « Time: 1775.

Ann is determined to aid the patriot cause by smuggling supplies past the British blockade. She meets Roger, a sailor, and falls in love before she realizes he is part of the British occupational force in Massachusetts. This light romance (the second in the author's Wild Rose Inn series) will introduce the Revolutionary War period to younger secondary students.

63.  Bailey, Anthony. **Major André**. Farrar, 1987. (0-374-19917-5) $15.95. « Time: 1780.

Late in September 1780, Major John André of the British army meets with Major General Benedict Arnold of the American forces at West Point. They agree to terms for Arnold's surrendering the fort, a treasonous act. After their meeting, André is captured, court-martialed, convicted of being a spy, and hanged on October 2d. Arnold escaped. This complex but vivid story of André's life, and the details of what went wrong with his plan with Arnold, is told by André to one of his captors.

13

64.  Benet, Stephen Vincent. **Spanish Bayonet**. Dorna, 1926. Repr. Scholarly, 1926. (0-685-27275-3) $29.00. « Time: Late 1770s.
Florida became an English colony as a result of the war that ended in 1763. This colorful adventure tale, concerning the development of Florida by the English and the exploitation of Minorcan Greek and Italian indentured laborers on indigo plantations, has the Revolutionary War as a backdrop.

65.  Callahan, North. **Peggy**. Cornwall Books, 1983. Associated Universities Press, 1983. (0-8453-4717-9) $14.95. « Time: 1778-1801
Peggy Shippen was pretty, vain, ambitious, devoted to fabulous clothes and entertainment, and quite empty-headed. Her marriage to Benedict Arnold was a good match, for he, too, was greedy and liked to live far beyond his means. Callahan, who has written many biographies of Revolutionary figures, wrote this account of Arnold's treachery for a popular audience.

66.  Churchill, Winston. **Richard Carvel**. Macmillan, 1899. Repr. Reprint Service, 1992. (0-7812-6687-4) Lib Bdg $99.00. « Time: ca. 1774-1783.
The hero fights alongside John Paul Jones in the battle between the *Bonhomme Richard* and the *Serapis* in this action-filled novel characterized by careful research, attention to detail, and a lively presentation of characters and events. The lovely and wealthy Dorothy Manners is Carvel's romantic interest, but her powerful uncle expects her to marry an affluent Englishman. Set in Maryland and London before and during the Revolution.

67.  Cooper, James Fenimore. **The Pilot**. Dodd, 1824. Several editions available. « Time: 1776-1783.
Cooper displayed his extensive knowledge of seamanship in this exciting story of naval warfare during the Revolution. The work caused great excitement at the time because its accuracy concerning the sea-faring life was unusual in fiction. This story of high adventure features Mr. Gray (based upon John Paul Jones), his shipmates, and the women they love.

68.  Cooper, James Fenimore. **The Spy**. Dodd, 1821. Several editions available. « Time: 1780-1812.
This adventure story of conflicting loyalties, intrigue, and military action is set primarily in Westchester County, New York, an area that lay between the camps of the Americans and the British, where the inhabitants affected neutrality. Peddler Harvey Birch, an American agent who is generally believed to be a British spy, risks capture by both sides as he strives to provide information to General Washington and at the same time protect a Loyalist family who have been good to him. This tale, which illustrates well the later Revolutionary period and the nationalistic spirit of the era, has been called the first American novel.

69.  Cornwell, Bernard. **Redcoat**. Viking, 1988. Tor, 1990. (0-8125-0247-7) Pb $4.95. « Time: Late 1770s.
Philadelphia's divided loyalties, the gaiety of Philadelphia's Loyalist society, and the grim reality of war are illustrated through this readable story about redcoat Sam Gilpin, rebel Jonathan Becket, and his heroic sister, Martha Crowl. British soldiers, and their leader General William Howe, are well portrayed.

70. Davis, William Stearns. **Gilman of Redford**. Biblo, 1922. (0-8196-1203-0) $20.00. « Time: 1770-1775.

Roger Gilman's story, set in Massachusetts on the eve of the Revolution, pictures rural and city life and customs, and is filled with famous people and events. Gilman, a patriotic student at Harvard, is a friend and helper of Paul Revere and Samuel Adams.

71. Edmonds, Walter D. **Drums Along the Mohawk**. Little, 1936. Repr. Buccaneer Books, 1981. (0-89966-291-9) Lib Bdg $25.95. Bantam, 1992. (0-553-27412-0) Pb $5.50. « Time: 1776-1784.

The effects of the Revolution on the farmers of the Mohawk valley in upstate New York is the focus of Edmonds' work. Unaided, these frontiersmen withstood the raids of British regulars from Canada and the Iroquois from the surrounding country. The battle of Oriskany (1777) plays an important part in the book. The flavor of pioneer days is well presented, but reviewers in 1936 noted Edmonds' negative presentation of Native Americans.

72. Fast, Howard. **April Morning**. Crown, 1951. Bantam, 1983. (0-553-27322-1) Pb $4.50. « Time: April, 1775.

During the battles of Lexington and Concord (Massachusetts) Adam Cooper, a 15-year-old farm boy, sees his father shot. Fast's memorable description of the beginning of the war is a concise, simple, and convincing account that captures the sights and sounds of the day that changes Adam rapidly from boy to man. Readers will learn, with Adam, the painful cost of patriotism, and the realities of war as it was then fought.

73. Fast, Howard. **Citizen Tom Paine**. Duell, 1943. Grove-Atlantic, 1987. (0-8021-3064-X) Pb $10.95. « Time: ca. 1775-1790.

Thomas Paine was always at his best in a time of crisis—seen as a rabble-rouser by many and a great patriot by others. His idiosyncrasies, strengths, weaknesses, and his ability to catch the imagination of a people—to make them grasp the "inevitability of America"—are all captured in Fast's revealing and balanced work. Paine's writings in support of independence were published during his residence in Philadelphia, where he was a friend of Benjamin Franklin.

74. Fast, Howard. **The Proud and the Free**. Little, 1950. Houghton, n.d. Pb. Write for information. « Time: 1781.

Unpaid, hungry, and wearing rags, the common soldiers of the 11th Pennsylvania Regiment protested against their officers, whom they saw as tyrannical opportunists. This vigorous account of their revolt tells a little-known story with rich detail and believable characters.

75. Fletcher, Inglis. **Raleigh's Eden**. Bobbs, 1940. Repr. Amereon, 1976. (0-89244-006-6) Lib Bdg $31.95. Bantam, 1986. (0-553-25950-4) Pb $4.50. « Time: 1764-1782.

John Paul Jones, Lord Cornwallis, kilted Highlanders, pirates, and other historic figures flash through the pages of this colorful and lengthy novel that is primarily about plantation life in North Carolina during the Revolution. Adam Rutledge, a gentleman plantation owner, is rigidly controlled by his discontented invalid wife; Mary Warden is married to a man near her father's age. Their story of elegant society is part of the author's series on the history of North Carolina.

76. Fletcher, Inglis. **The Scotswoman**. Bobbs, 1954. Repr. Queens House, 1976. (0-89244-008-2) Lib Bdg $21.95. « Time: 1746-1784.

As a young woman, Flora Macdonald rescued Bonnie Prince Charlie after the Battle of Culloden (1746). Later, her family settle in North Carolina, seeking prosperity and peace. But when the Revolution begins, their loyalty to their former enemies involves them in the action, and Flora once again shows her mettle. Based upon a true story.

77. Fletcher, Inglis. **Toil of the Brave**. Bobbs, 1946. Repr. Queens House, 1976. (0-89244-010-4) Lib Bdg $21.95. Bantam, 1986. (0-553-25875-3) Pb $4.50. « Time: 1779-1780.

The fourth in a series set in the Albemarle district of North Carolina. Scotsman Peter Huntley, a captain in the Continental army, is Washington's liaison officer to the Southern planters. The desperate military situation of the southern campaign is the background for a rich romance that includes a duel, a slave uprising, and abundant details of Southern life. The battle of King's Mountain concludes the story.

78. Forbes, Esther. **Johnny Tremain**. Houghton, 1943. Several editions available. « Time: 1775-1776.

Johnny Tremain, an orphan, is an apprentice silversmith in Boston at the beginning of the American Revolution. He plays his part in the early days of the Revolution as a courier for the rebel Committee of Public Safety and meets Paul Revere, the Adamses, and John Hancock. This award-winning novel moves quickly and presents a realistic picture of the times that will appeal to a wide range of readers.

79. Ford, Paul Leicester. **Janice Meredith**. Dodd, 1899. Repr. Reprint Service, 1992. (0-7812-2876-X) Lib Bdg $75.00. Airmont, 1967. (0-8049-0148-1) Pb $0.95. « Time: 1774-1783.

Beginning in New Jersey in 1774, this dramatic novel that spans the years of the American Revolution presents a realistic picture of the war and of the character of George Washington. The story centers on the daughter of a patriot who falls in love with a bondservant, only to discover that he is an officer in the Rebel army.

80. Gerson, Noel B. **The Swamp Fox, Francis Marion**. Doubleday, 1967. Amereon, n.d. (0-88411-642-5) $21.95. « Time: 1780-1783.

This well-researched novelized biography of the life of Francis Marion, the Swamp Fox of South Carolina, expertly interweaves the threads of warfare, romance, and politics. Marion was an effective leader in battles against the Cherokees before the Revolution. However, he is primarily noted for the daring and elusive fighting style of his guerrilla band against the British in the battle for the South, during which he and his men usually struck at night and then disappeared into swamps and wooded lands, out of British reach.

81. Gilman, Dorothy Butters. **Bells of Freedom**. Macrae Smith, 1963. Peter Smith, 1984. (0-8446-6162-7) $15.50. « Time: 1775-1776.

Jed is apprenticed to a friendly man who needs an intelligent, honest errand boy for his business of counterfeiting patriot money in Boston during the Revolutionary War. In this fast-moving novel, the boy-hero, who witnesses action at Breed's Hill, Concord, and Dorchester Heights, reevaluates his ideas of loyalty. For younger secondary students.

82. Grey, Zane. **Betty Zane**. Grosset, 1903. Several editions available. « Time: 1775-1783.

This tale of the hardships of life beyond the Allegheny Mountains on the Virginia frontier, including fights with Indians and the destruction of the settlement during the Revolution, is based on the experiences of the author's family.

83. Grimes, Roberta. **My Thomas: A Novel of Martha Jefferson's Life**. Doubleday, 1993. (0-385-42399-3) $20.00. « Time: 1772-1782.

Although Martha Jefferson's journals were destroyed because of her husband's concern for privacy, Grimes has carefully researched her account of their 10-year marriage and shows the events that led to the Jeffersons' support of independence and the Revolutionary War. Grimes challenges the belief that Jefferson sired Sally Hemmings's children.

84. Hodge, Jane Aiken. **Judas Flowering**. Coward, 1976. Ulverscroft, 1977. (0-7089-0077-1) Large type ed. $15.95. « Time: 1774-1783.

Mercy Phillips's father is killed by a revolutionary mob because he is a Loyalist printer, but she is rescued and goes to live with a Loyalist family in Savannah. However, when the family's son comes home from college in New England and reports British activity there, most of the family join the Rebels; Mercy becomes a pamphleteer for the Patriot cause. Believable characters and an exciting plot hold the reader's interest in this story that tells of the Revolution in the South.

85. Lambdin, Dewey. **The French Admiral**. Fine, 1990. (1-55611-208-4) $19.95. Windsor Publishing Corp., 1991. (1-55817-491-5) Pb $4.95. « Time: 1783.

The second in a series of the sea adventures of Alan Lewrie includes land events when Alan becomes involved in the bloody battle at Yorktown. The events are historically accurate, and the characters are lively in this action-filled series. Sequel to *The King's Coat*. Other titles in the series follow activities of the British Navy in other parts of the world after the American Revolution.

86. Lambdin, Dewey. **The King's Coat**. Fine, 1989. (1-55611-142-8) $19.95. Windsor Publishing Corp., 1990. (1-55817-389-7) Pb $3.95. « Time: 1780.

Alan Lewrie, 17, begins his naval career as an unwilling midshipman in the British Navy. He serves on several ships, gaining experience in dealing with stormy weather, battles against the American rebels, personnel clashes, and other difficulties. Naval jargon and realistic action scenes give appeal to this first novel in a new series. Followed by *The French Admiral*.

87. Lancaster, Bruce. **Blind Journey**. Little, 1953. Repr. Amereon, 1976. (0-88411-685-9) $21.95. « Time: 1781.

Descriptive detail and excellent research are features of this story about Ward Gratwick, a young American patriot who works as a courier for Benjamin Franklin in an effort to get money and supplies from France. Battles at sea add to the excitement, as Ward succeeds in getting to Yorktown in time to take part in the campaign against Cornwallis.

88.  Lancaster, Bruce. **Guns of Burgoyne**. Stokes, 1939. Repr. Amereon, 1975. (0-89190-881-1) Lib Bdg $24.95. « Time: 1777.

Lancaster tells the story of the defeat of Burgoyne at the Battle of Saratoga, New York, from the viewpoint of a Hessian officer in the English army. Exciting adventure, believable people, and a unique point of view set this work apart.

89.  Lancaster, Bruce. **Phantom Fortress**. Little, 1950. Repr. Amereon, 1976. (0-88411-683-2) Lib Bdg $21.95. « Time: 1780-1783.

This well-researched and stirring story of the guerrilla warfare of Francis Marion, the Swamp Fox from South Carolina, centers on a cavalry captain who has escaped from the British and joined Marion's troops. There he falls in love with a refugee from an uprising in the West Indies. She has pledged herself to the Colonial cause and is effective as a spy for the Rebels. This suspenseful and well-paced novel provides much information about military tactics during guerrilla warfare.

90.  Lancaster, Bruce. **Secret Road**. Little, 1952. Repr. Amereon, n.d. (0-89190-217-1) $21.95. « Time: 1780.

This story of the part George Washington's secret service played in exposing Benedict Arnold's treason and in the capture of Major André is told through the adventures of Captain Grant Ledyard. The accurate accounts of spies Robert Townsend and Major André, and of life in Connecticut and in British-occupied New York City will be of interest to readers.

91.  Lancaster, Bruce. **Trumpet to Arms**. Little, 1944. Repr. Amereon, 1976. (0-88411-681-6) Lib Bdg $23.95. « Time: 1775-1776.

Lancaster's story of how local militia from all the colonies merged into the first American army ends with the Battle of Trenton (New Jersey). The action centers on actual experiences of the 21st Regiment of the Massachusetts Infantry (John Glover's Marblehead Men). This lively, well-paced, and well-researched account also shows the gradual growth of trust and respect of the military men for their leader, George Washington.

92.  Melville, Herman. **Israel Potter: His Fifty Years in Exile**. Putnam, 1855. Several editions available. « Time: ca. 1776-1790.

Melville based this story on the life of a common soldier who fought at Bunker Hill, served as messenger to Benjamin Franklin, and served under John Paul Jones in the battle between the *Bonhomme Richard* and the *Serapis*. Later the soldier moved to England, where he was a gardener for George III. The story, which first appeared in serial form in *Putnam's Monthly Magazine*, is a low-key account of the struggle of an ordinary man for survival.

93.  Meyers, Maan. **The Kingsbridge Plot**. Doubleday, 1993. (0-385-46951-9) $18.50. Bantam, 1994. (0-553-56380-7) Pb $4.99. « Time: ca. 1775.

The setting, language, and political turmoil are authentic in this historical mystery that concerns an actual assassination attempt against George Washington and concurrent (fictional) gruesome murders. A young physician is the protagonist in this well-written novel, enhanced by short chapters with an abundance of white space. A concluding chapter separates fact from fiction.

94.   O'Dell, Scott. **Sarah Bishop**. Houghton Mifflin, 1980. (0-395-29185-2) $14.45. Scholastic, 1991. (0-590-44651-7) Pb $3.25. « Time: ca. 1770-1784.

Although Sarah Bishop has met some kind people on both sides of the conflict, she wants nothing to do with either side. Her father was lost at the hands of the Rebels, and her brother was killed by the King's men. Fearing both sides, she hides in a cave in the wilderness of New York State, gradually learning to take joy in her hard-won self-reliance. The carefully researched work is based on the life of a real woman.

95.   Pope, E(lizabeth) M(arie). **Sherwood Ring**. Houghton Mifflin, 1958. Peter Smith, n.d. (0-8446-6416-2) $19.00. Puffin, 1992. (0-14-034911-1) Pb $3.99. « Time: ca. 1775-1783.

Rich in mystery, romance, and historical lore, this is the story of Peggy. While visiting her ancestral home in Orange County, New York, she travels back in time to meet family ghosts who were involved in the Revolution. Guerrilla action, humor, and parallels of characters and relationships add to the appeal of this well-researched work. This novel won an award from the New York *Herald Tribune*.

96.   Rinaldi, Ann. **The Fifth of March: A Story of the Boston Massacre**. Harcourt Brace, 1993. (0-15-227517-7) Pb $3.95. « Time: 1770.

Political disagreements among Americans, the actions of mobs, and British retaliation are all examined in this well-researched story of the Boston Massacre. Rachel Marsh, servant in the John Adams household, is the story's central figure. She finds herself torn between positions: She is first apolitical, then fiercely American, then sympathetic to a British soldier who responded to violence with violence.

97.   Rinaldi, Ann. **Finishing Becca: The Story of Peggy Shippen and Benedict Arnold**. Harcourt Brace, 1994. (0-15-200880-2) $10.95. (0-15-200879-9) Pb $3.95. « Time: 1781.

Becca Synge, maid to the wealthy beauty Peggy Shippen, tells a story that shows how the spoiled Philadelphia socialite maneuvered her husband, Benedict Arnold, into betraying the American cause. This well-researched account is suited for younger secondary students.

98.   Rinaldi, Ann. **A Ride into Morning: The Story of Tempe Wick**. Harcourt Brace, 1991. (0-15-200573-0) $15.95. « Time: 1781.

After she protests her brother's dealing with the British, Mary Cooper, 14, is sent to visit her cousin Tempe Wick, whose farm is near the New Jersey camp of General Anthony Wayne. Tempe has been dispirited by the war—the death of her father, food shortages, and endless work and compromise. When soldiers threaten to take her horse, Tempe compromises no more and hides it in her house. This well-researched story, based upon legend, is suited for younger secondary students.

99.   Rinaldi, Ann. **The Secret of Sarah Revere**. Harcourt Brace, 1995. (0-15-200393-2) $11.00. (0-15-299392-4) Pb $5.00. « Time: 1770-1776.

Through the eyes and thoughts of Sarah, Paul Revere's daughter, readers see the political and social events that took place in Boston during the exciting and frightening days that led up to the Revolution. If the family of a friend supports the British, what happens to the friendship? How does the routine of daily life go on in a time of turmoil? Rinaldi's carefully researched work provides an excellent view of family life and makes historic figures come alive. Suitable for younger secondary students.

100.    Rinaldi, Ann. **Time Enough for Drums**. Holiday, 1986. (0-8234-0603-2)
$15.95. Troll, 1989 (0-8167-1269-7) Pb $2.50. « Time: ca. 1886-1783.

Events of the war as they affect her family in the Trenton, New Jersey, area are
related by Jemima. Her sister is married to a British officer; her mother writes patriotic
letters to the newspaper; her tutor, under the guise of being a Tory, is a spy for
Washington; one grandfather works for Indian justice; and the other is a real Tory.
Thus, Jemima's story provides a broad view of the people and events of the time.
Rinaldi's book provides an accurate picture of the culture and customs of the time.
Suitable for younger secondary students.

101.    Roberts, Kenneth L. **Arundel: Being the Recollections of Steven Nason of
Arundel, in the Province of Maine, Attached to the Secret Expedition Led by
Benedict Arnold Against Quebec**. Doubleday, 1930. Fawcett, 1981. (0-449-24456-
3) Pb $2.95. Fawcett, 1986. (0-449-21305-6) Pb $3.95. « Time: 1775.

Steven Nason has a personal interest in the success of the expedition led by
Benedict Arnold across Maine to Quebec, because the girl he loves has been taken
captive by the Indians and is held there. The blunders, failures, humor, and heroism
of Arnold's expedition into Canada in the first year of the Revolution are told with
Roberts's usual flair in this well-researched lengthy novel.

102.    Roberts, Kenneth L. **Oliver Wiswell**. Doubleday, 1940. Fawcett, 1983. (0-449-
21193-2) Pb $4.95. « Time: 1775-1784.

Oliver Wiswell tells the story of the American Revolution from the point of view
of a colonial who is loyal to the Crown. The bitterness of civil war is powerfully and
dramatically brought to life in this absorbing and lengthy novel. The complexity of
this work makes it suitable for mature readers.

103.    Sherman, Dan. **The Traitor**. Fine, 1987. (1-55611-000-6) $17.95. « Time: 1780.

Sherman's novel of espionage, politics, strategy, adventure, and treason is set
during a troubled time. Dissatisfaction with George Washington is growing, the
underpaid volunteer army is grumbling, and morale among the supporters of the
Revolution is low. An investigation of the murder of an English officer and his
mistress (American double agents) uncovers a conspiracy to subvert the revolution
for financial gain.

104.    Stone, Irving. **Those Who Love**. Doubleday, 1965. (0-385-00157-6) $19.95.
« Time: 1764-1801.

Stone's biographical novel tells the story of Abigail and John Adams through
Abigail's eyes, from their courtship through the close of his presidency. The chapters
that cover the Revolution and the Constitutional era are of particular interest. Stone's
careful research, based upon the numerous letters and diaries of the Adams, provides
details of local custom in Massachusetts.

105.    Thane, Elswyth Beebe. **Dawn's Early Light**. Duell, 1943. Repr. Amereon, n.d.
(0-88411-974-2) Lib Bdg $23.95. « Time: 1774-1783.

The picturesque village of Williamsburg is the setting for this sentimental
romance concerning a young girl who wears her twin brother's clothes to cross the
battle lines to find her love. Minor characters include Thomas Jefferson, the Randolphs,
and the Marquis de Lafayette. In this old-fashioned tale, suited for younger secondary
students, readers will learn about the southern campaigns and local customs.

106. White, Richard W. **Jordan Freeman Was My Friend**. Four Walls Eight Windows, 1994. (0-941423-73-5) $18.95. « Time: 1781.

Billy, son of Captain Latham, an American patriot, is good friends with Jordan Freeman, a former slave. They become involved in the building of Fort Griswold (Connecticut) in the days leading up to the massacre of its inhabitants by the British, led by the traitorous Benedict Arnold. This concise, simply written story will have a wide appeal as it emphasizes the virtue of loyalty to friends and country. The story is based on real events.

107. Williams, Ben Ames. **Come Spring**. Houghton, 1940. Buccaneer Books, 1976. (0-89966-197-1) Lib Bdg $32.95. « Time: 1776-1783.

The Robbins family lived in a remote Maine settlement during the Revolution. They were not far from the scene of war, but their daily affairs and their relations with neighboring Indians were of more immediate importance to them. The story is lengthy but presents a true, homely picture of customs, habits, modes of thought, and such routine activities as bear hunting, house raisings, land clearing, and home birthings.

108. Wolf, William J. **Benedict Arnold, A Novel**. Paideia, 1990. (0-913993-13-1) $30.00. « Time: 1780.

The complex and elusive character of Benedict Arnold is explored in this carefully researched novel. Wolf develops the story slowly, filling it with detail. As a result, both real and fictional characters are well developed, and the reader is given a fine portrait of the contradictions, from the highest idealism to the most self-serving pettiness, that surrounded the Revolutionary War.

# EVENTS ALONG THE FRONTIER

109. Altsheler, J. A. **Border Watch**. Appleton, 1912. Several editions available. « Time: Late 1770s.

Last in the Young Trailer series, this story concerns Henry Ware's adventures as part of the George Rogers Clark campaign against the Indians in Illinois and Indiana. The work presents a good picture of frontier life and border warfare. This sequel to *Scouts of the Valley* is suitable for younger secondary students.

110. Altsheler, J. A. **Eyes of the Woods**. Appleton, 1917. Several editions available. « Time: 1770s.

Henry Ware is assisted by animals and the elements in his escape from a thousand pursuing Indians in his adventures in the Kentucky and Ohio forests. Sequel to *Keepers of the Trail;* followed by *Free Rangers*. Suitable for younger secondary students.

111. Altsheler, J. A. **Forest Runners**. Appleton, 1908. Several editions available. « Time: 1770s.

In this sequel to *Young Trailers,* Henry Ware and his friends save a band of settlers from massacre. This stirring story gives a good picture of the courage of the frontiersmen. Suitable for younger secondary students; followed by *Keepers of the Trail*.

112. Altsheler, J. A. **Free Rangers**. Appleton, 1909. Several editions available. «
Time: 1770s.

Henry Ware and his friends help settlers in Kentucky and along the Mississippi.
They eventually journey down the Mississippi to New Orleans to talk to the Spanish
governor-general about the mistreatment of American settlers by Spanish agents. This
sequel to *Eyes of the Woods* is suitable for younger secondary students. Followed by
*Riflemen of the Ohio*.

113. Altsheler, J. A. **Keepers of the Trail**. Appleton, 1916. Repr. Buccaneer Books,
1992. (0-89966-932-8) Lib Bdg $25.95. Repr. Amereon, n.d. (0-88411-948-3) Lib
Bdg $21.95. « Time: 1770s.

Henry Ware and his friends seek to deter a large force of English and Indians
marching to attack Kentucky settlements. This sequel to *Forest Runners* is followed
by *Eyes of the Woods*. Suitable for younger secondary students.

114. Altsheler, J. A. **Riflemen of the Ohio**. Appleton, 1910. Several editions
available. « Time: ca. 1775-1778.

In the further adventures of Henry Ware and his friends, Daniel Boone, Simon
Kenton, and the renegade Simon Girty are characters, and Henry is captured by
Wyandot Indians. This sequel to *Free Rangers* is followed by *Scouts of the Valley*
and is suitable for younger secondary students.

115. Altsheler, J. A. **Scouts of the Valley**. Appleton, 1911. Several editions available. « Time: Late 1770s.

Henry Ware and his friends attempt to prevent the Wyoming Valley, Pennsylvania, massacre of 1778, and they participate in the battle of Chemung. This exciting
sequel to *Riflemen of the Ohio* may be read independent of others in the series; it is
suitable for younger secondary students. Followed by *Border Watch*.

116. Altsheler, J. A. **Young Trailers: A Story of Early Kentucky**. Appleton, 1907.
Several editions available. « Time: 1770s.

Henry Ware, a young frontiersman, gains skill in hunting, fishing, and wilderness
survival. Through his capture and release by the Shawnee, he learns Indian ways in the
Kentucky forest. Followed by *Forest Runners;* suitable for younger secondary students.

117. Boyd, Thomas Alexander. **Shadow of the Long Knives**. Scribner, 1928. Peter
Smith, n.d. (0-8446-1086-0) $10.25. Amereon, n.d. (0-88411-861-4) $22.95. « Time:
ca. 1760-1783.

Angus McDermott, raised by Indians, is an excellent frontiersman, scout, interpreter, and peacemaker in dealings between the British and Native Americans. The
characters of this adventure delineate the ethical struggles of 25 years of history along
the Ohio frontier, culminating with the Revolution and a battle between American
troops and the Shawnee and other Indian peoples.

118. Giles, Janice Holt. **Hannah Fowler**. Houghton, 1956. University Press of
Kentucky, 1992. (0-8131-1793-3) $28.00. (0-8131-0810-1) Pb $15.00. « Time: ca. 1778.

With her new husband, Hannah Moore makes a home on the Kentucky frontier.
Giles fills the story with authentic details of life in the backwoods, where events are
influenced by historical characters, but the reality of the struggle against the wilderness and unfriendly Indians defines the day.

119.   Giles, Janice Holt. **The Kentuckians**. Houghton, 1953. University Press of Kentucky, 1987. (0-8131-1639-2) $24.00. (0-8131-0177-8) Pb $12.00. « Time: 1769-1777.

Giles's carefully researched story of pioneer Kentucky focuses on the troubles with the Cherokee nation and the efforts of land speculators when settlers were agitating for statehood. Daniel Boone and many other historic characters are accurately presented.

120.   Receveur, Betty Layman. **Oh Kentucky!** Ballantine, 1992. (0-345-31717-3) Pb $5.99. « Time: ca. 1775-1776.

Daniel and Rebecca Boone welcome Kitty Gentry, 16, and her family to Boonesborough. The Gentrys and other new settlers build homes and carve farms out of the wilderness while they resist Indian attacks encouraged by the British in an attempt to halt the move toward independence. Details of the arduous but rewarding life of the pioneers enrich this engaging tale. Followed by *Kentucky Home*.

121.   Roberts, Elizabeth Madox. **Great Meadow**. Viking, 1930. Repr. AMS Press, 1980. (0-404-15235-X) $27.50. J. S. Sanders, 1992. (1-879941-07-4) Pb $10.95. « Time: 1774-1781.

Early settlers who traveled the Wilderness Road from Virginia to settle at Harrod's Fort, Kentucky, faced primitive living conditions and food shortages. For women who found themselves without the support and protection of a man, the times were especially perilous. Roberts's lyrical novel centers around Diony and Berk Jarvis, a newly married couple. When Berk fails to return from a journey, Diony must make a life-changing decision. This work was critically acclaimed at the time of its publication; today's readers may have difficulty getting past the poetic style of the early pages so that they may enjoy the informative story.

122.   Thompson, Maurice. **Alice of Old Vincennes**. Bowen-Merrill, 1900. Indiana University Press, 1985. (0-253-30402-4) $20.00 (0-253-20362-7) Pb $8.95. « Time: 1778.

Thompson's romance of life in the old French town of Vincennes, Indiana, has been popular since its initial publication. The difficulties with Indians and greedy white men, and the details of pioneer life in the Northwest Territory during the early days of the Revolution, are all based on incidents in the life of Alice Roussillon.

# Chapter 3

## The Age of Expansion, 1783-1860

For the convenience of the reader, entries in this chapter have been divided into the following categories:

◆ Inclusive Titles

◆ Life in the Young Nation:

• Eastern and Southern Living

• The Midwest

• The Plains and Mountain States

• California and the Pacific Northwest

## INCLUSIVE TITLES

123.   Alter, Judy. **Jessie: A Novel Based on the Life of Jessie Benton Fremont**. Bantam, 1995. (0-553-37465-6) Pb $9.95. « Time: Mid-1840s to mid-1860s.
    As the daughter of a senator from Missouri, Jessie Benton gained a great deal of knowledge about politics while she polished her writing skills by serving as her father's clerical assistant. Later she used these abilities to promote the career of her explorer/politician/soldier husband as she accompanied him to Panama, frontier military posts, the California gold mines, Paris, and London. All the while she wrote and spoke her mind. Her story reveals the growing pains of a nation struggling with the concept of Manifest Destiny. This well-researched work provides a good sense of the times.

124.   Charbonneau, Louis. **Trail: The Story of the Lewis and Clark Expedition**. Doubleday, 1989. (0-385-24211-5) $22.95. « Time: 1803-1805.
    This straightforward tale of the remarkable Lewis and Clark Expedition is told from the points of view of Meriwether Lewis, George Shannon (a fictional character), and Seaman, Lewis's Newfoundland retriever. The factual material is based on journals kept by Lewis, Clark, and other members of the expedition.

125.   Fisher, Vardis. **Tale of Valor**. Doubleday, 1958. Repr. Amereon, 1976. (0-89190-834-X) Lib Bdg $28.95. « Time: 1804-1805.
The Lewis and Clark Expedition traveled 8,000 miles from St. Louis to the Pacific Northwest and back again to explore the vast territory which, at that time, was almost unknown to the white people of the United States. Fisher's carefully researched, realistic account details dangers and hardships, the relationships among the explorers, their dealings with Native Americans, and the great sense of adventure and discovery they enjoyed.

126.   Melville, Herman. **Moby Dick**. Harper, 1851. Several editions available. « Time: Early 1800s.
In this classic tale of the sea, Captain Ahab pursues Moby Dick, the ferocious white whale that had earlier bitten off his leg. Moby Dick comes to symbolize the forces of nature, and Ahab's fury, which brings about the death of the whale, destroys him as well. This epic tragedy acquaints readers with the realities of life aboard a whaling vessel.

127.   Neihardt, John G. **Splendid Wayfaring: Jedediah Smith and the Ashley-Henry Men, 1822-1831**. Macmillan, 1920. University of Nebraska Press, 1970. (0-8032-5732-6) Pb $9.95. « Time: 1822-1831.
Jedediah Smith was a courageous explorer—the first American to discover the central overland route to California and to measure the length of the Pacific Coast from Los Angeles to the Columbia. Among his companions were men who established the fur trade in that region. Neihardt's lively chronicle of the adventures of these men who were responsible for opening the central United States to settlers is well researched and well written.

128.   O'Dell, Scott. **Streams to the River, River to the Sea: A Novel of Sacagawea**. Houghton, 1986. Several editions available. « Time: 1804-1806.
Sacagawea was a member of the Shoshone tribe. As a child she was captured by the Minnetarres, and later was forced to marry a French trader. She and her husband were hired by the Lewis and Clark Expedition, and she proved to be a remarkable guide. She accompanied the party across the northwest to the Pacific and guided them back through Yellowstone to the Minnetarre territory. Through Sacagawea's words the reader views the risks from both nature and man, as well as the personal relationships of this remarkable group of explorers.

129.   Roberts, Kenneth L. **Captain Caution: A Chronicle of Arundel**. Doubleday, 1934. Fawcett, 1982. (0-449-24509-8) Pb $2.95. « Time: 1812.
British impressment of American sailors was a primary cause of the War of 1812. Roberts's story centers on the experiences of a ship's captain who, returning to Arundel, Maine, from a voyage to China, is captured by the British. This carefully researched novel is full of action, suspense, and detailed information about naval life.

130.   Seifert, Shirley. **Three Lives of Elizabeth**. Repr. Amereon, 1976. (0-89190-139-6) Lib Bdg $21.95. « Time: ca. 1800-1865.
Elizabeth Moss married three men of distinction: Dr. Daniel Wilcox in pioneer Missouri; wealthy William Henry Ashley, a fur trader and Congressman; and the famous John Jordan Crittenden, an attorney and politician from Kentucky. Elizabeth was an ambitious woman; through her fictionalized biography, the reader enjoys an informative account of customs in mid-nineteenth-century America.

131.  Seton, Anya. **My Theodosia**. Houghton, 1941. Amereon, n.d. (0-8488-0624-7) $22.95. « Time: 1800-1805.

Careful research underlies Seton's novel about Theodosia Burr's marriage to a South Carolina planter; the political aspirations of her father, Aaron Burr; his duel with Alexander Hamilton; and the trial that followed. This is the first novel by a popular novelist.

132.  Stone, Irving. **Immortal Wife**. Doubleday, 1944, 1948. (0-385-04219-1) $24.95. « Time: Mid-1840s to mid-1860s.

Stone's well-researched fictional biography of Jessie Benton Fremont, wife of John Fremont, primarily covers John's part in the conquest and development of California and national politics. Action in the western campaigns of the Civil War is also a part of the story. The Fremonts' lives—fortunes made and lost, a presidential nomination, and two courts-martial—lend themselves naturally to fiction.

133.  Stone, Irving. **The President's Lady**. Doubleday, 1951. (0-385-04362-7) $24.95. NAL-Dutton, 1968. (0-451-15857-1) Pb $4.95. « Time: 1790-1845.

Stone's quietly sympathetic account of the romance of Rachel and Andrew Jackson, set against a background of American politics, provides a clear picture of the mores of the time. All the characters are historical figures, and the account is based upon careful research.

134.  Vidal, Gore. **Burr**. Random House, 1973. Ballantine, 1986. (0-345-33921-5) Pb $5.95. « Time: 1770s-1836.

Aaron Burr's role in history is revealed in this novel, written in the form of a memoir left by the aging Burr. Among the many prominent persons that were an important part of his life were Alexander Hamilton, Thomas Jefferson, and George Washington. This carefully researched work comprises a trilogy with *1876: The Nation Grows Up* and *Washington, D.C.: Chronicles*.

135.  Waldo, Anna Lee. **Sacajawea**. Avon, 1979, 1984. (0-380-84293-9) Pb $6.99. « Time: Mid-1780s-1884.

The social customs of the Native American tribes met on the Lewis and Clark Expedition, and the various tribes with whom Sacagawea lived, are detailed in this lengthy account of the life of Sacagawea. It traces her life from childhood to old age (estimated by the author to be from the mid-1780s to 1884). The expedition itself is a minor part of the book. The patient reader interested in Indian tradition and the role of Indian women will find this work very informative.

# *LIFE IN THE YOUNG NATION*

## Eastern and Southern Living

136.  Adams, Samuel Hopkins. **Canal Town**. Random House, 1944. Syracuse University Press, 1988. (0-8156-0228-6) Pb $15.95. « Time: 1820s.

Adams's lively, well-researched novel provides details of life in a New York canal town and the practice of medicine in the early nineteenth century, as a young physician struggles to combat ignorance and superstition.

137. Allis, Marguerite. **Not Without Peril**. Putnam, 1941. Repr. Old Fort Four, 1989. (0-9622471-0-3) $16.95. « Time: ca. 1790.

Pioneer hardships and customs are clearly presented in this well-researched, lively, and credible novel, which is based on the life and adventures of Jemima Sartwell, one of the first settlers in Vermont. Authentic in its detail concerning language, customs, and relations among settlers and Native Americans, this novel was highly recommended at the time of its initial publication.

138. Armstrong, Jennifer. **Steal Away**. Orchard, 1992. Several editions available. « Time: 1855.

Orphaned 13-year-old Susannah, sent from her Vermont home to live with her pious slave-owning relatives on a Virginia plantation, receives the unwanted gift of a slave girl named Bethlehem. The two unhappy girls conspire to pose as boys and escape north. The powerful story of their hazard-filled escape is told in alternating chapters, showing the perspectives of both Susannah and Bethlehem and how differing backgrounds may interfere with understanding. Suitable for younger secondary students.

139. Atherton, Gertrude. **The Conqueror: Being the True and Romantic Story of Alexander Hamilton**. Macmillan, 1902. Amereon, n.d. (0-88411-588-7) $30.95. « Time: ca. 1765-1804.

Atherton's carefully researched fictionalized biography of Alexander Hamilton is highly sympathetic. While many details of Hamilton's early years and his private life are romanticized, his public life, socially and politically, is well documented. Among major players in this work are George Washington, John Adams, Thomas Jefferson, James Madison, and Aaron Burr. Some editions are subtitled *A Dramatized Biography of Alexander Hamilton*.

140. Bacheller, Irving. **Eben Holden: A Tale of the North Country**. Lothrop, 1900. Several editions available. « Time: 1850s.

Life was simple in the Adirondack Mountain region of New York in the 1850s. This quiet, rambling story that focuses on a faithful old servant presents a charming picture of life in the woods. Abraham Lincoln and Horace Greeley are minor figures in the story.

141. Bontemps, Arna. **Black Thunder: Gabriel's Revolt: Virginia, 1800**. Macmillan, 1936. Beacon, 1992. (0-8070-6337-1) Pb $12.00. « Time: 1800.

In 1800, a slave who came to be known as "General Gabriel" planned an insurrection in which 1,100 slaves, armed with pikes, cutlasses, and firearms from the Arsenal, would capture Richmond. This well-planned undertaking failed because of a violent storm and betrayal by insiders. Bontemps's faithful, convincing, and fast-moving retelling of the incident received critical acclaim.

142. Bradley, David. **Chaneysville Incident**. Harper & Row, 1981. Several editions available. « Time: 1859.

When John Washington, a present-day Black professor, goes to a reunion in his hometown in southern Pennsylvania, just north of the Mason-Dixon line, he investigates a rumor he heard as a child. The rumor concerned 12 slaves who, having escaped via the Underground Railroad, learned they were about to be recaptured. Rather than being taken, they asked to be killed, and their request was honored. As Washington investigates this story he struggles with the realities of Black history and his own life, which is a success by white standards. The complexity of this novel makes it appropriate for mature readers.

143. Bristow, Gwen. **Deep Summer**. Crowell, 1937. Repr. Buccaneer Books, 1979. (0-89966-025-8) Lib Bdg $25.95. « Time: ca. 1775-1800.

The story of the marriage of Judith (the daughter of a Puritan Connecticut farmer) and Philip (from an aristocratic South Carolina family) traces the romance of two people of very different backgrounds. It ranges from their days in a cabin in the Louisiana wilderness to the time when they own a great plantation. Followed by *The Handsome Road,* a Civil War novel.

144. Brown, Rita Mae. **Dolley: A Novel of Dolley Madison and Love and War**. Bantam, 1994. (0-533-08890-4) $22.95. « Time: ca. 1800-1812.

Brown combines narrative with excerpts from a fictional diary to tell the story of Dolley Madison and the important role she played in the early days of the nation. Madison served as hostess during the Jefferson administration as well as during her husband's presidency. She smoothed many tense situations and had a strong influence on social attitudes and political decisions. The tensions in Washington during the War of 1812, leading up to the burning of the city, are well portrayed.

145. Byrd, Max. **Jefferson: A Novel**. Bantam, 1993. (0-553-09470-X) $22.95. « Time: 1785-1789.

Byrd examines Thomas Jefferson's years in Paris just preceding the French Revolution, when he served as the U.S. ambassador. The story, which includes many details of daily life in Paris, is told through the eyes of Jefferson's admiring secretary.

146. Carr, John Dickson. **Papa La-Bas**. Harper, 1968. Carroll & Graf, 1989. (0-88184-494-2) Pb $3.95. « Time: 1858.

The author is noted for his well-plotted mysteries. New Orleans, 1858, is the vividly and accurately portrayed setting for a tale that involves a British consul, a U.S. senator who uses logic to solve any problem, and the requisite Southern beauties and virile men. Mystery lovers will enjoy trying to spot the guilty party and will learn a great deal about life in this romantic city in the turbulent days before the Civil War.

147. Cary, Lorene. **The Price of a Child**. Knopf, 1995. (0-679-42106-8) $23.00. « Time: ca. 1855-1860.

The price of freedom is the theme of Cary's moving novel. When Ginnie is on a trip with her master, she is given the opportunity by workers in the Underground Railroad to escape to freedom. Fully realizing that her child remains on a plantation, Ginnie opts for freedom. She assumes a new name and becomes a speaker for the abolitionist cause. Cary's story is fully realized, showing Ginnie and those with whom she comes in contact as flawed humans who are doing the best they can. Details of life in Philadelphia at the time are well portrayed.

148. Cather, Willa. **Sapphira and the Slave Girl**. Knopf, 1940. Random House, 1975. (0-394-71434-2) Pb $9.00. Repr. Thorndike Press, 1992. (1-56054-482-1) Large type ed. Lib Bdg $19.95. « Time: Mid-1850s to late 1860s.

Virginia socialite Sapphira Dodderidge Colbert, who was considered to have married beneath her, was for many years a very active person. This story begins when events have caused her to become a nearly house-bound invalid. She is unjustifiably jealous of the mulatto slave girl Nancy. This concise, quiet story of manners and conflicting loyalties is beautifully told by an author noted for her character studies.

149. Charbonneau, Eileen. **In the Time of the Wolves**. Tor; distributed by St. Martin's Press, 1994. (0-812-53361-5) Pb $3.99. « Time: 1824.

Twins Joshua and Susannah are children of a Dutch-English mother and a French-Native American father who is a successful farmer. Joshua rejects his father's heritage and desperately wishes to attend Harvard. Their story centers on the summer of 1824, when the weather in New York's Catskill Mountains is so cold that the wolves come down from the mountains to seek food on the nearby farms. Charbonneau's story provides good characterizations and a strong sense of the time, and addresses ethnic and ethical issues that are of interest today.

150. Chase-Riboud, Barbara. **Echo of Lions**. Morrow, 1989. (0-688-06407-8) $19.95. « Time: 1839.

Issues of freedom and justice are argued in legal and moral terms in this account of the Amistad affair, in which slaves under the leadership of Joseph Cinque rebelled, seized a ship, were captured, and were put on trial for their lives. The story is told from the viewpoints of Cinque, a former slave who served as translator, and former president John Quincy Adams, who argued the case before the Supreme Court.

151. Chase-Riboud, Barbara. **The President's Daughter**. Crown, 1994. (0-517-59861-2) $23.00. « Time: ca. 1800-1863.

This sequel to *Sally Hemmings* concerns Harriet, daughter of Sally Hemmings, a slave in the household of Thomas Jefferson. At age 21, Harriet leaves Monticello and passes as white, which opens opportunities but fills her life with conflict. Through her experiences the reader sees events leading up to the Civil War and the Emancipation Proclamation.

152. Chase-Riboud, Barbara. **Sally Hemmings**. Viking, 1979. Several editions available. « Time: 1766-1826.

Chase-Riboud's well-researched love story of Thomas Jefferson and Sally Hemmings, his slave and reported mistress, spans 60 years. The social life and fashions of two continents are accurately portrayed as Sally goes to Paris with Ambassador Jefferson. Hemmings could have chosen to remain behind in freedom, but instead she re-enslaved herself by returning to Monticello, where she spent the remainder of her life.

153. Clemens, Samuel. **The Adventures of Huckleberry Finn**. Harper, 1885. Several editions available. « Time: Early 1800s.

After escaping from his drunken and brutal father, Huck meets Jim, a runaway slave. During their journey down the Mississippi and their forays into the society of towns along the banks, they meet con men, lynch mobs, thieves, and genteel bigotry. The moral development of Huck as he struggles with the current social structure is revealing and delightful.

154. Clemens, Samuel. **The Adventures of Tom Sawyer**. Harper, 1876. Several editions available. « Time: Early 1800s.

Tom has learned to function well both in polite society and in the company of his rough friend, Huck. When the two boys witness a murder, they are afraid to tell what they know, so they run away to Jackson's Island on the Mississippi. This exciting adventure of life in mid-nineteenth-century Missouri has been a favorite for more than 100 years.

155.   Clemens, Samuel. **Pudd'nhead Wilson**. American Publishing, 1894. Repr. Reprint Service, 1989. (0-7812-1119-0) Lib Bdg $79.00. Norton, 1981. (0-393-95027-1) Text ed. Pb $9.95. « Time: 1840s.

When a slave of mixed blood gives birth to a white son, she fears he will be sold away from her, and so exchanges him with the newborn son of the master's household. In later years the town eccentric, Pudd'nhead Wilson, solves a murder and the case of transposed identities. This sober tale condemns slavery while offering a taste of the renowned Clemens wit.

156.   Cochran, Louis. **The Fool of God: A Novel Based on the Life of Alexander Campbell**. Duell, 1958. College Press Publishing, 1992. 4th ed. (0-89900-275-7) Pb $10.95. « Time: 1811-1866.

Alexander Campbell, founder of the Disciples of Christ and president of Bethany College (West Virginia), was a friend of John Brown, Henry Clay, James Madison, and Thomas Jefferson. Cochran's fictional biography shows not only Campbell's life but also the experience of immigrants who came to the United States for religious freedom.

157.   Cooper, J. California. **Family**. Doubleday, 1991. (0-385-41171-5) $18.95. 1992. (0-385-41172-3) Pb $9.00. « Time: ca. 1850s.

The lot of many slave women was to bear numerous children, many fathered by their masters. These children were frequently sold. To remove herself and her children from this cycle, Clora, a plantation slave, attempts to poison herself and her children; she dies, but the children survive. Her spirit then follows her descendants as they struggle with the harsh realities of plantation life. The character development and rich dialogue strengthen this powerful story.

158.   Cooper, James Fenimore. **The Pioneers**. Dodd, 1822. Several editions available. « Time: ca. 1793.

Natty Bumppo, an older man who lives by the laws of nature, finds himself in conflict with the laws of civilization and moves west across the Alleghenies. This tale, set around Lake Otsego, New York, shows pioneer life on the frontier just after the Revolution. The story has historic importance as the first true romance of the frontier in American literature. Although it falls late in the Leatherstocking series, it was the first written. Followed by *The Prairie*.

159.   Cummings, Betty Sue. **Say These Names (Remember Them)**. Pineapple Press, 1984. (0-910923-15-9) $14.95. « Time: 1830s.

See-ho-kee, a young squaw, sees her tribe nearly exterminated in the second Seminole War. She follows Apayaka, the Indian leader who continues to defy the whites, and hides deep in the Everglades. The day-to-day lives of the Seminoles are presented here, with Indian history, folklore, religion, and family structure described in this narrative that takes See-ho-kee from her youth to late middle age.

160.   Dailey, Janet. **The Proud and the Free**. Little, Brown, 1994. Several editions available. « Time: 1830s.

The theft of Cherokee lands in Georgia by white settlers, followed by the forced journey of the Cherokee to the West that cost the lives of thousands, is the theme of this well-researched work. The story is told through the experiences of Temple Gordon, an educated Cherokee princess, and her future husband, The Blade Stuart, who owns a plantation. The conflict among the Cherokee as to the best way to save their people, and the realities of their situation, are presented in this work, which is stronger in historical background than in character development.

161.   De Blasis, Celeste. **Swan's Chance**. Bantam, 1986. (0-553-05092-3) $16.95. Bantam, 1986. (0-553-25692-0) Pb $5.95. « Time: 1836-1860s.
The English immigrant Falkoner family faces crisis after crisis, but still they thrive on the Maryland farm where they raise race horses. The Falkoners are opposed to slavery and run their business with free employees, but they are affected by political upheaval and divided loyalties as the Civil War nears, and by the turmoil of the war itself. Sequel to *Wild Swan*.

162.   Degenhard, William. **The Regulators**. Dial, 1943. Second Chance, 1981. (0-933256-22-1) $24.95. (0-933256-23-X) Pb $16.00. « Time: 1786-1787.
Between 1780 and 1787, many Massachusetts farmers lost their land because of high taxes and repressive monetary policies. Daniel Shays, a veteran of the Revolution, led a rebellion that prevented courts from meeting and halted a session of the Massachusetts State Supreme Court. The rebellion was suppressed, but supporters of reform won the next election. Degenhard tells the story of Shays' Rebellion with clarity and lively action.

163.   Dell, Floyd. **Diana Stair**. Farrar, 1932. Repr. AMS Press, n.d. (0-404-58419-5) $49.50. « Time: 1840s.
Diana Stair, a young widow, is concerned about the exploitation of young women in Massachusetts textile mills, but her consuming interest is abolition. Years ahead of her time, she is constantly at odds with society and the law, yet she attracts both men and women to her causes. This successful portrait of a Boston intellectual is a dramatic account of social conflict.

164.   Edmonds, Walter D. **Rome Haul**. Little, 1929. Syracuse University Press, 1987. (0-8156-0213-8) Pb $13.95. « Time: 1850s.
The unique way of life along the Erie Canal and the independent nature of the people attracted to canal life are successfully recaptured in this lively novel that shows the growing pains of a new nation. Action centers around Dan Harrow, a young farmer who becomes a "canawler," and the picturesque people he meets along the way. This well-researched work was highly recommended at the time of its publication because of its accuracy, its vibrant and picturesque language, and the unforgettable picture it presents of a little-known and long-gone era.

165.   Field, Rachel. **All This and Heaven Too**. Macmillan, 1938. Repr. Buccaneer Books, 1983. (0-89966-323-0) Lib Bdg $35.95. Amereon, 1976. (0-8488-0269-1) $32.95. « Time: 1850s.
As the wife of the Reverend Henry M. Field, Henriette Desportes (the author's great-aunt) presided over New York City literary gatherings frequented by Harriet Beecher Stowe, Samuel Morse, William Cullen Bryant, and other gifted persons of the 1850s. However, in the late 1840s she was governess in the home of a French duke and involved in a scandalous murder trial. This story, written in two parts that reveal the divided life of this fascinating woman, abounds with interesting details of mid-century social life in a novel that was well reviewed at the time of its publication.

166. Fletcher, Inglis. **The Queen's Gift**. Bobbs, 1952. Repr. Queen's House, 1976. (0-89244-005-8) Lib Bdg $27.95. Repr. Buccaneer Books, 1990. (0-89968-506-4) $25.95. « Time: 1781-1789.

This story of adventure and romance includes intense dialogues between Adam and Mary Rutledge about whether they should remain in North Carolina or pioneer in Illinois. It also contains discussions among the Rutledges and their friends about the political realities of life under the Articles of Confederation and the critical debates about the ratification of a constitution that would provide a strong central government. Details of Southern life in villages and on plantations are revealed in detail. This is the last of the author's series about life in North Carolina.

167. Giles, Janice Holt. **The Believers**. Houghton, 1957. University Press of Kentucky, 1989. (0-8131-0189-1) Pb $15.00. « Time: Early 1800s.

Giles's story of religious beliefs and social customs at a Shaker colony in Kentucky is told through the eyes of Rebecca, who follows her husband there. He becomes a fanatical believer, but Rebecca eventually leaves the colony, divorces, and remarries. This faithful recounting of Shaker life reflects the author's careful research and her sympathy for the good intentions of the best of the Shakers.

168. Giles, Janice Holt. **Land Beyond the Mountains**. Houghton, 1958. Repr. Cherokee, 1990. (0-87797-186-2) $29.95. Amereon, 1976. (0-88411-644-1) $22.95. « Time: 1783-1792.

In the late 1780s General James Wilkinson used his considerable charm and powers of persuasion to strengthen his political power and enhance his personal fortune. His schemes took advantage of the move for separate statehood for Kentucky, and the need for Kentuckians to trade in New Orleans markets controlled by the Spanish. Giles's account of the settling of Kentucky interweaves the true story of Wilkinson's schemes and the fictional story of Cass Cartwright, who establishes a settlement near Frankfort. Giles's portrait of life on the Kentucky frontier is enlivened by believable characters.

169. Graham, Heather. **Runaway**. Delacorte, 1994. (0-385-31264-4) $18.95. « Time: 1830s.

To escape trumped-up murder charges, Tara Brent runs from Boston to New Orleans and finally to a plantation deep in the wilds of Florida. In her Florida home, Tara must deal with an untamed wilderness and the battles between Seminoles and white settlers. This is the first of a projected series about Florida history.

170. Green, Julian. **The Distant Lands**. M. Boyars, 1991. (0-7145-2909-5) $24.95. « Time: 1850s.

Green began this work about the antebellum South in the 1930s, but laid it aside when *Gone with the Wind* covered his subject for that generation. He became a distinguished author and later returned to *The Distant Lands*, completing it in 1986. It is a lengthy, dramatic tale about penniless 16-year-old Elizabeth Escridge, newly arrived to Georgia from England, who immediately discovers passion and secrets beneath the social calm. Excellent characterizations and descriptions of the details of living enrich this spellbinder, which is suited for mature readers.

171.   Grey, Zane. **Western Union**. Harper, 1939, 1991. (0-06-100222-4) Pb $3.50. « Time: ca. 1860.

A prairie fire, a buffalo stampede, a flood, Indians, a bandit gang, and a body of hard-working laborers who successfully construct the first telegraph lines across the plains are all found in this fast-moving romance of the West. Suitable for younger secondary students.

172.   Hawthorne, Nathaniel. **The Blithedale Romance**. Dutton, 1852. Several editions available. « Time: 1841.

This novel is based on Hawthorne's experiences at Brook Farm, an idealistic transcendentalist experiment in communal living. The narrator, Miles Coverdale, is a dispassionate observer whose revelations about other members of the community reveal a great deal about himself.

173.   Heidish, Marcy. **Miracles: A Novel About Mother Seton, the First American Saint**. NAL Books, 1984. Ballantine, 1984. (0-345-29742-3) Pb $2.50. « Time: 1774-1821.

Elizabeth Ann Bayley, the well-educated daughter of an Episcopal physician, grew up in New York City, married, and raised five children. After she was widowed, she converted to Catholicism. Abandoned by her strongly anti-Catholic family, she accepted the assistance of a bishop in Maryland, and moved there to start a school for girls. Modern parochial schools are patterned after the system that she started. She also founded the first American community of the Daughters (Sisters) of Charity of St. Vincent de Paul. This fictionalized biography is told through the persona of a skeptical priest, who is examining her record to find reasons why she should not be canonized.

174.   Hergesheimer, Joseph. **Balisand**. Knopf, 1924. Repr. AMS Press, n.d. (0-404-15119-1) $28.50. « Time: 1790-1800.

Following the Revolutionary War, Richard Bale lives on a Virginia plantation known as Balisand. The political developments of the day are debated by admirers of Washington and Jefferson; a doomed romance ends in a tragic duel; and readers are informed about the customs of the day.

175.   Humphrey, William. **No Resting Place**. Delacorte, 1989. (0-385-29729-7) $18.95. Dell, 1990. (0-317-99667-3) Pb $10.95. « Time: 1838.

In 1838, the Cherokee people were exiled from their home in Georgia to a reservation in the Oklahoma territory. Humphrey tells the story through the eyes of a young Cherokee who, serving as interpreter and medical attendant, accompanies his grandparents on the death march that comes to be known as the Trail of Tears.

176.   Jakes, John. **North and South**. Harcourt Brace 1982. (0-15-166998-8) $24.95. Dell, 1985. (0-440-16205-X) Pb $6.99. « Time: 1842-1861.

George Hazard, financed by his family's ironworks in Pennsylvania, and Orry Main, supported by a rice plantation in South Carolina, meet at West Point, and the lives of their families become intertwined. Through the relationship of these two families, the reader views the Mexican War, the rising conflict between pro- and antislavery factions, and other complex disputes that lead to the confrontation between the Confederacy and the Union. This balanced and well-researched work is the first in a trilogy concerning events before, during, and after the war. Followed by *Love and War*.

177.  James, Henry. **Washington Square**. Modern Library, 1881. Several editions available. « Time: Early 1800s.

Social life in New York City is portrayed in this story of the relations between Catherine, a naïve girl; Dr. Sloper, her worldly-wise father; her devious and romantic aunt, Mrs. Penniman; and Morris Townsend, an irresponsible and self-absorbed suitor who is interested in Catherine's income. When Dr. Sloper becomes convinced of Townsend's motives, he threatens to disinherit Catherine. This short novel is considered by many critics to be a work of great quality.

178.  Lenski, Lois. **Bound Girl of Cobble Hill**. Lippincott, 1937. Amereon, n.d. (0-89190-632-0) $21.95. « Time: ca. 1784-1793.

Mindwell Gibbs is bound out to work for a tavern-keeper at the age of seven; she must work for him until she is sixteen. This readable work presents a detailed account of the manners and customs of late eighteenth-century Connecticut and the life of a bound child, who is at the mercy of his or her employer. Binding was a common practice during the colonial period and in the early days of our nation. Suitable for younger secondary students.

179.  Lyons, Mary E. **Letters from a Slave Girl: The Story of Harriet Jacobs**. Macmillan, 1992. (0-684-19446-5) $13.95. « Time: ca. 1850s.

The true story of Harriet Jacobs is told in the form of fictionalized letters that reveal her thoughts and feelings. Although teaching slaves to write was illegal in North Carolina, Jacobs's kindly mistress taught her when she was very young. At her owner's death, Harriet was bequeathed to a family where the safety of her own family was threatened if she did not submit to sexual molestation. Jacobs escaped but spent seven years hiding in a cubbyhole at her grandmother's cottage before she was finally able to flee to the North. The story has been extensively researched.

180.  Major, Charles. **Bears of Blue River**. Doubleday, 1901. Several editions available. « Time: 1820s.

Little Balser, age 13, lives with his parents, younger brother, and sister in a log cabin on the bank of the Big Blue River in Indiana. The story opens with his encounter with a fierce one-eared bear. Readers who like stories of nature and tales of early pioneer life will enjoy this adventure story.

181.  Meyers, Maan. **The High Constable**. Doubleday, 1994. (0-385-46984-5) $19.95. « Time: Early 1800s.

Lovers of historical mystery will delight in this well-written and carefully researched thriller that reveals the corrupt politics of early nineteenth-century New York. Using authentic details of local custom and dialogue, Meyers tells the story of a physician with family problems who gets to the underlying causes of the murder of a young woman. Sequel to *Dutchman* and *Kingsbridge Plot*.

182.  Monfredo, Miriam Grace. **Seneca Falls Inheritance**. St. Martin's Press, 1992. (0-312-07082-9) $19.95. « Time: 1848.

Seneca Falls, New York, was the setting for the First Women's Rights Convention in 1848. In setting a murder mystery at the same time as the Convention, Monfredo succeeds in telling an entertaining tale in which historical figures, including Elizabeth Cady Stanton, appear in a historically accurate setting. Librarian Glynis Tyron is the delightful detective who assists the sheriff in his investigations.

183.   Ogilvie, Elisabeth. **Jennie Glenroy**. Down East Books, 1993. (0-89272-326-2) $24.95. « Time: 1820s.

This sequel to *Jennie About to Be* and *The World of Jenny G.* stands on its own, but readers may wish to read all three novels about Alick Glenroy, a shipbuilder; his wife, Jennie; and their five lively children. This account of family life, set in early nineteenth-century Maine, provides an abundance of delightful detail about the customs, politics, joys, and adversities of the time.

184.   Partridge, Bellamy. **The Big Freeze**. Crowell, 1948. Repr. AMS Press, n.d. (0-404-58458-6) $16.00. « Time: 1840s.

A young engineer is the protagonist in this colorful and exciting account of the building of the Croton dam and aqueduct to supply water to New York City. Among the historical characters to appear are Horace Greeley and James Fenimore Cooper.

185.   Paulsen, Gary. **Nightjohn**. Doubleday, 1993. (0-385-30838-8) $14.00. « Time: 1850s.

Through the voice of 12-year-old Sarny, the atrocities of slavery are revealed: constant labor, public beatings and mutilations, atrocious living conditions, and, for women, rape. Nightjohn, an escaped slave, has returned to teach others to read—a forbidden practice that results in severe punishment. This violent story ends with hope as readers see Sarny and others continuing their effort to learn. Though strongly realistic in treatment, the reading level of this well-researched work is suitable for younger secondary students.

186.   Price, Eugenia. **Before the Darkness Falls**. Doubleday, 1987. (0-385-23068-0) $17.95. Jove, 1980. (0-515-10538-4) Pb $6.99. « Time: ca. 1845-1860.

Price's saga of three real families from Georgia's past is enhanced by fully developed characters and accurate descriptions of life in polite society and on the frontier. Natalie Browning Latimer faces unexpected tragedy, and her brother Jonathan flouts convention with his marriage to a half-Cherokee woman. Strong chapters, in which political ideas and the slavery issue are discussed by the family and their friend Robert E. Lee, clarify the conflicts that they faced. Other friends include President James Polk and his predecessor John Tyler. The first two volumes of Price's Savannah Quartet are *Savannah* and *To See Your Face Again*.

187.   Price, Eugenia. **Lighthouse**. Lippincott, 1971. Repr. Thorndike Press, 1992 (1-56054-185-7) Large type ed. Lib Bdg, $20.95. Bantam, 1972. (0-553-26910-0) Pb $5.99. « Time: ca. 1791-1830.

This first work in the author's Saint Simons Island trilogy focuses upon James Gould, brokenhearted because he lost his sweetheart to his brother. He moves from Massachusetts to the South, goes into business, struggles with his conscience about slavery, and eventually enters into a happy marriage with Jane Harris, a Southern girl. They have many adventures on the Georgia frontier before they finally settle on Saint Simons Island, where James has an opportunity to realize his dream by building a lighthouse there. This series is based on considerable research. Followed by *New Moon Rising*.

188.  Price, Eugenia. **Maria**. Lippincott, 1977. Thorndike, 1993. (1-56054-467-8) Large type ed. $20.95. Bantam, 1984. (0-553-26362-5) Pb $5.99. « Time: Late 1700s.

When Maria arrives in St. Augustine in 1763, she is determined to acquire wealth and status. Soon widowed, she struggles to overcome prejudice and hardship. The story provides information about life in colonial Florida under Spanish and British rule and in the early days following the American Revolution.

189.  Price, Eugenia. **New Moon Rising**. Lippincott, 1969. Repr. Thorndike, 1991. (1-56054-184-9) Large type ed. Lib Bdg $19.95. Bantam, 1985. (0-553-25017-5) Pb $4.50. « Time: ca. 1830-1861.

Horace Gould, dismissed from Yale for being involved in a student rebellion, returns to Saint Simons Island, Georgia, where he works on the family plantation, has nine children, and prepares to fight for the Confederacy though he has doubts about the institution of slavery. This second volume in the author's Saint Simons Island trilogy is a sequel to *Lighthouse*, and is followed by *Beloved Invader*.

190.  Price, Eugenia. **Savannah**. Doubleday, 1983. (0-385-15274-4) $19.95. Jove, 1984. (0-515-10486-8) Pb $6.99. « Time: Early 1812-1825.

Orphaned Mark Browning sails south to start a new life and meets Savannah businessman Robert Mackay, who takes him into his business. The War of 1812, romantic complications, and a secret from the past enliven this well-researched novel, which is the first in the author's Savannah quartet. Followed by *To See Your Face Again*.

191.  Price, Eugenia. **To See Your Face Again: A Novel, the Sequel to Savannah**. Doubleday, 1985. (0-385-15275-2) $21.95. Jove, 1986. (0-515-10564-3) Pb $6.99. « Time: 1838.

Natalie, a willful 16-year-old, is aboard a steam boat when it explodes, killing Natalie's great-uncle and her companion. Love flourishes as she and the charming Burke Latimer survive five days in the water. After their rescue, Burke labors to attain financial security through his work on the frontier, where he is a house builder. The impetuous Natalie does not want to delay their marriage, but finds that she may not be suited to the life of a pioneer. Price's atmospheric recreation of the antebellum South includes just the right amount of villainy. Sequel to *Savannah;* followed by *Before the Darkness Falls*.

192.  Price, Eugenia. **Where Shadows Go**. Doubleday, 1993. Several editions available. « Time: 1825-1839.

Price fans will enjoy this lengthy story, filled with period detail, that is set on Saint Simons Island off coastal Georgia. John Fraser, a military man, marries Anne Couper, and they live on her father's plantation. Fraser is a fine farmer and the plantation prospers, but he never reconciles himself to being part of the slave-owning elite. Eventually, Anne also comes to question the moral implications of the way she was raised. Sequel to *Bright Captivity*; followed by *Beauty from Ashes*.

193.  Receveur, Betty Layman. **Kentucky Home**. Ballantine, 1995. (0-345-31718-1) Pb $5.99. « Time: 1792-1825.

As the first American president establishes the government in Philadelphia, the senator from Kentucky, Roman Gentry, and his wife Kitty enter the social and political whirl in the new capital. They become acquainted with Aaron Burr, Alexander Hamilton, Thomas Jefferson, and other leaders. However, Kitty recognizes that the strength of her family is in Kentucky, and she determines to return there. The family flourishes, along with the new state, even though their son becomes involved in the Burr scandal and the later threat from the Shawnee, who support the British in the War of 1812. Sequel to *Oh, Kentucky!*

194.   Rice, Anne O. **Feast of All Saints**. Simon & Schuster, 1979. Several editions available. « Time: ca. 1850s.

The hard realities of class and color in antebellum New Orleans are seen in this well-researched novel that brings the time and place to life. The story concerns Free People of Color, persons descended from slaves and from the French and Spanish who had enslaved them. It was the custom to free these offspring, but they were never given full political or social freedom. Two of these children, Marcel and Marie, are raised as gentility but still are forever separated from their father's world by the prevailing social attitude.

195.   Rinaldi, Ann. **Broken Days**. Scholastic, 1995. (0-590-46053-6) $13.95. « Time: ca. 1810.

Following her mother's death, the half-Shawnee daughter of Thankful Chelmsford finds a home with her highly proper relatives in Massachusetts. Although the characterization is somewhat shallow, Rinaldi provides a good historic setting and shows the genuine struggle of a young person caught between two cultures. This sequel to *A Stitch in Time* is one of the author's Quilt Trilogy and is suited for younger secondary students.

196.   Rinaldi, Ann. **A Stitch in Time**. Scholastic, 1994. (0-590-46055-2) $13.95. (0-590-46056-0) $13.95. « Time: 1788-1791.

In the first volume of the Quilt Trilogy, readers are introduced to Hannah, who pieces a quilt as she looks after the family following her mother's death. Other characters in this well-researched novel include her sweetheart who is going to sea; her former romantic interest (who returns from the frontier with his motherless child for Hannah to care for); and Hannah's brother, two sisters, and puritanical father. In the upheaval following the Revolution, part of the family stays in Salem, Massachusetts; one sister elopes and moves South; and others head for the western frontier. Suited for younger secondary students.

197.   Rinaldi, Ann. **Wolf by the Ears**. Scholastic, 1991. (0-590-43413-6) $13.95. 1993. (0-590-43412-8) Pb $3.50. « Time: 1819-1822.

Harriet, daughter of Sally Hemmings, is a slave on the plantation of Thomas Jefferson. When she becomes a young woman, her mother begins to encourage her to leave the plantation at the age of 21, to seek the freedom that Jefferson promises. But Harriet believes that she can never leave Monticello, the home of all she loves, or pass for white, as others encourage her to do.

198.   Roberts, Walter. **Royal Street: A Novel of Old New Orleans**. Bobbs, 1944. Repr. AMS Press, n.d. (0-404-11415-6) $24.50. « Time: 1840s.

Victor Oliver, an expert fencer, is accepted as a leader of polite society in New Orleans until he falls in love with the daughter of an aristocratic Creole planter; then his nonaristocratic heritage is held against him. This story of romance and intrigue provides an opportunity to present a fine picture of the delightful houses, manners, and clothes that characterized certain parts of New Orleans in the 1840s.

199. Robson, Lucia St. Clair. **Light a Distant Fire**. Ballantine, 1988. (0-345-32548-6) Pb $8.95. 1991. (0-345-37561-0) Pb $5.99. « Time: Early 1800s.

The attitude of Lt. John Goode, a young graduate of West Point, toward the Seminole Indians changes gradually from contempt to admiration as he comes to know Osceola and his people. When the government sends troops against the Seminoles, Goode succeeds for a while in protecting them, but tragedy is inevitable. Through real and fictional characters, Robson presents an authentic picture of the complex issues involved.

200. Settle, Mary Lee. **Know Nothing**. Viking, 1960. Macmillan, 1988. (0-684-18847-3) Pb $9.95. Ballantine, 1981. (0-345-29313-4) Pb $3.50. « Time: ca. 1849-1860.

Settle clearly reveals the changing social mores and the complex political ideas (including the appeal of the short-lived Know-Nothing Party) in antebellum (West) Virginia in her story of the Beulah plantation and the unhappy romance between Johnny Catlett and his orphaned cousin Melinda. Sequel to *O Beulah Land*.

201. Slaughter, Frank G. **The Warrior**. Doubleday, 1956. Pocket Books, 1977. (0-671-81076-6) Pb $1.95. « Time: 1835.

At the time of the setting of this well-told story, the prevailing attitude was that the U.S. government was under no obligation to honor promises, treaties, and rules of warfare when dealing with Native Americans. Slaughter's lively story is told by a white settler and provides an accurate description of the feelings on both sides of the 1835 war with the Seminole Indians of Florida, culminating in the capture of their leader, Osceola.

202. Stolz, Mary. **Cezanne Pinto: A Memoir**. Knopf, 1994. (0-679-84917-3) $15.00 « Time: 1850s.

As an old man, Cezanne Pinto looks back on the days of his youth in slavery. When he was a young child, grieving because his mother was sold, he escaped to Canada on the Underground Railroad. Later he became a cowboy, continuing all the while to look for his mother. Through this memoir the reader sees the life of a slave and his determination to free himself from that stigma, and hears stories about the great African-American leaders of the time. Suitable for younger secondary students.

203. Stowe, Harriet Beecher. **Oldtown Folks**. Houghton, 1869. Several editions available. « Time: ca. 1783-1800.

Based on actual events, this quiet reminiscence of life in Oldtown (Natick), Massachusetts, in the years following the Revolutionary War is recognized for its value in showing the changing social life and religious movements of the time.

204. Stowe, Harriet Beecher. **Uncle Tom's Cabin**. Jewett, 1852. Several editions available. « Time: 1840s.

Before the Civil War began, more than 3 million copies of *Uncle Tom's Cabin* were in print. This daring domestic novel, whose message was that slavery destroys both master and slave, had a tremendous effect upon social attitudes in the 1850s. The story concerns the gentle old slave, Uncle Tom, who is devoted to his master's daughter, Little Eva. Upon her death, however, he is sold to the vicious Simon Legree. Another important character is the slave Eliza, whose escape to freedom across cakes of ice on the Ohio River is now a familiar image.

205. Styron, William. **The Confessions of Nat Turner**. Random House, 1967. Several editions available. « Time: 1831.

Nat Turner was raised and educated by a master opposed to slavery. The master's promise of freedom was broken when financial reverses caused him to sell Nat, whose subsequent experiences led to his leadership in a slave uprising at Southampton, Virginia in 1831. Styron bases this fictional account on Turner's confession to the defense counsel and tells the story from Turner's view. The psychological results of suppression are revealed in this powerful portrait of a gifted and proud man.

206. Warren, Lella. **Foundation Stone**. Knopf, 1940. University of Alabama Press, 1986. (0-8173-0288-3) Pb $16.95. « Time: 1820s-1865.

In a realistic panorama, Warren tells the story of the family of Yarborough Whetstone and his bride, who left a secure home in South Carolina to pioneer in the wilderness of Alabama. The story of the Whetstones and their descendants covers the settling of Alabama, the development of fine plantations, the turmoil of the war, and the realities of the days following the defeat of the Confederacy. Upon its publication, *Foundation Stone* was favorably compared with *Gone with the Wind*.

207. Yerby, Frank. **The Foxes of Harrow**. Dial, 1946. Buccaneer Books, 1976. (0-89966-210-2) Lib Bdg $20.95. « Time: 1825-1861.

Stephen Fox, a handsome hero, rises from poverty to great wealth in New Orleans in the decades preceding the war. He establishes a vast Louisiana plantation, loses it during the war, and prepares to start again. Realistic detail, lively action, colorful characters, romance (and more romance), politics, and racial conflict are all a part of the story.

## The Midwest

208. Aldrich, Bess Streeter. **A Song of Years**. Appleton, 1939. Several editions available. « Time: 1854-1865.

Aldrich is noted for her ability to provide a convincing picture of time and place, with all the details of home life, marriages, births, and deaths. This story, set in pioneer Iowa, concerns Wayne Lockwood, a lonely young settler; the neighboring Martin family of seven daughters and two sons; and the romance between Suzanne Martin and Lockwood.

209. Cooper, James Fenimore. **The Prairie**. Dodd, 1827. Several editions available. « Time: 1804.

This fifth and last volume of the Leatherstocking series is a story of life on the prairie beyond the Mississippi River at the time of Jefferson's administration. The aged trapper, Natty Bumppo; Ellen, a young girl from a family traveling westward; and her romantic interest, Paul Hover, are captured by a band of Sioux. They escape, but the Sioux have taken their horses and cattle, and the pioneers must depend on the assistance of Bumppo and an army officer who is searching for his kidnapped wife. Although it is full of unlikely coincidence and stilted dialogue, and Cooper was never known for lively female characters, *The Prairie* still catches much of the spirit of the old West. Sequel to *The Pioneers*.

210. DeHartog, Jan. **The Peculiar People**. Pantheon, 1992. (0-679-41636-6) $22.50. Repr. Thorndike, 1993. (1-56054-670-0) Large type ed. $17.95. « Time: 1830s.

Among the forces that drive Mordecai Monk and Lydia Best, Quakers whose activist ideas are unsettling to their more conservative brethren in faith, is the desire to correct injustices to slaves and Native Americans. Lydia, disgraced for her involvement with the Underground Railroad, accompanies Monk to Indiana, where he attempts to convert the Shawnee. Conflict concerning social attitudes of the day are seen, as each character deals with serious personal problems as well as with the conflicts created by their faith.

211. Derleth, August William. **Bright Journey**. Scribner, 1940. Repr. Buccaneer Books, 1993. (1-56849-1245-5) $21.95. « Time: 1812-1840.

The life of Hercules Dousman and the development of the fur trade in the Northwest territory provide the setting for this two-part story. Part I deals with Dousman's boyhood on Mackinac Island during the War of 1812. Part II chronicles his adventures in Prairie du Chien, Wisconsin, as he rises from obscurity to become a director of the American Fur Company. Derleth's balanced account of the fur trade and the role of Native Americans and French fur traders includes enough romance and poetic descriptions of the wilderness to sustain the reader's interest.

212. Derleth, August William. **Hills Stand Watch**. Duell, 1960. Repr. Buccaneer Books, 1993. (1-56849-124-7) $21.95. « Time: 1840s.

The development of the Wisconsin territory and its move to statehood are revealed in detail in this romance. Candace and David live a restricted life in an isolated lead mining village. The reader becomes acquainted with the trials of this life: problems with Indians who raid shipments, the details and dangers of lead mining, and the down-river journey to market. The author's knowledge of, and love for, the land and its people shines through this accurate history.

213. Eggleston, Edward. **The Circuit Rider**. Scribner, 1874. Several editions available. « Time: 1800-1825.

Eggleston's somewhat melodramatic account of a circuit rider among the Methodists in southern Ohio is based on his own experiences and those of Jacob Young, whose autobiography showed him to be a wild, irreligious youth who converted out of remorse and despair. Through the adventures of the fictional hero, Morton Goodwin, the reader becomes acquainted with daily life, customs, and religion on the frontier.

214. Eggleston, Edward. **The Graysons**. Scribner, 1887. Several editions available. « Time: ca. 1850.

In this detailed picture of daily life and customs in rural Illinois, Abraham Lincoln is introduced as counsel in a murder trial. The story is loosely based on an anecdote about the way in which Lincoln defended the accused by using information from an almanac. The characters include an indentured girl; a jaunty, well-dressed villain; and townspeople eager for a lynching.

215. Eggleston, Edward. **The Hoosier School-Boy**. Scribner, 1883. Several editions available. « Time: ca. 1840.

The difficulties of acquiring an education in frontier Indiana and Ohio are shown in this essentially plotless potboiler, based upon the author's boyhood memories, that has appeared on reading lists for more than 100 years. Readers will gain insight into the games and small pleasures of boys of the time.

216. Eggleston, Edward. **The Hoosier School-Master**. Scribner, 1871. Several editions available. « Time: 1850s.

This sentimental tale of Indiana backwoods life and education centers on the experiences of an itinerant teacher who boards around among the farmers. He falls in love with a servant girl whose mistress wants him as a husband for her daughter. The simple plot provides the setting for a portrayal of the character, morality, and customs of Midwesterners that many Hoosiers considered disparaging. Eggleston originally published this tale in serial form, and it was so popular that the book was published without revision.

217. Ellis, William D. **The Bounty Lands**. World, 1952. Landfall Press, 1981. (0-913428-20-5) Pb $5.95. « Time: ca. 1799-1819.

Following the Revolutionary War, western lands in the Northwest Territory were granted to veterans in recognition of their wartime service. However, land speculators had other ideas for use of that land, and conflict broke out between settlers and speculators in Ohio. Ellis's exuberant story is based on careful research, as is evident in the accuracy of detail.

218. Fuller, Iola. **The Loon Feather**. Harcourt Brace, 1967. (0-15-653200-X) Pb $10.95. « Time: Early 1800s.

This award-winning fictionalized autobiography of Oneta, Tecumseh's daughter (Ojibway), is set in the Mackinac region of Michigan during the busy fur-trading years. In telling the story of Oneta's education in a convent school in Quebec and her return to her people on the island, Fuller presents a rich picture of a time when people of many backgrounds intermingled to develop a new society.

219. Kirkland, Caroline M. **New Home—Who'll Follow? or Glimpses of Western Life**. C. S. Francis, 1839. Several editions available. « Time: 1830s.

Kirkland and her husband founded a pioneer village in Michigan during the 1830s, and this fictionalized account of their adjustment to frontier living was first published in 1839. Perceptive sketches of neighbors and daily events reveal customs and contemporary language. They also provide an accurate picture of the explosive growth of the area. Thousands of immigrants poured into Detroit each day, where land-sharks waited to take advantage of the fever for homesteads.

220. Lancaster, Bruce. **For Us the Living**. Stokes, 1940. Repr. Amereon, 1975. (0-89190-882-X) Lib Bdg $30.95. « Time: ca. 1810-1834.

Lancaster's convincing fictionalized biography of Abraham Lincoln during his days in Kentucky and Indiana is based on the few facts that are known about his boyhood. The rest of the story is based on a clear understanding of Lincoln's character and the manner in which boys grew up on the frontier. Details of daily life—superstition, tall tales, songs, and cookery—enrich the story.

221. McDonald, Julie. **Amalie's Story**. Simon & Schuster, 1970. Rev. ed. Sutherland Pub., 1985. (0-930942-08-6) $7.95. « Time: mid-1800s.

*Amalie's Story* begins with her parents' marriage in Denmark and ends with her widowhood in Iowa in the 1880s. The main part of the story concerns Amalie's difficult adjustment to her new home. McDonald's novel provides an excellent feeling for the factors that led to emigration to America and the difficulties of adjusting to life in pioneer Iowa.

222.   Quick, Herbert. **Vandemark's Folly**. Bobbs, 1922. University of Iowa Press, 1987. (0-87745-182-6) Pb $13.95. « Time: 1840-1860.

Quick's hero, Jake Vandemark, tells the story of his memorable life, first on the Erie Canal and then as an early settler on an Iowa farm. This is a well-researched novel that presents a rich account of life on the prairie, including claim jumping, frontier law, and the Underground Railroad.

223.   Richter, Conrad. **The Fields**. Knopf, 1946. Ohio University Press, 1991. (0-8214-0979-4) Pb $12.95. « Time: ca. 1800-1820.

The daughter of the family introduced in *The Trees* marries a Boston lawyer whose strength and integrity are instrumental in the transformation of the area from an economy based on hunting to one based on agriculture. Details of life, speech, and regional character strengthen this highly acclaimed work. Preceded by *The Trees*; followed by *The Town*.

224.   Richter, Conrad. **The Town**. Knopf, 1950. Ohio University Press, 1991. (0-8214-0980-8) Pb $14.95. Harmony Raine, 1981. (0-89967-048-2) Lib Bdg $17.95. « Time: ca. 1830-1850.

In the rich concluding volume of the Awakening Land trilogy, the town grows, the family moves from cabin to mansion, the children establish their own homes, and the pioneer days are over. The novels of the trilogy stand alone, but the sum is greater than its parts. Preceded by *The Fields*.

225.   Richter, Conrad. **The Trees**. Knopf, 1940. (0-394-44951-7) $18.95. Ohio University Press, 1991. (0-8214-0978-6) Pb $12.95. « Time: Late 1700s.

Details about pioneer life, travel, and trade are an integral part of this well-researched classic work that begins the classic Awakening Land trilogy, about a pioneer family that migrates from Pennsylvania to the virgin wilderness of southeastern Ohio. Followed by *The Fields* and *The Town*.

226.   Sinclair, Harold. **American Years**. Doubleday, 1938. University of Illinois Press, 1988. (0-252-06037-7) Pb $10.95. « Time: 1830-1861.

Humor and lively characters mark Sinclair's chronicle of life in a small Illinois town during the years when Lincoln was coming to local and national attention.

227.   Thoene, Brock. **The Legend of Storey County**. Thomas Nelson, 1995. (0-7852-8070-7) $16.99. « Time: ca. 1840-1900.

Jim Canfield is a 100-year-old ex-slave. When he tells a reporter the story of his life, the reader travels with him from the auction block to his life in Missouri, his friendship with two young men named Sam and Huck, his escape to Iowa, his involvement in the Civil War, and his western adventures. This spellbinding, often humorous story is well researched.

228.   Thom, James Alexander. **Panther in the Sky**. Ballantine, 1989. (0-345-30596-5) $19.95. 1990. (0-345-36638-7) Pb $5.95. « Time: Late 1700s.

Thom states that he "was looking especially for insights into the culture, morality, ceremony, and psychic condition of the Shawnee" in this work about Tecumseh, a noted Shawnee chief who used his remarkable skills as a leader and military strategist to unite the Native American people against the encroachment of white settlers in the Ohio valley. Respectful attention is given to the courage of Native Americans in their struggle to maintain their way of life.

229. West, Jessamyn. **The Friendly Persuasion**. Harcourt, 1945. Several editions available. « Time: Mid-1800s.

The life of a family of Indiana Quakers during the years leading up to the Civil War is told with warmth and charm in this episodic novel based upon West's family legends. Readers will find vivid metaphors, humor, and memorable characters and descriptions.

230. West, Jessamyn. **The Massacre at Fall Creek**. Harcourt Brace, 1975, 1986. (0-15-657681-3) Pb $6.95. Peter Smith, n.d. (0-8446-6274-7) $18.50 « Time: 1824.

In 1824, nine Seneca Indians were massacred near a pioneer settlement in Indiana by four white men and a boy. West's suspense-filled story describes the social climate of the time, the killings, the trial, and the effects of the incident on the families of those involved.

## The Plains and Mountain States

231. Aldrich, Bess Streeter. **A Lantern in Her Hand**. Appleton, 1928. Several editions available. « Time: Mid-1800s.

From her log cabin home in Iowa, Abbie Deal moves to the plains of Nebraska where she raises her family. Written as a tribute to the author's pioneer mother, this story of sacrifice, accomplishment, and family life on the plains has remained popular for more than 60 years.

232. Altsheler, J. A. **Texan Scouts**. Appleton, 1913. Several editions available. « Time: 1830s.

In the last book of the author's Texan trilogy, Ned Fulton continues his adventures in Texas. He is involved in the war for Texan independence, including the siege of the Alamo, but he escapes on a schooner bound for New Orleans. Davy Crockett, James Bowie, and Santa Anna are characters in this historically accurate novel. Suitable for younger secondary students.

233. Altsheler, J. A. **Texan Star**. Appleton, 1912. Several editions available. « Time: 1830s.

Fictional character Ned Fulton escapes from two Mexican prisons and finally reaches Texas, where he warns Sam Houston of an impending attack and joins his forces to fight Indians and Mexicans in the war for Texas independence. This well-researched first work of the Texan trilogy is suitable for younger secondary students.

234. Altsheler, J. A. **Texan Triumph**. Appleton, 1913. Several editions available. « Time: 1830s.

Ned Fulton is involved in the San Jacinto campaign in the war for Texas independence. This dramatic account of events is based on historic fact. Suitable for younger secondary students. Sequel to *Texas Star*; followed by *Texan Scouts*.

235.  Arnold, Elliot. **Blood Brother**. Duell, 1947. University of Nebraska Press, 1979. (0-8032-5901-8) Pb $11.95. « Time: 1856-1870.

Arnold's detailed and exciting fictionalized account of Cochise and the Apache wars in New Mexico and Arizona, and the efforts of Tom Jeffords, a famous peacemaker and Indian agent, is sympathetic to the Native American point of view. Among the real people included as characters is Oliver Otis Howard, a Union general.

236.  Arnold, Elliot. **Time of the Gringo**. Knopf, 1953. Repr. Amereon, n.d. (0-88411-180-6) Lib Bdg $28.95. « Time: 1830s-1840s.

Don Manuel Armijo was the Mexican governor of New Mexico just before the Mexican War (1848). Arnold's lengthy, exciting novel provides an authentic picture of life there, the events that led to the war, and the personality of Armijo. The development of the characters and situations is authentic and colorful.

237.  Becnel, Rexanne. **When Lightning Strikes**. Dell, 1995. (0-440-21568-4) Pb $5.99. « Time: 1855.

When Abigail's recently widowed father decides to join a wagon train headed west under an assumed name, Abigail is confused and frightened. The demands of the journey, however, give her little time to contemplate the mystery. This engrossing story provides a strong sense of time and place.

238.  Binns, Archie. **The Land Is Bright**. Scribner, 1939. Oregon State University Press, 1992. (0-87071-508-9) Text ed. $24.95. (0-87071-509-7) Pb $13.95. « Time: 1850s.

This colorful, realistic, and dramatic account of the Oregon Trail adventures of a family of Illinois farmers and their traveling companions clarifies the spirit of the people who made this tremendous journey. Memorable episodes and characters mark the tale, which begins with the loading of the wagons and closes in Oregon.

239.  Bittner, Rosanne. **Thunder on the Plains**. Doubleday, 1992. (0-385-42148-6) $15.00. Bantam, 1992. (0-553-29015-0) Pb $5.99. « Time: 1857-1869.

When Bo Landers hires Colt Travis, a handsome half-breed scout, to guide his workers as they build the transcontinental railroad, Landers's beautiful and innocent young daughter and the honorable scout inevitably fall in love. Recognizing the differences in their worlds, they separate. A war, imprisonment, marriage to others, and other impediments must be overcome before true love has its way in this well-written historical romance.

240.  Brackett, Leigh. **Follow the Free Wind**. Doubleday, 1963. Ballantine, 1980. (0-345-29008-9) Pb $1.75. « Time: ca. 1820-1860s.

Brackett's fictionalized biography tells the story of James Beckwourth, a man of mixed blood who went west as a blacksmith. He was adopted by the Crow Indians, lived and fought with them against the whites, joined Kearny's force in California, and took part in the stampede to riches in Colorado in 1859. Winner of the 1964 Western Writers of America Award.

241. Capps, Benjamin. **A Woman of the People**. Duell, 1966. University of New Mexico Press, 1985. (0-8263-0782-5) Pb $10.95. « Time: 1850-1870.

Texas is the setting for this story of Helen Morrison, a white girl captured by the Comanches at the age of nine. During her captivity, she adopts the Comanche ways while secretly planning to escape, until marriage finally convinces her that she has become Comanche. Helen's observations of the daily life and customs of the Comanche and their struggle against the white settlers are well presented.

242. Cather, Willa. **Death Comes for the Archbishop**. Knopf, 1927. Several editions available. « Time: 1850s.

Cather's simply told classic work, concerning two French priests who traveled to New Mexico shortly after the Mexican War to work with the settlers there, has received critical acclaim. The story of Fr. Latour and Fr. Vaillant is based on the lives of two priests who served the Vicarate of New Mexico. It presents a picture of the Mexican and Native American cultures, the landscape of the southwest, desperadoes, and frontier heroes such as Kit Carson.

243. Comfort, Will. **Apache**. Dutton, 1931. 2d ed. Repr. Amereon, 1976. (0-89190-851-X) $20.95. University of Nebraska Press, 1986. (0-8032-6319-8) Pb $9.95. « Time: ca. 1850s-1863.

Comfort's factual and simply told fictionalized biography is balanced in its presentation of the life of Mangas Colorado (Don-Ha), the famous Apache leader respected by both whites and Indians for his efforts to reunite the Indian nations against white encroachment in the New Mexico territory. Mangas Colorado, father-in-law to Cochise, was captured in 1863.

244. Conley, Robert J. **Mountain Windsong: A Novel of the Trail of Tears**. University of Oklahoma Press, 1992. (0-8061-2452-0) $19.95. « Time: 1830s.

Long after the events known as the Trail of Tears are over, a grandfather tells the tale to his grandson. In an accurate and moving account, the reader sees the story from the view of Waguli, who is forced to endure the migration, and his sweetheart, Oconeechee, who remains behind with a small group hiding in the mountains, hoping to retain their way of life. This highly recommended work reveals the values of Native Americans and their dignity as they were forced from their homeland.

245. Crook, Elizabeth. **Promised Land: A Novel of the Texas Rebellion**. Doubleday, 1994. (0-385-41858-2) $22.50. « Time: 1836.

The tragic e ents that led to Texas independence are the focus of this well-researched page-turner in which the homesteading Kenner family is forced to flee their home after the fall of the Alamo. Details of the natural world and the daily life of citizens and soldiers are all seen, as some of the family flee toward the U.S. border and others are involved in battle.

246. Crook, Elizabeth. **The Raven's Bride**. Doubleday, 1991. (0-385-41775-6) $19.95. Southern Methodist University Press, 1993. (0-87074-348-1) Pb $12.95. « Time: ca. 1829.

Sam Houston, advocate of Indian rights and supporter of Andrew Jackson, was governor of Tennessee when he married Elizabeth Allen, who left him after only 11 weeks. Houston never spoke of the marriage, despite much speculation that cost him the governorship. Author/researcher Crook examined the slim evidence to write a historically based work that is admittedly a literary invention. The strong characterizations of both Houston and Elizabeth, and an accurate sense of the time, add to the appeal of this moving story.

247.   Davis, Harold Lenoir. **Beulah Land**. Morrow, 1949. Repr. Greenwood, 1971. (0-8371-5212-7) $35.00. « Time: 1851.

For personal reasons, an odd assortment of people join to make a hazardous journey from North Carolina to the Southwest, to Kansas, and on to Oregon. Along the way, the reader is treated by the Pulitzer prize-winning author to a revealing picture of the developing nation and of local culture.

248.   Early, Tom. **Sons of Texas**. Berkley, 1989. (0-425-11474-0) Pb $4.99. « Time: 1816.

A fine sense of the time and good character development characterize this work concerning Michael Lewis and his brother Andrew, who seek revenge against a cruel Spanish officer who massacred a band of horse traders. First in the Sons of Texas series.

249.   Fisher, Vardis. **Children of God**. Harper, 1939. O. L. Holmes, 1977. (0-918522-50-1) $12.95. « Time: ca. 1820s-1850.

In his epic of the West, Fisher provides the background of the Mormon movement, which was founded by Joseph Smith in 1830. Under the leadership of Brigham Young, the group moved west in the 1840s, faced persecution in Illinois and Missouri, and made a heroic migration to Utah before founding an empire in the desert in 1847. Smith and Young are major characters in the story.

250.   Fisher, Vardis. **The Mothers**. Vanguard, 1943. Several editions available. « Time: 1846.

Fisher's well-researched account of the tragic Donner party, of its courage, endurance, and cowardice, is told from the point of view of the mothers who had to face disaster and the deaths of their families when trapped in the Sierra mountains by a blizzard.

251.   Fisher, Vardis. **Mountain Man**. Morrow, 1965. Several editions available. « Time: 1830s.

Returning home from a trapping expedition, a mountain man finds his Indian bride and child slain; he vows revenge on the Indian murderers, hunts them, and is hunted in return. The life of the self-sufficient trapper and mountain man of the early 1800s is faithfully presented in Fisher's story of Sam Minard, whose love of nature and personal freedom justifies his heroic struggle to survive.

252.   Garwood, Julie. **For the Roses**. Simon & Schuster, 1995. (0-671-87097-1) $23.00. « Time: 1860-1879.

A good sense of the Old West is found in this adventure of four streetwise boys (including a runaway slave) who find an abandoned baby girl. The boys decide to protect the child and raise her, so they head for Montana, where they live under an assumed name. When the baby becomes a young woman, she is found by an employee of her original family who romances her without revealing his true identity. She must then choose between wealth and those who have raised her.

253. Gordon, Leo V. **Powderkeg**. Presidio Press, 1991. Several editions available. « Time: 1857-1858.

During the presidency of James Buchanan, there was a little-known event called the "Utah War." Southern members of the president's cabinet, supported by false reports, pushed for a large contingent of the army, led by a Southern sympathizer, to be sent to Utah to quell a nonexistent rebellion. The real intent of the mission was to weaken the army, capture Salt Lake City, and, when the South seceded, assure that California and the southwest would be cut off from the Union. This exciting and informative novel features appealing characterizations.

254. Guthrie, A. B. **The Big Sky**. Sloane, 1947. Houghton, 1992. (0-395-61153-9) Pb $9.70. Repr. Buccaneer Books, 1993. (1-56849-121-2) Lib Bdg $24.95. « Time: 1830s.

Guthrie's classic work tells the story of a mountain man who lives in the Upper Mississippi River country. He is courageous and knowledgeable about the wilderness but unable to live comfortably in settled areas. In his characterization of the lives of trappers and Indians, Guthrie includes language and situations natural to the time and place.

255. Guthrie, A. B. **The Way West**. Sloane, 1949. Repr. Lightyear, 1992. (0-89968-305-3) Lib Bdg $32.95. Houghton Mifflin, 1993. (0-395-65662-1) Pb $10.95. « Time: 1840s.

Dick Summers, one of the principal characters of *The Big Sky,* accepts the responsibility of guiding a wagon train from Independence to the Willamette River in Oregon. By centering upon the lives of five couples, Guthrie realistically and faithfully reveals details of the overland journey, and the impact of cruelty and kindness on human relationships. This simple story is filled with the Western idiom.

256. Hotchkiss, Bill. **Ammahabas**. Norton, 1983. Comstock, n.d. (0-89174-112-7) Pb $7.95. « Time: 1830s-1850s.

In this sequel to *The Medicine Calf,* Beckwourth becomes restless in his role as a Crow chief, so he leaves his friends and his 10 wives to travel with a variety of companions to California and then back to his home in St. Louis. Ultimately he returns to the mountains and his Crow friends. The story is full of Indian lore and realistic derring-do.

257. Hotchkiss, Bill. **The Medicine Calf**. Norton, 1981. (0-393-01389-8) $13.95. Repr. Comstock, 1989. (0-89174-046-5) $4.95. « Time: 1820s.

The life of Jim Beckwourth, a mulatto mountain man and horse wrangler from Virginia, is fictionalized by Hotchkiss in this realistic, action-filled novel. When Beckwourth's wife is killed by a Blackfeet war party he vows revenge, joins the Crows (enemies of the Blackfeet), and becomes one of the chiefs of that nation. Followed by *Ammahabas.*

258. Hotze, Sollace. **A Circle Unbroken**. Houghton Mifflin, 1988. (0-89919-733-7) $13.95. 1991. (0-395-59702-1) Pb $4.95. « Time: 1838-1845.

Rachel Porter is captured by the Dakota Sioux when a small child. After initial mistreatment, she is raised by the chief as his own daughter. When she is rescued at age 17, she finds that in spite of her love for her white siblings, she has changed too much to be the person her white father wants her to be. Suited for younger secondary students.

259. Hough, Emerson. **The Covered Wagon**. Appleton, 1922. Amereon, n.d. (0-89190-617-7) $24.95. Reprint Service, 1992. (0-7812-6743-9) Lib Bdg $89.00. « Time: 1848.

Detailed descriptions of scenes and events add to Hough's account of the adventures of a caravan of pioneers making their way from Missouri to Oregon. Romantic and leadership rivalries, battles with swollen streams and prairie fires, fights with natives, internal dissension, the exhaustion of a pilgrimage that lasts many months, and the divisive effect of the news about the California gold strike are all well presented in this classic work.

260. Johnston, Terry C. **Dance on the Wind**. Bantam, 1995. (0-553-09071-2) $21.95. « Time: 1810-1815.

Life on the frontier and the restless qualities of those who were always pushing further west is strongly portrayed in Johnston's account of the coming of age of Titus Bass. Bass's father wants him to continue the family tradition in farming, but Titus decides to try his luck on the Mississippi, blacksmithing in St. Louis, and as a mountain man. Good characterizations and fast action ensure that this work will find a wide audience.

261. Kherdian, David. **Bridger: The Story of a Mountain Man**. Greenwillow, 1987. (0-688-06510-4) $11.75. « Time: 1822-1824.

A first-person narrative is used to tell the story of the early years of Jim Bridger, a mountain man who traveled up the Missouri and across the Rockies. The story concludes with Bridger's discovery of the Great Salt Lake in 1824. This well-researched work is suitable for younger secondary students.

262. Kirkland, Elithe. **Divine Average**. Little, 1952. Shearer Publishing, 1984. (0-940672-19-7) $15.95. « Time: 1838.

The story of Range Templeton, a man with a powerful hatred of Indians and Mexicans and an equally powerful hunger for land, is the setting for Kirkland's novel of racial conflict among American and Mexican settlers and the Native Americans in Texas. Historical characters inhabit the background of this story.

263. Kirkland, Elithe. **Love Is a Wild Assault**. Doubleday, 1959. Shearer Publishing, 1991. (0-940672-58-8) Pb $13.95. « Time: ca. 1840s.

This biographical novel is based upon the memoir of 80-year-old Harriet Ann Ames, married 3 times and mother of 18 children, who provides a colorful picture of life in the young Republic of Texas. Politics, violence, chicanery, romance, and the events of daily life are all part of this exciting account of frontier living.

264. Kunstler, James Howard. **Embarrassment of Riches**. Tor, 1988. (0-8125-8498-8) Pb $3.95. « Time: 1803-1804.

In a work reminiscent of *The Adventures of Huckleberry Finn,* Kunstler relates the adventures of Samuel and his botanist uncle. They are sent by President Jefferson into the unexplored wilderness of the southern part of the Louisiana Purchase in search of a legendary giant sloth. They meet a decidedly strange family of pirates on the Ohio, are rescued from Indians, witness a slave revolt, and participate in a battle against Spaniards. Readers will enjoy the high adventure while they learn about the flora and fauna of the wilderness.

265. L'Amour, Louis. **Comstock Lode**. Bantam, 1981-1982. (0-553-27561-5) Pb $5.50. Thorndike Press, 1993. (1-56054-648-4) Large type ed. Pb $16.95. « Time: 1849-1850.

Trevallian's family, newly arrived from Wales, seeks a fortune in the gold fields but meets with tragedy when drunken ruffians rob and murder both parents. Trevallian dabbles in various jobs to make a living while he seeks revenge. The story exposes the brutality and crooked financial deals that sprang from the gold fever surrounding the rise of boomtown Virginia City, Nevada.

266. Lasky, Kathryn. **Beyond the Divide**. Macmillan, 1983. (0-02-751670-9) $15.95. Dell, 1986. (0-440-91021-8) Pb $3.25. « Time: 1849.

Shunned by the other Amish in their Pennsylvania home town, Meribah and her father join a group of wagons headed west. When the wagon train leaves her and her ailing father alone in the Sierras, she survives through the kindness of the Yana, a small Indian tribe. Meribah's exposure to new ideas, her changing values, and a vivid sense of each of the characters on the trek are revealed through her diary. Lasky's story of the realities of the westward journey is based on careful research.

267. Laughlin, Ruth. **The Wind Leaves No Shadow**. Whittlesey, 1948. Caxton, 1948. (0-87004-083-9) Pb $8.95. « Time: 1840s.

Set in the time between the liberation of Mexico from Spain and the American occupation is this story of the life of Doña Tules (nee Maria Gertrudes Barceló), market girl, monte queen, and revolutionist in Santa Fe, New Mexico. Laughlin's account, based on historic records, legends, and imagination, shows insight into the character and culture of those who settled there: Spanish, Mexicans, Indians, and Yankees.

268. Long, Jeff. **Empire of Bones: A Novel of Sam Houston and the Texas Revolution**. Morrow, 1993. (0-688-12252-3) $22.00. « Time: ca. 1836.

Revealed in this fictionalized biography are Houston's experience with Andrew Jackson, which prepared him to assume leadership in Texas; the complexities, strengths, and weaknesses of Houston's personality; his brilliance and his blunders; and the situation in which he found himself the leader of a ragtag group of rebels. Suitable for mature readers.

269. Manfred, Frederick F. **Lord Grizzley**. McGraw, 1954. University of Nebraska Press, 1983. (0-8032-8118-8) Pb $8.95. NAL-Dutton, 1964. (0-451-08311-3) Pb $4.50. « Time: 1820s.

Mountain man Hugh Glass, trapping in the Upper Missouri River country, is deserted by his companions, who believe him dead after he is badly mauled by a grizzly. The injured man's obsession with revenge gives him the strength to struggle, sometimes on hands and knees, to reach safety. This powerful account is based on actual events.

270. McMurtry, Larry. **Dead Man's Walk**. Simon & Schuster, 1995. (0-684-80753-X) $26.00. « Time: ca. 1840.

Woodrow Call and Gus McCrae, novice Texas Rangers, endure many hardships during the early days of the Texas Republic, including struggles with nature, fellow Rangers, and Native Americans. Not daunted by the dangers in Texas, however, they set out to help rescue wealthy Santa Fe from the Mexicans. Prequel to *Lonesome Dove*.

271. Meyer, Carolyn. **Where the Broken Heart Still Beats: The Story of Cynthia Ann Parker**. Harcourt Brace, 1992. (0-15-200639-7) $16.95. (0-15-295602-6) Pb $5.95. « Time: 1836-1858.

In 1836, little Cynthia Ann Parker was captured by the Comanche. She was raised by them and adopted their ways, living first as a slave and later as a chief's wife and the mother of Quanah Parker. When she was rescued 24 years later, Cynthia Ann found reassimilation very difficult. In an afterword, Meyer explains the factual basis for the story.

272. Michener, James A. **The Eagle and the Raven**. State House Press, 1990. Several editions available. « Time: 1830s.

This previously unpublished excerpt from Michener's *Texas* concerns the lives of Sam Houston (arrogant speculator and frontiersman) and Santa Anna (vain and opportunistic general and politician) and their encounter at the battle of San Jacinto, which resulted in Texas independence and the U.S. annexation of Texas. The work includes a lengthy introduction in which the author discusses the story's development.

273. Morrow, Honore. **On to Oregon**. Morrow, 1926. Repr. Morrow, 1946. (0-688-21639-0) $16.00. Morrow, 1991. (0-688-10494-0) Pb $4.95. « Time: 1840s.

When 13-year-old John Sager and his family leave Missouri to join a caravan to traverse the Oregon Trail, John is an immature and disobedient child. However, the deaths of his parents and the responsibility of caring for six younger siblings, including a new baby, soon matures him. The story's simplicity, attention to historic detail, and excitement will appeal to younger secondary students.

274. Olds, Bruce. **Raising Holy Hell**. Holt, 1995. (0-8050-3856-6) $22.50. « Time: ca. 1850-1859.

Olds traces the life of slavery-hating John Brown from his childhood to his death by hanging at Harper's Ferry in 1859. Brown's lifelong abolitionist activities came to national attention when he, his sons, and other followers led guerrilla actions against armed proslavery groups in Kansas in 1856. Olds uses eloquent accounts recorded by Brown, his family, and associates in addition to other historical documents. This powerful novel requires a mature reader.

275. Owen, Dean. **The Sam Houston Story: A Swashbuckling Account of the Man Whose Daring Exploits Altered the Course of Texas History**. Monarch, 1961. Chivers North America, 1992. (0-7927-1208-0) Large type ed. $19.95. (0-7927-1207-2) Large type ed. Pb $17.95. « Time: 1812-1863.

Sam Houston lived for a time with the Cherokee, served in the army under Andrew Jackson during the War of 1812, and became a district attorney, member of Congress, governor of Tennessee, and leader in the fight to gain Texas's independence from Mexico. Houston found danger a tonic and deliberately chose a life of adventure and difficulty. This easy-to-read fictionalized biography presents a realistic view of Houston's relations with the men and women in his life.

276. Proctor, George W. **Walks Without a Soul**. Doubleday, 1990. (0-385-24470-3) $14.95. « Time: 1850s.

When a Comanche raiding party captures several white women, they also take the wife and daughters of slave Nate Wagoner. Nate is allowed to go with the other men in an attempt to free the women, but his slave status is never forgotten, although his valor in battle leads to grudging respect. Because the Comanche have no place in their world for a Black man, Nate is regarded as one who "walks without a soul," and consequently he is able to go places that other persons cannot. This engrossing story is well researched.

277. Robson, Lucia St. Clair. **Ride the Wind: The Story of Cynthia Ann Parker and the Last Days of the Comanches**. Ballantine, 1982. (0-345-29145-X) Pb $8.95. « Time: 1836-1870s.

The true story of the remarkable life of Cynthia Ann Parker and her son Quanah Parker is widely known. In this work, Robson tells the dramatic story of the young woman who was kidnapped by the Comanche, overcame her fears, learned to value the Indian ways, and married a tribal leader. Cynthia Ann was reclaimed by her original white family, but her son, Quanah Parker, became an important Comanche chief who opposed resettlement in the Indian Territories. Robson's compelling work brings the complexities of their story to life.

278. Sanders, Leonard. **Star of Empire: A Novel of Old San Antonio**. Delacorte, 1992. (0-385-29916-8) $22.00. Dell, 1993. (0-440-21635-4) Pb $5.99. « Time: 1850s.

Corrie McNair, a Charleston socialite, marries Tad Logan, and they go to the new Texas Republic to build a cattle ranch on the desolate frontier near San Antonio. Tad fights the Comanche and the Mexican Army, while Corrie raises their sons and rebuilds their war-damaged home. Sanders bases the story on journals, letters, and other documents and incorporates both fictional and real characters in the plot.

279. Schultz, James Willard. **Quest of the Fish-Dog Skin**. Houghton, 1913. Confluence Press, 1984. (0-8253-0321-4) Pb $7.95. « Time: 1861.

Two young boys, one a Blackfeet Indian and one white, test their mettle and their friendship as they make their way across the Rockies from Fort Benton, Montana, to the Pacific in search of seal skin (fish-dog skin). This sequel to *With the Indians in the Rockies* stands on its own.

280. Schultz, James Willard. **With the Indians in the Rockies**. Houghton, 1912. Confluence Press, 1984. (0-8253-0319-2) Pb $7.95. « Time: 1856.

An orphaned boy is taken by his fur trapper uncle to the Montana wilderness at the head of the Missouri River. Here he lives with the helpful Blackfeet Indians and becomes close friends with an Indian boy. After the two boys are kidnapped by the Kootenays and taken to the Rockies, they escape and make their way back home. This well-written adventure provides an excellent sense of time and place. Followed by *Quest of the Fish-Dog Skin*.

281. Searls, Hank. **Blood Song**. Ballantine, 1985. (0-345-30663-5) Pb $3.95. « Time: 1849.

The past and present are blended in this tale of a retired admiral's attempt to relive the journey made by his great-grandfather, Morgan, along the Emigrant Trail in 1849. As he and his granddaughter retrace the path of their ancestor, commentaries by the admiral and Morgan appear in alternating chapters. The dangers and emotions of both journeys are well presented in this readable tale.

282.  Seifert, Shirley. **The Turquoise Trail**. Lippincott, 1950. Repr. Amereon, 1976. (0-89190-140-X) Lib Bdg $25.95 « Time: 1846-1848.

Seifert's entertaining fictionalized biography is based on the diary of Susan Shelby Magoffin, who traveled overland from Independence, Missouri, to Santa Fe, El Paso, and on into Mexico at the time of the Mexican War. The rigors of the journey, hostile natives, and the war challenged the endurance of the travelers, especially the women, who were expected to be both ladies and hardy pioneers.

283.  Taylor, Robert Lewis. **The Travels of Jamie McPheeters**. Doubleday, 1958. Several editions available. (0-89966-835-6) Lib Bdg $36.95. « Time: 1849-1851.

Hair-raising adventures are encountered by an adolescent boy and his father as they make their way from Louisville to the California gold fields in 1849. They endure capture by bandits, torture by Indians, and a short stay with the Mormons before they finally settle on a ranch in California. This humorous and well-researched story is based on the journals of Dr. Joseph Middleton and other authentic documents.

284.  Taylor, Theodore. **Walking Up a Rainbow**. Dell, 1988. Several editions available. « Time: 1850s.

Lively 14-year-old Susan has been orphaned and left with her family land, a large herd of sheep, and an equally large debt. She hires a company of men to help her take the sheep from Iowa to California, where she hopes to sell them and pay off the debt. She nurses the men through Rocky Mountain spotted fever, guards the sheep against raiders, and survives the desert and an attempted gang rape. The story is told by Susan and by Clay, the youngest of the cowhands, whom she has chosen for her future husband. Their relationship adds lighthearted moments to the serious effort they have undertaken.

285.  Thom, James Alexander. **From Sea to Shining Sea**. Ballantine, 1984. (0-345-28479-8) Pb $8.95. Ballantine, 1986. (0-345-33451-5) Pb $5.95. « Time: ca. 1770-1820.

Anne Rogers Clark narrates this story of her 10 children, with emphasis on her most famous sons: George, the hero of the Revolution, and William, who explored the West with Meriwether Lewis. Readers also travel to the frontier in Kentucky with members of the Clark family and meet Jonathan Clark, who was at Charles Town during the smallpox epidemic. Based upon careful research of primary documents, this readable account brings to life a remarkable family that had a great impact on the new nation.

286.  Vliet, R. G. **Rockspring**. Viking, 1974. Southern Methodist University Press, 1992. (0-87074-334-1) Pb $7.95. « Time: 1830s.

Jensie, the daughter of poor white pioneers, is kidnapped from her East Texas home by Mexican bandits. Throughout her ordeal she faces rape, the violence of her captors toward her and each other, harsh weather, and inadequate food. Her ordeal changes her, and she fears that her family will not accept her or her unborn child.

287.  Whipple, Maurine. **Giant Joshua**. Houghton, 1941. Repr. Western Epics, 1976. (0-914740-17-2) $15.00. « Time: 1860s.

Clory is the third wife of 40-year-old Abijah MacIntyre. Her story of life in a polygamous Mormon household provides an account of pioneer life in the Utah desert, of Mormon beliefs, and of the disease, hunger, and other hardships they faced, including persecution from the government. All the while, Clory struggles to please her demanding husband and his selfish first wife, and to raise her children.

288.   White, Stewart Edward. **Long Rifle**. Doubleday, 1932. Several editions available. « Time: 1820s.

Andy Burnett, grandson of a friend of Daniel Boone, inherits the long rifle that Boone won in a shooting match. With that rifle, Burnett follows the example of his ancestors, moving ever westward. He is one of the early explorers of the Rockies and is captured by the Blackfeet and adopted into their tribe. Accurate information concerning the wildlife of the mountains and plains, and details about the ways in which Indians and trappers lived, add interest to an adventure story celebrating individualism and the free life.

289.   Zelazny, Roger, and Gerald Hausman. **Wilderness**. Tor, 1993. (0-312-85654-7) $21.95. Forge, 1994. (0-8125-3534-0) Pb $4.99. « Time: 1808.

Zelazny and Hausman alternate between two outstanding factually based survival stories. One concerns John Colter, once a part of the Lewis and Clark Expedition, who now finds himself in a battle of wits with the Blackfeet, his captors. He is stripped to a loincloth and given a small head start; he must elude their efforts to find him again and torture and kill him. The other account concerns trapper Hugh Glass, who has been badly mauled by a bear. He must fight the elements of nature and his mental and physical exhaustion as he attempts to crawl to the nearest settlement. Both exciting narratives play tribute to the wilderness and to the hardy independent frontiersmen who risked their lives there.

## California and the Pacific Northwest

290.   Berry, Don. **Moontrap**. Viking, 1962. Comstock, 1991. (0-89174-000-7) Pb $5.95. « Time: 1850s.

Realistic action and language characterize Berry's story of Johnson Monday, a mountain man who settles on an Oregon farm with his Indian wife. This novel, filled with vivid descriptions, presents an accurate picture of frontier life in Oregon.

291.   Berry, Don. **To Build a Ship**. Viking, 1963. Comstock Editions, 1977. (0-89174-029-5) Pb $3.95. « Time: 1850s.

Ben Thaler and his friends learn that the ship they expected to bring them provisions is not coming, so they set out to build their own. Emphasis in this accurate account is on the details of building the ship, which so absorbs the characters that its completion overrides all other interests and values.

292.   Berry, Don. **Trask**. Viking, 1960. Comstock Editions, 1976. (0-89174-001-5) Pb $3.95. « Time: Late 1840s.

Highly favorable reviews were accorded to *Trask* when it was published because of its well-researched and realistic presentation of white and Native American attitudes and actions when the first homesteaders came to the Oregon Territory. The novel, based on the life of early settler Elbridge Trask, is exciting, filled with details, and respectful of all persons and cultures.

293.  Binns, Archie. **Mighty Mountain**. Scribner, 1940. Binford & Mort, 1951. (0-8323-0110-8) $14.95. (0-8323-0259-7) Pb $9.95. « Time: 1850s.

Elmer Hale, a New Englander, did not intend to settle in Puget Sound when he visited his uncle there, but he stayed to establish a homestead. Binns's story of pioneer hardships and of the relations between the settlers and the Indians shows an understanding of the forces that drove both groups.

294.  Dana, Richard Henry, Jr. **Two Years Before the Mast**. Harper, 1840. Several editions available. « Time: 1830s.

Forced to leave college because of vision problems, the author served aboard a brig for two years. His adventures are recounted in this realistic novel that introduces the reader to events in the Spanish colony of California and life at sea at that time.

295.  Haycox, Ernest. **Earthbreakers**. Little, Brown, 1952. Amereon, 1976. (0-89190-977-X) $26.95. Windsor Publishing Corp., 1993. (1-55817-688-8) Pb $3.50. « Time: 1845.

At the end of a harrowing journey across the continent, a dozen families and three unattached men reach their town site near Oregon City. Here they build cabins and strive to create a community from the wilderness. Antagonisms and rivalries, weather, and disease strain their resources. This realistic romance is suitable for mature readers.

296.  Holland, Cecelia. **The Bear Flag**. Houghton Mifflin, 1990. (0-395-48886-9) $19.45. Windsor Publishing Corp., 1992. (1-55817-635-7) Pb $5.99. « Time: 1840s.

The main historic events that took place in California during the 1840s are well presented in this exciting story, which includes much information about real people and the idea of Manifest Destiny. The story centers upon Catharine Reilly, her brutal overland journey, and her efforts to promote California statehood while defeating the efforts of those who want to gain control of the state for their own ends.

297.  Holland, Cecelia. **Pacific Street**. Houghton Mifflin, 1992. Repr. Thorndike Press, 1992. (1-56064-434-1) Large type ed. $17.95. « Time: 1848.

The gold-driven lawlessness and vigor of the exploding population of San Francisco is clearly seen in this well-researched work that features those low on the social rung—women, Blacks, and Native Americans. As merchants and opportunists rush to supply endless needs, others seek to make their fortunes in the new gold fields, and Frances, Daisy, and Mitya use their considerable talents to get their share.

298.  Hough, Emerson. **54-40 or Fight**. Bobbs, 1909. Lightyear, 1976. (0-89968-043-7) Lib Bdg $17.75. « Time: Mid-1840s.

This rapidly moving story of the political and personal conflicts underlying the Northwest boundary treaty and the annexation of Texas interweaves real personages with fictional ones. It provides a readable account of events that threatened to once again bring the United States and Great Britain to war. The English minister Pakenham, President Tyler, John C. Calhoun, and Russian Baroness von Ritz play major roles.

299.  Jackson, Helen Hunt. **Ramona**. Little, 1884. Little, 1939. Several editions available. « Time: 1840s.

Ramona, daughter of a Scots father and an Indian mother, is cast out by her aristocratic guardian when she marries an Indian. Jackson's romantic story includes factual information on seizure of Mexican lands; the inhumane treatment of Native

Americans; and relations among Indians, Spanish, Mexicans, and white settlers in California at the time of the American conquest. The book is a passionate plea for just treatment of all persons.

300.   Johnston, Terry C. **Carry the Wind**. Caroline House, 1982. Green Hill, 1982. (0-89803-106-0) $18.95. Bantam, 1986. (0-553-25572-X) Pb $5.99. « Time: 1830s.
   Novice fur trapper Josiah Paddock and his guide Titus Bass take part in the famous rendezvous of trappers, traders, and Indians at Pierre's Hole in 1832. This realistic and detailed account of the lives of these mountain men, as they fight grizzlies, hunt buffalo, and bargain and skirmish with Indians in the Rockies and Grand Tetons, includes appearances by legendary mountain men Bill Sublette and Jim Bridger.

301.   Jones, Nard. **Swift Flows the River**. Dodd, 1940. Binford & Mort, 1964. (0-8323-0114-0) $14.95. « Time: 1856-1876.
   With careful detail, Jones tells the story of the development of eastern Washington along the Snake and Columbia Rivers, from Lewiston west to the Cascades. Action focuses on the life of Caleb Paige who, in maturity, becomes a steamboat captain. Beginning with an Indian attack on a frontier blockhouse, the story of one generation of the Paige family includes many lively characters, including a gambler, a Nez Percé named Cutmouth, and Mike Shea, an Irish ex-trooper. Jones's affection for the locale and its people shines through in this informative account of the history of the northwest.

302.   McCord. Christian. **Across the Shining Mountains: The Odyssey of Nathaniel Wyeth**. Jameson Books, 1986. Green Hill, 1987. (0-915463-31-8) $18.95. « Time: 1832.
   Novice Nathaniel Wyeth left his business in Massachusetts to set up trading posts in Oregon. Tormented by stiff competition, bad luck, and his own naiveté, he failed in his venture, but this "pioneer of pioneers" made it possible for others to settle there. Wyeth's experiences promoted public interest in Oregon, thus allowing the U.S. government to maintain American interests in the region. This fictionalized biography, based on primary sources, is the sixth in the publisher's Frontier Library series.

303.   Roesch, E. P. **Ashana**. Random House, 1990. (0-394-56963-6) $19.95. Ballantine, 1991. (0-345-37298-0) Pb $5.99. « Time: 1790s.
   In 1790, Russian hunters and traders established settlements in present-day Alaska and took many native hostages. The story of the suffering of the people is told in a first-person account by Ashana. In spite of her betrothal to a man of her own people, she is forced to become a mistress to the Russian leader and bear him two children. This carefully researched blend of fact and fiction includes much information about Inuit myth and tradition.

304.   White, Stewart Edward. **Stampede**. Doubleday, 1942. Repr. Amereon, n.d. (0-88411-886-X) Lib Bdg $15.95. « Time: 1850s.
   Andy Burnett, who was introduced in *Long Rifle*, is seen again in this story of the conflict between established landowners and squatters after California became a state. This colorful and fast-paced story is a sequel to *The Folded Hills* (out-of-print).

# Chapter 4

# The Civil War, 1861-1865

305.   Adicks, Richard. **Court for Owls**. Pineapple, 1989. (0-910923-65-5) $17.95.
« Time: ca. 1863-1865.

Lewis Powell, an idealistic Confederate soldier, becomes involved in the conspiracy to avenge the Confederacy by assassinating Abraham Lincoln. Based on a real person, this detailed and realistic novel depicts the chain of events to provide insight into the motives for Powell's actions. The charismatic John Wilkes Booth and other conspirators are vividly portrayed.

306.   Altsheler, J. A. **Guns of Bull Run**. Appleton, 1913. Buccaneer Books, 1990. (0-89968-458-0) Lib Bdg $21.95. Repr. Amereon, 1976. (0-88411-942-4) $22.95. « Time: Late 1850s-1862.

Through the story of Kentuckian Harry Kenton, son of a West Point officer, the reader sees how fiery speeches and newspaper articles encourage the growth of tension between North and South, the reasons why Kentucky remains a divided state, and why Kenton joins the Confederacy. He fights in many battles, including the first famous battle of Bull Run, which is portrayed in detail.

307.   Altsheler, J. A. **Guns of Shiloh**. Appleton, 1914. Repr. Buccaneer Books, 1990. (0-89968-459-9) Lib Bdg $21.95. Repr. Amereon, 1976. (0-88411-943-2) Lib Bdg $22.95. « Time: 1861-1862.

In a balanced and well-researched presentation, Altsheler tells the story of the great Western campaign. The hero is a descendant of Henry Ware (of the Young Trailers series) and set on the Kentucky frontier. This is the second in the author's Civil War series; it is the sequel to *Guns of Bull Run* and is suitable for younger secondary students.

308.   Altsheler, J. A. **Rock of Chickamauga**. Appleton, 1915. Repr. Buccaneer Books, 1993. (0-89968-567-6) Lib Bdg $21.95. Repr. Amereon, n.d. (0-8488-0071-0) $22.95. « Time: 1862-1863.

Dick Mason, introduced in *Guns of Shiloh,* is involved in the siege of Vicksburg and other dangerous events of the war in the West. George H. Thomas, a Union General, is among the real-life characters in this lively and well-researched work that is suitable for younger secondary students.

309.   Altsheler, J. A. **Scouts of Stonewall**. Appleton, 1914. Several editions available. « Time: 1862-1863.

The Valley of Virginia campaign is seen through the eyes of Henry Kenton, an aide on the staff of Stonewall Jackson. This work tells the story from the Southern view and presents a vivid portrait of Jackson. Followed by *Star of Gettysburg*, this readable work is suitable for younger secondary students.

310.   Altsheler, J. A. **Shades of the Wilderness: A Story of Lee's Great Stand**. Repr. Buccaneer Books, 1990. (0-89968-467-X) Lib Bdg $21.95. Repr. Amereon, n.d. (0-88411-940-8) Lib Bdg $22.95. « Time: 1983-1864.

Through the eyes of Henry Kenton, who is an aide to Lee, the reader is presented with a striking and romantic portrait of Lee and other Southern leaders as they strive to recover from the loss at Gettysburg. This story is suitable for younger secondary students. Sequel to *Star of Gettysburg*.

311.   Altsheler, J. A. **Star of Gettysburg**. Appleton, 1915. Repr. Buccaneer Books, 1990. (0-89968-469-6) Lib Bdg $22.95. Repr. Amereon, 1976. (0-88411-945-9) Lib Bdg $24.95. « Time: 1863.

Henry Kenton, part of the Confederate forces, sees action at Gettysburg. This work presents an insider's view of army life when the Southern forces were at their best. The death of Stonewall Jackson is recounted in this exciting story that is suitable for younger secondary students. Sequel to *Scouts of Stonewall*.

312.   Altsheler, J. A. **Sword of Antietam**. Appleton, 1916. Repr. Buccaneer Books, 1993. (0-89968-566-8) Lib Bdg $21.95. Amereon, 1985. (0-317-28286-7) Lib Bdg $24.95. « Time: 1862.

The Battle of Antietam was fought in Maryland, about 50 miles northwest of Washington, D.C., during the fall of 1862. This critical battle between the forces of Lee and McClellan stopped the surge of the Southern army into Northern territory. Altsheler's informed account captures the spirit of the time and is suitable for younger secondary students.

313.   Altsheler, J. A. **Tree of Appomattox**. Appleton, 1916. Repr. Buccaneer Books, 1993. (0-89968-568-4) Lib Bdg $21.95. Amereon, 1985. (0-317-28292-1) Lib Bdg $23.95. « Time: 1864-1865.

Northern hero Dick Mason is a participant in events leading up to Lee's surrender. Excellent portraits of Lee, Grant, and Sheridan highlight this work, which is suitable for younger secondary students.

314.   Andrews, Mary Raymond Shipman. **Perfect Tribute**. Scribner, 1906. Repr. Buccaneer Books, 1992. (0-89966-920-4) Lib Bdg $9.95. « Time: 1863.

Shortly after giving the Gettysburg Address, Lincoln visits a veterans' hospital and meets a soldier who had just read the speech in the morning's paper. A strong sense of the time is provided in this simple, moving story that has been heavily reprinted since its first edition.

315.   Bass, Cynthia. **Sherman's March**. Random House, 1994. (0-679-43033-4) $21.00. « Time: 1864.
Incorporating a fictionalized "primary source" format, Bass uses three narratives—by General William Tecumseh Sherman, Union army captain Nicholas Whiteman, and Annie Saunders, a Southern widow and refugee—to show the reasons for, and the results of, Sherman's March to the Sea, which destroyed the South's economic resources and drove civilians from their homes. Good characterizations are found in this well-written novel based on actual accounts.

316.   Bristow, Gwen. **Handsome Road**. Crowell, 1938. Repr. Buccaneer Books, 1979. (0-89966-028-2) Lib Bdg $23.95. « Time: 1859-1885.
Action in this novel centers on Corrie May Upjohn, who lives down by the docks of a small Louisiana river town, and Ann Sheramy Larne, local aristocrat. Vivid scenes, strong characterizations, and careful details are a part of Bristow's realistic account. Most of the action is set just before and during the Civil War, although one also sees the war's aftereffects and Reconstruction.

317.   Bromfield, Louis. **Wild Is the River**. Harper, 1941. Repr. Amereon, n.d. (0-88411-507-0) Lib Bdg $22.95. « Time: 1861-1865.
Bromfield's colorful potboiler of emotional upheaval and physical violence is set in wartime New Orleans during the Yankee occupation of the city. The seductive qualities of the city; its mix of French, Creole, Spanish, and Black peoples; and the idealism and materialism of both Northerners and Southerners are combined in a readable, accurate, and witty tale that features good characterizations. Among the real persons included as characters is Benjamin Franklin Butler, politician and military leader.

318.   Brown, Rita Mae. **High Hearts**. Bantam, 1987. (0-553-27888-6) Pb $4.95. « Time: 1861-1865.
Brown's careful research on Confederate military strategy and the lives of Confederate soldiers is evident in this realistic, detailed, and occasionally humorous account of Geneva Chatfield. She cuts her hair and, disguised as a boy, joins a Virginia cavalry regiment to fight beside her husband. Because of her great riding ability, Geneva becomes an excellent soldier, better than her husband. Through the experiences of energetic and interesting characters, Brown shows the effects of the war on women, including Geneva's mother and a family slave who tend the wounded.

319.   Catton, Bruce. **Banners at Shenandoah**. Doubleday, 1955. Repr. Amereon, 1976. (0-89244-019-8) Lib Bdg $19.95. « Time: 1861-1865.
Exciting action and the rough side of the daily life of a soldier are seen in this balanced account of young Bob Hayden, who was flag bearer for Phil Sheridan's fighting cavalry and close to many historic persons and events. The grim realities of war are included without being graphic; an engaging love story and a dry wit move the story along. This work by a Pulitzer prize winner noted for his nonfiction books about the Civil War will appeal to young readers.

320.   Clapp, Patricia. **Tamarack Tree: A Novel of the Siege of Vicksburg**. Lothrop, 1986. (0-688-02852-7) $11.95. Puffin, 1988. (0-14-032406-2) Pb $3.95. « Time: 1859-1863.

The horrors of life in a city under siege for months are clearly portrayed in this work. Action centers on 17-year-old Rosemary, who has come from England to join her brother at Vicksburg. Through Rosemary's efforts to understand both sides of the conflict, the reader receives a balanced presentation of the issues. Suitable for younger secondary students.

321. Collier, James Lincoln. **With Every Drop of Blood: A Novel of the Civil War**. Delacorte, 1994. (0-385-32028-0) $15.95. « Time: 1861-1865.

Johnny, a 14-year-old Confederate soldier, comes from a family too poor to own slaves, but he has the prevailing attitude toward them. When he is captured by Cush, a Black Union soldier, trust is slow to develop on both sides. Through the confusion and terror of battle, when the life of each depends upon the other, understanding grows, but the reality of racism is not forgotten.

322. Cornwell, Bernard. **Copperhead: A Novel of the Civil War**. HarperCollins, 1994. (0-06-017766-7) $15.95. Thorndike, 1994. (0-7862-0186-X) Large type ed. Lib Bdg $21.95. « Time: 1862.

The battle for Richmond is the setting for the sequel to *Rebel*. This time, Nathaniel Starbuck becomes involved in espionage at great risk to himself and his family. Cornwell's blend of battle scenes, romance, and authentic background will find many readers. Volume 2 of the Starbuck Chronicles.

323. Cornwell, Bernard. **Rebel**. HarperCollins, 1993. Several editions available. « Time: 1861-1862.

Nathaniel Starbuck, the son of an abolitionist preacher, flees south because of troubles with the law, and finds himself in Richmond when the war begins. Not trusted by either side, he becomes involved with a man named Faulconer, who is determined to raise an independent army to fight for the Confederate cause. Volume 1 of the Starbuck Chronicles.

324. Coyle, Harold. **Look Away**. Simon & Schuster, 1995. (0-684-80392-5) $24.00. « Time: 1859-1863.

A prosperous New Jersey businessman uses the excuse of a romantic tragedy to deliberately place his two sons on opposite sides of the Civil War. In this way, regardless of the outcome, he and his business interests will be protected. The accounts of the young men's military training and battlefield experiences are engrossing, as are the stories of the women they know, whose lives are forever changed. The brothers meet at the bloody battle at Gettysburg. The author's concluding note, in which he distinguishes between those events based on historic fact and those that are imaginary, adds to the value of this well-written work.

325. Crane, Stephen. **Red Badge of Courage**. Appleton, 1895. Several editions available. « Time: 1863.

At the battle of Chancellorsville, Henry Fleming, a young Union soldier, comes under fire for the first time. Overcome by fear, he runs from the battle. After a struggle with his conscience, he returns to lead a charge against the enemy. This extraordinary examination of the psyche of a soldier has remained a classic for 100 years.

326.   Dailey, Janet. **Legacies**. Little, Brown, 1995. (0-316-17205-7) $22.95. « Time: 1860-1865.

Lije Stuart, Harvard Law graduate and grandson of a wealthy Cherokee planta-tion owner, serves as a Confederate soldier and spy during the war. However, his romantic interest, Diane, sides with her father, who is an officer in the Union army. This predictable romance provides a strong account of the feud within the Cherokee nation resulting from the treaty that surrendered Cherokee land to the federal govern-ment and led to the horrors of the Trail of Tears. Sequel to *The Proud and the Free*.

327.   Dowdey, Clifford. **Bugles Blow No More**. Little, 1937. Repr. Cherokee, 1990. (0-87797-176-5) $24.95. « Time: 1861-1864.

In the excitement of Secession night, wealthy Mildred Wade is attracted to Brose Kirby—a totally unsuitable match. In telling their story, Dowdey describes the leaders of the Confederacy and the events of the Civil War as they were viewed by the residents of Richmond. This romance of social history and partisan passion chronicles it all: the early enthusiasm; the profiteering; the jealousies, anger, and fear; the privations of war; the bread riot; and the looting that followed the fall of the city.

328.   Eberhart, Mignon G. **Bayou Road**. Random House, 1979. Repr. Amereon, n.d. (0-88411-297-7) $18.95. Warner, 1987. (0-446-34402-8) Pb $3.95. « Time: 1864-1865.

Eberhart's picture of Southerners under siege focuses on occupied New Orleans in the closing days of the war. Young Marcy Chastain, trying to maintain her once-luxurious home and care for her family, negotiates with Union officer John Farrell to get a pass that will allow her to take her family up the Bayou Road to the Chastain plantation, and safety. Once there, she finds herself at the mercy of a killer who has adequate reason to wish to dispose of Marcy and her fiancé.

329.   Eberhart, Mignon G. **Family Fortune**. Random House, 1976. Repr. Amereon, n.d. (0-88411-769-3) Lib Bdg $20.95. « Time: 1863-1865.

In a swift-paced novel of historical insight, Eberhart examines the divisions caused by the war and the impending statehood of West Virginia. The Chance family of West Virginia has many relatives on both sides of the Civil War, all of whom are anxious to claim their share of the family fortune following the death of Pendleton Chance. His daughter Lucinda realizes that her greedy older brother is determined to cheat her and her brothers of their shares. She marries a distant cousin to claim adult status, but learns that greed can lead to murder.

330.   Eulo, Elena Yates. **Southern Woman**. St. Martin's Press, 1993. (0-312-08751-9) $21.95. « Time: 1861-1865.

When Elizabeth Crocker's husband Joe decides to fight for the Union, her Tennessee neighbors ostracize her. She and her baby are, however, befriended by Ama Hadley, the town's wealthiest citizen, whose liberal household includes free Black women. When Joe returns from the war injured and bitter, she struggles with poverty. When he is murdered, she kills the attacker and is held for trial. Eulo's picture of the life of poor Southern white women is accurate and engrossing.

331.  Fleischman, Paul. **Bull Run**. HarperCollins, 1993. (0-06-021446-5) $14.00. (0-06-121447-3) Pb Lib Bdg $13.89. « Time: 1862.

Most of the enlisted men who fought at Bull Run (Manassas), the first major battle of the Civil War, were ill-prepared and disorganized. Through the distinct voices of 16 narrators, whose thoughts and fears are powerfully expressed, the story of that fearful event and how it transformed their lives is told. This innovative, critically acclaimed work is an absorbing narrative.

332.  Foote, Shelby. **Shiloh**. Dial, 1952. Several editions available. « Time: 1862.

Through the views of several Union and Confederate soldiers, Foote, a noted scholar of Civil War history, reveals the thoughts of soldiers going into battle, their belief in their leaders, and details of the battle at Shiloh, one of the bloodiest in history. Accurate and balanced, this work includes many revealing incidents and provides a sense of the landscape and weather, the suffering of the wounded, and the strategies and backgrounds of the leading generals.

333.  Forman, James D. **Becca's Story**. Macmillan, 1992. (0-684-19332-9) $14.95. « Time: 1861-1865.

Basing his work on family letters and journals, Forman tells the story of 15-year-old Becca Case, who is romantically drawn to both Alex and Charlie. Although the war takes both young men to service, Becca remains sheltered in her small Michigan town. Through letters, the men recount the trials of battle and daily living; they share their thoughts about war and the Southerners who are the enemy. The characters ring true, as does the poignant conclusion.

334.  Forrester, Sandra. **Sound the Jubilee**. Lodestar/Dutton, 1995. (0-525-67468-1) $15.99. « Time: 1861-1865.

Maddie hears rumors of slaves who escape, but her mother believes that freedom is a fantasy and is obedient to her mistress. When the war threatens, the mistress decides that they will all find safety at Nags Head, North Carolina. When they arrive, however, the Union has captured nearby Roanoke Island, making it a safe haven for runaway slaves. Maddie and her family escape to the island, only to find that overcrowding and few jobs make survival a struggle. When, at the end of the war, the island is returned to its former owners, the freed slaves are forced to leave, with no place to go. This story is based on historic events and is suitable for younger secondary students.

335.  Fox, John, Jr. **Little Shepherd of Kingdom Come**. Scribner, 1903. Lightyear, 1976. (0-89968-039-9) Lib Bdg $23.95. « Time: Late 1850s-1865.

Chad Buford, a boy from the Kentucky mountains, believes he is illegitimate. He works as a shepherd in the valley of Kingdom Come Creek in the Cumberland Mountains. Later, on a trip to the Bluegrass region, he becomes acquainted with the aristocratic Major Buford, who finds that Chad is related to him. Chad's story shows his life before the war, conflict between mountaineers and flatlanders, the way in which Kentucky was torn by conflicting loyalties before and during the war, and the realities of war as seen by Morgan's Raiders, who caused great havoc with the Union Army.

336.   Garland, Hamlin. **Trail-Makers of the Middle Border**. Macmillan, 1926. Repr. Reprint Service, 1988. (0-7812-1249-9) $59.00. « Time: 1850s-1865.

Garland based this story on the experiences of his father Richard, who grew up on a farm in Maine and pioneered in Wisconsin, making a living by lumber rafting. Richard Garland was also a soldier under Grant at Vicksburg. Vivid details, in a direct and simply written account, bring the reader an honest account of the time.

337.   Gerson, Noel B. **Clear for Action! A Biographical Novel About David Farragut**. Doubleday, 1970. Amereon, n.d. (0-88411-641-7) $19.95. « Time: 1861-1865.

David Farragut (1801-1870) became a midshipman in the U.S. Navy at age 10. He was involved in the War of 1812 and is remembered for his statement, "Damn the torpedoes, full speed ahead." Farragut's great knowledge of seamanship, his devotion to duty, and his drive for perfection in all that he did assured his steady rise in rank to become the first man in the U.S. Navy to achieve the rank of Admiral. Gerson's fictionalized biography is suitable for younger secondary students.

338.   Gurasich, Marj. **House Divided**. Texas Christian University Press, 1994. (0-87565-122-4) Pb $9.95. « Time: 1861-1865.

Sixteen-year-old Louisa grew up as a tomboy in a family of brothers and nephews. Although her German immigrant family are Texans, they are also antislavery and staunch Unionists. With the coming of the war, the family is splintered; the two sons choose two very different paths. After one brother is killed, Louisa is swept up in the conflict when she masquerades as a hospital orderly in an attempt to rescue her surviving brother from a military prison. Louisa's story is based on the experiences of hundreds of women on both sides who actually went to war. This sequel to *Letters to Oma* is suitable for younger secondary students.

339.   Herrin, Lamar. **Unwritten Chronicles of Robert E. Lee**. St. Martin's Press, 1989. (0-312-03448-2) $17.95. 1991. (0-312-05983-3) Pb $9.95. « Time: 1861-1865.

The agonies of leadership, as faced by Robert E. Lee and Stonewall Jackson, are evident in Herrin's sympathetic study of these remarkable men. Lee's sense of duty and Jackson's sense of mission are presented in alternating narratives that provide valuable insights into the men and their historic roles.

340.   Holland, Isabelle. **Behind the Lines**. Scholastic, 1994. (0-590-45113-8) $13.95. « Time: 1863.

In 1863, the wealthy were allowed to pay the poor to take their place in the military draft. This injustice led to riots in New York City and conflict between rich and poor, Black and white. Holland tells the story from the viewpoint of Katie, a 14-year-old Irish immigrant. Suffering from harsh treatment because she is Irish, Catholic, and poor, she befriends Jimmy, a free Black groom whom the riots have endangered. This accurate, easy-to-read work is suitable for younger secondary students and will encourage discussion of the issues.

341.   Hunt, Irene. **Across Five Aprils**. Follett, 1964. Several editions available. « Time: 1861-1865.

Each member of the Creighton family is fully developed in this story of an Illinois farm family. After Father suffers a heart attack, and the older brothers go off to war, the responsibility for the farm falls on Jethro, who is only nine when Fort

Sumter is fired upon. This award-winning novel, based on the experiences of Hunt's grandfather, is suitable for younger secondary students.

342.   Jakes, John. **Love and War**. Harcourt Brace, 1984. (0-15-154496-4) $19.95. Dell, 1985. (0-440-15016-7) Pb $6.50. « Time: 1861-1865.

This second novel in Jakes's North and South trilogy focuses on the ways in which the war disrupts the lives and friendship of the Mains, a family of South Carolina planters, and the Hazards, who are industrialists from Pennsylvania. George Hazard accepts an important position in Washington, and brother Billy becomes an army engineer. Orry Main goes to Richmond to work in the Confederate government. Activities in both governments and both armies and on the home front are revealed through the involvement of some member of one of these intertwined families. Sequel to *North and South*; followed by *Heaven and Hell*.

343.   Jones, Douglas C. **Barefoot Brigade**. Holt, 1983. Tor, 1989. (0-8125-8459-7) Pb $4.95. « Time: 1861-1865.

Attention to the details of the daily lives of Confederate soldiers marks this fine story that concerns six men: two farmers, a judge, a professional soldier, and a slave owner and his cousin, who are there to fight a war without really understanding its basis. As their squad moves from Arkansas to Appomattox, the reader sees the battles of Antietam, Gettysburg, and Spotsylvania. More important, however, are the small events that provide the core of this work: the men's struggles to survive, the individual antagonisms, the squalid privations of daily life, and the bonding of the men into a family.

344.   Jones, Douglas C. **Elkhorn Tavern**. Holt, 1980. Tor, 1989. (0-8125-8457-0) Pb $4.95. « Time: 1862.

In a realistic novel, Jones tells the story of a strong Arkansas farm family— mother, son, and daughter—who must deal with the aftermath of the Battle of Elkhorn Tavern (also called the Battle of Pea Ridge) near their home while their father is away with the army. Jones's descriptions of the land and the realities of battle are memorable. Followed by *Roman*.

345.   Jones, Ted. **Grant's War: A Novel of the Civil War**. Presidio, 1992. (0-89141-434-7) $19.95. « Time: 1861-1865.

In an effort to gain understanding of generals Grant and Lee, historian Arthur Kelly, the novel's central character, taps the memories of old men, survivors of the war. Through their reminiscences, the personalities of the generals, the horrors of the battlefield, and the monotonous routine of daily life become clear. Kelly's interviews also bring forward the dramatic effect that the issue of slavery had on the commitment to victory by persons on both sides of the issue, and the unique ability of Grant to take advantage of the superior material resources of the North.

346.   Jones, Ted. **Hard Road to Gettysburg: A Novel**. Presidio, 1993. (0-89141-445-2) $21.95. « Time: 1861-1865.

Twin boys, separated at birth, do not know of each other. Samuel attends West Point and becomes an engineer with the Union Army. Simon attends the Virginia Military Institute and joins the Confederate Army. Exciting battle scenes are portrayed in detail, and suspense builds when Samuel, in a Confederate uniform, attempts to engineer the assassination of Stonewall Jackson. Powerful storytelling and excellent research underlie this exciting story.

347.   Kantor, MacKinlay. **Andersonville**. World, 1955. Several editions available. « Time: 1864-1865.

Andersonville, a prison for Union prisoners of war, was noted for its squalor and horrible conditions. The central character in this important work is Ira Claffey, a humane Georgian upon whose land the prison was constructed. Readers will not soon forget the searing detail of living conditions or the well-developed characters, whose actions range from cowardice and mindless viciousness to courage and deep compassion. The realism of this powerful work make it suitable for mature readers.

348.   Kassem, Lou. **Listen for Rachel**. Macmillan, 1986. Avon, 1992. (0-380-71231-8) Pb $3.50. « Time: ca. 1858-1865.

Rachel is in her adolescence when her parents are killed in a fire and she goes to live with relatives in the Appalachians. Although it is difficult to make the adjustment, she begins to learn folk medicine practices that she puts to good use when the Civil War comes. Several memorable characters, including the healer Granny Sharp, will be appreciated by readers. Suitable for younger secondary students.

349.   Keith, Harold. **Rifles for Watie**. Crowell, 1957. Several editions available. « Time: ca. 1861-1863.

The Union Army is being seriously challenged by the Confederate Cherokee 2nd Cavalry Regiment (1st Cherokee Mounted Rifles) under the leadership of General Stand Watie. Union soldier Jeff Bussey (age 16), from a Kansas farm, is involved in the entire Western campaign. His efforts to find the source of the cavalry's rifles leads to his becoming a spy and temporarily part of the Cherokee Regiment. This exciting and historically accurate novel, which includes information about the slave-owning Cherokee nation and details of a soldier's life, has effective characterization. It is suitable for younger secondary students.

350.   King, Benjamin. **Bullet for Lincoln**. Pelican, 1993. (0-88289-927-9) $19.95. « Time: 1865.

In speculative fiction, King examines the possibility that behind the conspiracy to assassinate Lincoln were Northern businessmen who wished to cast a pall over the South to assure that their investments in the West would be profitable. In this story, a spy named Anderson is hired by J. P. Morgan to make certain that a Southerner is blamed for the planned assassination. However, the plot is uncovered by two detectives in an action-packed thriller that provides a good sense of the times.

351.   King, Benjamin. **Bullet for Stonewall**. Pelican, 1990. (0-88289-768-3) $19.95. « Time: 1863.

History has it that Stonewall Jackson was accidentally killed by his own men. King, a military historian, speculates that he was actually the victim of a Union conspiracy to assassinate Jackson and change the course of the war. This gripping, well-written novel explores that possibility and presents a great deal of information about military life.

352.   Lancaster, Bruce. **Bride of a Thousand Cedars**. Stokes, 1939. Repr. Amereon, 1975. (0-89190-883-8) $22.95. « Time: 1861-1865.

The Northern blockade of Southern ports naturally led to profitable blockade running. This light novel presents a view of that action. It pictures life in Bermuda; the local beauty, Sally Cottrell; and a handsome British blockade runner. Amusing and picturesque, with lots of action and local color, this romance is a delightful change of pace for this noted author of historical fiction.

353.   Lancaster, Bruce. **Scarlet Patch**. Little, 1947. Repr. Amereon, 1976. (0-88411-682-4) Lib Bdg $27.95. « Time: 1861-1863.
There were many foreign-born volunteers who fought for the Union, including Baron de Merac from France who believed the survival of the Union was critical to world order. These volunteers faced prejudice in many forms, including denigration by their own commanding officers. In an acclaimed, well-researched, and action-filled novel, Lancaster shows the enormous price that was paid for the Union's inadequate training and incompetent leadership. Emphasis is on the eastern battles of the early years of the war.

354.   Lytle, Andrew. **Long Night**. Bobbs, 1936. University of Alabama Press, 1988. (0-8173-0413-4) $21.95. (0-8173-0415-0) Pb $14.50. « Time: 1859-1865.
Cameron McIvor, whose father was framed and murdered in 1859, devotes his life to vengeance. He lives in cane brakes and caves in the woods, strikes in the night, and retreats to hiding places during the day. With the coming of the Civil War, he becomes involved in the conflict and sees action at Shiloh, which is described in detail. This fast-paced drama, based on the life of a real person, presents a story of a young man's growth in character and a genuine picture of life in Alabama at the time.

355.   MacDonald, Robert S. **The Catherine**. Petrocelli, 1982. (0-89433-181-7) $12.95. « Time: 1861-1865.
Adventure lovers will enjoy this account of lively action aboard a Union ship that was specially built to be speedy enough to pursue Southern blockade runners and otherwise assist the Union effort. The *Catherine* is involved in rescues, captures Southern ships, and is a part of the Battle of New Orleans. The brother of the shipbuilder and captain of the ship is William Saunders, an excellent seaman who loves his wife but is attracted to the New Orleans widow who saves his life.

356.   Meriwether, Louise. **Fragments of the Ark**. Pocket Books, 1994. (0-671-79947-9) $21.00. « Time: 1861-1870.
Peter Mango and his fellow slaves are initially lauded for their action in stealing a Confederate steamboat and fleeing with their families to freedom. Mango continues to pilot the ship for the Union, while some of the former slaves enlist in the Massachusetts 54th Regiment, and others settle on small farms. They are all treated with the same bigotry they had known as slaves. Mango works to persuade the North to allow Blacks to fight in the Union Army. After the war he becomes a successful riverboat captain and a delegate to the Freedman's Convention. This engrossing, fact-filled work, which shows the impact of social, political, and economic factors on people's lives, is based on the life of Robert Smalls.

357.   Mitchell, Margaret. **Gone with the Wind**. Macmillan, 1936. Several editions available. « Time: ca. 1860-1872.
When the story begins, beautiful Scarlett O'Hara is 16, wealthy, selfish, willful, and incurably romantic. The realities of the war soon bring unceasing labor and poverty, but she is determined to use her considerable power over men to regain her position. The vigorous narrative, historic authenticity, and richness of the characterizations make this classic rendition of the Southern point of view a favorite in print and on film.

358. Perez, N. A. **Slopes of War: A Novel of Gettysburg**. Houghton Mifflin, 1984, 1990. (0-395-35642-3) $14.45. (0-395-54979-5) Pb $4.80. « Time: 1863.

The major events of the battle of Gettysburg are highlighted in this novel, which introduces a number of historical persons. The issues that caused the war and the details of battle are revealed from both the Union and Confederate viewpoints. This compelling novel, which concludes with Lincoln's Gettysburg Address and its meaning to a young battle-weary amputee, will appeal to younger secondary students.

359. Plain, Belva. **Crescent City**. Delacorte, 1984. (0-385-29354-2) $16.95. Dell, 1987. (0-440-11549-3) Pb $5.99. « Time: 1861-1865.

Most of the action in this novel is set against the backdrop of the Civil War, but the story begins nearly 25 years earlier, when eight-year-old Miriam and her brother David emigrate from Germany to live in their father's New Orleans mansion. Married at 16 to Eugene Mendez, an older man, Miriam's rigidly controlled life is predictable for a Jewish woman in that time and place. When David, now a physician, becomes an abolitionist and must flee north, Miriam is left to deal with an elderly blind husband, the care of her twins, and an illicit romance. When the war begins she takes her family to their country estate, where, through adversity, she gains in strength and independence.

360. Price, Eugenia. **Stranger in Savannah**. Doubleday, 1989. (0-385-23069-9) $19.95. Jove, 1990. (0-515-10344-6) Pb $6.50. « Time: 1854-1865.

This final volume in the author's Savannah quartet follows the Browning, Stiles, and Mackay families, from the first rumblings of secession in 1854 through the increasing tensions that cause divisions among family and friends, and finally through the tragedies of the war. Although a slow starter, this work includes well-developed characters and an accurate and moving sense of the time. The quartet provides an outstanding Southern family drama, but one need not read the other books to fully appreciate this work. Sequel to *Before the Darkness Falls*.

361. Rinaldi, Ann. **In My Father's House**. Scholastic, 1993. (0-590-44730-0) $13.95. « Time: 1852-1865.

Oscie, a proud daughter of the Old South, wants things to stay the same, but her stepfather thinks the South must change. Battles on the field and in the home weave history into a dramatic and factual story based on the experiences of a family whose Manassas farm was the scene of the first battle of the war and who lived in Appomattox at the time of Lee's surrender. Authentic period dialogue shows attitudes toward the underclasses in both North and South. This ALA Best Book for Young Adults is suited for younger secondary students.

362. Rinaldi, Ann. **Last Silk Dress**. Holiday, 1988. (0-8234-0690-3) $15.95. Bantam, 1990. (0-553-28315-4) Pb $3.99. « Time: 1861-1865.

Susan Chilmark believes vehemently in the Confederate cause; among her activities is the collection of women's silk dresses to be used in making a military balloon. Her brother, Lucien, however, believes that the Confederate cause is wrong, and their disagreements highlight the issues for readers. This romantic story provides accurate information about life in Richmond during the war and the medical treatment of the wounded who were brought there. Suitable for younger secondary students.

363. Safire, William. **Freedom**. Doubleday, 1987. Several editions available. «
Time: 1861-1862.

Journalist, political commentator, and Pulitzer prize-winner Safire uses his
professional experience to develop a lengthy novel that covers the experiences of nine
major players in the dramatic first two years of the war. During this time, Lincoln's
purpose evolves from the political/military process of saving the physical Union to
the acceptance of the complex moral, political, and military situation that demanded
the adoption of the Emancipation Proclamation. Prodigious research is reflected in
this work, which is especially informative concerning the political aspects of those
years. Suited for mature readers.

364. Schaefer, Jack. **Company of Cowards**. Houghton, 1957. Bantam, 1988. (0-
553-27350-7) Pb $2.95. « Time: 1861-1865.

Jared Heath, charged with cowardice, becomes the leader of a band of seven
other renegade soldiers assigned to a punishment battalion in the Union Army. He
works with them for months to form a cohesive unit. As the soldiers attempt to redeem
themselves, the reader sees the strain of battle from the view of each soldier. This
fast-paced account is based on actual events.

365. Schultz, Duane P. **Glory Enough for All; The Battle of the Crater: A Novel
of the Civil War**. St. Martin's Press, 1993. (0-312-09817-0) $22.95. 1994. (0-312-
11219-X) Pb $12.95. « Time: 1864.

In this powerful work, Schultz gives an account of the heroic efforts of a group
of Pennsylvania miners, led by Union Colonel Henry Pleasants (a mining engineer).
The miners dug a shaft under a Confederate fort at Petersburg, Pennsylvania, to blow
it up. With encouragement from the army but no support, the men had to design their
own tools and find their own supplies. It was planned that a division of Black troops
would lead the attack after the explosion, but poor leadership led to many unnecessary
deaths. This actual event has received little attention. Schultz's effective account will
appeal to mature readers.

366. Scott, Evelyn, **The Wave**. Cape & Smith, 1929. Repr. AMS Press. (0-404-
20230-6) $48.00. « Time: 1861-1865.

Rather than tell the story of the Civil War through the experiences of a few key
persons, Scott weaves together hundreds of vivid and poignant wartime narratives,
some quite short, to show the crisis of an individual at a particular moment. The length
and disjointed nature of the work requires a mature reader, who will be rewarded with
a panorama of the war as it affected people from all stations of society.

367. Seifert, Shirley. **Farewell, My General**. Lippincott, 1954. Repr. Amereon,
1976. (0-89190-136-1) $19.95. « Time: Mid-1850s-1864.

Details of Indian fighting, life on a military post, the importance of military
horses, and the strategy used in the Civil War are included in this fictionalized
biography of J. E. B. Stuart, who served with Stonewall Jackson at Chancellorsville
and commanded Lee's cavalry in the Wilderness Campaign. The novel covers the
years from the time of his courtship of Flora Cooke to his death during the battle of
Richmond.

368.   Shaara, Michael. **Killer Angels**. McKay, 1974. Several editions available. «
Time: 1863.

Using letters and other documents, Shaara reconstructs the four days of the Battle of Gettysburg in a fast-paced novel. The reader sees primarily the officers' point of view. The South is represented by Generals Robert E. Lee and James Longstreet; the Northern view is conveyed by Colonel Joshua Chamberlain and General John Buford. Among the topics clarified in Shaara's examination of this crucial battle are the historical pressures, military tactics, and personal motives that led to the battle; the problems caused by the terrain (helpful maps are included); and the cost in men and equipment.

369.   Stone, Irving. **Love Is Eternal: A Biographical Novel About Mary Todd and Abraham Lincoln**. Doubleday, 1961. (0-385-02040-6) $24.95. Ulverscroft, 1976. (0-85456-551-5) Large type ed. $16.95. « Time: ca. 1840-1865.

Mary Todd and Abraham Lincoln were complex personalities whose romance was not smooth. In telling their story, Stone includes details of daily living and family trials, political debates, and events of the war, along with many familiar Lincoln anecdotes. This warmly told account has found a wide audience.

370.   Stribling, T. S. **The Forge**. Doubleday, 1931. Several editions available. «
Time: Late 1850s-Late 1860s.

The reader gains a sense of the impact of events on ordinary people through this vivid and unsentimental account of the experiences of the middle-class Vaiden family of Alabama and their slaves and neighbors before, during, and after the war. The story has humor and vitality along with many details of daily living, such as life in a rude log cabin and in the even cruder slave quarters, the maintenance of farm animals and equipment, and the overarching impact of the wilderness and the vicissitudes of nature.

371.   Tate, Allen. **Fathers**. Putnam, 1938. Ohio University Press, 1984. (0-8040-0108-1) Pb $9.95. « Time: Late 1850s-1862.

Poet and biographer Allen Tate examines the impact of changing circumstances, conflicting ideas, and the disintegration of a great Virginia estate on its residents. Action is set in the years immediately before the war and during its early days; it centers around the Buchan and Posey families of Virginia, including the dignified and honorable Major Buchan, tradition-bound Sarah Buchan, arrogant George Posey, Lacy Buchan (the narrator), and various eccentric relatives.

372.   Thane, Elswyth Beebe. **Yankee Stranger**. Duell, Sloan, and Pearce, 1944. Repr. Amereon, 1976. (0-88411-963-7) Lib Bdg $22.95. « Time: 1861-1865.

Eden Day of Williamsburg, Virginia, is in love with a Yankee journalist from New Jersey. When she discovers he is a Union spy, her devotion is challenged, especially as she is doing some smuggling herself. Grandmother Day, met in *Dawn's Early Light,* is also a part of the story.

373.   Townsend, George A. **Katy of Catoctin: Or the Chain Breakers**. Appleton, 1886. Tidewater, 1959. (0-87033-037-3) Pb $5.00. « Time: 1859-1865.

The Catoctin Valley of the Blue Ridge Mountains of Maryland is the primary setting for this account of German-American settlers and the impact of the Civil War on them, from the time of John Brown's Raid to the execution of John Wilkes Booth. The author, who lived through these days and knew Booth personally, set the story in an area well known to him and based the story on real persons and events. Readers will find insight into the character of Booth and attitudes on both sides of the war. The old-fashioned style and reference to events well known to Americans at the time of publication will require a mature reader.

374.   Vidal, Gore. **Lincoln**. Random House, 1984. Several editions available. « Time: 1861-1865.

Vidal weaves a powerful tapestry as he tells the story of Lincoln during his presidency through the eyes of three associates: John Hay, Salmon P. Chase, and William H. Seward. Vidal's well-researched and lengthy account presents an ambitious, determined, and troubled Lincoln. Filled with historical detail and political insight, this work will appeal to mature readers.

375.   Whitney, Phyllis A. **Quicksilver Pool**. Appleton, 1955. Fawcett, 1981. (0-449-23983-7) Pb $3.95. HarperCollins, 1991. (0-06-100152-X) Pb $4.99. « Time: 1862-1863.

Wade Tyler, a Northern soldier, is devoted to the memory of his first wife. His loveless marriage to Lora Blair, a Southern girl, and his mother's determination to manage the household and her grandson result in serious family and political problems. This readable novel is set on Staten Island, New York, in the middle of the war.

376.   Whitney, Phyllis A. **Step to the Music**. Crowell, 1953. Fawcett, 1985. (0-449-70058-5) Pb $2.50. « Time: 1861-1865.

The divided allegiances of the Garrett family of Staten Island allow Whitney to show how people on both sides of the war were affected by it, and the way in which the realities of the war developed responsibility in young Abbie Garrett. An exciting account of the Battle of New York and a generous supply of romance will assure this novel's popularity with younger secondary students.

377.   Willis, Connie. **Lincoln's Dreams**. Bantam, 1987. (0-553-05197-0) Pb $15.99. 1992. (0-553-27025-7) Pb $4.99. « Time: 1861-1865.

This unusual novel blends past and present, truth and fiction, in the story of Annie, a modern young woman who seeks psychiatric help because she keeps having violent dreams of events during the Civil War, about which she knows almost nothing. Through this device, Willis develops a simple and riveting story in which Annie "becomes" a real Civil War hero through sharing the dreams of Robert E. Lee. This story will appeal to science fiction fans and will give them much information about the nation's bloodiest conflict.

378.   Yeager, Charles Gordon. **Fightin' with Forrest**. Dixie, 1987. Repr. Pelican, 1988. (0-88289-728-4) $19.95. « Time: 1853-1865.

The dedication of Lt. General Nathan Bedford Forrest to the Confederate cause was legendary, and he expected the same devotion from all the men under his command. This action-filled novel deals with two young sharpshooting friends, one from a wealthy plantation family and one from the Alabama hills, who ride close to Forrest though most of the war. The book provides a straightforward account of his actions and character and of events during the war from the Confederate point of view.

379.   Young, Stark. **So Red the Rose**. Scribner, 1934. J. S. Sanders, 1992. (1-879941-12-0) Pb $11.95. « Time: Late 1850s-1865.

Young's novel of life on two Mississippi plantations near Natchez in the days just before and during the war was highly acclaimed for its evocative and romantic presentation of the mind-set and gracious lives of the wealthy Southern aristocracy. The panorama of the war is seen through brief episodes that show how it touched this region.

380.   Zach, Cheryl. **Hearts Divided**. Bantam, 1995. (0-553-56217-7) Pb $3.99. «
Time: ca. 1860-1862.

Elizabeth Stafford's father, who owns a plantation in South Carolina, has very strong ideas concerning the proper role of women. He sends Elizabeth to an exclusive boarding school to be properly educated, but she is exposed to many ideas there that encourage her natural independence. While at school, she witnesses the firing on Fort Sumter and falls in love with a Union soldier. Later, while visiting a cousin in Washington, D.C., she witnesses the first Battle of Bull Run. This dramatic story provides information about the war and social attitudes of the time, including Elizabeth's relationship with her personal slave. Suitable for younger secondary students.

# Chapter 5

# The Expanding Frontier, 1866-1899

For the convenience of the reader, entries in this chapter have been divided into the following categories:

♦ Eastern and Southern States

♦ The Plains, West, Southwest, and Pacific Northwest

## EASTERN AND SOUTHERN STATES

381. Adams, Henry. **Democracy**. Holt, 1879. Repr. Amereon, n.d. (0-89190-525-1) $19.95. « Time: 1873-1877.

This story of Washington social life and the political scandals that occurred during the second administration of Ulysses S. Grant is of interest to any student of power, politics, and corruption. The story centers on Madeleine Leigh, a poised young widow whose romance with a senator is threatened when he compromises his reputation to gain political advantage.

382. Adams, Samuel Hopkins. **Tenderloin**. Random House, 1959. Repr. Amereon, n.d. (0-89190-894-3) $23.95. « Time: 1880s-1890s.

Based on true events, this is the story of Dr. Farr, a clergyman who undertakes a crusade against gambling and prostitution in New York City despite corrupt police and politicians. Young Tommy Howatt, a rough-hewn reporter, assists the reformer. Through their experiences, the reader gains a realistic picture of the rampant vice and crime that pervaded the city. The speech and attitudes of the characters reflect the times.

383. Alexander, Lawrence. **Speak Softly**. Doubleday, 1987. (0-385-23598-4) $16.95. « Time: 1890s.

In the late 1890s, Theodore Roosevelt was the president of the New York City Board of Police Commissioners. Based on this fact, Alexander spins an entertaining tale of mystery that includes murder, an experimental submarine, and a letter threatening a young student named Franklin, Roosevelt's distant cousin. The setting is accurate, and this complicated and entertaining story is replete with period detail.

384.   Bisno, Beatrice. **Tomorrow's Bread**. Liveright, 1938. Repr. AMS Press, n.d. (0-404-58407-1) $27.00. « Time: 1890s.

Jewish Sam Karenski emigrates from Russia, opens a garment sweatshop in Chicago, and later becomes a fanatical labor leader. Bisno's award-winning story of the conditions in the garment-making industry and of the effort to organize labor is a sweeping account of social change.

385.   Bjorn, Thyra Ferre. **Papa's Wife**. Rinehart, 1955. Repr. Buccaneer Books, 1992. (0-89966-883-6) $25.95. « Time: Late 1800s.

This wholesome story of family life and customs concerns a large Swedish family that migrates to America and settles in New England, where Papa becomes a minister. Followed by *Papa's Daughter*.

386.   Brewer, James O. **No Bottom**. Walker, 1995. (0-8027-3259-3) $20.95. « Time: ca. 1870.

In a dramatic story set on the Mississippi River following the Civil War, Luke Williamson tries to find the causes of the sinking of the *Mary Justice*, of which he is half owner. He is assisted by Masey Baldridge, an alcoholic insurance investigator. This first novel provides a strong picture of life in the South following the war. Prequel to *No Virtue*.

387.   Brewer, James O. **No Virtue: A Masey Baldridge/Luke Williamson Mystery**. Walker, 1995. (0-8027-3178-3) $19.95. « Time: ca. 1870.

Veterans on both sides of the Civil War cooperate to solve a murder in which a rare coin, part of the lost Confederate treasury, plays an important role. Well-developed characters, a good sense of the times, and a compelling story appear in Brewer's mystery, which is set on a Mississippi paddle wheeler. Sequel to *No Bottom*.

388.   Brock, Darryl. **If I Never Get Back**. Crown, 1989. (0-517-57345-8) $18.95. Ballantine, 1991. (0-345-37055-4) Pb $5.95. « Time: 1869.

In a delightful time-travel tale, modern crime reporter Sam Fowler finds himself in Cincinnati just as the Red Stockings are ready to begin their record-breaking year. He joins them on their tour, and the reader is treated to a view of many American cities in the summer of 1869. Of course, Sam runs afoul of those who do not wish him well, but he also gets to know many fascinating characters, including Mark Twain. Baseball lovers will have fun with this book while they learn a great deal about post-Civil War America.

389.   Christilian, J. D. **Scarlet Women**. Donald I. Fine, 1996. (1-55611-475-3) $22.95. « Time: 1871.

The corruption, danger, and destitution of life among the underclass in postwar New York City are revealed in this well-researched mystery concerning the murder of a prostitute and a restaurateur. The story is told through the adventures of a street-smart private detective who grew up among the people he is investigating.

390.   Coleman, Lonnie. **Legacy of Beulah Land**. Doubleday, 1979. Dell, 1981. (0-440-15085-X) Pb $2.95. « Time: 1879-1895.

Georgia planter Sarah Kendrick Troy and her son and grandson struggle to maintain their plantation under trying circumstances, including the efforts of a newly wealthy farmer to take it away. A large cast of characters and complex circumstances blend into a satisfying romance of the Reconstruction. Sequel to *Beulah Land* and *Look Away, Beulah Land.*

391.  Conroy, Sarah Booth. **Refinements of Love: A Novel About Clover and Henry Adams**. Pantheon, 1993. (0-679-42050-9) $22.00. « Time: Late 1880s.
    Clover Adams was a lively young woman of proven literary ability. Her cold and egocentric husband, Henry Adams, noted author and descendant of two presidents, insisted that she suppress her talents and show absolute devotion and obedience to him. After 13 years of marriage, Clover died; Henry destroyed all her writings and omitted all mention of her in his autobiography. Conroy presents a detailed account of late-nineteenth-century social customs in Washington, D.C. in this mix of fact and fiction that explores the possibility that Clover's death was not suicide. President Grover Cleveland is among the characters in this story.

392.  Cooney, Caroline B. **Both Sides of Time**. Delacorte, 1995. (0-385-32174-0) Pb $10.95. « Time: 1895.
    Cooney uses time-travel, romance, and mystery to powerfully examine the role of women and racial and ethnic prejudice at the turn of the century. When Annie Lockwood of the late-twentieth-century falls through time and finds herself in a Victorian mansion, she is thrilled. Then, when the sexist and racist attitudes and legal and cultural norms become clear to her, Annie must deal with the realities of life in both centuries. This exciting work is suitable for younger secondary students.

393.  DeForest, J. W. **Playing the Mischief**. Harper, 1875. Repr. Reprint Service, 1988. (0-78112-1161-1) $59.00. « Time: 1870s.
    During Grant's administration, Josephine Murray, an amoral widow, successfully duped Congress out of $100,000 via her fraudulent claim for a barn destroyed in the War of 1812. DeForest based this popular novel on careful research and realistically depicts the many corrupt factions that were found in Washington, D.C. The work was first serialized in a popular magazine.

394.  Dreiser, Theodore. **The Financier**. Harper, 1912. Several editions available. « Time: ca. 1850-1874.
    Frank Cowperwood's interest is making money. He is realistic, aggressive, and amoral, believing that to succeed one must maintain the appearance of propriety while carrying on ruthless business practices. His enterprises lead finally to his arrest and conviction for embezzlement, which he regards only as a setback. Dreiser's story of the business career and love affair of a Philadelphia financier is based on the life of Charles Tyson Yerkes. Followed by *The Titan.*

395.  Dreiser, Theodore. **Jennie Gerhardt**. Harper, 1911. Several editions available. « Time: Late 1800s.
    Jennie, a beautiful and hardworking young woman, loses her daughter and the two men she loves, yet she grows in generosity of spirit and gives all that she has to help her family. Circumstances and social attitudes, however, destroy her chances for a happy and meaningful life. Dreiser's naturalistic story, set in Chicago and the Midwest, is enriched by the inclusion of many social and economic details.

396. Dreiser, Theodore. **Sister Carrie**. Doubleday, 1900. Several editions available. « Time: 1889.

Carrie's goals are money, clothes, and fame. She cares little about how she achieves her goals, and she is never satisfied, always seeking more excitement and someone new whose love for her will be useful. Although she glimpses a more meaningful life, Carrie is essentially satisfied with her self-centered world. Dreiser's realistic and powerful account of poverty, duplicity, and social climbing depicts life in the lower middle classes in New York and Chicago, with insights into the business world as well.

397. Dreiser, Theodore. **The Titan**. Lane, 1914. Repr. AMS Press, n.d. (0-404-20084-2) $27.50. NAL-Dutton, 1985. (0-452-00756-9) Pb $5.95. « Time: 1870s.

After leaving prison, Frank Cowperwood moves to Chicago, where he again enters the world of high finance and continues to acquire the beautiful—whether it be women or art. His pragmatic approach to life is based on his ultimate goal: to please himself. Sequel to *The Financier*.

398. Dykeman, Wilma. **The Tall Woman**. Holt, 1962. Wakestone Books, 1982. (0-9613859-1-X) Pb $8.95. « Time: ca. 1862-1892.

Lydia McQueen, a woman from the Smoky Mountains of North Carolina, marries a Union soldier even though the men of her family are Confederate soldiers. Toward the end of the war, her husband is imprisoned at Andersonville, and she is left to fend off predators alone. During the Reconstruction years following the war, Lydia works to establish a church and a tax-supported school in their remote community and to raise her mentally impaired son. The difficulties faced by women, regional speech patterns, and the details of daily living are well presented in this serious novel.

399. Ferber, Edna. **Saratoga Trunk**. Doubleday, 1941. Repr. Amereon, n.d. (0-89190-323-2) $19.95. Fawcett, 1980. (0-449-24115-7) Pb $1.95. « Time: 1880s.

Wealthy Clint Maroon, once a Texas cowboy, meets the dazzlingly beautiful Clio in New Orleans. When they go to Saratoga, New York, to attend the races, they meet the Vanderbilts and many other wealthy Easterners. Clint enters the railroad business and becomes an enormous success. Ferber's lively story is filled with details of social and business life in New Orleans and Saratoga.

400. Ferber, Edna. **Show Boat**. Doubleday, 1926. Repr. Lightyear, 1992. (0-89968-281-2) Lib Bdg $21.95. Fawcett, 1979. (0-449-23191-7) Pb $1.95. « Time: 1870s-1880s.

Ferber carefully researched life on a Mississippi River showboat for this lively story of the Hawks-Ravenal family and the *Cotton Blossom*, a floating palace theater.

401. Fleming, Thomas J. **The Spoils of War**. Putnam, 1985. Avon, 1986. (0-380-70065-4) Pb $4.50. « Time: 1866-1899.

Detailed references to historic figures and events allow the reader to view the tumultuous times between the end of the Civil War and the beginning of the twentieth century. Through three decades, the family of Cynthia Stapleton is affected by those happenings that influence the nation: the freeing of the slaves, yellow journalism, political and financial skullduggery, women's suffrage, the growth of unions, and changes in social standards. Set in the South and New York City.

402.   Gerard, Philip. **Cape Fear Rising**. Blair, 1994. (0-89587-108-4) $18.95. «
Time: 1898.

Newspaperman Sam Jenks and his schoolteacher wife are only in Wilmington, North Carolina, for three months, but during that time they witness a great racial conflagration. Social, political, and economic conflict occurs among the factions within each of the community's three major groups: the established white community, the working-class redshirts, and the city's Black community, which includes an African-American newspaper publisher who insists on full equality. This important novel provides a clear picture of the roots of American racism.

403.   Harris, Marilyn. **American Eden**. Doubleday, 1987. (0-385-18816-1) $18.95.
« Time: 1889.

Mary Eden Stanhope, of noble British birth, and her Southern aristocrat husband live just outside of Mobile, Alabama, but they are isolated from the community because of their progressive beliefs. Thus, when a vigilante group attacks them and abducts Eve, their 17-year-old daughter, they find no support in the community. Eve is rescued by the head of a theatrical troupe and travels with them across the southwest, suffering various types of abuse. Her fiancé Stephen follows her and gets involved in much violent action. A fast-moving plot, gritty action, lively characters, and vivid descriptions of the landscape make this a page-turner. Sequel to *Eden Rising*.

404.   Howells, William Dean. **A Hazard of New Fortunes**. Dutton, 1890. Several editions available. « Time: Late 1800s.

This novel of manners, which centers on persons connected with a literary magazine, shows how varied point of view concerning the rights of workers led to the streetcar strike in New York City.

405.   Jakes, John. **Heaven and Hell**. Harcourt Brace, 1987. (0-15-131075-0) $19.95. Dell, 1988. (0-440-20170-5) Pb $5.95. « Time: ca. 1865-1880.

As in other volumes of Jakes's North and South trilogy, the story centers on the Hazards of Pennsylvania and the Mains of South Carolina, this time dealing with the realities of the Reconstruction. Displaced by the war, Charles Main goes west and scouts for Custer, hoping to make a life for his infant son. Other members of his extended family also struggle to rebuild their disrupted lives. Steelmaker George Hazard, his abolitionist sister, and his politician brother tell the story of these years in the North. This entertaining tale is filled with historical details that show the economic and geographic growth of the nation and its political corruption and racist attitudes. Sequel to *Love and War*.

406.   Jakes, John. **Homeland**. Doubleday, 1993. (0-385-41724-1) $25.00. « Time: 1892-1902.

In a lengthy novel, Jakes tells of the adventures of Pauli, an orphaned German immigrant who comes to Chicago expecting to find a perfect new home. Instead, he finds a sometimes violent labor union movement, crime, greed, poverty, the women's rights struggle, action in the Spanish American War, and national expansionism. Through his experiences he meets Theodore Roosevelt, Eugene Debs, Thomas Edison, Clara Barton, and Jane Addams, all shown as three-dimensional personalities. Pauli aspires to be a photographer, and he eventually becomes involved with the developing motion picture industry. His view of an expanding United States will enlighten and entertain the reader.

407.   James, Henry. **The Bostonians**. Macmillan, 1886. Several editions available. « Time: 1870s.

The painful effort that went into winning the right of women to vote is clarified in James's satirical view of Boston society. The story centers on Basil Ransom, a conservative old-fashioned Southerner; his New England cousin, Olive; and Verena, an attractive young woman who is a forceful advocate of suffrage.

408.   Jones, Douglas C. **Remember Santiago**. Holt, 1988. Tor, 1992. (0-8125-0386-4) Pb $5.99. « Time: 1898.

When attorney Eban Pay and his Osage friend Joe Mountain become involved in the Cuban invasion, they experience mayhem, confusion, politics, egos, petty jealousies, and ineptitude. Jones's picture of the Spanish American War, seen from the viewpoints of several witnesses, shows the underlying callous political maneuvering that had no concern for the lives or fortunes of others. Among the real people who play an active role in the action are Theodore Roosevelt and Clara Barton.

409.   Lewisohn, Ludwig. **The Island Within**. Harper, 1928. Repr. Ayer, 1975. (0-405-06730-5) $30.00. « Time: 1870s.

Arthur is the son of a Jewish family that immigrated to New York from Poland in the 1870s and has since risen to affluence. Arthur becomes a successful psychiatrist and marries a Gentile, then finds that the conflict between family heritage and American values is too great. After an intense struggle, he leaves his family and goes on a Jewish mission. This authentic history of intellectual and emotional struggle was critically acclaimed at the time of publication.

410.   Lynch, Daniel. **Yellow**. Walker, 1992. (0-8027-1226-6) $19.95. « Time: 1898.

The dying Ambrose Bierce tells the story, told to him by Frederic Remington, of the experiences that Remington and fellow journalist Richard Harding Davis had while representing the Hearst and Pulitzer newspapers during the Spanish-American War. This enjoyable, action-filled story presents a historically accurate account of the power of the press and the arrogance of major newspaper publishers at that time.

411.   Mallon, Thomas. **Henry and Clara**. Ticknor & Fields, 1994. (0-395-59071-X) $21.95. « Time: ca. 1864-1900.

Henry and Clara Rathbone, stepbrother and stepsister, overcome social objections to their marriage. However, they can never overcome their memories of the night they were guests in President Lincoln's box at Ford's Theater in April 1865, or the rumors and innuendo that have surrounded them. With attention to detail, Mallon provides a clear picture of social life in the last half of the nineteenth century; he also shows the way that a person's life is shaped by events.

412.   Mark, Grace. **Dream Seekers**. Morrow, 1992. (0-688-11223-4) $22.00. « Time: 1890s.

Siblings Josef and Hannah Chernik, adult children of Russian immigrants, seek to improve their lives to flee a Chicago tenement. Hannah works as a seamstress and takes a wealthy lover, but is abandoned when she becomes pregnant. When Josef becomes involved in a union movement that leads to the Pullman Strike of 1894, he is accused of murder, and Hannah hires noted attorney Clarence Darrow to defend him. Careful research lies behind this novel. In addition to Clarence Darrow, many real-life characters, including Jane Addams, Eugene Debs, and George Pullman, are involved in the story.

413.   Morrison, Toni. **Beloved**. Knopf, 1987. (0-394-53597-9) $27.50. NAL-Dutton, 1988. (0-452-26446-4) Pb $10.00. « Time: Late 1860s-1870s.
   Before the Civil War, the pregnant slave Sethe sent her children to their grandmother in Ohio (their father paid for their freedom). When she escapes and her capture is imminent, she murders her infant daughter to prevent the child's recapture. Eighteen years later, Sethe's trauma and searing memories, and the reactions of others to her deed, are revealed in splintered pieces that coincide with the psychological horror suffered by Sethe.

414.   Norris, Frank. **The Pit**. Doubleday, 1903. Several editions available. « Time: 1890s.
   Carrying forward the theme of how the force of events affects the individual, Norris tells the story of Jadwin, a weak person who becomes a famous speculator on the Chicago Board of Trade. He manages to corner the wheat market, but his prosperity is lost when a bumper crop of wheat is harvested. His wife, alienated by his obsession with finance, reconciles with him in his time of need. Sequel to *The Octopus*.

415.   Page, Thomas Nelson. **Red Rock: A Chronicle of Reconstruction**. Scribner, 1898. Several editions available. « Time: Late 1860s.
   Southern resistance to the Reconstruction is the theme of *Red Rock*, which was a bestseller at the turn of the century. Virginian author Page provides romantic heroes and satanic villains, along with realistic details of daily living in his home state.

416.   Pratt, Theodore. **The Barefoot Mailman**. Duell, 1943. Ulverscroft, 1970. (0-85456-010-6) Large type ed. $15.95. R. Bemis, 1980. (0-89176-034-2) Pb $3.95. « Time: 1880s.
   Vivid descriptions of the coast, exciting adventures, and interesting characters enhance this delightful romance concerning Steve Pierton, who carries mail on foot between Palm Beach and Miami. When the great Florida land development boom is imminent, he becomes involved with land promoters.

417.   Price, Eugenia. **The Beloved Invader**. Lippincott, 1965. Several editions available. « Time: ca. 1865-1870.
   The Saint Simons Island church was vandalized during the Civil War. When Anson Dodge came to Georgia to see about his family business, he worked to rebuild the church. This somewhat sentimental fictionalized biography provides a good sense of life on Saint Simons Island following the war. Sequel to *New Moon Rising*.

418.   Ripley, Alexandra. **Charleston**. Doubleday, 1981. Avon, 1982. (0-380-57729-1) Pb $4.95. Warner, 1991. (0-446-36000-7) Pb $5.99. « Time: ca. 1861-1880.
   Two families coping with the effects of the Civil War and Reconstruction are the focus of this novel set in Charleston. Central to the story are Lizzie, who matures from a frightened child to a competent businessperson, and Pinckney Tradd, who goes North to make his fortune and shake his poor-white-trash image.

419.   Steuber, William. **The Landlooker**. Bobbs, 1957. Prairie Oak Press, 1991. (1-879483-04-1) Pb $12.95. « Time: 1871.

Pa Rohland, a Chicago manufacturer of harnesses, sends his two sons into frontier Wisconsin to test the market for the family business. Fifteen-year-old Emil narrates their many adventures, including a terrible forest fire. Back home, Pa is dealing with the effects of the devastating Chicago Fire (October 1871).

420.   Stratton-Porter, Gene. **Laddie: A True Blue Story**. Grosset, 1913. Several editions available. « Time: ca. 1880s.

This evocative portrait of post-Civil War Indiana farm life was a bestseller shortly after its publication. It is based on the experiences of the author's family; all the chief characters were real people, and most of the events actually occurred. The story concerns Laddie, who needs to change Princess's mind; a mystery that surrounds the Pryors; and finding out what went wrong with Shelley in Chicago.

421.   Stribling, T. S. **The Store**. Doubleday, 1932. Repr. Buccaneer Books, 1991. (1-56849-056-9) Lib Bdg $21.95. University of Alabama Press, 1985. (0-8173-0251-4) Pb $13.95. « Time: 1884.

The end of the old South and the development of the new is the theme of this sequel to *The Forge*. Colonel Vaiden, a Civil War Veteran and member of the Ku Klux Klan during Reconstruction, has become shiftless in his middle age. This novel of manners, set in Alabama, is filled with details of time and place.

422.   Tarkington, Booth. **The Magnificent Ambersons**. Doubleday, 1918. Several editions available. « Time: 1870s.

The social changes following the Civil War are reflected in this Pulitzer prize-winning epic of family life in Indiana. Isabel, trapped in a loveless marriage, is attracted to Eugene, her widowed former sweetheart. Her grown son George falls in love with Eugene's daughter Lucy but values his social position more than happiness for himself or his mother. Changes in his social position and in society require George to reevaluate his ideas.

423.   Terris, Susan. **Nell's Quilt**. Farrar, 1987. Scholastic, 1988. (0-590-41914-5) Pb $2.50. « Time: 1899.

Nell, age 18, feels she cannot avoid the marriage her family has arranged for her to an older widower with a small child. Still, she dreams of going to college and avoiding the fate of the women she sees in her Massachusetts community. In her efforts to control herself and to win the approval of her parents, Nell becomes increasingly rigid, working on an intricate quilt while she starves herself. Nell expects to die when she finishes her quilt, and comes very close to this state before taking charge of her own life.

424.   Thane, Elswyth Beebe. **Ever After**. Duell, Sloan & Pearce, 1945. Repr. Amereon, n.d. (0-88411-958-0) $23.95. « Time: 1890s.

Journalist Bracken Murry and his cousin Fitzhugh Sprague cover the jubilee of Queen Victoria and the Spanish-American War in Cuba for the New York *Star*. Lively, if unlikely, romances add interest to this work, which is set in Williamsburg, London, and Cuba. Sequel to *Yankee Stranger*; followed by *The Light Heart*.

425.   Tippett, Thomas. **Horse Shoe Bottoms**. Harper, 1935. Repr. AMS Press, n.d. (0-404-58479-9) $18.00. « Time: 1870s.

Life in the Illinois coal fields is shown through the story of John Stafford, who becomes a vital factor in the early history of the miners' labor union. This is a simple and convincing story of hope and terror, based on the author's experiences and those of his family and friends.

426.   Tourgee, Albion W. **A Fool's Errand**. Fords, Howard, and Hulbert, 1879. Several editions available. « Time: 1865-1870s.

This story takes place after the Civil War, when Colonel Comfort Servosse and his family move from Michigan to North Carolina. He plans to practice law and encourage the education and economic development of the freedmen. The author, an active member of the "carpetbag" convention of 1868, wrote many novels and articles supporting the Northern view of Reconstruction. This semiautobiographical novel, like other Tourgee works, is primarily of interest for its expression of the carpetbagger view of social and political conditions in the South at the time. It shows the mixed reception of carpetbaggers by Southerners, and the various attitudes of Northerners, ranging from genuine altruism to greed to self-righteous intellectual and religious pride. This powerful book was very popular at the time of its publication and is considered one of the most comprehensive novels of the era.

427.   Vidal, Gore. **1876**. Random House, 1976. (0-394-49750-3) $19.95. Ballantine, 1987. (0-345-34626-2) Pb $5.95. « Time: 1876.

The self-congratulatory Centennial Exposition of 1876 was not enough to obscure the scandals of the Grant administration, a bitter national election, and the events at Little Bighorn. Through the eyes of Charley Schuyler, an American who has been in France for nearly four decades, and his French-born daughter, the reader views the American social scene and political chicanery and comes to know many leading personalities, including Mark Twain. Sequel to *Burr*. Followed by *Washington D.C.*

428.   Vidal, Gore. **Empire**. Ballantine, 1988. (0-345-35472-9) Pb $5.95. « Time: ca. 1898-1910.

The actions of Caroline Sanford, a newspaper publisher, highlight the turn-of-the-century political and social life of the nation's rich, powerful, and famous. Action encompasses the Spanish-American War (1898), the United States assumption of the Philippines (at the cost of 100,000 Philippine lives), the assassination of President McKinley, and the presidency of Theodore Roosevelt. Along the way, the influence of William Randolph Hearst, Henry James, Henry Adams, and John Hay (Secretary of State, 1898-1905) are revealed.

429.   Wharton, Edith. **Age of Innocence**. Appleton, 1920. Several editions available. « Time: 1870s.

In a Pulitzer prize-winning story of manners set in New York, the smug hypocrisy of the time is revealed through the life of Newland Archer. Bound to his marriage through the narrow and rigid customs of his class, he is unable to violate the social code to seek happiness.

430. Yerby, Frank. **The Vixens**. Dial, 1947. Ulverscroft, 1981. (0-7089-0628-1) Large type ed. $12.00. « Time: Late 1860s.

Laird Fournois, a Southern aristocrat, fought with the Union Army. In this fast-paced romance, he returns home to New Orleans following the war. To improve his situation, he marries a beautiful woman who becomes mentally unbalanced. Jealousy, illicit romance, and the requisite villains characterize this dramatic novel. Nonetheless, it portrays the Reconstruction period well. Suitable for mature readers.

431. Zaroulis, Nancy. **Last Waltz**. Doubleday, 1984. Zebra, 1986. (0-8217-1777-4) Pb $4.50. « Time: 1890s.

The role of women in Boston's high society in the last years of the nineteenth century is the theme of Zaroulis's novel. Marian, who acts as companion to members of a wealthy family, tells the story of women imprisoned in loveless marriages by social mores, misdiagnosed and overmedicated by physicians, and leading useless and unhappy lives.

# THE PLAINS, WEST, SOUTHWEST, AND PACIFIC NORTHWEST

432. Adams, Andy. **Log of a Cowboy**. Houghton, 1903. Several editions available. « Time: 1880s.

Adams spent 12 years on the range and wrote this story to counter contemporary romantic nonsense about life on the range. His realistic account concerns a cattle drive from Texas through Arkansas and Wyoming to the Blackfoot Agency in Montana. Adams's accurate literary picture of this phase of our history has become a classic.

433. Aldrich, Bess Streeter. **Lieutenant's Lady**. Appleton, 1942. Repr. Amereon, 1975. (0-88411-252-7) Lib Bdg $21.95. University of Nebraska Press, 1987. (0-8032-5914-X) Pb $9.95. « Time: Late 1860s.

Aldrich's bestselling account of the experiences of a young army wife on the Indian frontier in Nebraska just after the Civil War is based on a diary that recorded its author's innermost thoughts. The story is told in so artless a fashion that it rings true.

434. Bakst, Harold. **Prairie Widow**. Evans, 1992. (0-87131-694-3) $16.95. « Time: 1870s.

Jennifer Vandermeer did not want to leave the comforts of Ohio to settle in Kansas, but her husband saw opportunities for them there. She unhappily denigrates the fledgling community and snubs her neighbors, but when her husband dies of a fever, she and her children are dependent on them for the winter. Although Jennifer plans to return east in the spring, the winter's events and her father's death change her mind. This realistic account shows the determination needed to make a home on the prairie.

435. Beach, Rex Ellingwood. **Barrier**. Harper, 1908. Buccaneer Books, n.d. (0-685-00931-9) Lib Bdg $14.85. « Time: ca. 1896.

The rough life at an Alaskan trading post during the gold rush is accurately portrayed in Beach's story of a romance between a young soldier and a woman whose part-Indian heritage is a barrier to their marriage.

436.   Beach, Rex Ellingwood. **Spoilers**. Harper, 1906. Repr. Irvington, n.d. (0-8398-0157-2) Lib Bdg $9.25. « Time: ca. 1898.

This brutally realistic account of life on the Alaskan frontier during the gold rush concerns a conspiracy among a group of mine owners. Street brawls, riots, battles at the mines, and murderous fights are a part of the tension-filled drama.

437.   Berger, Thomas. **Little Big Man**. Dial, 1964. Several editions available. « Time: 1876.

Jack Crabb, age 111, reflects on his frontier adventures as a gunfighter, Indian scout, and buffalo hunter, and on events leading up to the Battle of the Little Bighorn. Characters include General Custer, Wild Bill Hickok, Calamity Jane, and Wyatt Earp. This frequently humorous story reflects the attitudes of the frontier.

438.   Blake, James Carlos. **The Pistoleer**. Berkley, 1995. (0-425-14782-7) Pb $12.00. « Time: ca. 1868-1895.

Using newspaper accounts and excerpts from the autobiography of John Wesley Hardin, Blake recounts the controversial life of the notorious gunman, whom some regarded as a thug and others as a romantic Robin Hood. Hardin's career as a murderer began in his early teens and continued until his arrest at age 25; he is reputed to have killed more than 40 persons. Unlike many gunfighters, Hardin's fame rested primarily on a willingness to kill not for financial gain, but to avenge friends and family members. Blake's balanced account will find a wide audience.

439.   Blake, Michael. **Dances with Wolves**. Newmarket, 1991. Several editions available. « Time: ca. 1863-1868.

In an epic novel, Blake relates the adventures of Dunbar, a Civil War hero who finds himself alone at an abandoned fort on the western frontier. He befriends the Comanche, is adopted by them, and becomes the warrior named Dances with Wolves. Blake's tale is filled with accurate detail that reveals his appreciation for the Comanche way of life.

440.   Blevins, Win. **Stone Song: A Novel of the Life of Crazy Horse**. Forge/Tor; distributed by St. Martin's Press, 1995. (0-312-85567-2) $22.95. Forge, 1995. (0-614-05528-8) Pb price not available. « Time: 1870s.

Mature readers seeking an understanding of the Lakota Sioux people and the motives that drove Crazy Horse, the leader of the warriors who defeated Custer at the Little Bighorn, will enjoy this well-researched biographical novel. The appended glossary and list of characters increase understanding of the work.

441.   Bojer, Johan. **The Emigrants**. Appleton, 1925. Repr. Greenwood, 1974. (0-8371-6194-0) $35.00. Minnesota Historical Press, 1991. (0-87351-260-X) Pb $12.95. « Time: ca. 1870-1890.

Bojer's simple story of a colony of Norwegians who settled the Red River Valley of North Dakota, and their fight with drought, frost, poverty, and isolation, emphasizes the efforts of pioneers making small but sure gains against great odds.

442.   Bonner, Cindy. **Lily**. Algonquin, 1992. Several editions available. « Time: 1883.

Lily DeLony, the dutiful and hardworking daughter of a respectable family, is fascinated by Marion, the youngest of the Beatty gang, brothers implicated in theft and murder. When the citizens of McDade, Texas, decide that they have had enough of the infamous gang, the Beatty brothers flee, and Lily must choose between respectability and romance. This award-winning version of the classic conflict is loosely based on historic events and provides a good sense of the time and place. Followed by *Looking After Lily*.

443.   Bonner, Cindy. **Looking After Lily**. Algonquin, 1994. (0-56512-045-0) $18.95. « Time: ca. 1885.

When Lily's husband is sent to serve two years in jail for his involvement in a fight, he asks his footloose brother Haywood (Woody) to look after his young, pregnant bride. As these two mismatched souls travel 400 miles to a farm in north Texas, they face the hardships and dangers of pioneer life. This account is told from the point of view of Woody, who falls in love with his brother's hardworking and resourceful wife. This sequel to *Lily* is to be followed by a third story.

444.   Brady, Joan. **Theory of War**. Knopf, 1993. (0-679-41966-7) $21.00. « Time: 1865-early 1900s.

In 1865, four-year-old Johnny Carrick, a white boy, was indentured by his father to a Kansas tobacco farmer for $15. Brady, the granddaughter of Johnny Carrick, tells the painful story of Johnny's continual mistreatment by the farmer and his jealous son, and the hatred that consumed and destroyed Johnny. She also explores the psychological damage to the descendants of Johnny, and all enslaved persons, in a powerful novel suitable for mature readers.

445.   Broome, H. B. **Dark Winter**. Doubleday, 1991. (0-385-26568-9) $14.95. « Time: 1884.

Tom English, Texas rancher and gunfighter, is searching for the murderer of five ranch hands when he enters the lawless town of Frisco, New Mexico. There he meets a colorful Shakespeare-quoting patent medicine salesman and 19-year-old Elfego Baca, who is determined to bring law and order to the area. The novel is based on true events, in which Baca won out in a 36-hour standoff against 80 men.

446.   Burks, Brian. **Runs with Horses**. Harcourt Brace, 1995. (0-15-200264-2) $11.00. (0-15-200994-9) Pb $5.10. « Time: 1886.

An Apache youth, Runs with Horses, must complete a series of trials to become a warrior. He is determined to succeed, for he knows that Geronimo, the tribe's leader, needs all available warriors. Burks's factual account shows the struggle of an Apache community to keep their culture alive in a compact story that is suitable for younger secondary students and reluctant readers. A bibliography concludes the work.

447.   Burroughs, Edgar Rice. **Apache Devil**. Grosset and Dunlap, 1933. Repr. Buccaneer Books, 1976. (0-89966-043-6) Lib Bdg $16.20. « Time: Late 1800s.

The Apache Devil is a fictional young white man, brought up by the Apaches, who is involved in Geronimo's last campaign. The colorful, action-filled story, sympathetic to the Indian cause, is given authenticity through the author's own experiences as a cowboy, ranger, and soldier in the U.S. Cavalry.

448.   Capps, Benjamin. **Sam Chance**. Duell, 1965. Southern Methodist University Press, 1987. (0-87074-250-7) $22.50. (0-87074-251-5) Pb $10.95. « Time: Late 1800s.

Sam Chance, a Civil War veteran, wants to get far away from the North/South squabbles. He settles on the plains just west of the village of Dallas and rounds up wild cattle to begin his life as a cattleman. Chance is a good family man and a shrewd businessperson, but he must deal with buffalo, Indians, and the dangers of cattle drives to assure the growth of his cattle empire.

449. Capps, Benjamin. **The Trail to Ogallala**. Duell, 1964. Texas Christian University Press, 1985. (0-87565-012-0) $16.95. (0-87565-013-9) Pb $9.95. « Time: ca. 1866.

Before fences and railroads marked the western landscape, cattle drives from Texas to Nebraska were important to the economy of the nation. Capps's detailed account of a three-month struggle to travel 1,800 miles with 3,000 cattle is faithful to this dangerous, dirty, stressful, and colorful time in our history.

450. Capps, Benjamin. **White Man's Road**. Harper, 1969. Southern Methodist University Press, 1988. (0-87074-281-7) $22.50. (0-87074-272-8) Pb $10.95. « Time: 1890s.

Joe Cowbone, a young Comanche who remembers when his people were free to roam the plains, must now stand in line for food on an Oklahoma reservation. As he searches for his identity in a society controlled by white men, the reader learns about the life of a conquered people in the 1890s.

451. Carlile, Clancy. **Children of the Dust**. Random House, 1995. (0-679-44132-8) $23.00. « Time: 1889.

At the time of the Oklahoma Land Rush, Gypsy Smith, a gunfighter and lawman of Cherokee/African-American heritage, agrees to lead a group of poor Black share-croppers to the new territory, but they are not welcome there. When Smith recovers from an attack by the Klan, in which they castrate him and leave him for dead, he leaves a trail of bodies as he exacts his revenge. His actions trigger a massive manhunt, led by the Klan and the local law. The setting is based on careful research.

452. Carter, Forrest. **Gone to Texas: The Rebel Outlaw, Josey Wales**. Delacorte Press/Eleanor Fieide, 1975. Buccaneer Books, 1985. (0-89966-561-6) Lib Bdg $25.95. « Time: Late 1860s.

Josey Wales, whose family was murdered during the Kansas-Missouri border conflict, becomes an outlaw in Texas, joining Comanche chief Ten Bears, bandits, and former Confederate soldiers who refuse to surrender. Readers will enjoy Carter's fast-paced morality play that pits underdogs against a repressive military establishment and an untrustworthy government. First published in 1973 under the title *The Rebel Outlaw*.

453. Carter, Forrest. **Watch for Me on the Mountain**. Delacorte, 1978, 1990. (0-385-30082-4) Pb $10.00. Ulverscroft, 1982. (0-7089-0771-7) Large type ed. $15.95. « Time: Late 1800s.

Geronimo, the Chiricahua Apache chief, fought a desperate hit-and-run war against white settlers in the Southwest. Carter, who holds the title of "Storyteller in Council to the Cherokee Nations," bases this sympathetic, balanced novel on Geronimo's oral autobiography and other historical sources.

454. Cather, Willa. **My Antonia**. Houghton, 1918. Several editions available. « Time: Late 1800s.

The family of Antonia Shimerda emigrates from Bohemia to the Nebraska frontier, where they are swindled by being sold poor land. When her overworked father commits suicide, Antonia supports the family. After she is deserted by a philanderer, she marries a neighbor and raises a large, happy family. This classic of American literature is based on the life of a friend of the author.

455.    Cather, Willa. **O Pioneers!** Houghton, 1913. Several editions available. « Time: 1880s.

The closeness of Alexandra Bergson to the land she loves allows her to convert the virgin prairie into rich, productive farm land. Others in her family, however, do not share her vision and passion for the land. Cather's story of Bohemian and Swedish pioneers on the Nebraska prairie, which includes clear and detailed observations of life, is a powerful account of struggle and attainment on the untamed prairie.

456.    Charyn, Jerome. **Darlin' Bill: A Love Story of the Wild West.** Arbor House, 1980. Fine, 1985. (0-917657-40-3) Pb $8.95. « Time: Late 1860s-early 1870s.

Salome Blackburn's life seems perfect for treatment in a novel. Born in New Orleans in 1848, she saw occupation of the city by both Confederate and Union troops. From there, she traveled throughout the West—Texas, Kansas, South Dakota, and Oklahoma. At various times in her life she was a schoolteacher, hotel manager, fortuneteller, adventurer, and lover of Wild Bill Hickok. Charyn tells her story in a delightful mix of fact and fiction, with hilarious moments set in a revealing portrait of life in the West. Suitable for mature readers.

457.    Clark, Walter Van Tilberg. **The Ox Bow Incident.** Random House, 1940. Several editions available. « Time: 1885.

This account of the lynching of three men accused of murder and cattle rustling is told from the viewpoint of a cowboy who wanders into a frontier Nevada town for refreshment and finds himself part of a posse. Clark combines psychological insight, deft characterizations, and descriptions of the desolate and beautiful land in a fast-paced story.

458.    Conley, Robert J. **Ned Christie's War.** Evans, 1991. Pocket Books, 1993. (0-671-75969-8) Pb $3.99. « Time: 1880s.

While awaiting a conference, Cherokee leader Ned Christie and his friend pass the time drinking. When he awakens, his friend is gone and a dead U.S. marshal is found nearby. While Christie is on the run from the law, a legend grows up about his savagery and cunning, and his flight ends in a bloody confrontation.

459.    Cotton, Ralph. **While Angels Dance: The Life and Times of Jeston Nash.** St. Martin's Press, 1994. (0-312-11098-7) $21.95. « Time: 1860s.

A vivid sense of life on the Missouri/Kansas frontier is provided through the story of Jess Nash, who flees from his Kentucky home to relatives in Missouri following his involvement in the death of a Union soldier. A cousin of the James brothers, Jess rides with Quantrill's Raiders during the war and later with the James-Younger gang. The plot is predictable, but the strong characterizations will appeal to mature readers.

460.    Cummings, Jack. **The Deserter Troop.** Walker, 1991. Several editions available. « Time: 1872.

Continued service at a remote cavalry post in Arizona becomes impossible for Sergeant Joe Madden and six troopers under the rigid and cruel command of Captain

Falk. The men desert and turn to a life of crime to survive. This causes conflict among them. Meanwhile, Falk must track them down. Powerful characterizations and a strong sense of time and place strengthen this appealing Western.

461. Cummings, Jack. **The Indian Fighter's Return**. Walker, 1993. (0-8027-1268-1) $19.95. « Time: 1892.

Cummings's action-filled story and its good character development provide an easy introduction to early feminists, small-town politics, and civil rights. The plot concerns Ella, an Indian rights activist; Jon, who wishes to rescue her from her Shoshone captor; and escaping bank robbers, all of whom find themselves united to fight a hostile Indian tribe in Idaho. Suitable for younger secondary students.

462. Edmonds, Janet. **Rivers of Gold**. St. Martin's Press, 1991. (0-312-06453-5) $18.95. « Time: 1890s.

The Klondike River Valley of Alaska is the setting for this dramatic story of Amity Jones, who seeks to improve her life by becoming a mail-order bride. Although her life with Samuel York is demanding, Amity is content until an attack by marauders leaves Samuel dead and herself pregnant. She then learns that her marriage is not legal and her home is not her own. Still, she tries to make a home for her family by running a boardinghouse that she hopes will prosper during the gold rush. This absorbing tale is based on extensive research and presents a clear picture of life on the Alaskan frontier.

463. Ell, Flynn J. **Dakota Scouts**. Walker, 1992. (0-8027-4130-4) $18.95. « Time: ca. 1870.

The government opened the Dakota Territory to settlers in 1863; by 1870 they had to send troops to protect them. In a realistic story of conflict between cultures, Ell tells of John Benson, a Seventh Cavalry scout who dreams of having his own ranch; his Black mentor, an army mule driver named Isaiah Dorman; and Lone Bear, a Sioux warrior and scout who dreams of peace and of having enough resources to marry Little Moon. Benson and Lone Bear respect one another, but each fears the people of the other. Their story, based on accurate history and a deep knowledge of the landscape, will inform and entertain Western fans.

464. Erdman, Loula. **The Edge of Time**. Dodd, 1950. Texas Christian University Press, 1989. (0-87565-031-7) Pb $13.95. « Time: 1885.

Bethany and Wade Cameron leave Missouri to homestead in the Texas Panhandle. Here they farm in cattle country, where they are not welcome. Life on the Texas prairie includes living in a sod house, prairie fires, and water shortages. This quiet novel, which Erdman based on true stories of those whose families homesteaded the area, has remained popular over the years.

465. Estleman, Loren D. **Bloody Season**. Bantam, 1987. Several editions available. « Time: 1881.

Estleman's intense research, which is the basis for this detailed and realistic account of the events leading to and following the action at the O.K. Corral, allows the reader to feel and smell Tombstone, Arizona, in 1881. This portrait of the greedy womanizer Wyatt Earp, the alcoholic woman-beater Doc Holiday, and the rival McLaury-Clanton gang will destroy many romantic myths about the gunfight and its participants.

466.  Estleman, Loren D. **This Old Bill**. Doubleday, 1984. Ultramarine, 1984. (0-385-19165-0) $25.00. Windsor Publishing Corp., 1990. (1-55817-422-2) Pb $3.95. « Time: ca. 1860s-1890s.
Details of the exciting life of Buffalo Bill Cody fill this lively fictionalized biography that presents his experiences as buffalo hunter, Indian fighter, and entertainer, and his friendships with Kit Carson, Annie Oakley, and Wild Bill Hickok.

467.  Fackler, Elizabeth. **Billy the Kid: The Legend of El Chivato**. Tor; distributed by St. Martin's Press, 1995. (0-312-85559-1) $24.95. « Time: 1870s.
The murderous career of Billy the Kid (Henry Antrim, a.k.a. William H. [Billy] Bonney) is recreated in Fackler's balanced account, which reveals the hard life Billy lived as a cattle rustler and gunman. A sociopath whose only interest was his own welfare, Billy's death was a relief to many powerful people who had used his skills for their own purposes.

468.  Fulton, Len. **The Grassman**. Thorp Springs Press, 1974. Repr. Dustbooks, 1974. (0-914476-26-2) $7.95. « Time: 1886.
Andrew Finn's travels to the Wyoming Territory to meet relatives provides the setting for a story about a place where a family's livelihood depends on scarce grass and water, and range wars flare over the rights to the Ten Smoke River. Throughout the story, the harshness of life in the frontier plains is evident.

469.  Garfield, Brian. **Manifest Destiny**. Penzler, 1989. Warner, 1990. (0-445-40815-4) Pb $5.95. « Time: 1884.
Following the deaths of his wife and his mother on the same day, Theodore Roosevelt, a young New York politician, goes to the North Dakota Badlands to become a rancher and recover his health. While there, he becomes involved in a fight for land and defends a number of small ranchers against a wealthy Frenchman who wants to build a cattle empire. This story is based on careful research and provides a strong sense of the time and place.

470.  Garland, Hamlin. **A Little Norsk, or Old Pap's Flaxen**. Appleton, 1892. Reprint Service, 1988. (0-7812-1218-9) Lib Bdg $59.00. « Time: 1880s.
Two bachelor homesteaders on the South Dakota prairie adopt an orphaned immigrant child and raise her lovingly. The sentimental story is realistic in its portrayal of the countryside and farm work.

471.  Garland, Hamlin. **Main Traveled Roads**. Harper, 1890. Several editions available. « Time: 1880s-1890s.
Garland shows clearly the beauty of the country, the high spirits of the young, and the unending toil and monotonous lives of many farmers and their wives in his realistic novel based on his personal experiences. Details of work, housing, food, customs, and manner of speech are accurate and convincing. *Main Traveled Roads* is set in South Dakota, Wisconsin, and Iowa.

472.  Gibbons, Reginald. **Sweetbitter**. Broken Moon, 1994. (0-913089-51-6) $21.95. « Time: 1890s.
Racism, hatred, and love are the theme of this powerful novel set in Texas. Ruben, an orphan of Choctaw and white blood, is raised by a Black woman of generous spirit, who teaches him to read. Because of her influence, he becomes astute

in navigating the complex political and social worlds of Blacks, Native Americans, and whites. However, when his love for a prominent white girl is reciprocated, they are both in grave danger.

473. Giles, Janice Holt. **The Plum Thicket**. Houghton, 1954. Fawcett, 1978. (0-449-23767-2) Pb $1.95. « Time: 1890s.

The visit of middle-aged Katherine Rogers to the Southern farm and village where she spent a happy summer is warm with remembrances of the time. It reveals that each generation, as it grows up, must face the same choices as its predecessors. Religious revivals, Confederate reunions, and baseball contribute to the setting.

474. Gipson, Fred. **Old Yeller**. Harper, 1956. Several editions available. « Time: 1870s.

Fourteen-year-old Travis is left in charge of the family farm in Texas while his father drives a herd of cattle to the market in Abilene. His experiences, which lead him from childhood to manhood, are shared by an ugly stray dog. This classic tale has been a favorite since it was first published.

475. Gorman, Edward. **Night of Shadows**. Doubleday, 1990. (0-385-24561-0) $14.95. « Time: 1895.

Cedar Rapids, Iowa, is the setting for a mix of history, suspense, and romance in a Western format. Based on the life of the first female police officer in the city, the story concerns Ann Tolan, whose role as a police officer is resented by the men. Assigned to keep track of an alcoholic retired gunfighter, Ann is convinced that he is innocent of a recent murder, but she is the only one who believes in him.

476. Grey, Zane. **Nevada**. Harper, 1928. Bantam, 1946. (0-553-24343-8) Pb $2.95. « Time: 1880s.

Nevada and Ben Ide were partners in an effort to capture wild horses. That exciting story was told in Grey's *Forlorn River*. This formulaic, action-filled story features an accurate and colorful portrayal of Western culture and scenery. It concerns the romance between Nevada and Ben's sister, which is threatened when Nevada's enemies bring up past accusations of rustling and gunfighting.

477. Grey, Zane. **Riders of the Purple Sage**. Harper, 1913. Several editions available. « Time: 1871.

Beset by troubles, Jane Withersteen is ably assisted by Lassiter, a mysterious gunman. Confrontations with evil teach Jane that she must fight to protect her own; Lassiter learns from her the healing power of love. Grey's romance of the conflicts between Mormons and Gentiles and the depredations of cattle rustlers in southwestern Utah includes classic descriptions of the landscape.

478. Grey, Zane. **The U. P. Trail**. HarperCollins, 1918, 1991. (0-06-100176-7) Pb. $3.50. « Time: 1860s.

Massacre, kidnapping and escape, gamblers and other villains, high adventure and colorful characters abound in Grey's epic tale of the building of the Union Pacific Railroad. In spite of the melodramatic style, the work is very informative concerning the realities of the task. Suitable for younger secondary students.

479. Halacy, Dan. **Empire in the Dust**. Walker, 1990. (0-8027-4108-8) $18.95. Thorndike, 1991. (1-56054-189-X) Large type ed. Lib Bdg. $15.95. « Time: ca. 1890.

Rustlers, plague, drought, encroaching farmers, poor markets, and labor problems are all part of this rousing Western. Texas rancher Frank Cullen has one of the biggest spreads around, but the arrival of homesteaders threatens his livelihood. The reader will enjoy the story and come away with a better understanding of economic problems on the frontier.

480. Hall, Oakley. **Bad Lands**. Athenaeum, 1978. Bantam, 1988. (0-553-27265-9) Pb $4.50. « Time: 1880s.

The true story of the Johnson County Cattle War is the basis for Hall's account of the violent conflict between the free-rangers and those who favored barbed wire and other modern improvements. The story shows the impact of settlers on the fragile ecology of the Dakota Badlands.

481. Hall, Oakley. **Warlock**. Viking, 1958. Bantam, 1988. (0-553-27114-8) Pb $4.50. « Time: 1880s.

In an unnamed southwestern state, the town of Warlock is under the control of anarchistic forces led by power-hungry Abe McQuown. When a group of citizens bring in Clay Blaisedell to serve as marshal, he has no real legal authority. This critically acclaimed novel is based on events in Tombstone, Arizona.

482. Hansen, Ron. **Assassination of Jesse James by the Coward Robert Ford**. Knopf, 1979. Norton, 1990. (0-393-30679-8) Pb $8.95. « Time: 1880s.

A long flashback depicts the early history of the James-Younger gang, but the emphasis of this account is on James's last days. Jesse James was already a mythical hero to the 19-year-old Bob Ford when they met. Hansen tries to unravel some complex truths about James and his killer, who found himself pardoned for his crime but never respected.

483. Hansen, Ron. **Desperadoes**. Knopf, 1979. Norton, 1990. (0-393-30680-1) Pb $8.95. Ulverscroft, 1981. (0-7089-0644-3) Large type ed. $12.00. « Time: 1890s.

The lives of the Dalton boys, peace officers turned outlaws, are recalled by the elderly Emmett Dalton, the only brother to survive the aftermath of their robbery of the bank at Coffeyville, Kansas. Hansen received critical acclaim for the writing style and authoritative tone of this, his first novel.

484. Haycox, Ernest. **Bugles in the Afternoon**. Little, 1944. Windsor Publishing Corp., 1990. (1-55817-455-9) Pb $3.95. « Time: 1870s.

In 1875, Kern Shafter enlists as a private in Custer's command. Through his story, the reader gains a sense of the atmosphere that led to the confrontation between Custer and the Sioux on the Dakota frontier.

485. Henry, Will. **Alias Butch Cassidy**. Random, 1968. Bantam, 1991. (0-553-24101-X) Pb $3.99. « Time: Late 1800s.

Robert LeRoy Parker, later known as Butch Cassidy and George Parker, was the son of a Mormon bishop who was a strict father. At the age of 16, he teamed up with rustler Mike Cassidy and fled with him to Robber's Roost, a notorious outlaw hideout in Utah. From there, he and other outlaws robbed gold shipments throughout Utah and Wyoming. Henry won a Western Writers of America special award for this work.

486.   Henry, Will. **From Where the Sun Now Stands**. Random, 1960. Bantam, 1991. (0-553-29084-3) Pb $3.99. « Time: 1877.

The fictional hero, Hayets, narrates this work that is widely considered Henry's masterpiece. The story concerns Chief Joseph of the Nez Percé as he led his people on a 113-day, 1,300 mile retreat from the White Bird Canyon in Idaho toward the Canadian border. This attempt to find freedom failed when starvation led to Chief Joseph's surrender in Montana. In a captivating, historically accurate account, Henry honors the Nez Percé.

487.   Henry, Will. **No Survivors**. Random House, 1950. Bantam, 1992. (0-553-23698-9) Pb $3.99. « Time: 1865-1878.

Following the Civil War, Confederate Colonel John Buell Clayton becomes a scout for the army. He is captured by Sioux under the leadership of Crazy Horse and allowed to live because of his courage. Crazy Horse eventually adopts Clayton, renames him Cetan Mani (Walking Hawk), and allows him to marry an Indian woman. For years Cetan Mani supports the Indian cause, but when the Battle of Little Bighorn is imminent, he warns Custer of the danger. Custer ignores the warning. This factually based account shows Henry's sympathy for the Sioux cause.

488.   Highwater, Jamake. **The Eyes of Darkness**. Lothrop, 1985. (0-688-41993-3) $13.00. « Time: ca. 1860s-early 1900s.

Charles Alexander Eastman (Indian name Ohiyesa), taken from his Sioux people to attend white schools at the age of 17, determined to learn white man's medicine to help his people. As a physician, Eastman served at a number of reservations and wrote several books. In this fictionalized biography, Highwater shows how the tragedy at Wounded Knee in 1890 led to Eastman's disillusionment with his influence in a white man's world.

489.   Horgan, Paul. **A Distant Trumpet**. Farrar, 1960. Godine, 1991. (0-87923-863-1) Pb $16.95. « Time: 1880s.

Matthew and Laura Hazard, a young married couple, live at a remote Arizona Territory army post under constant threat of attack by Apaches. This vivid and informative account of the time is based on extensive research.

490.   Hough, Emerson. **Heart's Desire: The Story of a Contented Town, Certain Peculiar Citizens, and Two Fortunate Lovers**. Macmillan, 1905. Several editions available. « Time: 1880s.

In a parody of formulaic Western romances, Hough tells an episodic story based on his own experiences in New Mexico. The hero of the story is Dan Anderson, a lawyer and journalist who came to the town of Heart's Desire for a peaceful life. Heart's Desire is a paradise, where there is no official law but plenty of order, and life is a series of pranks and hilarious tales. Then come capitalists, the railroad, and women, plus an effort to corrupt Dan to the benefit of the wealthy. He resists and nearly loses his true love, until he is wounded by Billy the Kid. Hough's humorous prose provides delightful reading while still producing a sense of place and convincing characterizations.

491.   Houston, James. **The White Dawn: An Eskimo Saga**. Harcourt, 1971, 1989. (0-15-696256-X) Pb $6.95. « Time: 1897.

Outstanding descriptions of wildlife and Eskimo customs are provided in Houston's carefully researched tale. It concerns the changes to the social structure of a small Eskimo village brought about by the arrival of three stranded whalers.

492. Hoyt, Edwin P. **The Last Stand**. Tor; distributed by St. Martin's Press, 1995. (0-312-85533-8) $22.95. « Time: 1876.

Military historian Hoyt presents a well-balanced account of the career of George Armstrong Custer. He shows Custer as a complex man: a rigid military disciplinarian as well as a romantic who risked his life and career to care for his wife. Also revealed are the complexities of postwar politics and the realities of life on the plains.

493. Johnston, Terry C. **Cry of the Hawk: A Novel**. Bantam, 1992. (0-553-08936-6) $17.50. 1993. (0-553-56240-1) Pb $5.99. « Time: 1860s.

Confederate Jonah Hook, seeking release from a Union prison, agrees to go west to fight Indians. Following the war, he returns home to find that his family has been kidnapped by marauding Mormon Danites. Johnston's account of Hook's efforts to find his family, and his other violent adventures as an Indian fighter and buffalo hunter, is well written and historically accurate.

494. Jones, Douglas C. **Come Winter**. Holt, 1989. University of Arkansas Press, 1992. (1-55728-259-5) Pb $14.95. « Time: 1870s.

Roman Hasford has progressive ideas about the future of his home town in western Arkansas. He builds a bank, starts a horse farm, and enters politics, but finds that his ideas are strongly opposed by those who wish the sleepy hamlet to remain as it had been. When one of his workers is murdered, Hasford's efforts to wield his power result in a bitter feud. This realistic picture of a nineteenth-century frontier community reveals social hypocrisy and violence in politics. Sequel to *Roman*.

495. Jones, Douglas C. **A Creek Called Wounded Knee**. Scribner, 1978. Macmillan, 1984. (0-684-18257-2) Pb $7.95. « Time: 1890.

This dramatic story of the personalities and events that made inevitable the massacre at Wounded Knee Creek (in the South Dakota Badlands) has been thoroughly researched. It is well told by Jones, a prolific author of powerful historical fiction. This book completes Jones's chronicle, which includes *The Court Martial of George Armstrong Custer* and *Arrest Sitting Bull*.

496. Jones, Douglas C. **Gone the Dreams and the Dancing**. Holt, 1984. Tor, 1987. (0-8125-8453-8) Pb $3.95. « Time: ca. 1875.

Liverpool Morgan, a Confederate Civil War veteran, is asked by Kwahadi, a wise Comanche chief, to locate the white woman who is his mother. Morgan comes to feel at home in the Comanche culture. The reader learns the fate of the people who were forced to surrender at Fort Sill (1875) because of wars with white settlers and the decimation of their buffalo herds. Based on the life of Quanah Parker. Sequel to *Season of the Yellow Leaf*.

497. Jones, Douglas C. **Roman**. Tor, 1989. (0-8125-8455-4) Pb $4.95. « Time: ca. 1865-1870.

Following the Civil War, Roman leaves his Arkansas home to see the West. Here he breaks horses, fights Indians at Beecher Island, and makes a fortune as a garbage entrepreneur in Lawrence, Kansas, before returning home to find true love. Although the action is predictable, the historic setting, language, and characterizations are accurate. This work will be enjoyed by younger secondary students and adventure fans. Sequel to *Elkhorn Tavern*; prequel to *Come Winter*.

498.   Jones, Douglas C. **Search for Temperance Moon**. Holt, 1991. Repr. Thorndike Press, 1991. (1-56054-244-6) Large type ed., Lib Bdg $22.95. « Time: ca. 1880.

June Moon is the madam at Arkansas's most famous bordello, which is located at Fort Smith, just next to Indian Territory, where only the tribal police and the federal government have jurisdiction. When her mother, the outlaw Temperance, is murdered and the authorities refuse to act, June hires a hot-tempered former lawman to find some answers. Jones fills this mystery/Western with rich details of life on the frontier, where vice and corruption were as common as they are in our modern world.

499.   Jones, Douglas C. **Winding Stair**. Holt, 1979. Tor, 1991. (0-8125-8461-9) Pb $4.95. « Time: 1875-90s.

In the late 1800s, an area that included western Arkansas was one of the last strongholds of western lawlessness. Under Isaac C. Parker, history's "hanging judge," federal marshals began in 1875 to restore order in the border town of Fort Smith, Arkansas. This story is narrated by a young lawyer who is involved in bringing to justice a group of murdering desperadoes. Strong characterizations are featured in this authentic account.

500.   Kelton, Elmer. **The Day the Cowboys Quit**. Doubleday, 1971. Several editions available. « Time: 1883.

When Eastern banks demand changes in business management by landowners before lending money, the cowhands react angrily to the threat to their traditional independence. This lively and informative novel is based on an actual cowboy strike in Texas.

501.   Kelton, Elmer. **Slaughter**. Doubleday, 1992. (0-385-24894-6) $22.00. « Time: Late 1860s.

With the end of the Civil War, Northerners and Southerners moved west, renewing interest in the concept of Manifest Destiny. Hostility between them and the native peoples was inevitable. This novel concerns the conflict over the buffalo; their slaughter was very profitable for white business people, while their loss meant death to the Comanche way of life. Kelton shows several points of view—featuring a Confederate veteran, an English gambler, a freed slave, a young businesswoman, and Crow Feather, a proud Comanche warrior—in a well-written saga that will appeal to many readers.

502.   Kissinger, Rosemary K. **Quanah Parker: Comanche Chief**. Pelican, 1991. (0-88289-785-3) $12.95. « Time: 1845-1911.

Quanah Parker, son of a Comanche chief and the white Cynthia Ann Parker (who had been abducted as a child), was dedicated to his people and did everything in his power to keep his promise to drive the whites from the Indian lands. This fictionalized biography deals with a number of those conflicts, followed by Parker's final surrender to keep his people from starvation. Ultimately he adopted many white ways, becoming a cattle rancher and working with Theodore Roosevelt and others to promote peaceful coexistence between Indians and whites.

503.   Kluge, P. F. **Season for War**. Freundlich, 1984. (0-88191-017-1) $15.95. « Time: 1884-1900.

Lucy Lawson wants to be known for accomplishing something, so she persuades her journalist friend to build up her husband's achievements in his newspaper.

Consequently, Captain Henry Lawson and his buffalo soldiers become popular heroes, as they are involved in the last pacification of the Native Americans and the Philippine-American War. Horrifying war action is vividly detailed. This complex story presents an engrossing picture of the limitations on the freedom of African Americans following the Civil War, and the role of women in a society where protection meant control.

504. L'Amour, Louis. **The Cherokee Trail**. Bantam, 1982. (0-553-20846-2) Pb $3.50. 1982. (0-553-27047-8) Pb $3.99. « Time: Late 1860s.
Left a widow with a child, Southern-born Mary Breydon determines that she will run a station on the Cherokee Trail in Colorado. With the support of friends, she battles enemies with her brains, and guns when necessary. The history, characters, and language of the story ring true.

505. Landis, Jill Marie. **Jade**. Jove, 1991. (0-515-10591-0) Pb $4.95. « Time: 1870s.
Set in San Francisco, this story includes a great deal of information about the Victorian standards of the day and about Chinese lore, myth, and culture. The somewhat contrived plot involves Jade Douglas's efforts to regain possession of the Chinese art treasures that her grandfather collected and her father used as collateral for his debts. Her efforts lead to a romantic involvement with the wealthy J. T. Harrington and danger from a mysterious party who is willing to murder Jade to get possession of the treasure. Younger secondary students will enjoy this romance that deals with a little-known segment of San Francisco society.

506. Lane, Rose Wilder. **Free Land**. Longmans, 1938. University of Nebraska Press, 1984. (0-8032-7914-0) Pb $8.95. « Time: 1880s.
Leaving their Minnesota home, David Beaton and his bride homestead in the territory that is to become South Dakota. *Free Land*, a realistic and simple story of the pioneer spirit, presents a clear picture of the land and the struggle to change the prairie sod into wheat farms.

507. Lane, Rose Wilder. **Let the Hurricane Roar**. Longmans, 1933. Harper & Row, 1985. (0-06-4401-58-8) Pb $3.50. « Time: 1870s.
A dugout on the South Dakota prairie is the home of 16-year-old Caroline and Charles, her 19-year-old husband. They face a grasshopper plague, prowling wolves, and many other hardships, but show true pioneer spirit and love for their land. The romance and the reality of the time are seen in Lane's simply told story.

508. Lea, Tom. **The Wonderful Country**. Little, 1952. Repr. Texas A&M Press, 1984. (0-89096-185-9) $15.95. « Time: 1880s.
Exciting action, well-developed characters, and vivid descriptions of the countryside add to this thoughtful story of Texan Martin Brady. As a boy, he flees to Mexico after killing his father's murderer, but later returns to become a Texas Ranger. A fine presentation of time and place.

509. LeMay, Alan. **The Searchers**. Harper, 1954. Berkley, 1992. (0-425-13481-4) Pb $3.99. « Time: 1860s.
This authoritative and exciting novel of life on the Texas frontier just after the Civil War includes fine characterizations. The story centers on the harrowing five-year

search for 10-year-old Debbie, the only survivor of a massacred family, who has been living with the Comanche.

510.  Matheson, Richard. **Journal of the Gun Years**. Evans, 1991. Several editions available. « Time: 1864-1876.

Matheson tells his story about the deterioration of a good man through the detailed and personal journal that fictional Civil War veteran Clay Halser begins in 1864. After the war, Halser is unable to settle into the routine of his quiet hometown. He is a superior gunman, so he goes west and uses his skills to operate on both sides of the law. He loses friends and family through the years as newspaper accounts exaggerate his prowess and he tries to live up to his publicity.

511.  McMurtry, Larry. **Anything for Billy**. Simon & Schuster, 1988. Pocket Books, 1991. (0-671-74605-7) Pb $5.99. « Time: 1878-1881.

Ben Sippy is a dime novelist from Philadelphia. In 1878, he leaves his large and demanding family and goes west to find the life about which he has been making up stories. Here he meets a buck-toothed 17-year-old who already has a reputation as a killer. Later Sippy writes less-than-admiring stories about the boy and gives him the name of Billy Bone (known to us as Billy the Kid). The first-person delivery and episodic chapters give an accurate sense of the time and the harsh lives of criminal and victim.

512.  McMurtry, Larry. **Buffalo Girls**. Simon & Schuster, 1990. Several editions available. « Time: Late 1800s.

A series of never-mailed letters written by Calamity Jane reveal authentic details of Western life in the transitional days between the Old West and the new. The letters show how Jane, Buffalo Bill Cody, Wild Bill Hickok, and an assortment of fur trappers and Indians exploited their past for a profit, just as the entertainment industry exploited them, knowing they were the last of an era.

513.  McMurtry, Larry. **Lonesome Dove**. Simon & Schuster, 1985. Several editions available. « Time: Late 1870s.

Horse theft, gunfights, hangings, and stampedes are found in this lengthy Pulitzer prize-winning novel that concerns two former Texas Rangers on a cattle drive from south Texas to Montana. The story is peopled with all the characters one would expect in this setting, but the characterizations are exceptional, and McMurtry's realistic treatment of events results in a credible and exciting account.

514.  McMurtry, Larry. **Streets of Laredo: A Novel**. Simon & Schuster, 1993. (0-671-79281-4) Pb $25.00. « Time: Late 1890s.

In an action-filled and sometimes humorous sequel to *Lonesome Dove*, Captain Woodrow Call tracks a train robber across Texas and into northern Mexico. Accompanying him is an oddly assorted cast, including a naive bookkeeper, Call's exhausted old sidekick, and a Shoshone who can track anybody, even the elusive, Apache-trained Joey Garza. Memorable scenes include Call's visits with Judge Roy Bean and John Wesley Hardin, and a stopover at Crowtown in west Texas. Leland Stanford, a politician and builder of railroads, is also a character.

515. Morris, Gilbert. **The Yukon Queen**. Bethany House, 1995. (0-55661-393-8) Pb $8.99. « Time: 1896-1899.

Cass, a rebellious young member of the Winslow family, leaves his Wyoming home and spends three years traveling about the country. He supports himself by doing menial labor, but he dreams of wealth. On the death of his friend, Fletcher Stevens, Cass finds himself responsible for Fletcher's daughter, who turns out to be attractive and self-sufficient. Together they head for the Klondike, where they are joined by two Winslow cousins. Although the story is somewhat predictable, Morris provides a good sense of the times in a story that is suitable for younger secondary students. Book 17 in the House of Winslow series.

516. Nixon, Joan L. **High Trail to Danger**. Bantam, 1991. (0-553-07314-1) $16.00. 1992. (0-553-29602-7) Pb $3.50. « Time: 1870s.

Accurate information about late-nineteenth-century frontier living conditions is found in this formula novel about an extremely plucky heroine. Fearing that she and her sister are being done out of their inheritance by greedy relatives, Sarah runs away to a wild mining town in Colorado to find her father. On the way, she encounters all types of danger, but finds help and romance in the guise of two very different young men. Suitable for younger secondary students needing an introduction to the time.

517. Norris, Frank. **McTeague**. Doubleday, 1899. Several editions available. « Time: Late 1800s.

McTeague, a scoundrel from a California mining town, learns enough dentistry to make a living in San Francisco. His free-spending habits and his wife's obsession with hoarding money culminate in violent tragedy. Norris's realistic novel presents a powerful picture of degeneracy because of greed, as well as life among the lower classes in northern California at the turn of the century.

518. Norris, Frank. **The Octopus**. Doubleday, 1901. Several editions available. « Time: 1870s-1880s.

Norris intended to write a trilogy about the wheat industry to show how the problems of society affect individual lives. The theme of *The Octopus* is the planting, growing, and harvesting of the crop; *The Pit* deals with its marketing (Norris died before the third volume was written). Set in California, *The Octopus* concerns the war between the San Joaquin Valley wheat growers and the railroad monopoly that had corrupted the government and controlled the newspaper and the bank. This fast-moving story provides an authentic picture of the vanishing Spanish culture. Norris's naturalistic treatment of unpleasant subject matter caused his work to be largely ignored at the time of its writing.

519. Osborn, Karen. **Between Earth and Sky**. Morrow, 1996. (0-688-14123-4) $23.00. « Time: 1867-1930.

Abigail Conklin's letters to her sister provide a chronicle of her experiences after she leaves her Virginia home to settle on the frontier in New Mexico. Abigail details frontier living, but she is an unconventional woman who has an appreciation for the stark beauty about her. Consequently, her story provides a good sense of place and the expectations of society for women.

520. Paulsen, Gary. **Canyons**. Delacorte, 1990. Several editions available. « Time: 1884.

In alternating chapters, Paulsen tells two coming-of-age stories. In 1884 Coyote Runs, an Apache youngster, must succeed in a grueling horse raid to prove his readiness to join the men of his Apache tribe. While in a canyon, the boy is deliberately shot by two soldiers from Fort Bliss. One hundred years later, Brennan Cole finds the skull with a hole through its forehead. With the help of a pathologist and others, he sets about finding out what happened. This informative and powerful story will involve the readers in the lives of both characters.

521. Portis, Charles. **True Grit**. Simon & Schuster, 1968. NAL-Dutton, 1969. (0-451-16022-3) Pb $3.95. « Time: 1880s.

This delightful high adventure of a 14-year-old girl (Mattie Rose) and a U.S. Marshal (Rooster Cogburn) whom she bribes to help her avenge her father's death was serialized and made into a movie. A fine example of nineteenth-century Americana, the setting of this moving and humorous tale ranges from Arkansas to the Indian Territory. Suitable for younger secondary students.

522. Richter, Conrad. **The Lady**. Knopf, 1957. Repr. Amereon, n.d. (0-89190-332-1) $17.95 University of Nebraska Press, 1985. (0-8032-8918-9) Pb $6.50. « Time: 1880s.

Set in the Mexican-American society of northern New Mexico, Richter's critically acclaimed, concise tale of violence, revenge, and rivalry between cattlemen and sheepmen focuses on a vital, charming, and enduring woman.

523. Rolvaag, Ole. **Giants in the Earth**. Harper, 1927. Harper & Row, 1965. (0-06-083047-6) Pb $7.00. « Time: 1880s.

In a moving, critically acclaimed narrative of everyday events, Rolvaag has created a classic account of the mental and physical hardships of pioneer life on the South Dakota plains. Norwegian immigrant farmer Per Hansa Holm exults in wresting a living from the virgin prairie. However, his wife Beret hates the hard and lonely life and longs for the comfort and security of Norway. She becomes increasingly fanatical about religion. Followed by *Peder Victorious*.

524. Rolvaag, Ole. **Peder Victorious**. Harper, 1929. University of Nebraska Press, 1982. (0-8032-8906-5) Pb $10.95. Repr. Greenwood, 1973. (0-8371-7067-2) $57.50. « Time: Late 1890s.

Although the Holm family and their neighbors have settled in their new homes enough that survival is no longer a problem, they still must deal with issues of assimilation. The boy, Peder, has the joyous vision of his pioneer father, and wants to become one with the new community and find a girlfriend. His mother, Beret, runs a prosperous farm but still clings to the old ways and resists Americanization. Sequel to *Giants in the Earth*; followed by *Their Father's God*.

525. Sandoz, Mari. **Miss Morissa, Doctor of the Gold Trail**. McGraw, 1955. University of Nebraska Press, 1980. (0-8032-9118-3) Pb $8.95. « Time: 1870s.

Epidemics, gunshot wounds, and snake bites are part of the routine of a physician in frontier Nebraska, to be faced along with violent weather, Indian attacks, and range wars. As a woman physician, however, Dr. Morissa Kirk has additional personal and professional problems. Sandoz's accurate and detailed account of life in the North

Platte River country, based on the lives of three persons, provides vivid portrayals of the varied people that lived in Nebraska or who passed through on their way to the gold fields in the Black Hills.

526.  Sandoz, Mari. **Son of the Gamblin' Man**. Potter, 1960. University of Nebraska Press, 1976. (0-8032-0895-2) $29.95. « Time: Late 1800s.
    Ex-gambler and promoter *par excellance* John Cozad brought his family west to found the Nebraska town that bears their name. Cozad wanted the town to become the new capital of the United States. (It is located where the 100th meridian crosses the Platte River.) His style and temper made many powerful enemies, however, and when he shot a man in self defense, he had to run for his life. Sandoz's fictionalized account of the Cozad family, which is carefully based on actual events, is also the story of many pioneer families who endured financial difficulties, turbulent weather, and violent neighbors.

527.  Schaefer, Jack. **Shane**. Houghton, 1949. Several editions available. « Time: 1889.
    The development of character, situation, and mood make *Shane* a classic account of life on a homestead farm in Wyoming. In this tightly woven story, a boy tells about a mysterious former gunman who hires on to help with the farm work and is ultimately drawn into the conflict between the farmers and cattle ranchers.

528.  Svee, Gary D. **Single Tree**. Walker, 1994. (0-8027-4142-8) $19.95. « Time: 1880s.
    Vigilante madness rules Montana in the late 1880s, where cattle rustling, real or suspected, results in almost certain death. Award-winning author Svee tells an engrossing story of the adventures of itinerant cowboy Eli Gilfeather and his adopted son Runs Towards. Their powerful neighbor heads a group of marauding vigilantes that hangs the innocent Sam Wilder. Runs Towards then helps the Wilder family to achieve a semblance of justice.

529.  Welch, James. **Fools Crow**. Viking, 1986. Viking Penguin, 1987. (0-14-008937-3) Pb $11.00. « Time: ca. 1865-1899.
    This powerful novel examines the subtle and inevitable destruction of the Blackfeet nation in the post-Civil War years and reveals what has been lost. Details of tribal culture—the physical, mental, and spiritual life—are evoked by a part-Blackfoot author in a story of an uncertain boy who hopes to deserve the esteem of his people.

530.  Williams, Jeanne. **Home Mountain**. St. Martin's Press, 1990. Several editions available. « Time: 1881.
    Williams based this account of frontier life on an Arizona dairy ranch on accounts of women who lived in Arizona at that time. The story concerns the 16-year-old orphaned Katie McLeod, who takes her younger siblings and their livestock from Texas to Arizona, determined to make a life for them there. Her enterprise and hard work, along with help from the neighbors, get her through troubles with raiding Apaches, predators, and the weather. This well-written story provides an excellent sense of time and place.

531.  Williamson, Penelope. **Heart of the West**. Simon & Schuster, 1995. (0-671-50822-9) $22.50. « Time: 1880s.
    Life on the Montana frontier is seen through the experiences of three women: naïve and romantic Clementine from Boston; Hannah, a prosperous landowner who

had been a prostitute; and Erlan Woo, a Chinese bride whose heart remains in China. As these women and their families struggle to change the harsh frontier into an organized community that provides safety and comfort for growing children, the reader gains an appreciation for their determination.

532.    Woolley, Bryan. **Sam Bass**. Corona, 1983. (0-931722-25-X) $16.95. 1991, 2d ed. (0-931722-38-1) Pb $9.95. « Time: 1870s.

Bass, a real Texas outlaw, progresses from gambling on horses to bank and train heists. Betrayed by a companion when he robs a Union Pacific train in Nebraska, he dies of gunshot wounds at the age of 27. The story of his last years, told through the voices of a sheriff, a gang member, and several other people who knew him, provides an honest look at life on the edge of society at that time.

533.    Yep, Laurence. **Dragon's Gate**. HarperCollins, 1993. (0-06-022972-1) Lib Bdg $14.89 (0-06-022971-3) $15.00. « Time: 1860s.

During the late 1860s, many Chinese immigrants were recruited to work on the transcontinental railroad. Their treatment was harsh, their pay was low, and they faced constant prejudice. Yep's story concerns 14-year-old Otter, from a wealthy Chinese family, who joins his father and uncle on a work crew; their purpose is to learn American technology that they can take back home. Otter's unforgettable, historically accurate story reveals the conditions faced by these immigrants and explains the reasons for the Chinese workers' strike, which has been all but forgotten.

# Chapter 6

# Progressive Era, Twenties, and Depression, 1900-1939

For the convenience of readers, entries in this chapter are divided into the following categories:

- ◆ Inclusive Titles
- ◆ Early Twentieth Century
- ◆ World War I
- ◆ The Twenties
- ◆ The Thirties

## *INCLUSIVE TITLES*

534.   Estleman, Loren D. **Whiskey River**. Bantam, 1990. (0-553-07042-8) $17.95. 1991. (0-553-29025-8) Pb $4.99. « Time: 1920s-1930s.

Journalist Connie Minor tells the story of the rise and fall of Jack Dance, a Detroit gangster whose overconfidence led him to take on the major-league bootleggers. Minor, who is cynical and morally ambiguous, finds his career tied to the fate of Dance. He exploits that fact as best he can, just as Dance uses him to his own ends. Estleman's character development and authentic sense of the atmosphere created by the Eighteenth Amendment provide an excellent chronicle of the time and place.

535.   Goldreich, Gloria. **West to Eden**. Macmillan, 1987. Avon, 1989. (0-380-70601-6) Pb $4.95. « Time: ca. 1900-1930.

In this authentic story of a Jewish immigrant, the reader meets Emma Coen. After her father's reputation and fortune are lost in Amsterdam, Emma makes her way to Galveston, Texas, where she establishes a boardinghouse. After their marriage, Emma and Isaac move to Phoenix, where they open a business and struggle for their rights and statehood for Arizona.

536.  Killens, John Oliver. **Youngblood**. Trident, 1966. University of Georgia Press, 1982. (0-8203-0602-9) Pb $12.95. « Time: 1900-1941.

Petty discrimination and racial violence are found in this novel concerning a Black family from Georgia. Black folk tales incorporated into the story provide humor and reveal attitudes of the Black community toward the meaning of manhood. Followed by *And Then We Heard the Thunder*.

537.  Lewis, Sinclair. **Main Street**. Harcourt, 1920. Several editions available. « Time: 1912-1920.

In telling the story of the collegiate, professional, and married life of Carol Milford-Kennicott, Lewis covers the years 1912-1920, showing how America responded to World War I and the Jazz Age. While she works in St. Paul, Carol is exposed to the art, music, and political ideas of the city. After marriage, she and Dr. Kennicott make their home in Gopher Prairie, Minnesota, which he considers a fine place to live, but Carol finds it ugly, smug, and dull. Her attitudes and her unsuccessful efforts to change it reflect Lewis's own attitude toward what he called the "village virus."

538.  Puzo, Mario. **The Fortunate Pilgrim**. Macmillan, 1965. Fawcett, 1982. (0-449-23456-8) Pb $2.50. Bantam, 1985. (0-553-24859-6) Pb $3.95. « Time: 1920s-1930s.

Puzo's chronicle of immigrant Italian-American life features Lucia Santa Angeluzzi-Corbo, an indomitable, hard-working widow. Her struggles to assure the survival of her large family are both comic and painful. The picture of Italian community life is warmly realized in this entertaining novel.

539.  Rose, Howard. **The Pooles of Pismo Bay**. Raymond Saroff, 1990. (1-878352-04-0) $20.00. (1-878352-05-9) Pb $10.00. « Time: ca. 1908-1918.

Cora Elliot Poole is a leader in the organization of the Industrial Workers of the World (IWW), and her son Reuben is a labor agitator. This fictionalized view of the history of the IWW includes real characters, such as Emma Goldman, the American anarchist. The complexity of the political arguments in this novel make it suitable for mature readers interested in the history of labor movements.

540.  Tax, Meredith. **Rivington Street**. Morrow, 1982. Avon, 1990. (0-380-70907-4) Pb $4.95. « Time: ca. 1900-1918.

Set in New York City's Lower East Side, this account of the experiences of a Russian immigrant family focuses on Hannah Levy, a forceful woman, and her daughters Ruby (a creative fashion designer) and Sarah (a social activist). The repressive conditions and low pay in the garment industry, and the violent reaction to demands for better pay, are shown in this engrossing story. It includes a garment workers' strike, the Triangle Shirtwaist Factory fire, and the jailing of suffragists. Followed by *Union Square*.

541.  Tax, Meredith. **Union Square**. Morrow, 1988. Avon, 1990. (0-380-70906-6) Pb $4.95. « Time: 1920s-1930s.

In this continuing saga of the Russian immigrant Levy family, the energetic Levy girls and their husbands and friends experience all the political and social changes that occurred in New York's Lower East Side during the 1920s and 1930s. Sarah marries a Marxist, which causes a rift with her parents. While Sarah campaigns for unions and women's rights, her sister Ruby rises to prominence in the fashion industry. This sequel to *Rivington Street* is both entertaining and informative.

542.   Turpin, Waters Edward. **O Canaan!** Doubleday, 1939. Repr. AMS Press, n.d. (0-404-11420-2) $23.00. Ayer, n.d. (0-8369-9179-6) $15.75. « Time: ca. 1916-mid-1930s.

Early in the twentieth century, thousands of African Americans migrated from the South to northern cities, seeking to improve their lives. This story is set in Chicago and shows the effect of the migration, the subsequent social unrest, and the Great Depression on Joe Benson and his family.

543.   Watson, Larry. **Justice**. Milkweed, 1995. (1-57131-002-9) $17.95. « Time: 1899-1930s.

When the teenage sons of Bentrock, Montana, Sheriff Julian Hayden go to North Dakota on a hunting trip, they find that his reputation and power extend throughout the West. As they seek to understand their family history, they also learn about many other people in Bentrock and about the settling of the West. Using an episodic style and strong characterizations, Watson weaves an engrossing story. Prequel to *Montana 1948.*

# EARLY TWENTIETH CENTURY

544.   Borland, Hal. **When the Legends Die**. Lippincott, 1963. Bantam, 1984. (0-553-25738-2) Pb $3.99. « Time: 1910-1920s.

After the death of his parents, a young Ute boy from southwestern Colorado lives in the wilderness with only a tame bear for companionship. Befriended by an ex-bronco buster, the boy becomes noted on the rodeo circuit for his murderous riding style. He eventually finds himself by accepting his Indian heritage.

545.   Boyd, Brendan C. **Blue Ruin: A Novel of the 1919 World Series**. Norton, 1991. (0-393-03020-2) $19.95. HarperCollins, 1993. (0-06-097514-8) Pb $10.00. « Time: 1919.

A number of historical figures appear in Boyd's examination of a great sporting event fixed by gamblers and crooked players, revealing the way owners cheated their players and players cheated each other. It was also an era of scandal in government, when everyone tried to get something for nothing on the stock market. Baseball fans and readers interested in popular culture will enjoy this well-researched book.

546.   Brinig, Myron. **Wide Open Town: A Novel**. Farrar, 1931. American World Geographic, 1993. (1-56037-034-3) Rev. ed. Pb $12.95. « Time: ca. 1900.

The copper mining town of Silver Bow, Montana, in its roughest days provides the setting for this powerful novel. It is a love story of John Donnelly, a young Irishman and ardent Catholic, and Zola, a prostitute. The violence of the times, the exuberance and humor of the characters, and the outstanding portrayal of the beauty of the setting and the ugliness of the mines, are all well drawn.

547.   Bristow, Gwen. **This Side of Glory**. Crowell, 1940. Repr. Buccaneer Books, 1979. (0-89966-026-6) Lib Bdg $25.95. « Time: 1885-1919.

Kester Larne, cultured but poor, and Eleanor Upjohn, affluent but plebeian, fall in love and marry against the wishes of both families. Their story is the backdrop for Bristow's third story of life on a Louisiana plantation. This account concludes with the flu epidemic of 1918. Sequel to *The Handsome Road.*

548. Burns, Olive Ann. **Cold Sassy Tree**. Ticknor & Fields, 1984. Several editions available. « Time: 1906.

In a charming period piece, Burns tells the story of the scandal caused when 14-year-old Will Tweedy's grandfather marries a lovely young milliner. Will loves the eccentric old man and does his part to keep the peace. In the process he learns many lessons about life, death, and love, and readers see life in a small Georgia town at the turn of the century.

549. Byron, Gilbert. **The Lord's Oysters**. Little, 1957. Johns Hopkins, 1977. (0-8018-1959-8) Pb $9.95. « Time: 1910-1914.

Noah Martin's father believes in the freedom to work at fishing as he chooses, making funds chronically scarce in this loving household. Byron's autobiographical account of a boy's life among the oyster men of Chester River in the eastern-shore region of Maryland is filled with warmth and humor, and a bit of the cruelty of young boys.

550. Caldwell, Janet Taylor. **Answer As a Man**. Putnam, 1981. Amereon, 1976. (0-88411-143-1) $27.95. Fawcett, 1982. (0-449-20050-7) Pb $4.95. « Time: 1900-1910.

Jason Garrity, the son of devout Irish Catholic immigrants, faces religious hypocrisy and ethnic prejudice as he rises from delivery boy to resort hotel entrepreneur in a small Pennsylvania boomtown. He must also deal with financial scandals, political corruption, and family problems. Well-developed characterizations and a good sense of the time enrich Caldwell's novel.

551. Caldwell, Janet Taylor. **Testimony of Two Men**. Doubleday, 1968. Several editions available. « Time: 1901.

Incisive characterizations and an engrossing account of nineteenth-century medical practices enhance Caldwell's account of the problems of an outspoken physician in a small Pennsylvania town following the death of his wife after a botched abortion.

552. Chase, Mary Ellen. **The Lovely Ambition**. Norton, 1960. (0-393-08477-9) Pb $5.95. 1985. (0-393-30234-2) Pb $5.95. « Time: ca. 1900.

This is a nostalgic account of the family of an English Methodist minister that emigrates to Maine at the turn of the century. A quiet story, it has well-delineated characters and an outstanding picture of life on the rocky Down East shore.

553. Davis, Donald. **Thirteen Miles from Suncrest: A Novel**. August House, 1994. (0-87483-379-5) $19.95. « Time: 1910-1913.

Medford Henry McGee, age 10, begins a daily journal at his grandfather's insistence and continues for more than three years, when family responsibilities bring it to a close. Through these delightful pages the reader sees life on a farm in western North Carolina and (via newspaper accounts) major national events. The homey details of growing up, killing a pig, building a privy, a first train ride, weddings, births, and sorrows ring true.

554. Davis, Harold Lenoir. **Honey in the Horn**. Harper, 1935. Repr. AMS Press, n.d. (0-404-20074-5) $34.50. « Time: 1906-1908.

Humorous anecdotes and metaphors fill this episodic account of homesteading in Oregon, in which Clay Calvert meets herders, farmers, mill workers, storekeepers, horse traders, Indians, and desperadoes. The conversations among the men are filled with exaggeration and wry humor. They reflect the spirit of the times and are reminiscent of the stories of Bret Harte. Winner of the Harper Biennial Prize.

555.   Dinneen, Joseph. **Ward Eight**. Harper, 1936. Repr. Ayer, 1976. (0-405-09331-4) $26.50. « Time: ca. 1910-1919.
     The people who lived in Ward Eight in northern Boston, before and during World War I, were mostly immigrants, unsure of their status. The Ward Boss controlled the area, finding jobs for people, keeping them out of jail, and depending on their votes. He lined his own pockets but also spent a lot taking care of people. Dinneen's vigorous novel is filled with political insight. It concerns Hughie Donnelly, a ward boss, and Timothy O'Flaherty, initially Donnelly's opponent who becomes his friend and successor.

556.   Doctorow, E. L. **Ragtime**. Random House, 1957. Several editions available. « Time: ca. 1900-1910.
     Robert Peary, J. P. Morgan, Harry Houdini, Henry Ford, and many other well-known people of the day appear in this story of an upper-middle-class family living in New Rochelle, New York. The even tenor of their lives is disrupted by the changing social mores of the time and their interaction with an anarchist, a Black ragtime piano player, and a poor Russian immigrant.

557.   Dreiser, Theodore. **An American Tragedy**. Boni and Liveright, 1925. Several editions available. « Time: Early twentieth century.
     Teenaged Clyde Griffiths, from a poor family, learns to value what money can provide when he has a job as a bellboy. A tragedy that occurs while he and his friends are joy-riding causes him to flee to Chicago, where an uncle gives him work. Clyde's obsession with social climbing and his wish to marry a young socialite are threatened when his working-class girlfriend becomes pregnant. He drowns her, but is convicted and dies in the electric chair. Dreiser's tragedy, which he blames on the capitalist system, is based on an actual case.

558.   Edmonds, Walter D. **The Boyds of Black River**. Dodd, 1953. Syracuse University Press, 1988. (0-8156-2454-9) Pb $12.95. « Time: early 1900s.
     Edmonds's warm and gently humorous story set in upstate New York concerns a horse-loving family that views with disdain the coming of the horseless carriage. A touch of nostalgia and an appreciation for the food, drink, and social life at the turn of the century characterize this portrait of the times as seen by an adolescent boy.

559.   Falstein, Louis. **Laughter on a Weekday**. Obolensky, 1965. Astor-Honor, 1965. (0-8392-1147-3) $14.95. « Time: Early 1900s.
     The story of a Russian Jew's escape from early-twentieth-century pogroms is told with a fresh perspective by the son of one such family. He records their wanderings and their difficulties in establishing themselves in a small town in the American Midwest.

560.   Fergus, Charles. **Shadow Catcher**. Soho, 1991. (0-939149-55-9) $19.95. 1993. (0-939149-91-5) $12.00. « Time: 1913.
     Fergus based his first novel on the 1913 Wannamaker Expedition of Citizenship, which toured 75 Indian reservations to encourage Indians to become citizens and to obtain formal photos. Ansel Fry, a young stenographer, is at constant risk as he uses a hidden camera to obtain unposed photos that he sends to newspapers. He also records

what is said off the record to present a realistic account of the Indian experience and the duplicity of the government. This informative work examines the young nation's growing self-awareness and will find a wide audience.

561. Hughes, Langston. **Not Without Laughter**. Knopf, 1930. Macmillan, 1986. (0-02-052200-2) Pb $6.95. Amereon, 1976. (0-8488-1055-4) $21.95. « Time: Early 1900s.

Just before World War I, Sandy, an African-American boy, grows up in a small Kansas town under the wing of his loving grandmother. The author based this novel on his own experiences and reveals the ways in which his community helped him appreciate his heritage.

562. Janus, Christopher G. **Miss 4th of July, Goodbye**. Sheffield Books, 1990. (0-934831-00-9) Pb $12.95. « Time: 1917.

The author's sister migrated from Greece to West Virginia in 1917 and wrote letters to her grandfather back home. Based on these letters, Janus tells the story of 16-year-old Nikki, whose lively curiosity and strong sense of justice lead her to make many revealing comments about the customs and racist attitudes of her new home.

563. Kirkpatrick, Katherine. **Keeping the Good Light**. Delacorte, 1995. (0-385-32161-9) $14.95. « Time: ca. 1910.

Daily life in a lighthouse in Long Island Sound is filled with isolation and unending responsibility, and teenager Eliza Brown yearns to get away. Her story, filled with lively detail, provides an excellent picture of the times.

564. Litvin, Martin. **The Impresario**. Western, 1995. (0-938463-07-1) Pb $5.00. « Time: 1901.

After Ed Jackson, a Black man, stabs white Charley Rowe in a confrontation following a racial slur, Jackson is saved from a lynch mob by a Jewish junk dealer. Through the dealer's efforts, Jackson is able to rejoin society and live a productive life. Litvin's appealing novel is based on actual events in Illinois at the turn of the century.

565. Marshall, Catherine. **Christy**. McGraw, 1967. Avon, 1976. (0-380-00141-1) Pb $5.99. Repr. Buccaneer Books, 1994. (1-56849-309-6) Lib Bdg $27.95. « Time: 1912.

Marshall's account of a young teacher in Appalachia is based on the experiences of her mother. The story presents the joys and difficulties of Scots-Irish mountaineer life, the beauty of the hills, and the faith that sustains Christy through her experience in a community far from home.

566. Marshall, Catherine. **Julie**. McGraw, 1984. Avon, 1985. (0-380-69891-9) Pb $5.50. « Time: 1930s.

Eighteen-year-old Julie Wallace and her family move from Alabama to Pennsylvania, where her father runs a small newspaper. Julie's growth in experience as a writer and her romantic entanglements will sustain reader interest. As well, the story contains a great deal about steel plants, dam construction, and economic and political pressures from big business. The story is based on the author's own experience.

567. Owens, William A. **Fever in the Earth**. Putnam, 1958. Shearer, 1984. (0-940672-20-0) Pb $9.95. « Time: 1901.

The Spindletop oil strike is the background for this story of how the promise of wealth affects the lives of an itinerant preacher and a young schoolteacher. Owens's forceful account of booms and busts is based on a thorough knowledge of the time and place and its language and lore.

568. Schaefer, Jack. **Monte Walsh**. Houghton Mifflin, 1963. Several editions available. « Time: Early 1900s.

Schaefer's accurate picture of life in the western cattle country concerns a cowboy who spent most of his life on the open range and finds it difficult to adjust to the disappearance of the range. Action takes place across the plains of eastern Colorado and nearby regions at the turn of the century.

569. Settle, Mary Lee. **The Scapegoat**. Random House, 1980. (0-394-50477-1) $11.95. « Time: 1912.

By allowing different characters to narrate the story, Settle shows the relationships among the various segments of society in a small West Virginia town—the white gentry, African Americans, immigrants, Protestants, Catholics, and "outsiders"—and the events surrounding an imminent coal strike. The complex narrative technique makes this work suitable for mature readers. A real-life character who appears in this work is Mary Harris Jones (Mother Jones), who was a leader in the union movement. The fourth of the author's Beulah Quintet; followed by *The Killing Ground*.

570. Shuken, Julia. **In the House of My Pilgrimage**. Crossway Books, 1995. (0-89107-839-8) Pb $9.95. « Time: ca. 1900.

Refugees from oppression, war, and famine in Russia, Piotr and Fenya settle with a small group of Russian immigrants in Los Angeles. Obstacles to their financial and emotional stability seem overwhelming in the strange land, yet those who remained behind are having even more terrifying experiences. The challenges of making a new life and maintaining faith when everything seems impossible are honestly handled in this engrossing novel.

571. Sinclair, Upton. **The Jungle**. Doubleday, 1906. Several editions available. « Time: Early twentieth century.

A Lithuanian-American, new to the country, finds work at a Chicago stockyard. However, through misfortune and mistreatment, his fortunes sink until he finds himself a former convict on the verge of starvation. Sinclair's powerful indictment of deplorable working conditions and the subjugation of those who have no power has received mixed reviews. The strength of the telling is applauded by some, while others consider the work unbalanced and polemic.

572. Sinclair, Upton. **King Coal**. Macmillan, 1917. Repr. AMS Press, 1980. (0-404-58469-1) $30.00. Bantam, 1994. (0-553-21433-0) Pb $4.95. « Time: 1914-1915.

Wealthy Hal Warner assumes a new identity as Joe Smith and takes a job in the Colorado coal mines to determine the truth about working conditions. Sinclair's exciting, well-documented story is filled with interesting characters. It shows how a company is able to control the financial, legal, and political situation to its own advantage.

573.   Smith, Betty. **A Tree Grows in Brooklyn**. Harper, 1943. Several editions available. « Time: 1910s.

Francie Nolan knows the common people of Brooklyn because she lives in a tenement there. She also knows hunger, cold, and the thrill of learning. The details of daily life are set forth with warmth and humor as Francie, her family, and their neighbors steadfastly deal with their problems. This autobiographical story is set before and during World War I.

574.   Stein, Harry. **Hoopla**. Knopf, 1983. St. Martin's Press, 1986. (0-312-38983-3) Pb $7.95. « Time: 1912-1919.

The furor surrounding the Black Sox Scandal is chronicled through the points of view of two men ambitious for success—Luther Pond, a fictional investigative reporter, and Buck Weaver, a real Chicago White Sox ballplayer—in this well-researched, fast-paced, exciting novel.

575.   Stratton-Porter, Gene. **Freckles**. Grossett, 1900. Several editions available. « Time: ca. 1900.

A homeless boy, maimed and abandoned as an infant, is allowed to guard the precious timber of the Limberlost, a swamp in Northern Indiana. Through his stewardship of the woods, he finds happiness in the companionship of birds and other wild creatures.

576.   Stratton-Porter, Gene. **Girl of the Limberlost**. Grosset, 1909. Several editions available. « Time: ca. 1900.

Elnora Comstock, a poor Indiana girl and a friend of Freckles (see entry 575), lives on the edge of the Limberlost swamp. She is encouraged in her education by a kindly teacher and pays for her schooling by gathering moth specimens for the Bird Woman. This warmly told story has been a favorite of readers since its publication.

577.   Stratton-Porter, Gene. **The Harvester**. Doubleday, 1911. Several editions available. « Time: ca. 1900.

When David, a young man who raises and sells medicinal herbs, meets his dream girl, he must rescue her from a cruel uncle before he can make her his own. Stratton-Porter's sentimental romance reflects her own experiences of wholesome family life.

578.   Taber, Gladys. **Spring Harvest**. Putnam, 1959. Amereon, n.d. (0-89190-599-5) $21.95. « Time: 1914.

Life on the campus of a small Wisconsin coed college in the spring of 1914, before the United States entered the war, is told by one who grew up and lived her adult life in such a setting. Taber's picture of the time is warm and authentic, without stereotypes.

579.   Tarkington, Booth. **Penrod**. Doubleday, 1914. Several editions available. « Time: ca. 1900.

The humorous adventures of Penrod Schofield, a mischievous 12-year-old, and his friends in turn-of-the-century Indiana have been highly popular with several generations of adults and young readers. A strong sense of time and place, plus memorable characters, add to the strength of the work.

580.   Tucker, Augusta. **Miss Susie Slagle's**. Johns Hopkins University Press, 1987. (0-8018-3419-8) Pb $9.95. « Time: 1912-1916.

Attention to detail marks this story, which concerns the education and lives of a group of Johns Hopkins medical school students who live at Susie Slagle's boardinghouse. Readers interested in medical topics will enjoy this honest and realistic work.

581.   Warren, Robert Penn. **Night Rider**. Houghton, 1939. J. S. Sanders, 1992. (1-879941-14-7) Pb $11.95. « Time: 1905.

Warren's powerful first novel is a story of the violent tobacco war in Kentucky between growers and manufacturers. Vivid scenes and authentic detail make this work memorable.

582.   Wood, Jane Roberts. **A Place Called Sweet Shrub**. Delacorte, 1990. Several editions available. « Time: Early 1900s.

The story begins with Lucy's efforts to save the family hardware store, her care for an ailing aunt, and her concern about whether she will find a husband. After Lucy marries school principal Josh Arnold, they move to Sweet Shrub, Arkansas. While living at a boardinghouse, they become painfully aware of the bigotry that keeps the African-American population from any semblance of economic or civic equality. This sequel to *The Train to Estelline* presents a clear picture of the racial issues of the time.

583.   Yerby, Frank. **The Serpent and the Staff**. Dial, 1958. Ulverscroft, 1978. (0-7089-0241-3) Large type ed. $12.00. « Time: 1900s.

Medical practice in New Orleans at the turn of the century is challenging to Vienna-trained Dr. Duncan Childers, who scrambled his way up the social ladder from lowly beginnings to become a fashionable and wealthy surgeon. Yerby researched medical practice and social settings thoroughly for this dramatic tale.

584.   Yount, Steven. **Wandering Star**. Ballantine, 1994. (0-345-39437-2) Pb $5.99. « Time: 1910.

As an adult, Tom looks back on his days as an undisciplined boy who skipped school to work at the local newspaper in High Plains, Texas. Here he was encouraged to see both sides of many issues, including racial prejudice and other common practices. An important community issue in the spring of 1910 was the popularity of a traveling preacher who had convinced many citizens that the world would end with the coming of Haley's Comet. This credible account of small town life early in the century is revealing and very readable.

# *WORLD WAR I*

585.   Cather, Willa. **One of Ours**. Knopf, 1922. Random House, 1991. (0-679-73744-8) Pb $12.00. « Time: ca. 1910-1918.

Claude, an idealistic Nebraska farm boy, has never felt fully comfortable or purposeful in his prosperous home. However, the call to war that takes him to France allows him to serve in a glorious cause. Most critics hailed this account of life in Nebraska, but many were disappointed with the author's resolution of Claude's problems.

586. Dos Passos, John. **1919**. Houghton, 1932. NAL-Dutton, n.d. (0-451-52248-6) Pb $4.95. Amereon, n.d. (0-88411-345-0) $25.95. « Time: 1918-1919.

Dos Passos uses the "newsreel" and "camera eye" techniques in his realistic chronicle of life in America through the war years, with glimpses of five young Americans at home and at war. This powerful and controversial novel, which received critical acclaim upon publication, includes anecdotes about such public figures as Theodore Roosevelt, J. P. Morgan, Woodrow Wilson, and the Unknown Soldier. Sequel to *The 42nd Parallel*. Followed by *The Big Money*. Together, the three novels form Dos Passos's U.S.A. trilogy.

587. Dos Passos, John. **Three Soldiers**. Doran, 1921. Carroll & Graf, 1988. (0-88184-413-6) Pb $9.95. « Time: 1917-1918.

In a realistic and energetic novel, Dos Passos follows the experiences of three American soldiers who suffered the tyranny and misery of war. This novel was controversial at the time of its publication because of its revelations about military life.

588. Fleming, Thomas J. **Over There**. HarperCollins, 1992. (0-06-017983-X) $20.00. « Time: 1918-1919.

In a lengthy and somewhat complex novel, Fleming tells the story of Peggy Warden, an idealistic young college graduate who goes to the war zone to do what she can to help. Her assignment as an ambulance driver and nurse brings her in touch with a disillusioned French surgeon, General Pershing, and many other characters. She sees the war-torn countryside, the suffering of the innocent, and the political machinations of those wishing to assure their own fortunes and glory.

589. Goodrich, Marcus. **Delilah**. Rinehart, 1941. Repr. Naval Institute Press, 1985. (0-87021-145-5) $32.95. « Time: 1916-1917.

This award-winning book concerns the U.S. destroyer *Delilah*, which cruised the waters of the South Pacific in the six months preceding U.S. entry into the war. The story deals with the sometimes brutal realities of life aboard ship and "Victory or Death," the code of naval tradition.

590. Grey, Zane. **Desert of Wheat**. HarperCollins, 1919, 1991. (0-06-100167-8) Pb. $3.50. Amereon, 1976. (0-8488-276-4) $23.95. « Time: 1914-1918.

Kurt Dorn resents his German heritage and revels in his wheat ranch and his ability to send grain to nourish American soldiers during the war. After his crop is ruined in a clash · /ith the IWW (Industrial Workers of the World), he joins the army. Following horrendous experiences, he returns to his beloved ranch to heal both body and spirit. Distinctive characters and effective word pictures mark this work, which presents a controversial view of the IWW.

591. Hemingway, Ernest. **A Farewell to Arms**. Scribner, 1929. Several editions available. « Time: 1914-1918.

An American ambulance officer serving on the Austro-Italian front becomes involved with an English nurse and continues the romance while convalescing from a severe wound. This tragic story is told with minimal descriptions, staccato sentences, and natural dialogue.

592.   Trumbo, Dalton. **Johnny Got His Gun**. Lippincott, 1939. Several editions available. « Time: 1918+.

Trumbo's award-winning book concerns the thoughts of a soldier who lost limbs, speech, and hearing in the war. His thoughts include memories and his attempts to communicate with those around him. The story is uncompromising in its reality.

593.   Voigt, Cynthia. **Tree by Leaf**. Macmillan, 1988. (0-689-31403-5) $14.95. Fawcett, 1989. (0-449-70334-7) Pb $3.95. « Time: ca. 1918-1920.

When Clothilde's father goes to war against the wishes of her wealthy grandparents, she and the other family members are forced to leave their luxurious home and try to survive as best they can. Clothilde's mother maintains her façade of being a gracious lady; her brother is seduced by their grandparents' riches; and Clothilde is left with the work. She hopes that things will improve when her father returns, but he comes back so badly scarred by the war that he chooses solitude. Voigt's story presents a fine picture of the class distinctions that prevailed at the time. Suitable for younger secondary students.

## THE TWENTIES

594.   Adams, Samuel Hopkins. **Revelry**. Boni and Liveright, 1926. Reprint Service, 1992. (0-7812-6914-8) Lib Bdg $89.00. « Time: 1921-1923.

This fictionalized version of the political corruption and scandals of the Harding administration, written from an insider's view, spares none of the players, except perhaps Harding. The book was suppressed in Washington, D.C., and condemned by several state legislatures; a dramatization was banned in Philadelphia. Subsequent works have proven its accuracy.

595.   Asch, Nathan. **Pay Day**. Brewer, 1930. Repr. Omnigraphics, 1990. (1-55888-268-5) Lib Bdg $38.00. « Time: 1927.

The Sacco-Vanzetti trial and execution are in the background of this story as a young clerk named Jim lives from payday to payday. Through Jim's experiences the reader gets a strong sense of New York City at the time: the speakeasies, the subway, the dirt, the noise, and everyone discussing the Sacco-Vanzetti case. The writing style makes this work appropriate for mature secondary readers.

596.   Bradbury, Ray. **Dandelion Wine**. Doubleday, 1957. Knopf, 1975. (0-394-49605-1) $24.95. Bantam, 1985. (0-553-27753-7) Pb $4.99. « Time: 1928.

The essence of an Illinois summer in 1928 is presented through the adventures of a 12-year-old boy, who discovers that summer that he is alive. Ordinary events and emotions are honestly portrayed in this acclaimed novel.

597.   Burnett, William Riley. **Little Caesar**. Dial, 1929. Several editions available. « Time: 1920s.

A gangster tells the story of the Chicago gangs in the 1920s in his own language in this authentic action-filled story that became a famous movie. After Sam Vettori is eliminated in the struggle for gang leadership, Cesare Bandello (Rico) becomes the unquestioned leader until a policeman is killed during a nightclub holdup. This work is based on the author's experiences in Chicago during the 1920s.

598.   Caldwell, Janet Taylor. **Eagles Gather**. Scribner, 1940. Repr. Amereon, n.d. (0-88411-165-2) Lib Bdg $28.95. « Time: 1920s.

The multitudinous and antagonistic Buchard family are featured in this dramatic novel that examines the efforts of ruthless and greedy munitions barons to control international events for their own profit. A fast pace and powerful characterizations of fascinating, if unpleasant, people characterize the work. Sequel to *Dynasty of Death*.

599.   Davis, Harold Lenoir. **Winds of Morning**. Morrow, 1952. Repr. Greenwood, 1972. (0-8371-5785-4) $38.50. « Time: 1927.

The middle Columbia River country, near the southern border of the state of Washington, is the locale for a work that is both a mystery and a Western. Sheriff's assistant Amos Clarke tells of an unintentional murder and the relationship between a classic cattleman, Old Hendricks, and his difficult daughter. Humor and social criticism are a part of this critically acclaimed work, with the natural setting—a sparsely populated region of desert, sheep and cattle ranches, wheat farms, and Indian reservations—making an important contribution to the story.

600.   Dos Passos, John. **The Big Money**. Houghton, 1936. Several editions available. « Time: 1920s.

Many of the characters in this work were introduced in *The 42nd Parallel* and *1919*. Here their lives converge in the boom years as they travel widely across the land and are involved in activities as diverse as moviemaking and Communist Party rallies.

601.   Fitzgerald, F. Scott. **The Beautiful and the Damned**. Scribner, 1922. Several editions available. « Time: 1920s.

The glittering and reckless lives of wealthy Anthony Patch and glamorous Gloria Gilbert lead to excess and degradation. Fitzgerald's account of life in Manhattan during the Roaring Twenties documents the tragedy of life without direction.

602.   Fitzgerald, F. Scott. **The Great Gatsby**. Scribner, 1925. Several editions available. « Time: 1920s.

The glamour and moral barrenness of the Jazz Age underlie this story about Jay Gatsby, a self-made man who spends his ill-gotten fortune on disreputable parties. The only loyalty he shows is to Daisy, and this costs him his life. *The Great Gatsby*, set in Long Island, is often considered Fitzgerald's finest work.

603.   Giardina, Denise. **Storming Heaven**. Norton, 1987. Ivy, 1988. (0-8041-0297-X) Pb $4.99. « Time: 1921.

The 1921 armed confrontation between 10,000 United Mine Workers and the mine owners soon involved the U.S. Army. Giardina's powerful, authentic novel is based on this actual event, in which the army used airplanes and poison gas to control the miners. Narrators include the mayor of Annadel, West Virginia; a union organizer; a nurse; and a woman who lost four sons in a mining accident.

604.   Grosser, Morton. **The Fabulous Fifty**. Macmillan, 1990. (0-689-31656-9) $14.95. « Time: 1921.

Fifteen-year-old Sol Janus and his club buddies go all out to win an all-expense-paid trip for one to the 1921 World Series. The boys are not ethical in their efforts, and Grossner is effective in presenting life in an ethnic neighborhood at the time. The well-researched and detailed description of each game of the Series will appeal to fans. The story is based on experiences of the author's father.

605.　Guy, Rosa. **Measure of Time**. Holt, 1983. Bantam, 1986. (0-553-25611-4) Pb $4.50. « Time: 1920s.

Dorine grew up in the South. As a young adult in Harlem, she meets head-on the obstacles to achieving a comfortable life. She maintains financial responsibility for her distant family and makes a living by shoplifting and similar activities on the edge of the underground, but she lacks personal happiness. Glimpses of the history of Harlem and life there make this a worthwhile read.

606.　Halper, Albert. **The Foundry**. Viking, 1934. Repr. AMS Press, n.d. (0-404-58519-1) $37.50. « Time: 1929.

Halper examines events that preceded the crash of 1929 through incidents in the lives of foundry workers and their employers. This realistic work is rich with authentic details of the work accomplished in a Chicago foundry and of the home lives of those involved.

607.　Harris, Julie. **The Longest Winter**. St. Martin's Press, 1995. (0-312-13115-1) $23.95. « Time: 1926.

Through the fictional biography of an aviator who crashed on an Alaskan island in 1926 and spent 17 years there, Harris examines the native culture and the difficulties of a person who must adapt to a new life without understanding even its rudiments, including the language.

608.　Herbst, Josephine. **The Executioner Waits**. Harcourt, 1934. Repr. AMS Press, n.d. (0-404-58440-3) $34.00. « Time: 1918-1929.

In her sequel to *Pity Is Not Enough,* Herbst continues the story of the Trexlers, a large middle-class family from the Midwest, through the days during and following the war. The reader sees daily events, economic upheaval, labor unrest and strikes, and powerful changes in social attitudes. Herbst based this important social commentary on the experiences of her own family. Followed by *Rope of Gold.*

609.　Hogan, Linda. **Mean Spirit**. Macmillan, 1990. (0-689-12101-6) Text ed. $19.95. Ivy Books, 1992. (0-8041-0863-3) Pb $4.99. « Time: 1920s.

When it is discovered that the Oklahoma land owned by the Osage is rich with oil, it is only a matter of time until powerful white men try to take it away. The murder of Nora Blanket's mother is the first of many in this account of duplicity. The Osage attempts to protect themselves and their culture become hopeless when government authorities seem to be among the guilty. This gripping and thought-provoking story of injustice and prejudice will not be soon forgotten.

610.　Levin, Meyer. **The Old Bunch**. Viking, 1937. Carol Publishing Group, 1985. (0-8065-0974-0) $19.95. (0-8065-0967-8) Pb. $14.95. « Time: 1921-1934.

The story follows the adventures of a group of Jewish high school students for 13 years, from the time of their graduation to the Century of Progress Fair in 1934. Using a kaleidoscopic style, colloquial prose, and sharp characterization, this lengthy novel presents a citizen's eye view of Chicago during the riotous 1920s.

611.  Lewis, Sinclair. **Babbitt**. Harcourt, 1922. Several editions available. « Time: Early 1920s.

Lewis attacks sham and hypocrisy in his story about the empty and vulgar life of George F. Babbitt, a seemingly self-satisfied middle-class businessperson. Babbitt is in reality a shallow conformist whose identity depends on owning the latest gadget, a condition that Lewis felt was widespread across the nation. This classic work of social satire, set in the imaginary Midwestern city of Zenith, was both praised and reviled upon its publication.

612.  Lewis, Sinclair. **Elmer Gantry**. Harcourt, 1927. NAL-Dutton, 1967. (0-451-52251-6) Pb $4.95. Amereon, 1976. (0-8488-0827-4) $21.95. « Time: 1920s.

Former football star Elmer Gantry, experienced in religious chicanery, uses popular advertising methods to make himself and his church a power in the community. In Lewis's uncompromising satiric indictment of religious practices in the early twentieth century, Gantry regards his converts only as stepping-stones to be used for his own purposes. Like all true hypocrites, he convinces himself of his own sincerity.

613.  Marks, Percy. **Plastic Age**. Century, 1924. Repr. Illinois University Press, 1980. (0-8093-0984-X) $12.95. « Time: Early 1920s.

Marks addresses the realistic and idealistic aspects of college life as he recounts the experiences of Hugh Carver at Sanford. Daily routines, religious and philosophical discussions, thoughts, worries, and sexual exploits all appear in this almost photographic attempt at truth-telling.

614.  Maxwell, William. **The Folded Leaf**. Harper, 1945. Repr. AMS Press, n.d. (0-404-61510-4) $32.50. Godine, 1981. (0-87923-351-6) Pb $11.95. « Time: 1920s.

Lymie is the studious type; Spud is extroverted and athletic. Their friendship is firm through high school and college, until they both fall in love with the same girl. Lymie's attempted suicide leads them to maturity. In his highly acclaimed story of friendship, Maxwell presents a distinctive, rich, and moving social commentary.

615.  McKenna, Richard. **The Sand Pebbles**. Harper, 1963. Several editions available. « Time: 1920s.

McKenna's realistic novel of life aboard the gunboat *San Pablo*, which became embroiled in the Chinese revolution that brought Chiang Kai-shek to power, is told from the viewpoint of Jake, a man who hates military life but has a great love for ship engines. Jake tries to exclude himself from the problems of "gunboat diplomacy" but is caught up in the turmoil.

616.  McSorley, Edward. **Our Own Kind**. Harper, 1946. Repr. Ayer, 1976. (0-405-09350-0) $24.50. « Time: 1920s.

Ned McDermott does not have much education, and he is determined that his grandson Willie will have more advantages. McSorley's novel of an Irish-American family living in Providence, Rhode Island, is both humorous and tragic in its examination of the American Dream.

617.  Morris, Wright. **The Huge Season**. Viking, 1954. University of Nebraska Press, 1975. (0-8032-5805-4) Pb $7.95. « Time: 1920s.

The problems of the Jazz Age generation are seen as Peter Foley and his friends examine the impact of the ultra-idealistic 1920s on their lives from the vantage point of the conformist 1950s. The intermingling of the 1920s and 1950s provides an entertaining and enlightening view of a generation.

618.   Morrison, Toni. **Jazz**. Knopf, 1992. Several editions available. « Time: 1920s.

In a novel of profound emotional depth, Morrison takes the reader back to turn-of-the century Virginia to show the impact on individuals and families of the unending emigration of African Americans from the rural South to the urban North. Rage and repercussions surround the murder of a young woman by her 50-year-old married lover. Mature students will find this novel set in Harlem an unforgettable experience.

619.   Murray, Albert. **Train Whistle Guitar**. Northeastern University Press, 1989. (1-55553-051-6) Text ed. Pb $10.95. « Time: 1920s.

Growing up Black in Alabama in the 1920s is the theme of this novel that has autobiographical overtones. As 12-year-old Scooter looks for a style to live by and learns about life and his own background, the reader is immersed in the music (especially the blues), folklore, superstitions, and oral traditions of Southern life.

620.   Parks, Gordon. **The Learning Tree**. Harper, 1963. Fawcett, 1987. (0-449-21504-0) Pb $4.95. « Time: 1920s.

Teenaged Newt is growing up in a small Kansas town. His experiences are similar to those of any other adolescent, but he and his family must also endure the fact that being African American relegates them to the status of second-class citizens. This charming and memorable work, with its moments of humor, violence, and insight, is based on the experiences of the author, who is also a renowned photographer.

621.   Parini, Jay. **The Patch Boys**. Holt, 1986, 1988. (0-8050-0770-9) Pb $8.95. « Time: 1925.

Sammy di Cantini lives in Pennsylvania. His father died in a mining accident, and his brother Vince is working to organize a miners' union. Sammy's other brother is involved with mobsters. This lazy summer of his fifteenth year Sammy spends swimming, talking baseball, and wondering about girls, but he knows he must begin to plan his future. He does not wish to follow his father or either of his brothers, but he cannot find a way out. Should he consider the priesthood?

622.   Peck, Robert Newton. **A Day No Pigs Would Die**. Knopf, 1972. Several editions available. « Time: 1920s.

The realistic details of life and death on a Shaker farm in Vermont provide the setting for this coming-of-age story in which a boy must accept the slaughter of his beloved pig. No detail of life on the farm is avoided. The reader shares the economic and physical hardships, the butchering of the animals, the seasonal beauty and peace of rural living, and the wit and common sense of its inhabitants. Prequel to *A Part of the Sky*.

623.   Powell, Dawn. **The Golden Spur**. Viking, 1962. Random, 1990. (0-679-72687-X) Pb $8.95. « Time: 1920s.

This entertaining novel provides a glimpse of the life of the arts crowd in New York in the 1920s and the 1950s. Jonathan Jaimison is a young man who seeks to find the truth about his heritage by trying to retrace his mother's steps during the glamorous year she spent in Greenwich Village.

624. Schroeder, Ralph E. **A Glory from the Earth**. Pearl-Win, 1986. (0-9606240-8-2) Pb $9.95. « Time: 1918-1925.

The Mueller family—Ma, Pa, bossy Johnny, musical Jenny, intellectual Harry, and adventurous Ben—live on a Wisconsin farm. Grandparents who speak their minds live close by. Realistic details provide a moving portrait of daily life centered on farm work, church, and family. Adam, the illiterate hired man who loves horses, provides added interest.

625. Sinclair, Upton. **Boston**. Boni, 1928. Repr. Scholarly, n.d. (0-403-00295-8) 2 vol. $59.00. Repr. Bentley, 1978. (0-8376-0420-6) $32.00. « Time: ca. 1927.

Sinclair's two-volume work combines fiction and nonfiction in a passionate indictment of prejudice and injustice. Written shortly after the Sacco-Vanzetti execution, the story is told through the eyes of Cornelia, who left her position of privilege at the age of 60 and became friends with the two humble anarchists, especially the courageous and dignified Vanzetti. By telling the story through Cornelia, the reader is provided a balanced picture of social attitudes on several levels.

626. Sinclair, Upton. **Oil!** Boni, 1927. Repr. Bentley, 1981. (0-8376-0444-3) $32.00. « Time: Early 1920s.

In telling the story of the oil scandals of the Harding administration (1921-1923), Sinclair provides a rich picture of the oil industry of Southern California. The story centers around Dad Ross, an entrepreneur whose rise to wealth makes him an inadvertent oppressor of his workers, and Ross's son Bunny, whose love for his father is challenged when he is exposed to the radical political ideas of Paul Watkins. Bunny's efforts to work for social reform through nonviolent means add reality to this vigorous novel, which is an indictment of big business, government, and the greed of powerful individuals. In addition to the oil industry, the reader sees the emergence of Hollywood society and the growth of charlatanism in religion.

627. Slone, Verna Mae. **Rennie's Way**. University Press of Kentucky, 1994. (0-8131-1855-7) $17.95. « Time: ca. 1917-1927.

Slone provides detailed descriptions of life among the Appalachian mountain people of eastern Kentucky. The story concerns a 12-year-old girl who assumes the responsibility for the care of her father and infant sister following the death of her mother. Woven within the story are folkways: the preparation of food and medicine, social events, cultural attitudes, and family history. This appealing work will find a wide audience.

628. Smith, Betty. **Tomorrow Will Be Better**. HarperCollins, 1948, 1971. (0-06-080049-6) Pb $2.50. Amereon, n.d. (0-8488-1171-2) $21.95. « Time: 1920s.

Margy Shannon is the daughter of a factory worker who lives in Brooklyn. Through her story—her loves, job, marriage, and problems—Smith presents a warm account of the lives of ordinary people who, like Margy, believe that tomorrow will bring better things. This charming story provides a strong sense of time and place.

629. Vidal, Gore. **Hollywood: A Novel of America in the 1920s**. Random House, 1990. (0-394-57659-4) $19.95. Ballantine, 1991. (0-345-37013-9) Pb $5.95. « Time: 1917-1924.

Fictional and real people mingle comfortably in this account of the years during and after World War I. The primary events of the war, the national flu epidemic that killed more than 500,000 people, President Wilson struggling for the adoption of his plan for peace, and Warren Harding and the Teapot Dome scandal are all presented. Also included are information about the fledgling movie industry and notable Hollywood figures of the day. As action moves from Hollywood to Washington, the reader sees how much make-believe can be found in either city.

630. Walker, Charles Rumford. **Bread and Fire**. Houghton, 1927. Repr. AMS Press, n.d. (0-404-58482-9) $18.00. « Time: 1920s.
     Following the war, a young man works as an editor in a socialist paper and then in a Pennsylvania steel mill. This realistic account of mill work, which reveals the author's opinions on the labor movement and strikes, is based on his work experience.

631. Welty, Eudora. **Delta Wedding**. Harcourt, 1946, 1979. (0-15-625280-5) Pb $7.95. Amereon, n.d. (0-89190-516-2) $20.95. « Time: 1923.
     An impressionable young cousin visits during a wedding at the Fairchild plantation on the Mississippi Delta. The conversations among three generations of Fairchilds provide a realistic glimpse of a Southern family in decline.

632. Williams, Jeanne. **The Unplowed Sky**. St. Martin's Press, 1994. (0-312-11361-7) $22.95. « Time: 1920s.
     The technical aspects of farming and the routine aspects of daily living are woven nicely into this complex romance. Orphaned Hallie Meredith, 19, cares for her 5-year-old half-brother and makes a living as assistant cook on a traveling threshing team. In her new job Hallie witnesses the power of the local Ku Klux Klan, which opposes the hiring of Native Americans, leftists, and recent immigrants from Central Europe.

633. Yep, Laurence. **The Star Fisher**. Morrow, 1991. (0-688-09365-5) $12.95. Puffin, 1992. (0-14-036003-4) Pb $3.99. « Time: 1927.
     Joan Lee and her family are newcomers to a small West Virginia town; they are also Chinese American and discriminated against. As Joan tries to find her place in the school, she also works to bridge the gap between her proud and lonely mother and a well-meaning neighbor. Yep's picture of prejudice, as seen from many angles, is based on the experiences of his own family. Suitable for younger secondary students.

## *THE THIRTIES*

634. Adams, Alice. **A Southern Exposure**. Knopf, 1995. (0-679-44452-1) $23.00 « Time: 1939.
     Adams provides an excellent view of life in the South toward the end of the Depression by telling her story through the eyes of Harry and Cynthia Baird. The couple flee their debts and social obligations in Connecticut to look for an idyllic new life in North Carolina. As they settle into their new lives and become involved with their neighbors, the reader experiences a time when one's role was determined by race, gender, class, and religion.

635. Algren, Nelson. **A Walk on the Wild Side**. Farrar, 1956. Repr. Greenwood, 1978. (0-313-20294-X) $47.50. Thunders Mouth, 1990. (0-938410-80-6) Pb $12.95. « Time: 1931.

The savagery and poignancy of life in a New Orleans slum during the Depression is seen through the experiences of Dove Linkhorn, a country boy who becomes involved in the debasement required for survival. Algren includes a number of dubious characters, some comic interludes, pathos, and realistic scenes to reveal how unpleasant and cruel living conditions were.

636. Anderson, Edward. **Hungry Men**. Penguin, 1935. University of Oklahoma Press, 1993. (0-8061-2556-X) $12.95. « Time: 1930s.

Anderson called upon his own experiences in writing his stark, realistic account of the experiences of Acel Stecker, an unemployed musician who takes to the road. Acel's experience of catching freights, sleeping wherever he finds shelter, and standing in soup lines is straightforward; his account of those he meets in similar circumstances is revealing and disturbing.

637. Baldwin, James. **Go Tell It on the Mountain**. Knopf, 1953. Dell, 1985. (0-440-33007-6) Pb $5.99. « Time: 1930s.

Life in Harlem is vividly portrayed in this powerful and moving account that uses flashbacks to reveal the lives of three generations, showing the migration of Blacks from the rural South to the urban North and the impact of this cultural change. The central figure of the story is John Grimes, a 14-year-old boy. Through his spiritual awakening, John struggles to find a meaning for his life within a racist society and a religious structure that condemns his individuality.

638. Brush, Katherine. **Don't Ever Leave Me**. Farrar, 1935. Repr. Reprint Service, 1993. (0-7812-5438-8) Lib Bdg $89.00. « Time: 1930s.

Set during a Labor Day dance in a Pennsylvania mill town, where rich mill owners control the fate of the mill workers, this story of the past and present of wealthy Mrs. Billy Cunningham is a study of the manners of the time.

639. Collins, Max Allan. **Murder by the Numbers**. St. Martin's Press, 1993. (0-312-08856-6) $17.95. « Time: 1930s.

This fact-based account deals with the efforts of Eliot Ness to clean up the numbers rackets in Cleveland's Black ghetto. In taking on the Mayfield Road Gang, Ness must cope with corrupt politicians and mob violence. The hard-boiled tough-guy dialogue and unyielding code of honor, plus a fast-moving plot, will appeal to many readers.

640. Collins, Max Allan. **True Detective**. St. Martin's Press, 1983. (0-312-82051-8) $14.95. « Time: 1930s.

In a fast-paced private-eye story filled with accurate historic detail, Nate Heller starts a detective agency and becomes involved with gangsters and politicians in Prohibition-era Chicago. Among the real persons included in this reality-based work is Anton Cermak, the mayor of Chicago.

641. Connell, Evan S. **Mr. Bridge**. Knopf, 1969. Farrar, 1990. (0-86547-054-5) Pb $9.95. G. K. Hall, 1991. (0-8161-5205-5) Pb $15.95. « Time: 1930s.

This companion to the author's *Mrs. Bridge* delves into the life of her husband, a no-nonsense, authoritarian, self-righteous, lonely man. Told in vignettes of experiences, the life of the proper Bridges is revealed as essentially empty.

642.   Connell, Evan S. **Mrs. Bridge**. Knopf, 1959. Farrar, 1990. (0-86547-056-1) Pb $9.95. G. K. Hall, 1991. (0-8161-5206-3) Large type ed. Pb $15.95.« Time: 1930s.

A gentle, well-bred woman, Mrs. Bridge seems to have everything. Her husband is a successful lawyer, her house is fashionable, her children are healthy, and the maid does the housework. But when Mrs. Bridge tries to find meaning in her life, she is unsuccessful, for she has no idea how to avoid the prison of comfort. Connell's humorous insight into his characters and WASP life in the Midwest was critically acclaimed at the time of publication.

643.   Corcoran, Barbara. **The Sky Is Falling**. Macmillan, 1988. (0-689-31388-8) $14.95. Avon, 1990. (0-380-70837-X) Pb $2.95. « Time: 1931.

Annah, daughter of a banker, lives a comfortable life and enjoys her private school, until the Depression ruins the bank and her father cannot find work. When the family must separate, Annah is sent to live in New Hampshire with her widowed aunt. Expecting the worst, Annah has a hard time adjusting, but when she meets Dodie, whose life has always been difficult, Annah begins to mature. This work presents a good picture of the effects of the Depression. Suitable for younger secondary students.

644.   Dallas, Sandra. **The Persian Pickle Club**. St. Martin's Press, 1995. (0-312-13586-6) $20.95. « Time: ca. 1935.

Life in a small Kansas town during the Depression is seen through the interactions of the women in the local quilting circle. The long-term relationships within the circle are shaken when a new member, a novice newspaper reporter, begins to examine town secrets.

645.   Deal, Bordon. **The Least One**. Doubleday, 1967. University of Alabama Press, 1992. (0-8173-0673-0) Pb $19.95. « Time: 1932.

Boy Sword and his family are caught in the vise of poverty. Though their cotton crop was excellent, it brought only four cents a pound, and the family has to accept government commodities to survive. Their struggle, that of their neighbors, and the sights and sounds of the South at the time are portrayed through the eyes of Boy, who also must deal with the fact that, at the age of 12, he still has no first name.

646.   Doctorow, E. L. **World's Fair**. Random House, 1985. Several editions available. « Time: 1930s.

Revealing detail marks Doctorow's account of growing up in New York City during the Depression. Innocent nine-year-old Edgar, his more realistic older brother, and their mother tell the story. Edgar is thrilled because he has won an essay contest and can attend the World's Fair, but they must all deal with reality: a business failure causes their father to leave home, and their elderly grandmother is dying.

647.   Dos Passos, John. **Grand Design**. Houghton, 1949. Repr. Queens House/Focus Service, 1977. (0-89244-036-8) Lib Bdg $24.95. « Time: Late 1930s-early 1940s.

The New Deal years provide the setting for this novel of politics, ambition, idealism, and self-seeking. It shows how the coming of war places power in the hands of the few. Third in a series that includes *Adventures of a Young Man* and *Number One*.

648. Drury, Allen. **Toward What Bright Glory?** Morrow, 1990. Windsor Publishing Corp., 1992. (1-55817-581-4) Pb $5.99. « Time: 1939.

The European war, and the personal, political, and racial issues it raises, loom over Willie and his fraternity brothers as he begins his senior year of college in California. Through Drury's cast of typical characters, the American attitudes and fears of the time are portrayed.

649. Estes, Winston M. **Another Part of the House.** Lippincott, 1970. Texas Christian University Press, 1988. (0-87565-027-9) Pb $10.95. « Time: 1933-1934.

Texas during the Depression, with its poverty, drought, and dust storms, is seen through the eyes of nine-year-old Larry. He idolizes his older brother, resents his parasitic Uncle Calvin, and, with the help of his family, learns to deal with the sorrow that comes with the death of a loved one. The details of the time—O'Cedar furniture polish, Saturday afternoon movies, stickers in bare feet, covered dish suppers, and summer revival meetings—are presented as a normal part of the daily life of a decent and loving family.

650. Fante, John. **1933 Was a Bad Year.** Black Sparrow, 1985, 1991. (0-87685-656-3) $20.00. (0-87685-655-5) Pb $8.50. « Time: 1930s.

High school senior Dominic Molise has typical fantasies: professional basketball and girls. His worries are normal, too; his religious beliefs and his short stature. His Italian immigrant parents are struggling to make a living during the Depression and have their own problems. This sometimes humorous autobiographical novel has good character development and provides realistic details of time and place.

651. French, Albert. **Billy.** Viking, 1993. Several editions available. « Time: ca. 1937.

It is a blistering hot day in Mississippi when 10-year-old Billy Lee Turner and his friend Gumpy cross the railroad bridge into the white part of town. They are unable to resist cooling themselves in the pond, and when they are discovered by Lori, a 15-year-old white girl, and her friend, the girls attack the smaller boys. Gumpy escapes, but in the struggle Billy stabs Lori and she dies, setting off a racial conflagration. This fast-paced stark tragedy is told in realistic language; it will be long remembered.

652. Gwaltney, Frances I. **Idols and Axle-Grease.** Bobbs, 1974. Macmillan, 1974. (0-672-51877-5) $5.95. « Time: 1930s.

This gentle series of vignettes about a small town in Arkansas presents a delightful cast of characters, including one who lives in a tree. Other memorable residents are Miss Doll, a crippled teacher who never lost touch with her many students, and a World War I veteran who made himself into a hero. A warm sense of place makes the reader feel at home.

653. Halper, Albert. **The Chute.** Viking, 1937. Repr. AMS Press, n.d. (0-404-58434-9) $43.50. « Time: 1930s.

In a Chicago mail-order house, order pickers dart madly about filling orders. On the half hour, packages are sent from the top floor down through the building to the shipping floor, where an endless stream of packages is prepared for mailing to rural customers. Halper invites the reader to share in the lives of the young men and women who must meet the demands of the system while trying to maintain personal dignity.

654. Herrick, William. **Hermanos!** Simon & Schuster, 1969. Repr. Second Chance, 1983. (0-933256-38-8) $21.95. 1985. (0-933256-42-6) Pb $16.00. « Time: 1936-1939.

Jake Starr, a union organizer, uses his many skills when he becomes a member of the International Brigade, fighting against fascism in the Spanish Civil War. The vivid battle scenes and the clear picture of powerful people taking cynical advantage of others are based on the author's own experiences in Spain.

655. Hotchner, A. E. **King of the Hill: A Memoir.** HarperCollins, 1972, 1993. (0-06-092405-5) A Reissue ed. Pb $10.00. « Time: 1933.

The misadventures of adolescent Aaron, who is growing to manhood in St. Louis during the Depression, are amusing and poignant. References to the popular culture of the day, Aaron's basic decency, and his thrill in surviving by his own devices provide an appealing look at this time and place.

656. Hudson, Lois Phillips. **The Bones of Plenty.** Little, 1962. Minnesota Historical Society, 1984. (0-87351-175-1) Pb $9.95. « Time: 1933-1934.

The Custer family works hard to succeed on the North Dakota farm they rent, but drought, dust storms, wheat smut, and falling prices take their toll. This autobiographical story is filled with daily events and shows the effects of the economic crash and the Dust Bowl on the personal relations and futures of families like this one.

657. Hunt, Irene. **No Promises in the Wind.** Follett, 1970. Berkley, 1987. (0-425-09969-5) Pb $3.99. « Time: 1932-1933.

Fifteen-year-old Josh Grondowski's out-of-work father releases some of his economic fear and frustration by becoming harshly critical of Josh. Eventually Josh decides that the family would be better off without having to provide for him, so he and his smaller brother take to the road. They scrounge for food, hitchhike, ride freights, work in a carnival, and have many other experiences of the homeless, including deprivation, illness, and death, before reaching home again. Suitable for younger secondary students.

658. Jones, Douglas C. **Weedy Rough.** Holt, 1981. Tor, 1989. (0-8125-8463-5) Pb $4.95. « Time: 1930s.

Duny and Hoadie are best friends as they grow up in a small Arkansas town during the Depression. They are separated after an angry fight over a girl, and when they are reunited there is tragedy. A resulting murder trial reveals small-town hatreds and prejudices. Believable events of daily living and authentic characters make this bittersweet story a memorable one.

659. Kelly, Jack. **Mad Dog.** Macmillan, 1992. (0-689-12145-8) Text ed. $19.95. « Time: Early 1930s.

A dead ringer for John Dillinger is arrested. Upon his release he decides to capitalize on the resemblance and takes to the vaudeville circuit with a stage show based on Dillinger's criminal activities. Through this device, Kelly allows the narrator to delve into Dillinger's psyche and provides insight into the times.

660. Keyes, Frances Parkinson. **All That Glitters.** Messner, 1941. Repr. Lightyear, 1981. (0-89968-238-3) Lib Bdg $18.95. « Time: 1925-1940.

This lengthy, entertaining novel is set primarily in Washington, D.C., and follows several characters of high social and political standing through 15 years of their lives.

661.  Lee, Harper. **To Kill a Mockingbird**. Lippincott, 1960. Several editions available. « Time: 1930s.

When a Black man is accused of raping a white woman, attorney Atticus Finch takes the case in an effort to assure justice. Told with clarity from the point of view of the lawyer's young daughter Scout, the insightful account is filled with local color, dialogue, attitudes, and customs of the time. Winner of the Pulitzer Prize for fiction (1961), the Brotherhood Award of the National Conference of Christians and Jews (1961), and several other major awards.

662.  Litwak, Leo. **Waiting for the News**. Doubleday, 1969. Wayne State University Press, 1990. (0-8143-2274-3) Text ed. $39.95. (0-8143-2275-1) Text ed. Pb $19.95. « Time: 1939.

As the news brings word of Hitler's marches across Europe, Jake determines to oppose tyranny in Detroit in the guise of union-busting thugs. The combination of humor and suspense, likable characters, and strong sense of time and place makes this a worthwhile novel.

663.  McIntyre, John Thomas. **Ferment**. Farrar, 1937. Repr. AMS Press, n.d. (0-404-58448-9) $33.75. « Time: 1930s.

Steve and Tom Brown are half brothers. Flashy and opportunistic, Steve is an undercover worker for a strike-breaker. Dependable, plodding Tom is the treasurer of his cabbies' union. Through their story, McIntyre allows a variety of characters to speak from many points of view about strike-breaking and labor racketeering in Philadelphia, and the difficulty of the workingman's struggle against political forces and industrial might.

664.  Meriwether, Louise. **Daddy Was a Numbers Runner**. Prentice-Hall, 1970. Feminist Press, 1986. (0-935312-57-9) Pb $10.95. « Time: 1930s.

The way African Americans communicated with one another in Harlem of the 1930s; their customs, traditions, and attitudes; and the role of Black women are well portrayed in Meriwether's first novel. The story centers around Francie and her family. Her father is a numbers runner; one brother believes that the way to justice is through violence; and another brother drops out of school because prejudice makes it impossible to compete with white students. The role of a young Adam Clayton Powell in Harlem politics is part of the story.

665.  Moore, Ruth. **Spoonhandle**. Morrow, 1946. Blackberry: Salted in the Shell, 1986. (0-942396-49-9) Pb $9.95. « Time: Mid-1930s.

Moore generates a genuine Down East flavor in her novel about the Stilwells, who live in a small fishing village in Maine. Willie and Hod fish for a living and enjoy their independent life, while the greedy Agnes and Pete will do almost anything for money. The story centers around a conflict created when Pete plans to swindle his neighbors out of their property for the benefit of wealthy "summer people," who have a great deal of political power in the decaying community.

666.  Myrdal, Jan. **Another World**. Translated by Alan Bernstein. Ravenswood; distributed by Independent Publishers Group, 1994. (1-884468-00-4) $19.95. « Time: 1930s.

In an autobiographical novel, Myrdal tells of life in New York in the 1930s. His parents were sociologists who wrote about class and race relations, so Myrdal's youth was unusually involved with issues of social justice. This look at the lives of an unusual family will appeal to mature readers interested in political and cultural change.

667.   Olsen, Tillie. **Yonnondio**. Delacorte, 1974. Several editions available. « Time: Early 1930s.

The Holbrook family tries to make a living at mining in Wyoming, as tenant farmers in North Dakota, and in a slaughterhouse in Chicago. Anna and Jim do their best to shield their young brood from hunger and the insults that society heaps upon those unable to defend themselves.

668.   Peck, Robert Newton. **A Part of the Sky**. Knopf, 1994. (0-679-43277-9) $18.00. « Time: 1930s.

This autobiographical sequel to *A Day No Pigs Would Die* sees Rob as the head of the household at age 13, following the death of his father. The drought destroys the farm crops in spite of the family's hard work, and the Depression means that there are no jobs to help them meet the mortgage. A strong Shaker message comes through in a story that has appeal for all ages but is suitable for younger secondary students.

669.   Potok, Chaim. **Davita's Harp**. Knopf, 1985. (0-394-54290-8) $16.95. Fawcett, 1986. (0-449-20775-7) Pb $5.95. « Time: 1930s.

Ilana Davita Chandal's parents are preoccupied with the radical communist movement and have abandoned their Jewish heritage. Throughout her parents' involvement with labor union activists during the Depression and the Spanish Civil War, Davita visits the local synagogue and her aunt's Christian mission seeking a meaning for her own life. She attends the yeshiva and earns highest honors, only to be rejected because she is a girl. Through Davita's story, Potok offers a fine picture of the upheaval of the time and a young girl's search for purpose.

670.   Robinet, Harriette Gillen. **Mississippi Chariot**. Macmillan, 1994. (0-689-31960-6) Text ed. $14.95. « Time: 1930s.

Twelve-year-old Shortning Bread Jackson, whose wrongly accused father is serving on a chain gang, is determined to set him free and help the family escape from the Mississippi Delta. His tricks and disguises and some fortuitous circumstances occasionally lighten a drama that presents a vivid description of the life of a sharecropper, where life is a constant struggle against poverty and racism.

671.   Sinclair, Upton. **Dragon's Teeth**. Viking, 1942. Repr. Buccaneer Books, 1992. (0-89966-956-5) $18.95. « Time: 1930-1934.

In this lengthy Pulitzer prize winner, Sinclair shows the rapid slide of Germany into Nazism. Lanny Budd, a wealthy American, travels with his millionaire wife across Europe. He becomes acquainted with Hitler, Goering, and other Nazis, and recognizes what lies ahead for Europe. He is unable to convince other people of the danger, but he must try to get his Jewish brother-in-law out of Germany.

672.   Steinbeck, John. **Cannery Row**. Viking, 1945. Several editions available. « Time: 1930s.

In this episodic work, Steinbeck uses a rambling style to tell of the adventures of socially outcast workers in a California cannery. They are people of low taste and bad habits, but their intentions are good. A strong sense of time and place is provided in this work for mature readers.

673.   Steinbeck, John. **The Grapes of Wrath**. Viking, 1939. Several editions available. « Time: 1930s.

Steinbeck's description of the Dust Bowl of the mid-1930s is told through the experiences of Tom Joad and his family, who leave their desolate Oklahoma farm to work in California. However, they find themselves confined to a migrant camp with no work to be found, and efforts at organization defeated by force. The experience of the homeless is symbolized in this realistic novel.

674.   Steinbeck, John. **In Dubious Battle**. Viking, 1936, 1979. (0-14-004888-X) Pb $6.00. 1992. (0-14-018641-7) Pb $9.95. « Time: 1930s.

Raised with the brutalizing effects of poverty, Jim Nolan becomes a member of the Communist Party. As a migrant fruit worker in California, he works to organize other workers to strike for higher wages and better living conditions. The police and strikebreakers hired by the landowners do everything in their power to break the strike, including the use of all legal machinations and intimidation, violence, and murder.

675.   Steinbeck, John. **Of Mice and Men**. Viking, 1937. Several editions available. « Time: 1930s.

The memorable story of two California migrant workers—slow-witted, good-hearted Lennie and his friend George—is played out in three days. Lennie's great strength, which he cannot control, has driven them from one job to another, always in search of a piece of land of their own where they may raise rabbits. Tragedy is inevitable when the lonely young wife of a vicious ex-prizefighter turns her attention to Lennie. The story is evocative of the conditions of bums and vagabonds who can claim no rights.

676.   Strunk, Frank C. **Jordon's Showdown**. Walker, 1993. (0-8027-3222-4) $19.95. « Time: Mid-1930s.

Strunk provides a strong sense of time and place in his account of a Kentucky coal town in the 1930s. The town is controlled by the mine owners, but President Roosevelt has voiced support for the unions. Berkley Jordon, a World War I veteran, wants to stay out of the fracas and quietly supervise the gambling operation at Della's roadhouse, but a sniper's bullet that kills Berkley's best friend draws him into the fight. Sequel to *Jordon's Wager*.

677.   Taylor, Mildred D. **Roll of Thunder, Hear My Cry**. Dial, 1976. Several editions available. « Time: 1930s.

Like their neighbors, the Logans are struggling for economic survival during the Depression. It is rare for African Americans to own land in Mississippi in the 1930s, and the fact that the Logan family possesses a small farm makes them a target for racist attacks. Taylor's moving account of a loving and dignified family reveals rural Mississippi society at that time. Suitable for younger secondary students.

678.   Vance, James. **Kings in Disguise**. Kitchen Sink Press, 1990. (0-87816-106-6) $25.00. (0-87816-107-4) Pb $14.95. « Time: 1930s.

Freddie Bloch, 13, must cross the country in search of his father. He allies himself with a hobo known as the King of Spain. Together the two ride the rails, trying to get along and to protect themselves from other homeless wanderers, local police, and frightened townspeople. They see some kindness and much violence in this fully illustrated graphic novel.

679.   Van Raven, Pieter. **A Time of Troubles**. Macmillan, 1990. (0-684-19212-8) $13.95. « Time: 1930s.

Following his release from prison where he served a term for arson, Harlow Purdy convinces his 14-year-old son Roy to leave his job on Chesapeake Bay and go with him to California, where jobs are plentiful and they can make a new start. Their money exhausted, they ride the rails or travel with other families headed the same way. During their travels Roy sees that his father is still not trustworthy. When they reach California and face the realities of migrant labor work, they are divided; Harlow becomes a strike-breaker for the owners, and Roy works to help the laborers. This action-filled novel presents an excellent picture of the Depression and the hopelessness felt by homeless, jobless people. Suitable for younger secondary students.

680.   Vogel, Joseph. **Man's Courage**. Knopf, 1938. Syracuse University Press, 1989. (0-8156-0233-2) Text ed. Pb $14.95. « Time: 1930s.

A Polish immigrant family is denied its dream of owning a farm of its own. Instead, they depend on Adam's work as a day laborer, until the Depression denies even that support. The red tape of the relief system and the ineffectiveness of "simple good intentions" in a complex world are clearly presented in this story filled with irony, humor, and passion.

681.   Walker, Alice. **Color Purple**. Harcourt Brace, 1982. Several editions available. « Time: 1930s.

Incest victim Celie, instructed by her father to "tell nobody but God," begins a series of letters to God that document her struggle. Later, her letters are to her missionary sister, and these provide perspective on the struggles of poor Black women in both Georgia and Africa. The authentic voice of Walker's critically acclaimed novel is powerful and poignant.

682.   Warren, Robert Penn. **All the King's Men**. Harcourt, 1946. Several editions available. « Time: Late 1920s–early 1930s.

The story of Willie Stark, a Southern political demagogue modeled on Louisiana politician Huey Long, is narrated by a young intellectual journalist. Fine characterizations and powerful action characterize this Pulitzer prize winner, which deals with the destructive powers of ambition, greed, and cynicism.

683.   Welty, Eudora. **Losing Battles**. Random House, 1970. Several editions available. « Time: 1930s.

The characters are real—clannish, innocent, and occasionally dull or stupid—and the story includes both humor and tragedy in this account of two days of a Mississippi family reunion. Welty is noted for her evocation of life in the South.

684.   Williams, Jeanne. **The Longest Road**. St. Martin's Press, 1993. (0-312-08838-8) $21.95. 1994. (0-312-95239-2) Pb $4.99. « Time: 1930s.

After the death of their mother, Laurie Field and her brother are left with a grandfather who is so disinterested in their welfare that they leave and travel the rails all over the Southwest in search of their father. Here they find others who are also seeking a home and a place to belong. They share what they have, learn to live with hunger and fear, spend time in shantytowns, and live as outlaws. Williams's story is filled with accurate period detail.

685.  Wolfe, Thomas. **You Can't Go Home Again**. Harper, 1940. Several editions available. « Time: Early 1930s.

This sequel to *The Web and the Rock* continues the somewhat autobiographical adventures of George Weber from the late 1920s through the middle 1930s. His travels to his old home town in North Carolina, to New York to see former friends, to Germany during the early Nazi years, and to England, leave him disillusioned by the corruption and lack of morality everywhere.

686.  Wright, Richard. **Native Son**. Harper, 1940. Several editions available. « Time: 1930s.

Raised in Mississippi, Bigger Thomas, a young African American, seeks a better life in Chicago, only to become involved in violent criminal activity and murder. Bigger's cowardice and criminal acts are undeniable, but Wright's objective and brutally realistic account of the ways in which social injustice and racism pervade human relationships makes Bigger's actions plausible, if not acceptable.

687.  Wright, Sarah E. **This Child's Gonna Live**. Delacorte, 1969. Feminist Press, 1986. (0-935312-67-6) Pb $9.95. « Time: 1930s.

The lives of the residents of a Black ghetto in Maryland are revealed through this story of Mariah Upshur, who is determined that her hard work and faith will rescue her children from their environment of despair, disease, and deprivation. The author's representations of Black speech, culture, and religion at the time add greatly to the value of this work.

688.  Yount, John. **Hardcastle**. Southern Methodist University Press, 1980, 1992. (0-87074-341-4) Pb $10.95. St. Martin's Press, 1984. (0-312-36207-2) Pb $6.95. « Time: 1930s.

Award-winning author Yount has written another acclaimed novel that brings alive the experiences of coal miners in fictionalized Switch County, Kentucky. In colloquial prose, Yount tells of the miner's hopes, beliefs, and economic distress through the story of Music, a young man hired by the mine owners as a guard. However, he finds himself sympathizing with union organizers.

# Chapter 7

---

# World War II, 1939-1945

---

For the reader's convenience, entries in this chapter are divided into the following sections:

- ◆ Inclusive Titles
- ◆ At Home
- ◆ Military Personnel Stateside
- ◆ European Theater
- ◆ Pacific Theater

---

## *INCLUSIVE TITLES*

689.   Appel, Allen. **Till the End of Time**. Doubleday, 1990. (0-385-24944-6) $19.95. « Time: Early 1940s.

Using a time-travel device, Appel's character, historian Alex Balfour, travels back to World War II in the Pacific. Here he is involved in the attack on Pearl Harbor, meets John F. Kennedy in a PT boat, sees a POW camp where prisoners are used in medical experiments, and participates in the development of the Atomic Bomb. Other characters he meets along the way include Albert Einstein, Franklin D. Roosevelt, Orson Welles, and Betty Grable. This mix of science fiction and historical fiction will please many readers.

690.   Piercy, Marge. **Gone to Soldiers**. Summit, 1987. Fawcett, 1988. (0-449-21557-1) Pb $5.95. « Time: 1941-1945.

In an episodic overview, Piercy introduces many characters who are involved in various facets of the war, both at home and around the globe. On the home front, the reader finds rationing, race riots, and broken families; on the battlefield, one finds loneliness, grief, bloodshed, and friendship. The role of resistance fighters is also revealed. Although there are a dozen or so characters, most readers of this lengthy novel will be interested in the characters' efforts to win the war and find some measure of happiness.

691.   Rylant, Cynthia. **I Had Seen Castles**. Harcourt Brace, 1993. (0-15-238003-5) $10.95. « Time: 1942.

John Dante is 18 in 1942. His father, a professor, moves the family so he can work on the atomic bomb, and his mother begins a factory job. John is caught up in the war fever and yearns to enlist, until his new girl friend, a pacifist, urges him to stay out of it. They eventually part, but her memory is alive throughout his wartime experience. The battle scenes are strong, and the work provides a good sense of the time, but the complexity of the issues addressed make this a work for mature readers.

692.   Wouk, Herman. **War and Remembrance**. Little, Brown, 1978. (0-316-95501-9) $19.95. 1992. (0-316-95515-9) Pb $6.99. « Time: 1941-1945.

The fictitious Henry family sees the war from around the globe. Captain Henry continues to be in contact with President Roosevelt and other historic personalities, and rises in rank through the war. His sons see action, and his Jewish daughter-in-law and grandchild are caught up in the Nazi juggernaut. This epic account will hold the reader while providing a great understanding of the times. Sequel to *The Winds of War*.

693.   Wouk, Herman. **The Winds of War**. Little, Brown, 1971. (0-316-95500-0) $24.95. 1992. (0-316-95516-7) Pb $6.99. « Time: 1939.

Early in 1939, USN Commander Victor Henry is assigned to Berlin as naval attaché. Over the next two years he works with Roosevelt and meets Hitler, Goering, Stalin, and Churchill. Following the bombing of Pearl Harbor, he sees his sons go to war and contemplates the effect of industrialized armed forces. Followed by *War and Remembrance*.

# *AT HOME*

694.   Childress, Mark. **V for Victor**. Knopf, 1988. (0-394-56871-0) $18.95. « Time: 1942.

Victor lives with his grandmother near the Gulf of Mexico in Alabama. He is bored with his humdrum life until a nighttime disturbance leads to his discovery of a Nazi submarine in the Gulf. Soon he is caught up in a network of spies and double agents, with more excitement than he had bargained for.

695.   French, Albert. **Holly**. Viking, 1995. (0-670-85746-7) $21.95. « Time: 1945.

Holly is engaged to Billy, who is serving in the South Pacific, but she finds it impossible to be faithful. After Holly's brother returns home with a head wound and Billy is killed, Holly suffers deep psychological wounds. In telling Holly's story, French provides a revealing picture of life in a small North Carolina town during the war, including sacrifices on the home front and the racial bigotry accepted by the white population as the norm. Mature readers will enjoy this well-written novel that develops slowly to a powerful finish.

696.   Goldreich, Gloria. **That Year of Our War**. Little, Brown, 1994. (0-316-31943-0) $22.95. Wheeler, 1994. (1-56895-081-0) Large type ed. Pb $20.95. « Time: 1944.

Sharon Grossberg's father is a physician with the army in Europe. Following the death of her mother, Sharon lives with relatives. She and her extended family try to live normal lives while they follow the war news and worry about her father. Letters from her father, who is involved with liberating the concentration camps, confirm their worst fears, and when the Red Cross begins to make available lists of names of survivors, Sharon takes her grandparents to look for names of relatives.

697.    Greene, Bette. **Summer of My German Soldier**. Dial, 1973. Several editions available. « Time: ca. 1944.

Plain and little noticed by her parents, lonely Patty Bergen remembers the kindness of a German prisoner of war that she meets at her father's store. When he escapes, she does all in her power to shelter him, which scandalizes the community and horrifies her Jewish parents. Suitable for younger secondary students.

698.    Knowles, John. **A Separate Peace**. Macmillan, 1959. Several editions available. « Time: 1942-1943.

At age 16, Phineas and Gene, who are close friends at their exclusive school, are still too young for the war, but they are old enough to feel its impact. Gene, the narrator, tends to be bookish and envies his personable friend, whose confidence and vigorous free spirit make him seem capable of handling any situation with poise. Gene's jealousy results in an act of betrayal and tragedy for Finny.

699.    Leffland, Ella. **Rumors of Peace**. HarperCollins, 1979, 1985. (0-06-091301-0) Pb $13.00. « Time: 1941-1945.

The opinionated tomboy Suse Hansen is 11 when the war begins. In this quiet novel set in California, Suse experiences the panic of the early war years, the violent news of the war, and a growing understanding that the war is real and that catastrophe can strike her well-ordered life. She begins to feel hatred for the neighboring Japanese Americans. Excellent characterizations, accurate detail, and a strong sense of the time are found in this outstanding novel in which Suse grows from youthful ignorance to social consciousness and mature honesty.

700.    Levitin, Sonia. **Annie's Promise**. Macmillan, 1993. (0-689-31752-2) $14.95. « Time: 1945.

Thirteen-year-old Annie is having a difficult time with her Jewish immigrant parents, who are overprotective. Annie's normal conflicts with her older sisters, her parents' struggle as refugees, and the changes in friends returning from the war are all believably rendered. After Annie's parents finally allow her to attend a Quaker summer camp, she is shocked when they reveal racist attitudes toward a Black friend she makes there. Suitable for younger secondary students. Sequel to *Silver Days*.

701.    Ogilvie, Elisabeth. **Ebbing Tide**. Crowell, 1947. Repr. Amereon, 1976. (0-88411-185-7) Lib Bdg $22.95. Down East, 1985. (0-89272-218-5) Pb $9.95. « Time: 1941-1945.

After Joanna Bennett's husband Nils is sent to the Pacific, she continues to work at their lobster business in Maine with the help of family and friends. When Nils returns wounded, they must deal with many changes in their lives. Sequel to *Storm Tide*.

702.    Ogilvie, Elisabeth. **Storm Tide**. Crowell, 1945. Repr. Amereon, 1976. (0-88411-184-9) Lib Bdg $23.95. Down East, 1985. (0-89272-217-7) Pb $9.95.« Time: ca. 1940-1941.

The impending war and the submarine menace threaten Joanna Bennett's plans to return to her island home and work with her husband and her brothers to restore its lobster business to its former prosperity. Ogilvie succeeds in presenting a vivid picture of life on the coast of Maine in the 1940s. Sequel to *High Tide at Noon*; followed by *The Ebbing Tide*.

703. Poynter, Margaret. **A Time Too Swift**. Macmillan, 1990. (0-689-31146-X) $14.95. « Time: 1941-1945.

Marjorie's adolescent years coincide with the years of the war. As she grows to maturity, she sees the impact of the war all around her: the father of a friend is killed at Pearl Harbor, a Japanese family is interned, a woman becomes an alcoholic after her husband is reported missing, a 4F friend is accused of cowardice, and Marjorie's brother is wounded. The reader will gain a good sense of life in California during the war years. Suitable for younger secondary students.

704. Ross, Alice. **Whistle Punk**. Texas Christian University Press, 1994. (0-87565-123-2) Pb $9.95. « Time: 1944.

German POWs are working in the lumber camps of East Texas. Twelve-year-old Mac, angry and grieving for his brother, a pilot shot down over Germany, is determined to get his revenge on one of the prisoners, who looks enough like his brother to be his twin.

705. Sanders, Dori. **Her Own Place**. Algonquin, 1993. Several editions available. « Time: 1942-1950.

Mae Lee, child of Black tenant farmers, marries in her teens and works at a munitions plant as she awaits her husband's return from World War II. Afterward, he is restless and finally leaves after their fifth child is born. Calling upon inner resilience, she raises her family alone, builds a successful farm in South Carolina, and becomes an established member of her small rural community.

706. Saroyan, William. **The Human Comedy**. Harcourt, 1943. Dell, 1966. (0-440-33933-2) Pb $4.99. Harcourt Brace, 1989. (0-15-142301-6) $15.95. « Time: 1941-1942.

Homer is a 14-year-old messenger for the local telegraph office. An older brother is off to war, and Homer helps his widowed mother care for four-year-old Ulysses. In a gentle story set in California, Saroyan tells the story of all the normal happenings to family and friends.

707. Swarthout, Glendon. **The Eagle and the Iron Cross**. New American Library, 1966. Ulverscroft, 1981. (0-7089-0570-6) Large type ed. $12.00. « Time: ca. 1944.

Two young prisoners, whose role in the war was as tuba players in the Afrika Korps band, flee the brutality of a POW camp in Arizona to live with a small tribe of Apache Indians. Although the Indians make the young men welcome, they are themselves persecuted by local men who profit by returning escapees to camp after beating them unmercifully. Swarthout's tragic work provides strong characterizations and a good sense of place.

708.   Taylor, Mildred D. **The Road to Memphis**. Dial, 1990. (0-8037-0340-6) $14.95. Puffin 1992. (0-14-036077-8) Pb $3.99. « Time: 1941.

The racist social and legal system of the United States in the 1940s is clearly shown in this work about 17-year-old Cassie and her brother Stacy. This continuation of the saga of the Logan family is set in Mississippi. Sequel to *Roll of Thunder, Hear My Cry*.

709.   Villars, Elizabeth. **Wars of the Heart**. Doubleday, 1987. (0-385-19569-9) $16.95. « Time: 1941-1945.

While the men went to war, the women left at home had to do the best they could. Villars tells the story of three women who grow to maturity: a rich woman who becomes a radio reporter, a homemaker who becomes an advertising executive, and a young movie star.

## *MILITARY PERSONNEL STATESIDE*

710.   Cozzens, James Gould. **Guard of Honor**. Harcourt, 1948, 1964. (0-15-637609-1) Pb $8.95. « Time: 1943.

The differences between the civilian-in-uniform and the career soldier are evident in Cozzens's lengthy novel, which concerns three eventful days at an air base in Florida. A near accident leads to a serious racial confrontation; a group of paratroopers die; and the big brass from Washington make a visit.

711.   Dailey, Janet. **Silver Wings, Santiago Blue**. Poseidon, 1984. Pocket Books, 1989. (0-671-70280-7) Pb $5.95. « Time: 1941-1945.

The role of the Women Airforce Service Pilots (WASPs) on the home front is portrayed in this readable work. Four young women of dissimilar backgrounds combine their sense of duty and love of flying to undertake many crucial noncombat missions.

712.   Griffin, W. E. B. **Call to Arms**. Jove, 1987. (0-515-09349-1) Pb $5.99. « Time: 1941.

Shortly before Pearl Harbor, Marine Ken McCoy is assigned to spy on a Lieutenant Colonel who may have communist leanings. This exciting story, filled with details of military procedures, is a sequel to *Semper Fi* (volume 2 of The Corps series).

713.   Jones, James. **Whistle**. Delacorte, 1978. Dell, 1991. (0-440-39262-4) Pb $5.99. « Time: 1943.

The four veterans who are the focus of this novel have had experiences similar to those of the characters in *From Here to Eternity* and *The Thin Red Line*; this volume concludes Jones's trilogy. All four are returned from the Pacific Theater, wounded and war-weary, to a hospital in Tennessee and must now deal with their physical and psychological problems, exhaustion, and the changes that the war has wrought upon their families.

# EUROPEAN THEATER

714. Arnold, Elliott. **The Commandos**. Duell, 1942. Dorchester, n.d. (0-8439-2009-2) Pb $2.75. « Time: 1941.

In a grimly realistic novel, Arnold tells the story of a commando group that attacks Nazi fortifications along the Norwegian coast with the assistance of a beautiful leader of the Norwegian underground. Accurate detail and exciting storytelling make this action-filled story a winner.

715. Borden, G. F. **Seven Six One**. Burning Gate, 1992. (1-878179-03-9) $22.95. « Time: 1944-1945.

America's first all-Black tank regiment is advancing from France across Germany. Their fear of the Germans is balanced by their certainty that the rest of their own army has little use for them. The perseverance of the characters, the realism of their experiences, and the power of Borden's taut story make this a title that will appeal to mature readers.

716. Brown, Harry. **A Walk in the Sun**. Knopf, 1944. Several editions available. « Time: 1943.

An American platoon lands on a beach in Italy and must travel through enemy territory to an inland farmhouse to complete their mission. One after another, they lose their leaders, until a corporal must take the responsibility for their success or failure. Each member of the platoon is individually drawn in this simply told story filled with accurate detail. Although not pleasant reading, it is gripping and real.

717. Deighton, Len. **Goodbye Mickey Mouse**. Knopf, 1982. Ballantine, 1983. (0-345-31146-9) Pb $5.95. « Time: 1944.

Captain Jamie Farebrother, Lieutenant Mickey Morse (a.k.a. Mickey Mouse), and other aviators are a part of a bomber-escort mission over Germany. They are stationed in England and have friends there, but the well-researched story centers on scenes of their missions over enemy territory.

718. Denny, Robert. **Night Run: A Novel in Honor of the Famed Night Witches of World War II**. D. I. Fine, 1992. (1-55611-336-6) $21.00. « Time: ca. 1943.

The "night witches" were young Russian women who flew old biplanes at night to drop bombs over Nazi positions. Denny's story concerns American pilot Mike Gavin, who is able to bring his damaged plane down in Soviet territory and join the Red Air Force while waiting to return to his own unit. He becomes acquainted with the night witches and sees the role of women in the Soviet military. Exciting battle scenes and accurate detail characterize this informative work.

719. Eastlake, William. **Castle Keep**. Simon and Schuster, 1965. Carroll & Graf, 1989. (0-88184-499-3) Pb $4.95. « Time: 1944.

The war, and life itself, are bewildering to the assortment of nobility, American soldiers, and villagers in the Ardennes who are determined to defend an ancient, art-filled castle against the coming German onslaught. The characters are well developed, and the final battle scene is riveting.

720. Forester, C. S. **The Good Shepherd**. Little, Brown, 1955. Naval Institute Press, 1989. (0-87021-230-3) $32.95. « Time: 1942.

With only four destroyers, Captain Krause of the *Keeling* must protect a convoy of 37 merchant ships against German submarines in the Atlantic. Forester provides accurate technical detail, a strong sense of the character of the men who did the impossible, and vivid descriptions of action at sea.

721. Goodman, Mitchell. **The End of It**. Horizon, 1961. Second Chance, 1984. (0-933256-10-8) Pb $22.00. (0-933256-50-7). Pb $5.95. « Time: ca. 1943.

Young Lieutenant Freeman expects the war to provide a meaningful sense of participation and sacrifice. His involvement in the destruction of a vital German position results in the slaughter of many Italians who had been forced to go there as workmen. He is recognized by others as a hero but experiences severe psychological problems.

722. Heller, Joseph. **Catch-22**. Simon & Schuster, 1961. Dell, 1985. (0-440-11120-X) Pb $5.95. 1989. (0-440-20439-9) Pb $6.99. « Time: 1945.

Using grotesque comedy, Heller attacks the hypocrisy of the bureaucracy, military psychiatrists and physicians, and commanding officers. Notable among the hypocrites is Colonel Cathcart who, regardless of an increasing death toll, keeps raising the number of missions that his exhausted men must fly so that he can receive recognition.

723. Hersey, John. **A Bell for Adano**. Knopf, 1944. Several editions available. « Time: 1944.

The realities of Americans who must occupy areas formerly at war with the United States are presented with humor and insight in Hersey's account of the experiences of Major Joppolo. The major wishes to replace a beloved church bell that was melted down for bullets by the fascists, and thus gain the affection and respect of the Sicilian people. He has some success but finds himself up against the orders of an American general who is as dictatorial as any in the Axis armies.

724. Higgins, Jack. **Luciano's Luck**. Stein & Day, 1981. Dell, 1982. (0-440-14321-7) Pb $4.95. Pocket Books, 1992. (0-671-67618-0) Pb $5.50. « Time: 1943.

Higgins provides a good sense of time and place in this adventure-filled novel. The story concerns the efforts of General Eisenhower to enlist the Sicilian Mafia to support the Allied invasion of Italy. Convicted mobster Lucky Luciano is released from prison to make the contact. While the fictionalized Luciano is presented as a good guy, the story is informative and will find an appreciative audience.

725. Lay, Beirne and Sy Bartlett. **Twelve O'Clock High!** Harper, 1948. Repr. Ayer, 1979. (0-405-12187-3) Lib Bdg $23.00. « Time: 1942.

Brigadier General Frank Savage has the responsibility of shaping a demoralized group of aviators into a fighting unit that can make a significant strike early in the war. When they are ready, he must fight politicians and his superior officers when it is discovered that the Nazis know of their plan. Authentic detail and exciting action characterize this novel.

726.   Mazer, Harry. **The Last Mission**. Doubleday, 1979. Dell, 1981. (0-440-94797-9) Pb $3.99. « Time: 1942-1945.

Jack Rabb is only 15 when he lies about his age and joins the Air Force as a tail gunner. On his 25th mission, his plane is shot down; he is the only survivor and is sent to a POW camp. This fast-moving work, based on the author's experiences, provides a vivid picture of Jack's military experiences and his fears as a Jewish American prisoner. Suitable for younger secondary students.

727.   Merrick, Gordon. **The Strumpet Wind**. Morrow, 1947. Repr. Buccaneer Books, 1992. (0-89966-892-5) Lib Bdg $18.95. « Time: 1945.

Roger Chandler, an Intelligence officer who speaks French, is sent to France to work with an ex-Vichyite to send misinformation to the Germans. Unable to separate the evils of the Vichy regime from his friendship for the family of the man he was sent to contact, Chandler finds himself in a tragic position.

728.   Phillippi, Wendell C. **Dear Ike**. Two-Star Press, 1991. (0-9630859-0-5) $15.75. (0-9630859-1-3) Pb $10.50. « Time: 1939-1945.

The author served in the infantry in Europe during World War II, holds the rank of Major General (ret.), and has made a thorough study of the war. His work is not a novel but a collection of fictional letters between Eisenhower and other leaders important in the war (e.g., Marshall, MacArthur, Montgomery, Patton, Roosevelt, Churchill) that provide information about the personal and professional relationships among them and the strategies that won the war.

729.   Shaw, Irwin. **The Young Lions**. Random House, 1948. Dell, 1984. (0-440-39794-4) Pb $4.95. « Time: 1938-1945.

Three soldiers—one Austrian Nazi, one Jewish American, and one American playwright—make their individual ways through the war. Strong characterizations keep the reader interested in their separate stories until their final confrontation in the last days of the war. This engrossing book is lengthy, but it moves quickly and will find a wide audience.

730.   Shepard, Jim. **Paper Doll**. Knopf, 1986. Several editions available. « Time: 1942.

In England, early in the war, an inexperienced flight crew trains in preparation for bombing ball bearings factories in Germany. Friendships and rivalries develop, and the days leading up to their goal are both tedious and tense. The climactic bombing mission makes for riveting reading for mature students.

731.   Shreve, Anita. **Resistance**. Little, Brown, 1995. (0-316-78999-2) $21.95. « Time: 1943.

When his plane goes down in Belgium, fighter pilot Ted Brice is taken to the home of a Resistance fighter, Claire Daussois, who hides him in the attic. Over time, they fall in love, but they are turned in to the Gestapo by Claire's jealous husband. Excellent character development and descriptions of life under Nazi occupation distinguish this work, which is suitable for mature readers.

732.   Tregaskis, Richard. **Stronger Than Fear**. Random House, 1945. Amereon, n.d. (0-88411-878-9) $16.95. « Time: 1944.

Captain Paul Kreider, U.S. Army, has already been decorated for action in battle. Now, war-weary, he commands a company that is ordered to take a German-held city.

The story takes place in one day, with vividly realistic scenes of street fighting. The author was a reporter who moved with front-line troops.

733.   Wharton, William. **A Midnight Clear**. Knopf, 1982. Ballantine, 1983. (0-345-31291-0) Pb $4.99. « Time: 1944.

Will Knott is one of a group of near-geniuses drafted for a special project. Through a mix-up they find themselves in battle, and most are killed. The survivors are sent to a chateau in the Ardennes to maintain an observation post. Through long hours of boredom they talk, play cards, and build snowmen. Eventually the enemy makes contact, and a bloody battle ensues.

## PACIFIC THEATER

734.   Beach, Edward. **Dust on the Sea**. Holt, 1972. Zebra, 1989. (0-8217-2580-7) Pb $3.95. « Time: 1945.

The USS *Eel*'s Captain Richardson and his crew are assigned to destroy Japanese shipping in the Pacific. The enemy is gaining in proficiency in antisubmarine attacks; the commander of a sister sub is timid; and the captain of the pack's leading submarine is showing signs of war fatigue. The author is a former submarine commander; he provides an abundance of realistic detail in his account of the adventures of the *Eel* and her crew.

735.   Beach, Edward. **Run Silent, Run Deep**. Holt, 1955. Several editions available. « Time: ca. 1942.

Submarine life in wartime is filled with infighting among the men, tedious combat readiness drills, and the critical demand for a highly skilled team once battle is engaged. Beach, a World War II submarine captain, presents a novel filled with the details of running the ship and the demands of battle upon men, officers, and machines as seen through the eyes of a new officer.

736.   Clavell, James. **King Rat**. Little, Brown, 1962. Several editions available. « Time: 1945.

The horrors of life in a POW camp are vividly portrayed in this novel set in Singapore near the end of the war. As the Japanese become preoccupied with the advancing Allies, the camp comes increasingly under the control of the inmates. Notable among them are the "King," an American whose streetwise survival techniques are not always appreciated by others, and a British officer whose gentlemanly beliefs put him in conflict with the King. Other strong, and sometimes disturbed, characters are portrayed in a novel that is suitable for mature readers.

737.   Endo, Shusaku. **The Sea and Poison**. New Directions, 1992. (0-8112-1198-3) Pb $10.95. « Time: ca. 1942-1944.

The morality of actions under the pressure of wartime is the theme of this bleak and disturbing account of events in a POW camp where Japanese physicians perform a ghastly vivisection on an American prisoner. The action centers on a naïve young Japanese medical intern who finds himself pulled into the crime by his cynical superior. The novel reveals the tedious routine of daily life in a military hospital and the terror and moral decline of people at war. Suitable for mature readers.

738.  Ferry, Charles. **Raspberry One**. Houghton Mifflin, 1983. (0-395-34069-1) $13.45. « Time: 1941-1945.

Nick makes quite a transition from his routine life in Rhode Island to being stationed on a carrier in the Pacific, and his experiences help him grow in confidence and maturity. In this action-filled story, the reader comes to know and care about the aviators and seamen who face kamikaze attacks in the last months of the war.

739.  Fleming, Thomas J. **Time and Tide**. Simon & Schuster, 1987. Bantam, 1989. (0-553-27456-2) Pb $4.95. « Time: 1942.

Life aboard the fictional cruiser USS *Jefferson City* is detailed in Fleming's action-filled novel set in the South Pacific. The *Jefferson City* is involved in the Battle of Savo Island and emerges with a cowardly reputation, which the officers and crew struggle to erase through their valor in battles from Guadalcanal to Okinawa. Despite their efforts, the ship seems jinxed. Throughout this authentic account, the reader follows the personal and private lives of a number of diverse characters.

740.  Gobbell, John J. **The Last Lieutenant**. St. Martin's Press, 1995. (0-312-13108-9) $23.95. « Time: 1942.

On Corregidor, survivors of the Japanese invasion of the Philippines are holding out in spite of the lack of food and medical supplies. When the intelligence officer begins to suspect that the Navy cryptographer is a Nazi spy, he and his friend must combine their survival efforts with the added burden of keeping vital information secret. In this fast-paced thriller, Gobbell acknowledges the contribution of the Filipinos in resisting the Japanese.

741.  Green, Gerald. **East and West**. D. I. Fine, 1986. (0-917657-56-X) $18.95. « Time: 1940-1945.

Kenji Tamba is sent by the Japanese government to study in the United States. He meets and marries Julie Varnum. During their honeymoon the Japanese attack Pearl Harbor, and the Tambas are caught between the two nations. First they are sent to the internment camp at Manzanar; later they return to Japan. Kenji's brother Masao is filled with the fighting spirit, while his younger sister Yuriko resists the traditional Japanese role for women. The events from the beginning to the end of the war are seen through these characters, providing a satisfactory overview of Japanese attitudes and behavior during the war.

742.  Griffin, W. E. B. **Battleground**. Putnam, 1991. (0-399-13550-2) $19.95. Jove, 1991. (0-515-10640-2) Pb $5.99. « Time: 1942.

Rather than place his story in the middle of the action, Griffin chooses characters that provide readers with a different view as the battles move from Midway to Guadalcanal. A captain travels to many headquarters, reporting to the Secretary of the Navy; a specialist in Japanese works on an intelligence assignment; and a new captain forms a fighter squadron. Volume 4 of The Corps series.

743.  Griffin, W. E. B. **Counterattack**. Putnam, 1989. Jove, 1990. (0-515-10417-5) Pb $5.99. « Time: 1941-1942.

Griffin is noted for his books filled with accurate military detail. In *Counterattack* the reader sees the military changing from peacetime to wartime, the adjustments made by enlisted men who suddenly become officers, and the development of a new parachute battalion. Action begins with Pearl Harbor and extends through the Battle of Guadalcanal about a year later. Volume 3 of The Corps series.

744.   Heggen, Thomas. **Mister Roberts**. Houghton, 1946. Amereon, n.d. (0-88411-696-4) $18.95. Repr. Naval Institute Press, 1992. (1-55750-723-6) $32.95. « Time: ca. 1942-1943.

The USS *Reluctant* is a Navy cargo ship that goes back and forth among the Pacific islands, supplying the provisions for other ships on their way to battle. The men are bored beyond endurance and share a great loathing for their captain. They do, however, respect Lt. Roberts, the *Reluctant*'s peacemaker, who wants desperately to join a fighting ship. Memorable characters include Ensign Pulver, Quartermaster Dolan, and the ship's physician. The characterization and vocabulary are reminiscent of the time and place.

745.   Homewood, Harry. **O God of Battles**. Morrow, 1983. Bantam, 1984. (0-553-24363-2) Pb $3.95. « Time: 1941-1945.

Andy O'Connor is a fighter pilot who rises in rank and responsibility through his actions in battles in the Pacific. His brother Mike is a submariner who also is recognized for his leadership abilities. This exciting novel is filled with battle action; it also deals with Mike's problems with an exceptionally difficult captain, and with Andy's emotional, marital, and religious problems when he finds that he is infertile.

746.   Homewood, Harry. **Silent Sea**. McGraw-Hill, 1981. Bantam, 1989. (0-553-27985-8) Pb $4.50. « Time: 1943.

Captain Mike Brannon leads the men of the submarine *Eelfish* in battles that destroy a small Japanese convoy and seriously damage Japanese warships. The high command, however, reprimands him for wasting torpedoes. The *Eelfish* finds itself in the midst of a conflict concerning the proper use of submarines, including General MacArthur's plan to develop a submarine ferry service.

747.   Jones, James. **From Here to Eternity**. Scribner, 1951. Dell, 1991. (0-440-32770-9) Pb $5.99. « Time: 1941.

Private Prewitt is an excellent bugler, but his pride forces him to join the infantry. He soon finds himself alienated from the sergeant, who demands strict obedience to army regulations. However, Prewitt came from the Kentucky coal fields and is handy with his fists; he refuses to allow himself to be "broken." Jones thoroughly and vividly records the dark side of barracks and stockade life among the enlisted men in Hawaii in 1941, before the attack on Pearl Harbor. Using a realistic soldiers' vocabulary and a variety of characters, including a general with fascist leanings and an inmate of the stockade who argues that Evolution is God, this lengthy novel is an interesting read for mature students.

748.   Jones, James. **The Thin Red Line**. Scribner, 1962. Macmillan, 1985. (0-02-559780-9) $20.00. Dell, 1991. (0-440-38876-7) $5.99. « Time: 1942.

The role of the Army's Company C in the last few weeks of the amphibious campaign on Guadalcanal, in which the author was a participant, is the setting for this many-leveled story. Two major assaults over endless hills involve a large cast of characters that is so well drawn that the reader is able to follow them individually. Each man shows normal qualities of good and bad in responding to events. Thus, there are no heroes, but lots of realistic action and vocabulary.

749.   Keith, Agnes Newton. **Beloved Exiles**. Little, Brown, 1972. Ulverscroft, 1979. (0-7089-0385-1) Large type ed. $15.95. « Time: 1936-1950.

Events in British North Borneo before, during, and after the war are revealed in Keith's novel. For years, American-born Sara Evans and her husband, the British District Officer, live happily in Borneo, and Sara learns which local customs she can and cannot accept with equanimity. When she violates the custom of sending fatherless children to the orphanage by adopting the child of her husband and his Sino-Japanese mistress, she creates quite a social stir. Action centers primarily on the years that Sara spends in a Japanese prison camp. Keith's portrayal of the relations between Asians and Europeans and the breakup of the British empire are balanced; her account of Sara's experiences as a war prisoner is based on her own.

750.   Kelly, Jack. **The Unexpected Peace**. Gambit, 1969. Dorchester, 1983. (0-8439-2003-3) Pb $2.50. « Time: 1945.

Following the last few weeks of fierce fighting in the Philippines, action moves to occupied Japan, where neither the conquered nor the occupiers really know what is expected of them. Kelly, who was a part of the occupation forces, speaks with authority about the behavior exhibited on both sides—venality, honor, and struggles for political and economic power. This novel presents an authentic picture of Tokyo at that time. Suitable for mature readers.

751.   Killens, John Oliver. **And Then We Heard the Thunder**. Knopf, 1963. Howard University Press, 1984. (0-88258-115-5) Pb $9.95. « Time: 1941-1945.

Although Black men were expected to serve and die as soldiers, they were also expected to remain willingly in segregated units and to accept the same—or worse—racist treatment that they received as civilians. In this powerful novel, Soloman Saunders, an idealistic, educated, and ambitious African American, believes that he can use his considerable ability to rise to a position of leadership. Instead, he finds flagrant discrimination. The book's characters are well drawn, and the battle scenes are vivid. The author served in the amphibian forces during the war and realistically describes the life of an African-American soldier. This sequel to *Youngblood* is suitable for mature readers.

752.   Mailer, Norman. **The Naked and the Dead**. Rinehart, 1948. Holt, 1980. (0-8050-0521-8) Pb $14.95. 1990. (0-8050-1273-7) $30.00. « Time: 1944.

Through the actions of several well-drawn characters, the reader feels the fear and confusion of the troops aboard ship as they watch the bombardment of the island that is their target. The story follows them onto the beach and up the hills as they try to eliminate the desperate Japanese. Cold-blooded killing, souvenir hunting among corpses, and the torment of jungle warfare are all part of this realistic novel. Characters are as varied as a military genius with fascist leanings, a disillusioned liberal who recognizes his own desire for power, a petty gangster, and a cocky enlisted man who realizes that his nerve is gone. This powerful work is generally considered one of the most important books about the war. Mailer saw action as a rifleman in Leyte and Japan.

753.   Matthiessen, Peter. **Raditzer**. Viking, 1961. Random House, 1987. (0-394-75343-7) Pb $5.95. « Time: 1944.

Raditzer is aboard a troop ship headed for the Pacific. He is a self-pitying malingerer who takes advantage of the pity the others feel toward him because of his impoverished background. Raditzer's duties are mostly assumed by Charlie Stark, whose privileged life makes him particularly vulnerable to Raditzer's manipulations. This short novel, primarily about the relationship between two men, addresses the question of good and evil.

754.  Salisbury, Graham. **Under the Blood-Red Sun**. Delacorte, 1994. (0-385-32099-X) $15.95. « Time: 1941.

The experiences of Japanese Americans who were living in Hawaii when Pearl Harbor was bombed are masterfully handled in this episodic work. Tomikazu Nakaji's family has always enjoyed Grandfather's stories of family tradition and culture, but now, even though they are loyal citizens, this heritage makes them suspect. Like all adult Japanese American males, Tomi's father is imprisoned. His mother loses her job, and the lives of the children are dramatically altered. Salisbury's account is well balanced, showing empathy and eschewing easy answers. This work is suitable for younger secondary readers.

755.  Taylor, Theodore. **The Bomb**. Harcourt, 1995. (0-15-200867-5) $16.00. « Time: 1944-1945.

After the Bikini Atoll is liberated from Japanese occupation, life for the islanders begins to return to normal. Then the Americans decide that this would be a perfect place to test the experimental atomic bomb, and they propose to move the islanders to a new location. The islanders are told that the move will be temporary, but not all believe this. Abraham, the uncle of 14-year-old Sorry Rinamu, is one of the unbelievers. When Abraham dies, Sorry decides to work with others to resist the Americans. Taylor, who was in Bikini at the time the island was being prepared for the test, presents a balanced picture of the island culture and challenges readers to consider many important issues. Suitable for younger secondary students.

756.  Toland, John. **Gods of War**. Doubleday, 1985. (0-385-18007-1) $17.95. Tor, 1986. (0-8125-8900-9) Pb $4.95. « Time: 1941-1945.

The McGlynns and the Todas are related by marriage. Through these families, the entire saga of the war is seen—political maneuverings at high levels in Tokyo and Washington, military promises, military realities, and the torment of Japanese prison camps—from before Pearl Harbor through the horrors of Nagasaki.

757.  Toland, John. **Occupation**. Doubleday, 1987. (0-385-19819-1) $19.95. Tor, 1988. (0-8125-8902-5) Pb 4.95. « Time: 1945-1950.

In *Gods of War,* Toland introduced the American McGlynns and the Japanese Todas, whose families are linked by marriage, and followed their lives through the war. In the sequel *Occupation*, he shows how the American occupation of Japan affects both families. Cultural differences are explored, as are the understandings of the Japanese about the causes of Pearl Harbor. There is detailed coverage of the Tokyo war crimes trials and of changes in Japan immediately following the war.

758.  Uris, Leon. **Battle Cry**. Putnam, 1953. Bantam, 1982. (0-553-25983-0) Pb $6.99. « Time: 1941-1945.

Uris's pride in the Marines Corps, of which he was a part, is evident in this fine work that vividly portrays Marine training and their effectiveness in battle. The story concerns the radio squad of a battalion of the Sixth Regiment, led by a hard-headed commander who pushes his men to do whatever is necessary to gain the victory. Mac, the narrator, acquaints readers with a wide assortment of civilians-turned-marines in this lengthy, engrossing work set in Guadalcanal, Saipan, Tarawa, and New Zealand.

759. Wouk, Herman. **The Caine Mutiny**. Doubleday, 1951. Several editions available. « Time: 1944.

Ensign Willie Keith, a casual, fun-loving Princeton graduate in the Naval Reserve, is aboard the *Caine* as it patrols the Pacific. The *Caine*, dating from World War I, has been patched together for further service, but it is run in a slovenly fashion that increases the men's discomfort. The ship runs many boring routine missions and sees fierce action, but the primary problem of the crew is that the captain is a petty tyrant who proves himself incompetent during crises. Eventually, during a typhoon that has sunk other ships, the men push the second-in-command to assume control—mutiny in wartime. Outstanding descriptions of life at sea and the typhoon strengthen this exciting work.

# Chapter 8

# The Late Twentieth Century, 1945-1995

For the convenience of readers, entries in this chapter are divided into the following categories:

♦ 1945-1962 (Including the Korean War)

♦ 1963-1995 (Including the Vietnam War)

## *1945-1962 (INCLUDING THE KOREAN WAR)*

760.   Abbey, Edward. **Fire on the Mountain**. Dial, 1962. Avon, 1992. (0-480-71460-4) Pb $10.00. « Time: 1950s.

John Vogelin owns the Bar V Ranch, a large tract of semidesert land in New Mexico. He and his grandson, 12-year-old Billy, love the land and resist the efforts of the government to acquire it to use as a missile range. The story is told through Billy's eyes.

761.   Anania, Michael. **Red Menace**. Thunders Mouth, 1984. (0-938410-19-9) $13.95. Moyer Bell, 1993. (1-55921-088-5) Pb $7.95. « Time: 1950s.

While the nation showed its power with the atomic bomb, and Senator McCarthy was frightening Americans about the Communist threat, the author grew up in an ethnically mixed housing project in Nebraska. This episodic, fictionalized autobiography shows the nation coming to grips with its own international role and falling in love with extravagant cars and fashions. Flashes of humor and wit highlight this picture of where we were in the 1950s.

762.   Bissell, Richard Pike. **High Water**. Little, Brown, 1954. Minnesota Historical Society, 1987. (0-87351-221-9) Pb $8.95. « Time: 1940s.

From the viewpoint of the second mate, this is the story of a Mississippi towboat that is trying to take eight barges of coal upriver, from St. Louis to St. Paul, during a late winter flood. The years the author spent aboard such a vessel means that the dialogue, action, setting, and relationships between the members of the crew are authentic in this exciting, occasionally humorous adventure.

763.   Bissell, Richard Pike. **A Stretch on the River**. Little, Brown, 1950. Minnesota Historical Society, 1987. (0-87351-220-0) Pb $8.95. « Time: 1940s.

The author, an experienced river man, uses a first-person narrative to tell the story of a young man who, against the wishes of his family, chooses to become a deckhand on the *Inland Coal*, an Upper Mississippi freighter. Although the work is hard, he finds himself infected with an incurable love for steamboating, and feels sorry for those tied to the land. Authentic settings, language, and situations fill this story suitable for mature readers.

764.   Brooks, Gwendolyn. **Maude Martha**. Harper, 1953. Third World, 1992. (0-88378-061-5) Pb $9.95. « Time: ca. 1950.

Pulitzer prize-winner Brooks tells the episodic story of a young Black girl growing up in Chicago. She faces the usual problems of adolescence, wonders about death, and deals with the realities of living in a racist society. The grace and beauty of the writing raise this simply told story above the norm.

765.   Choi, Sook Nyul. **Gathering of Pearls**. Houghton Mifflin, 1994. (0-395-67437-9) $13.95. « Time: 1954.

This semiautobiographical novel concerns the adjustment of Sookan Bak when she travels from her Korean home to a women's college in New York. Her letters home emphasize the cultural differences she has found. This work, suitable for younger secondary students, would provide background for multicultural study.

766.   Cobb, William. **A Walk Through Fire**. Morrow, 1992. (0-688-11366-4) $22.00. Avon, 1993. (0-380-71832-4) Pb $5.50. « Time: 1961.

Hammond, Alabama, is the setting for this novel that shows the impact of efforts to eliminate segregation in the South. O. B. Brewster, a white businessman, and Eldon Long, an African-American minister, have been friends since childhood. In this time of racial tension, Eldon pushes O. B. to run for mayor, believing that he is the only person who can keep the peace. O. B. is reluctant, preferring to stay neutral and deal with his personal problems. However, when white students from the North arrive to help register Black voters, the Ku Klux Klan reacts, and O. B. must become involved.

767.   Cormier, Robert. **Tunes for Bears to Dance To**. Delacorte, 1992. (0-385-30818-3) $15.00. « Time: Early 1950s.

Shortly after the war, the return of service people makes jobs and housing scarce in Massachusetts, which compounds the problems of 11-year-old Henry, who works for a grocer to he p his mother support the family. Henry becomes friends with Mr. Levine, a Holocaust survivor, who is carving out of wood a replica of his home village, which was destroyed by the Nazis. The bigoted grocer puts pressure on Henry to destroy the handiwork of the "crazy" Jew. This moving account of the struggle between good and evil is suitable for younger secondary students.

768.   Davis, Thulani. **Nineteen Fifty Nine: A Novel**. Grove, 1992. (0-8021-123-7) $18.95. HarperCollins, 1994. (0-06-097529-6) Pb $10.00. « Time: 1959.

The growing integration movement in a small Virginia town is seen through the eyes of Willie Tarrant, a 12-year-old Black girl who is chosen to be one of the students to attend a white school. Nonviolent civil rights activities and violent confrontations are both a part of Willie's world, along with learning the actions and attitudes necessary to survive. Reading the diary of her great-aunt gives Willie insight into the world of Black women of the 1800s.

769.   Ellison, Ralph. **Invisible Man**. Random House, 1952. Several editions available. « Time: 1940s–early 1950s.
The unnamed narrator tells the story of his development from a trusting Black youth living in the South through his disastrous college experience. After wide social and political experiences in Harlem, he realizes that the powerful, both white and Black, want to use him to their own ends. This complex, symbol-filled work is considered to recapitulate African-American history from slavery through the migration to a Northern urban setting.

770.   Estleman, Loren D. **Edsel: A Novel of Detroit**. Mysterious Press, 1995. Several editions available. « Time: 1950s.
Connie Minor, a noted journalist in Detroit during the 1920s, falls on hard times during the Depression. But when Henry Ford wants someone whom he can trust to secretly manage the ad campaign for the Edsel, he remembers Minor. All begins well, but soon Minor finds himself caught between the labor union and management when he uncovers a murder as well as a scheme to undermine the Edsel. This entertaining story presents an authentic picture of the auto industry and life during the 1950s.

771.   Fast, Howard. **The Establishment**. Houghton Mifflin, 1979. Dell, 1987. (0-440-13988-0) Pb $4.50. « Time: ca. 1948.
In this sequel to *The Immigrants* and *Second Generation*, Fast chronicles the further adventures of the Levette family of San Francisco. Action centers around Barbara, a successful author, who is subpoenaed to testify before the Congressional Committee on Un-American Activities (and ends up in jail), and her husband Bernie, who is delivering weapons to the newly formed nation of Israel, fighting for its life against the Palestinians. Fast provides a good sense of life in postwar America. Followed by *The Immigrant's Daughter*.

772.   Filene, Peter. **Home and Away**. Zoland Books, 1992. (0-944072-22-4) $19.95. « Time: 1951.
High school junior Murray Baum investigates the history of his German immigrant parents as part of a report for school. In the process, Murray learns about the complexity of life in prewar Germany, the realities of the communist scare and American politics in the 1950s, and the impact of political events on ordinary families.

773.   Hazelgrove, William Elliott. **Tobacco Sticks**. Pantonne Press, 1995. (0-9630052-8-6) $18.95. (0-9630052-7-8) Pb $10.95. « Time: 1945.
The Virginia hometown of 12-year-old Lee is struggling with the aftermath of World War II, including the economic and social impact of many soldiers returning home, racial tensions, and conflicts between labor and management. When an innocent young Black woman is accused of a crime and Lee's attorney father decides to defend her, the family's standing in the community is threatened. Underlying all the action is the loving relationship between 12-year-old Lee and his father, which helps Lee weather the storms of adolescence. The many changes in American social attitudes that were developing at the end of the war are well presented in this revealing novel.

774. Hinojosa, Rolando. **The Useless Servants**. Arte Publico Press, 1993. (1-55885-068-6) text ed. $17.95. « Time: Early 1950s.

In a straightforward war diary, Texas Mexican Rafe Buenostro tells of his experiences in the Korean War. All the issues faced by a soldier in that war are related, including racism, loyalty, intense discomfort, fear, boredom, disorientation, and horror.

775. Hobbs, Valerie. **How Far Would You Have Gotten If I Hadn't Called You Back?** Orchard/Richard Jackson, 1995. (0-531-09480-4) $19.95. (0-531-08780-8) Lib Ed $19.99. « Time: Late 1950s.

Following her father's botched suicide attempt, Bron's family moves to California. There she becomes involved with a group that enjoys drag racing, drinking, and dating. She is soon torn between her feelings for JC and the fast life, and Will, who is headed for West Point. She must also decide whether she will develop her own musical gifts, which are extraordinary. This realistic, well-written work provides a strong sense of the times and the agonies of growing up.

776. Hobson, Laura Z. **Gentleman's Agreement**. Simon & Schuster, 1947. Repr. Cherokee, 1979. (0-87797-210-9) $18.95. « Time: 1946.

A journalist for a liberal newspaper in New York City is assigned to write a piece on anti-Semitism. Because this is a frequently discussed topic just following World War II, he wishes to find a new angle. He decides to pose as Jewish to see what will happen. The bigotry that he faces in social and professional situations and in seeking housing reveal a reality that was completely unknown to him.

777. Honig, Donald. **The Plot to Kill Jackie Robinson**. NAL-Dutton, 1992. (0-525-93530-4) $18.00. « Time: 1947.

The atmosphere and period detail are excellent in this exciting mystery written by a well-published baseball historian. Action centers on Joe Tinker, a New York sportswriter who investigates a murder, only to discover it is more complex than anyone thought and has hidden racial overtones. The casually accepted bigotry of the time is clearly presented.

778. Hooker, Richard. **MASH**. Morrow, 1968. Repr. Amereon, n.d. (0-88411-198-9) Lib Bdg $18.95. « Time: Early 1950s.

The serious and frightening moments in a mobile army surgical hospital serving on the front lines of the Korean War are leavened by antic high jinks. *MASH* characters are introduced in this novel that spawned a movie and a television series.

779. Irwin, Hadley. **Kim/Kimi**. Macmillan, 1987. (0-689-50428-4) $14.95. Puffin, 1988. (0-14-032593-X) Pb $3.99. « Time: 1950s.

Kim Andrews's mother is Irish American, and her deceased father was Japanese American. Although her family is loving and supportive, Kim has reached her teens and needs to understand what she calls her "Japaneseness." She travels to Sacramento, where she meets the grandparents who rejected her father after his marriage to a Caucasian, and she learns about the Japanese-American experience in detention camps during World War II. This well-written novel reveals a great deal about racial attitudes and growing up.

780.   Jen, Gish. **Typical American**. Houghton Mifflin, 1991. NAL-Dutton, 1992. (0-452-26774-9) Pb $10.00. « Time: Late 1940s.

Ralph Chang, his sister Theresa, and their friend Helen are three young Chinese who must remain in the United States when the communists take over their homeland. They decide to work hard and adapt to their new land while retaining their own values. Resilience, humor, and growing maturity help them deal with their own confusion, ambition, naïveté, and culture shock, as well as the prejudice faced by all immigrants.

781.   Jones, Madison. **Cry of Absence**. Crown, 1971. Louisiana State University Press, 1989. (0-8071-1579-7) Pb $9.95. « Time: Late 1950s

Wealthy Hester Glenn thinks she has raised her sons, Cam and Ames, to ideals of goodness. When the move for integration comes to her Tennessee town, Hester opposes it, believing that peace will return if the agitators will only go away. The involvement of Cam in the murder of a Black civil rights worker, however, forces Hester to face the consequences. This gripping novel presents all points of view of the tension-filled early years of the civil rights movement.

782.   Just, Ward S. **Jack Gance**. Houghton Mifflin, 1989. Ivy Books, 1990. (0-8041-0571-5) Pb $4.95. « Time: 1941-mid 1960s.

Political life in Chicago and Washington, D.C., are well presented in this novel of a man who is involved in Chicago politics and rises to become a U.S. Senator. Through the experiences of Jack Gance, an honorable man, Just presents a realistic picture of American politics and the difficulty of weighing conflicting loyalties to meet the demands of public and private life.

783.   Kay, Terry. **The Year the Lights Came On**. Houghton Mifflin, 1976. University of Georgia Press, 1989. (0-8203-1127-8) $25.00 (0-8203-1128-6) Pb $10.95. « Time: 1947.

Two rival gangs live on either side of Highway 17 in a rural community in north Georgia. One group, led by Dupree Hixon, represents the Haves—their homes have electricity and indoor plumbing. Collin Wynn leads the Have-nots, who live on the poor side of town. When the Rural Electric Administration brings electricity to all the area homes, the core of the rivalry, and the camaraderie that it generated, dissolves. This sentimental autobiographical account of life in Georgia in the late 1940s is filled with accurate period detail.

784.   Kesey, Ken. **Sometimes a Great Notion: A Novel**. Viking, 1964, 1977. (0-14-004529-5) Pb $12.00. « Time: Late 1950s.

Korean War veteran Hank Stamper is now the head of a family that has a long history of logging in the Oregon timber country. Faced with a strike among his workers, problems with the river and the weather, and a deadline on a critical contract, Hank asks his brother to return from Yale to help. This lengthy story of the conflict between the two men features rich characterizations and realistic dialogue; it provides a fine picture of the lumbering business and the struggle to succeed against the odds. The complexity of the story and the writing style suggest that *Sometimes a Great Notion* is for mature readers.

785.  Krisher, Trudy. **Spite Fences**. Delacorte, 1994. (0-385-32088-4) $14.95. «
Time: Late 1950s.

Life in a small Georgia town in the 1950s is restricted by cultural and racial
limitations. When 13-year-old Maggie, who is physically and psychologically abused
by her mother, becomes friends with a Black man who gives her a camera and
encourages her photographic skills, the town is scandalized—especially when Maggie's
photos reveal the racial violence around them. The racial cruelty, and Maggie's
mistreatment at home and by the community, make this a difficult, sobering book,
suitable for mature readers.

786.  Laurents, Arthur. **The Way We Were**. Harper, 1972. Repr. Amereon, n.d.
(0-88411-446-5) Lib Bdg $19.95. « Time: 1940s-1950s.

Katie Morosky abandons her role in the Communist Party when she marries
Hubbell Gardiner during World War II. During the McCarthy era, however, Hubbell's
job is endangered because of Katie's background. Laurents presents a clear picture
of the days of the Hollywood blacklist and its impact on those caught in the hysteria.

787.  MacInnes, Helen. **I and My True Love**. Harcourt, 1953. Several editions
available. « Time: 1950s.

In Europe during World War II, Sylvia falls in love with Czechoslovakian Jan
Brovic. Following the war, she marries a man who becomes a powerful official in the
U.S. government. When Brovic comes to Washington as a representative from the
communist Czech government during the height of the Cold War, he inevitably meets
Sylvia and her husband in the course of their diplomatic duties. Along with an
accurate picture of the social life in the city, MacInnes's novel provides a strong sense
of the tension in Washington in the late 1940s and early 1950s, and the dangers to
national security of even the most innocent comment.

788.  Michener, James A. **Bridges at Toko-Ri**. Random House, 1953. (0-394-
41780-1) $16.95. 1984. (1-449-20651-3) Pb $5.95. Fawcett, 1988. (0-679-41649-8)
Pb $5.95. « Time: 1950-1953.

Harry Brubaker was a lawyer in civilian life. Now he is a pilot stationed on a
carrier during the Korean War. In Michener's concise, action-filled novel, the reader
joins Brubaker as he makes daily bombing or strafing runs in a seemingly pointless
war. Other memorable characters include Beer Barrel, the landing officer whose
miracles bring planes down safely, and Mike Forney, a helicopter rescue pilot who
must try to reach downed aviators before they die in the icy waters. If they are already
dead, he must rescue their bodies.

789.  Nason, Tema. **Ethel: The Fictional Autobiography**. Delacorte, 1990. Dell,
1991. (0-440-21110-7) Pb $4.99. « Time: Early 1950s.

Ethel Rosenberg was convicted of giving atomic secrets to the U.S.S.R. and
executed in 1953. In this well-researched fictional autobiography written in the form
of a prison journal, Nason reveals Rosenberg's life story: her early hopes, her move
into radical political activity, and the difficulty of her decision to remain true to her
ideals, knowing that if she did so, she would not be able to raise her young sons.

790.  Oughton, Jerrie. **Music from a Place Called Half Moon**. Houghton Mifflin, 1995. (0-395-70737-4) $13.95. « Time: 1956.

When 13-year-old Edie Jo's father insists that the Baptist Vacation Bible School should be open to all the town residents, including the Native Americans who live on shacks at the edge of town, their North Carolina community goes up in arms. Edie Jo is as angry at her father as her mother is for putting the family in the center of such an uproar. Then she comes to know her classmate, Cherokee Fish, whose music seems somehow related to Edie's poetry. This balanced work reveals the ugliness and violence created by prejudice and anger.

791.  Roth-Hano, Renee. **Safe Harbors**. Four Winds, 1993. (0-02-777795-2) $15.95. « Time: 1951.

In this fictional autobiography, Roth-Hano, a Jew, tells the powerful story of her life in New York City, where at age 19 she came to serve as a governess after being hidden by Catholic nuns during World War II. Placed with a Jewish family, Renee grapples with her many conflicting feelings: her amazement at religious freedom in the United States, her own conflicting religious ideas, her guilt over her father's death, her resistance to the efforts of her mother and her employer to control her life, and her desire to return to France to Fernand, her first love. Roth-Hano presents a vivid picture of life in New York shortly after the war. Sequel to *Touch Wood*.

792.  Shange, Ntozake. **Betsy Brown**. St. Martin's Press, 1985. (0-312-07727-0) $12.95. 1986. (0-312-07728-9) Pb $8.95. « Time: 1957.

When school desegregation comes to St. Louis, Betsy Brown, who has been sheltered by her prosperous, middle-class Black family, encounters prejudice face-to-face for the first time. Her normal adolescent fancies and problems, her physician father's pride, her mother's fears, and her grandmother's strength are all brought to life in this well-written novel.

793.  Shaw, Irwin. **The Troubled Air**. Random House, 1951. Dell, 1987. (0-440-18608-0) Pb $4.95. « Time: 1950s.

The impact of the Communist scare of the 1950s on one group of people is the theme of *The Troubled Air*. Clement Archer, director of a radio program, is instructed to fire five people on unsubstantiated charges of Communist activity. Archer believes unquestioningly in the innocence of his friends, and his efforts to help them result in tragedy.

794.  Siddons, Anne Rivers. **Heartbreak Hotel**. Simon & Schuster, 1976. Ballantine, 1984. (0-345-31953-2) Pb $5.99. HarperCollins, 1993. (0-06-104278-1) Pb $5.99. « Time: 1956.

In a compelling story, Maggie Deloach, a Southern girl who expected to succeed in society as her parents had, is completely changed by experiences during her senior year in college. Her socially acceptable racism is challenged by anti-integration riots and a confrontation with a Black escaped convict. Siddons presents a fine picture of Southern college life at the time.

795.  Silko, Leslie Marmon. **Ceremony**. Viking, 1977. Viking, 1986. (0-14-008683-8) Pb $9.00. « Time: Late 1940s.

The recognition and acceptance that Native Americans received as a part of the nation's military establishment during World War II vanished with the end of the war.

Tayo returns home to the Navajo reservation in New Mexico after being hospitalized for battle fatigue. A half-breed, he finds acceptance nowhere until an old medicine man helps him find meaning in ancient ceremonies. This intricate story reveals the bitterness of relations between the white community and Native Americans, and divisions within the Native American community itself.

796.  Sinclair, Jo. **The Changelings**. McGraw, 1955. Feminist Press, 1985. (0-935312-40-4) Pb $8.95. « Time: Early 1950s.

On a lovely street in an Ohio city, the primarily Jewish residents are horrified to realize that Black families are moving into the neighborhood. Some racial disturbances occur, but understanding and acceptance come through the efforts of teenagers, including Judith Vincent and Jules Golden, who use humor to pave the way. This upbeat story of respect for other people is filled with homely details of Jewish life.

797.  Slaughter, Frank G. **Sword and Scalpel**. Doubleday, 1957. Ulverscroft, 1979. (0-7089-0386-X) Large type ed. $12.95. « Time: 1950-1953.

Captain Paul Scott, an army physician, is captured by the Chinese during the Korean War. He is eventually released but then is court-martialed, accused of collaboration.

798.  Styron, William. **The Long March**. Random House, 1968. (0-394-43387-4) $10.95. « Time: ca. 1950.

Lt. Tom Culver is a reservist called back to duty because of the Korean conflict. He is one of a group of civilian soldiers involved in a forced 36-mile night march near their base in the South. The concise and simply told story shows the contrast between civilian and military life. Other primary characters include the ultra-military Battalion Commander Templeton and Captain Mannix, who forces the men to finish the march because of personal pride.

799.  Unger, Douglas. **Leaving the Land**. Harper & Row, 1984. Ballantine, 1985. (0-345-32112-X) Pb $3.50. « Time: Late 1940s-1950s.

The Hogan family farms in South Dakota. When Marge Hogan's two brothers are killed during World War II, she is forced to help her father raise turkeys for a nearby processing plant. She is ground down by unceasing labor, loneliness, and economic reality. Characters and situations are well developed in Unger's first novel, which has as its theme the destruction of the family farm by the growth of huge corporation-owned farms.

800.  Verdelle, A. J. **The Good Negress**. Algonquin, 1995. (1-56512-085-X) $19.95. « Time: 1950s-1960s.

After Denise Palms, an intelligent Black girl, moves from her home in rural Virginia to Detroit, her teacher encourages her to study on her own when she must care for her mother's newest baby and cannot attend school. Verdelle explores the social and economic limitations caused by "backwoods" ways and manners of speaking, and the role of the Black woman in society. The complexity of this well-written work makes it suitable for mature secondary students.

801. Voigt, Cynthia. **David and Jonathan**. Scholastic, 1992. (0-590-45165-0) $14.95. « Time: 1950s.

In a complex and intense novel, Voigt examines the effect of the Holocaust on its survivors and their families. Henry, a Massachusetts WASP, is close friends with Jonathan Nafiche, from a Jewish family. The friendship of these intelligent boys is severely challenged, however, when Jonathan's cousin David comes to live with the Nafiche family. David was in a Nazi concentration camp and saw all his family die. Now he rejects Henry and Jonathan while demanding their attention, and causes great disruption in Jonathan's family by his need to talk about his experiences and their meaning for the human race.

802. West, Dorothy. **The Wedding**. Doubleday, 1995. (0-385-47143-2) $20.00. « Time: 1950s.

The divisions caused by race, social class, and generational differences are convincingly addressed by West in this moving novel set in a wealthy Black community in Massachusetts. The story features the Cole family, whose high social position is challenged by the forthcoming marriage of their daughter to a white man. Subplots woven through the story provide powerful characterizations and a strong sense of time and place.

# *1963-1995 (INCLUDING THE VIETNAM WAR)*

803. Agee, Jonis. **Strange Angels**. Ticknor & Fields, 1993. (0-395-60835-X) $21.95. « Time: 1980s.

The story of the struggle of the three Bennett siblings to retain control of their ranch in the Nebraska sandhills provides a strong sense of the realities of modern ranching. The two half-brothers and their half-sister (offspring of the deceased Heywood Bennett and three different mothers, one Sioux) each have different dreams for the ranch. They must deal with shadows of the past as well as horse thieves, blizzards, and personal conflict. Suitable for mature secondary students.

804. Amos, James. **The Memorial: A Novel of the Vietnam War**. Crown, 1989. Avon, 1990 (0-380-71195-8) Pb $3.95. « Time: Late 1960s.

Amos's straightforward telling of the experiences of Jake Adams, a marine lieutenant who saw a great deal of action in Vietnam, begins with Adams standing before the Vietnam Memorial pondering his own survival and the loss of so many that he knew. Through flashbacks, the story of brutal action, numbing boredom, and the vital role of camaraderie in life-or-death situations is told.

805. Barry, Lynda. **The Good Times Are Killing Me**. Real Comet Press, 1988. (0-941104-22-2) Pb $16.95. HarperCollins, 1992. (0-06-097424-9) Pb $17.00. « Time: Late 1960s.

Seventh-grader Edna Arkins tells how it is for the children to grow up in a Seattle neighborhood that is gradually moving from all white to a mix of neighbors, including white, African American, and Asian American families. Occasional racist incidents disturb the calm and friendly neighborhood, where Edna's adolescent days are marked by special music.

806.  Bryant, Dorothy. **Ella Price's Journal**. Lippincott, 1972. A.T.A. Books, 1982. (0-913688-08-6) Pb $9.95. « Time: ca. 1970.

Ella Price is an unhappy California housewife who decides to take a creative writing course at the community college. Her assignment, to keep a journal, provides the format for Bryant's account of a woman's painful struggle to move from innocent dependence to self-assurance. Many of the questions of the late 1960s and early 1970s are addressed, including peace marches and women's liberation.

807.  Bunting, Josiah. **The Lionheads**. Braziller, 1972. (0-8076-0632-4) $14.95. « Time: 1968.

This novel, filled with details of military activity, is set in Vietnam just after the Tet Offensive. General Lemming is ambitious and arrogant, interested only in his own rise in rank. This rise depends on showing success on the battlefield without regard for the welfare of his troops. To impress a visiting Secretary of the Navy, he schedules an action without providing proper support. The unnecessary mission succeeds, but at great cost. The author was an officer who served in Vietnam.

808.  Burke, Phyllis. **Atomic Candy**. Atlantic; distributed by Little, Brown, 1989. (0-87113-364-4) Pb $9.95. « Time: ca. 1952-1974.

Kate Albion, husband Joe, and daughter Marilyn play their part in the political scene of blue-collar Boston. Through the experiences of these ordinary people, the reader views the rivalry between Kennedy and Nixon, the hopes of the Kennedy presidency, assassinations, civil rights and women's movements, and antiwar protests. The Watergate era and the downfall of Nixon receive good treatment. The humorous tale is told with a slightly wacky flair that will appeal to some readers; others might prefer a more straightforward telling.

809.  Cook, Thomas H. **Streets of Fire**. Putnam, 1989. Warner, 1991. (0-446-35972-6) Pb $4.95. « Time: 1963.

Dr. Martin Luther King, Jr. is in Birmingham, Alabama in the early 1960s, leading another nonviolent civil rights demonstration. Detective Ben Wellman, who had been assigned to observe the marchers, is reassigned to investigate the murder of a little Black girl. This entertaining murder mystery presents a vivid view of the bigotry and racial tension of the South in the 1960s.

810.  Coonts, Stephen. **Flight of the Intruder**. Naval Institute Press, 1986. (0-87021-200-1) $16.95. Pocket Books, 1990. (0-671-70960-7) Pb $5.95. « Time: 1972.

Navy pilot Jake Grafton flies an Intruder attack plane on bombing raids over North Vietnam late in the war. The raids are often technical nightmares that are exceedingly dangerous and of little strategic importance. In frustration, Jake decides to take out a worthwhile target on his own. Exciting action scenes, accurately portrayed by a former Navy flyer, reveal the realities and complexities of life for a pilot in wartime.

811.  Covington, Dennis. **Lasso the Moon**. Delacorte, 1995. (0-385-32101-5) $15.95. « Time: 1980s.

April and her recovering-alcoholic physician father have moved to a new home on Saint Simons Island, Georgia, to start life afresh, but it is not easy. When she and her father attempt to shelter Fernando, an illegal alien from El Salvador, her eyes are opened to the realities of life in a nation where torture and death are common. She gains an understanding of how different her definition of a normal life is from his.

812.   Crew, Linda. **Children of the River**. Doubleday, 1989. Several editions available. « Time: 1970s.
Sundara and her aunt's family flee the terrors of the Khmer Rouge in Cambodia and settle in Oregon. Here Sundara faces loneliness for family left behind, the difficulties in choosing between her old and new cultures, and the normal concerns of adolescence. This fine story shows clearly the refugee experience and the discrimination faced by most newcomers.

813.   DeLillo, Don. **Libra**. Viking, 1988. Several editions available. « Time: ca. 1950s-1963.
DeLillo's meticulous research into the life of Lee Harvey Oswald is apparent in this fictionalized biography that investigates the events the led to the assassination of John F. Kennedy. Although speculative as to certain political connections of Oswald, and the involvement of the CIA, basically the story is factual. The portrait of Oswald is fully drawn; other characters, such as Jack Ruby, are presented in a realistic manner.

814.   Del Vecchio, John M. **The Thirteenth Valley**. Bantam, 1982, 1984. (0-553-26020-0) Pb $5.95. « Time: 1970.
The members of A Company, 7th Battalion, 402nd Infantry, have a mission against the last enemy stronghold in northern South Vietnam. Using a documentary style, Del Vecchio (a Vietnam correspondent) provides strong characterizations and detailed, realistic scenes of action and personal interaction. The primary characters include a cynical sergeant who is counting the days to the end of this tour of duty, a Black lieutenant who has serious personal problems, and a naïve, frightened new radio man.

815.   De Mille, Nelson. **Word of Honor**. Warner, 1985. (0-446-30158-2) Pb $6.99. « Time: 1968.
This somewhat complex novel concerns Ben Tyson, whose commission in the Army is reactivated in 1983 so he can be brought up on charges concerning a massacre in a hospital in Vietnam in 1968. Tyson's sense of honor impedes his attorney, and this powerful courtroom drama provides a perceptive account of American civilians in the military in wartime.

816.   Doctorow, E. L. **Book of Daniel**. Random House, 1971. Several editions available. « Time: 1967-1968.
The complexities of life during the Cold War years are seen through the experiences of Daniel Lewin, who was a child when his parents were executed as Soviet spies in the 1950s. Now an adult doctoral student studying the twentieth century, Daniel is trying to discover the truth about his parents and himself. Although Doctorow does not state that this novel is based upon the Rosenberg case, the situation is parallel. Suitable for mature readers.

817.   Ehrlichman, John. **The China Card**. Simon & Schuster, 1986. (0-446-34577-6) Pb $4.50. « Time: Late 1960s.
Ehrlichman, who was an aide to Richard Nixon, uses his considerable knowledge as an insider to provide a fictional account of how the normalization of relations

between the United States and China was brought about. Central to the story are Matt Thompson, a young attorney who grew up in China, and a skilled Chinese diplomat who has known Matt's family for years. Ehrlichman shows how Nixon, Kissinger, and Chou En-lai used the two subordinates to accomplish their political purposes and made sure that the recognition for their considerable accomplishment would fall on the national leaders. This story of political intrigue provides a good sense of the times.

818.   Gaines, Ernest J. **A Gathering of Old Men**. Knopf, 1983. (0-394-51468-8) $22.00. Random House, n.d. (0-394-72591-3) Pb $8.00. « Time: 1980s.

The relations between Blacks and whites in Louisiana in the early 1980s is revealed in Gaines's moving account of 20 elderly Black men who each claims to be responsible for the murder of a racist white Cajun, to protect the guilty man. Each man tells his own version of events, revealing his individuality and his past experiences of humiliation and social degradation. This short but complex work (with 15 first-person narratives) is a powerful picture of human relationships in a racist society.

819.   Garland, Sherry. **Shadow of the Dragon**. Harcourt Brace, 1993. (0-15-273532-1) Pb $3.95. « Time: 1980s.

Teenager Danny Vo and his family have lived in Houston for 10 years, and Danny has adjusted well to American ways, although there is still some conflict with the Vietnamese traditions of his family. When his cousin Sang Le comes to the United States from a Vietnamese refugee camp, Sang becomes involved with a Vietnamese gang and wants Danny to join, too. Further complicating things is Danny's romantic interest in a girl whose brothers are involved in a white supremacist group. Suitable for younger secondary students.

820.   Griffin, W. E. B. **The Aviators**. Putnam, 1988. Jove, 1989. (0-515-10053-6) Pb $5.95. « Time: 1963.

After distinguished service as a helicopter pilot in Vietnam, Captain Oliver is assigned to the Army Aviation Center in Alabama. There he uses his experience to train flyers, investigate crashes, and test equipment. In telling the story of this eventful year in Oliver's career, Griffin presents a detailed and engrossing picture of military life. Book 8 in the Brotherhood of War series.

821.   Griffin, W. E. B. **The New Breed**. Putnam, 1988. Jove, 1988. (0-3515-09226-6) Pb $5.99. « Time: 1964.

Colonel Sandy Felter returns from a secret mission and convinces President Johnson that the Congo may become as dangerous as Vietnam to the United States. He and his friend, Lieutenant Colonel Craig Lowell, gather a top group of warriors to fight the Congolese rebellion and rescue American and Belgian hostages. The characters are well drawn in Book 7 of the Brotherhood of War series, which provides a great amount of information about military tactics, equipment, and training procedures.

822.   Heath, William. **The Children Bob Moses Led**. Milkweed, 1995. (0-57131-008-8) $21.95. « Time: 1964.

In the summer of 1964, Bob Moses, a leader of the Student Nonviolent Coordinating Committee, directed the work of volunteers who came to Mississippi to help disenfranchised Black residents register to vote. Their actions were violently opposed by many local racists, and lives were lost in the South during this time. Heath's realistic novel alternates chapters telling the story from the view of Bob Moses and the fictional Tom Morton, an idealistic white college student. Suitable for mature secondary students.

823. Hillerman, Tony. **Finding Moon**. HarperCollins, 1995. (0-06-017772-1) $24.00. « Time: 1975.

Moon Mathias, the editor of a small Colorado newspaper, goes to Vietnam at the end of the war in an attempt to trace the Vietnamese daughter that his deceased brother left there. The powerful story of his journey reveals the turmoil left by the war and its impact on the Vietnamese and the Americans who were a part of it.

824. Huggett, William Turner. **Body Count**. Putnam, 1973. Dell, 1988. (0-440-20093-8) Pb $4.95. « Time: 1960s.

Chris Hawkins, a new lieutenant, is sent to Vietnam and given command of a Marine platoon in a combat sector. His developing leadership skills, relations with his men, and growing sense of the futility of their sacrifice is well presented in this realistic account, written by a Vietnam veteran.

825. Ignatius, David. **Agents of Innocence**. Norton, 1987. Avon, 1988. (0-380-70593-1) Pb $4.50. « Time: 1960s-1970s.

Tom Rogers is a CIA agent who penetrates a Palestinian unit and recruits an Arab agent. Action centers around CIA activities in Beirut and related events in Jordan. Former CIA agent Ignatius has written a suspenseful novel that is also very informative about the complexities of foreign policy in the Mideast and the loss of American prestige in Arab nations.

826. Jones, Adrienne. **Long Time Passing**. HarperCollins, 1990, 1993. (0-06-447070-9) Pb $3.95. « Time: 1969.

Jones presents a balanced picture of the anguish of the late 1960s in this novel about Jonas Duncan, a student at a university in California. His father is a marine on duty in Vietnam; Jonas loves Auleen Delange, a mixed-race peace activist. Jonas's struggle with his past and his attempts to deal with family and social expectations are well presented, with strong characters and a good sense of time and place.

827. Keras, Phyllis. **The Hate Crime**. Avon, 1995. $3.99. (0-380-78214-6) $3.99. « Time: 1990s.

Since Zach's father is the district attorney, he sees events from the inside when a Boston Jewish temple is defaced by racists, and Zach learns that his girlfriend is the daughter of Holocaust survivors. This novel, based on actual events, is suitable for younger secondary students.

828. Kerr, M. E. **Linger**. HarperCollins, 1993. (0-06-022878-2) $14.89. « Time: 1991.

Bobby never expects to see battle when he joins the military in the relatively quiet days of 1990, and is surprised and angry when he is sent to the Persian Gulf in the war against Iraq. Through Bobby's journal the reader sees the war; through the experiences of his brother Gary, at home in Pennsylvania, Kerr reveals how greed leads to manipulation and corruption. Action centers around the Linger Restaurant, which is the focal point of the town. It is owned by a wealthy man who uses political power and propaganda to enrich himself and destroy his opponents. His beautiful daughter Lynn dominates the teen set but is enamored of an antiwar teacher who plays piano at the Linger. Through this fine novel, Kerr clearly shows small-town politics at work, and offers an antiwar message.

829.   King, Sara. **An Irregular Moon**. Winston-Derek, 1990. (1-55523-346-5) Pb $8.95. « Time: Early 1960s.
Jason and his sister Valerie move with their father Frank to North Carolina after their mother leaves the family. Frank becomes police chief, and the family comes to revolve around Lucy, a Black woman who becomes their housekeeper. A local murder, Ku Klux Klan activities, and early stirrings of the desegregation movement are seen in this coming-of-age story.

830.   Kingman, Lee. **Peter Pan Bag**. Houghton, 1970. Dell, 1972. (0-440-96822-1) Pb $1.25. « Time: Late 1960s.
The hippie scene of Boston is seen through the experiences of Wendy Allardyce, who rebelliously leaves her comfortable home and joins the Big Scene on Beacon Hill. Here she meets a variety of vividly presented individuals, some of whom she finds fascinating while others are infuriating. This authentic, objective presentation reveals the hippie scene—the runaways, drugs, suicides, mental problems, and slovenly living conditions. Suitable for younger secondary students.

831.   Liotta, P. H. **Diamond's Compass**. Algonquin, 1993. (0-945575-74-2) $18.95. Mercury House, 1993. (1-56279-036-6) $20.00. « Time: 1978.
The opposing values and unresolvable conflicts of the United States and Iran are well portrayed in this spellbinding novel. In 1978, just before the revolution in Iran, Air Force cadet Dante Diamond goes to Tehran to visit his father, who serves as a military adviser to the Shah. After the revolution, Dante is there again to witness the violent cultural war that pits fundamentalist Islamic religious and political ideas against Western attitudes.

832.   Mason, Bobbie Ann. **In Country**. Harper & Row, 1985, 1986. (0-06-091350-9) Pb $10.00. « Time: Late 1960s–mid-1980s.
The impact of the culture of the 1960s on life in the 1980s is recounted in the story of Sam Hughes, whose father was killed in Vietnam. Sam lives in rural Kentucky with her uncle, a veteran who has symptoms similar to those of other soldiers who were exposed to Agent Orange. No one in the family will talk to Sam about the war, but she needs to understand why her father's life was lost, why returning veterans were shamefully treated, and why the nation was so divided. A visit to the Vietnam Memorial helps in her quest.

833.   Michener, James A. **Space**. Random House, 1982. Several editions available. « Time: 1970s.
Prodigious research is evident in this account of the space program. Although the characters are fictional (except for a few real-life people such as Werner Von Braun and Dwight Eisenhower), the situations faced by the administrators, engineers, politicians, and astronauts involved in the space program are real.

834.   Moore, Yvette. **Freedom Songs**. Watts, 1991. Several editions available. « Time: 1963.
African-American ninth grader Sheryl and her family visit relatives in rural North Carolina. Sheryl loves the South—until she has her first experience with

segregation. When her uncle announces that he intends to become a Freedom Rider that summer, the family is deeply divided, well aware that this is a dangerous thing to do. This strong story of family relationships provides an excellent view of how the civil rights struggle affected ordinary people.

835.   Mukherjee, Bharati. **Jasmine**. Grove, 1989. (0-8021-1032-0) $17.95. Fawcett, 1990. (0-449-21923-2) Pb $4.95. « Time: 1980s.

Married at 14 and soon widowed by religious fanatics, Jasmine leaves her native India to seek a new home in the United States. She lives for a time in immigrant ghettos in Florida and New York, allowing the reader to view a little-known side to American life. Award-winning author Mukherjee's realistic yet humorous novel is suitable for mature readers.

836.   Myers, Walter Dean. **Fallen Angels**. Scholastic, 1988, 1989. (0-590-40942-5) Pb $13.95. (0-590-40943-3) Pb $3.95. « Time: Late 1960s.

In a first-person narrative, 17-year-old Richard Perry from Harlem tells of his experiences during the Vietnam War. He and his companions are courageous soldiers, fighting tedium and fear as well as the enemy and the system. Although Richie does not use drugs, he sees many who do. Myers's realistic account, both dramatic and touching, reveals political, economic, religious, and social attitudes in the military and on the home front. Recommended for mature readers.

837.   Namioka, Lensey. **April and the Dragon Lady**. Harcourt Brace, 1994. (0-15-276644-8) $10.95. « Time: 1980s.

Grandma Chen holds rigidly to traditional Chinese ideas about the roles of men and women. Consequently, 16-year-old April Chen, who wishes to become a geologist, is severely torn between her desire to be respectful and loving to her family, and her own need for independence. While her spoiled brother is allowed to do as he wishes (so long as he follows tradition), April is expected to care for her ailing grandmother. Subplots concern the relations of the Chen family to the Caucasian world and the normal adolescent struggles faced by April and her brother. This story, set in Seattle, Washington, is suitable for younger secondary students. It is filled with authentic detail, and the characters are well developed.

838.   Nelson, Theresa. **And One for All**. Watts, 1989. Several editions available. « Time: 1966-1968.

The national conflict over the Vietnam War separated families as surely as did the Civil War. Nelson's poignant story concerns Geraldine, whose brother Wing leaves school, joins the Marines, and goes to Vietnam. Sam, a close family friend whose father died in Korea, is an antiwar activist. After the death of Wing in Vietnam, the friends must deal with their grief and their political estrangement.

839.   Okimoto, Jean Davies. **Talent Night**. Scholastic, 1995. (0-590-47809-5) $14.95. « Time: 1990s.

Rodney Suyama, of Japanese-American/Polish-American descent, is a typical teen living in Seattle. Rodney wants to become famous as the first Asian-American rap star. He hopes the money he expects to inherit from his uncle Hideki will further his plans, until he learns that the money comes with a catch—living according to his Japanese heritage. Another complication is his romantic interest in the beautiful Ivy, also biracial. This light and humorous story explores the themes of prejudice and stereotypes. Suitable for younger secondary students.

840.   Piercy, Marge. **Vida**. Summit Books, 1979. Fawcett, 1985. (0-449-20850-8) Pb $4.95. « Time: 1967-1974.

During the 1960s, Vida was a radical antiwar activist. She is now wanted by the FBI for her involvement in a 1970 bombing. Using flashbacks, Piercy reveals Vida's political evolution—the events that caused this strong, attractive, and intelligent woman to become a fugitive, always on the run, dependent on old friends for temporary assistance. Piercy's picture of 1960s radicals is suitable for mature readers.

841.   Proffitt, Nicholas. **Gardens of Stone**. Carroll & Graf, 1983, 1987. (0-88184-312-1) Pb $4.50. « Time: Mid-1960s.

Longtime veteran Sgt. Clell Hazard befriends the new recruit, Pfc. Jackie Willow. Hazard has lost one son to the Vietnam War and is beginning to question his role in the military machine. Willow, raised on romantic novels of battlefield glory, cannot wait to show his bravery. They see duty together in the honor guard at Arlington cemetery before Willow has his chance at active duty in Vietnam. Told with an abundance of humor, this novel nonetheless reveals the horrors of war. Realistic dialogue and action make this novel suited to the mature reader.

842.   Qualey, Marsha. **Come in from the Cold**. Houghton Mifflin, 1994. (0-395-68986-4) $14.95. « Time: 1969.

Jeff's brother died in Vietnam. Maggie's sister died in an antiwar protest. As Jeff and Maggie struggle to find meaning in the social conflict around them, they learn to love and respect each other. Through various characters in this well-written story set in Minnesota, Qualey presents a balanced view of the upheaval of the 1960s.

843.   Sidhwa, Bapsi. **An American Brat**. Milkweed Editions, 1993. (0-915943-73-5) $21.95. « Time: Late 1970s.

Feroze is a college student and a new immigrant to the United States from Pakistan. She is alternately charmed and appalled by the American culture—delighted by the shopping, restaurants, and appliances, and dismayed by the disregard of things of traditional value. As Feroze seeks to find a place for herself in her new homeland, the reader gains insight into the American way of life.

844.   Smith, Steven Phillip. **American Boys**. Putnam, 1975. Avon, 1984. (0-380-67934-5) Pb $4.95. « Time: Late 1960s.

This disturbingly realistic account of foot soldiers in Vietnam involves four men who became buddies before going to the war. Their varied horrific experiences as they walk the tightrope between ennui and death, and their efforts through alcohol, drugs, and brothels to escape for a moment, are portrayed for the mature reader.

845.   Soto, Gary. **Jesse**. Harcourt Brace, 1994. (0-15-240239-X) $14.95. « Time: 1968.

To get away from his abusive stepfather, Jesse, a 17-year-old Mexican American, drops out of school and moves in with his older brother, Abel. The boys do field work and odd jobs, which are all that is available to them. They also take classes, go to church, and become involved in the farm workers' movement. The draft hangs over them, and they face prejudice and poverty daily. Soto's episodic story includes well-developed characters and vivid descriptions in an engrossing account of Mexican Americans in California at the time.

846.   Thomas, D. M. **Flying in to Love**. Scribner, 1992. (0-684-19510-0) $20.00. « Time: 1963.

Fact and fiction are merged in this novel that concerns the assassination of John F. Kennedy. Thomas delves into the thoughts of the major characters, explores the myth that surrounds Kennedy, and raises many questions about the causes and results of this tragedy. The complexity of this novel makes it suitable for mature readers.

847.   Truscott, Lucian K. **Army Blue**. Crown, 1989. Warner, 1990. (0-446-35980-7) Pb $5.95. « Time: 1969.

Lt. Matthew Nelson Blue IV is the son of a colonel and grandson of a general. As the leader of a platoon that sustains losses from friendly fire, he is court-martialed, being accused of cowardice and fleeing from combat. When his father and grandfather come to Vietnam to help in his defense, their eyes are opened concerning the nature of this war. Truscott's suspenseful novel, which includes an extensive trial, is informative about military protocol and the realities of the Vietnamese War.

848.   Van Peebles, Melvin. **Panther**. Thunder's Mouth; distributed by Publishers Group West, 1995. (1-56025-096-8) Pb $10.95. « Time: 1960s.

A Vietnam veteran, Judge Taylor, drops out of college to join the California Black Panther Party. In time, he becomes a double agent, spying for both the Panthers and the government. Through this fast-paced story, Van Peebles capably recounts real events and familiarizes the reader with the movement and many real people.

849.   Wartski, Maureen. **The Face in My Mirror**. Fawcett, 1994. (0-449-70443-2) « Time: 1980s.

Mai Jennifer Houston, adopted when she was small by a middle-class family in Iowa, feels very American until, when she is 15, a group of skinheads make her their target. Her adopted family is very supportive, but Mai feels that she must visit her birth mother's sister in Boston to understand her Vietnamese heritage. There, through volunteer work with immigrants from many lands, and by seeing the inner-city problems faced by her cousins and aunt, Mai comes to understand the challenges faced by all immigrants.

850.   Webb, James H. **Fields of Fire**. Prentice Hall, 1978. Bantam, 1982. (0-553-25679-3) Pb $4.95. « Time: 1968-1969.

Authentic dialogue and action characterize this account of the experiences of a platoon of Marines slogging through the rice paddies and jungles of Vietnam. Through these men, the reader sees why their miserable living conditions and the violence and uncertainty that surrounded them engendered in most of them a great loyalty and love for one another. Based on the author's own experiences.

851.   Webb, James, H. **A Sense of Honor**. Prentice Hall, 1981. Bantam, 1981. (0-533-24104-4) Pb $4.50. « Time: 1968.

Annapolis is the setting for this novel that explores the reasons why some men willingly subject themselves to the rigor of officer's training. The primary characters are Bill Fogarty, a gung-ho midshipman who likes things the way they are; a Marine captain who was wounded in Vietnam and hates his new desk job; and a brilliant plebe who resists the traditional hazing. With the war in Vietnam in the background and antiwar activities and changing social attitudes at home, this examination of military tradition during a time of stress and change is insightful, informative, and entertaining.

852.   White, Ellen Emerson. **The Road Home**. Scholastic, 1995. (0-590-46737-9) $15.95. « Time: Late 1960s.

Becky Phillips, a newly graduated nurse, goes to Vietnam. Here, the horrors of dealing with large numbers of severely wounded people, too much death, and a shattered romance lead Becky to solve her problems with alcohol. When she returns home and finds that society regards her as a warmonger, her problems deepen. This moving work recounts the trials of women who are Vietnam veterans.

853.   Williams, Jana. **Scuttlebutt**. Firebrand Books, 1990. (0-932379-89-3) $18.95. (0-932379-88-5) Pb $8.95. « Time: Early 1970s.

A mixed group of women gets to know each other and the system when they enlist as naval recruits in the 1970s. Their experiences in boot camp raise questions about the role of women, racial conflict, homophobia, and unquestioned obedience to authority.

854.   Wouk, Herman. **Inside, Outside**. Little, Brown, 1985. (0-316-95504-3) $19.95. Avon, 1986. (0-380-70100-6) Pb $5.95. « Time: Early 1970s.

Israel David Goodkind, lawyer and writer, is serving as a consultant to President Nixon during Watergate. As an emissary to Israel, he meets Golda Meir. In the quiet times, he writes a memoir, covering the experiences of his Russian immigrant parents, his own childhood in a devout Jewish home in the Bronx, his education at Columbia, and happenings that draw him into the political activities of the time. This lengthy novel provides a fine picture of twentieth-century social history.

855.   Yamanaka, Lois-Ann. **Wild Meat and the Bully Burgers**. Farrar, 1996. (0-374-29020-2) $20.00. « Time: 1970s.

Lovey Nariyoshi and her family live on the big island of Hawaii. She tells the story of their lives, revealing the damage caused by the social restrictions imposed on Japanese Americans there. Yamanaka tells this touching, sometimes funny, episodic story in "Pidgin"—a mingling of Hawaiian and English. In so doing, she affirms the role of language in the forming of culture.

# Chapter 9

# Epic Novels

In the preceding chapters, the main part of the action of the entries has fallen within the time frame of the chapter where they are found. Entries in the Epic Novels chapter cross two or more of these natural divisions of our history. These works may be multigenerational or cover a theme that crosses time. Titles are arranged alphabetically by author, and are indexed in the same fashion as entries in other chapters.

856.   Aldrich, Bess Streeter. **Spring Came On Forever**. Appleton, 1935. Several editions available. « Time: 1866-1930s.

Two German-American families come to Nebraska by covered wagon in 1866 and settle on adjacent homesteads. This chronicle of two families shows life on the Nebraska prairie from pioneer days to the Depression in 1933. Clear characterizations and a respect for the land are features of this work. Suitable for younger secondary students.

857.   Atherton, Sarah. **Mark's Own**. Bobbs, 1941. Repr. AMS Press, n.d. (0-404-58404-7) $29.50. « Time: 1849-1929.

Through the story of mine laborers, labor organizers, and a mine owner and his descendants, the author reveals how unionization and changes in the price of coal affect life in a Pennsylvania coal mining town. Many details about mining practices and social customs in coal mining towns create additional interest in this enlightening and enjoyable work.

858.   Bell, Thomas. **Out of This Furnace**. Little, 1941. University of Pittsburgh, 1976. (0-8229-5273-4) Pb $14.95. 1991 (50th Anniv. Ed.) (0-8229-3690-9) $29.95. « Time: 1881-1930s.

The steel industry in Homestead, Pennsylvania, is seen through five generations of a Hungarian immigrant and his family. This sympathetic and entertaining story relates the development of the labor movement and the organizing of the Congress of Industrial Organizations.

859.   Blakely, Mike. **Shortgrass Song**. Forge, 1994. (0-312-85541-9) $23.95. « Time: ca. 1860-1899.

This exciting story of the opening of the West concerns the Holcomb family and their friend Buster Thompson, a runaway slave. The action deals realistically with battles with Native Americans, cattle drives, and wild animals and the weather in a remote area. It takes place in the Pike's Peak region of the Colorado territory.

159

860. Bromfield, Louis. **Mrs. Parkington**. Harper, 1943. Repr. Amereon, 1976. (0-88411-502-X) Lib Bdg $22.95. Thorndike, 1992. (1-56054-354-X) Large type ed. Lib Bdg $20.95. « Time: 1875-1942.

Susie, the daughter of a Nevada mining town hotelkeeper, marries a rich robber baron. She becomes a noted New York hostess, famous on two continents. Through the details of her life, the reader glimpses social attitudes of the time.

861. Caldwell, Janet Taylor. **The Captains and the Kings**. Doubleday, 1972. Fawcett, 1983. (0-449-20562-2) Pb $5.95. « Time: 1850-1915.

The overwhelming ambition of Irish immigrant Joseph Armagh is to make money and provide social position for his family. In his rise from complete poverty to wealth and political power, the story depicts how the few wield economic, political, and military power over the many.

862. Caldwell, Janet Taylor. **Never Victorious, Never Defeated**. McGraw, 1954. Repr. Amereon, 1976. (0-88411-162-8) Lib Bdg $29.95. « Time: ca. 1860-1935.

The DeWitt family of Pennsylvania gained its fortune through a railroad empire and struggled against each other, bankers, and the labor union to retain control. Caldwell's saga of four generations of the DeWitt family covers the rise of American capitalism and the exploitation of labor in the 75 years from the Civil War to the Depression.

863. Carroll, James. **Memorial Bridge**. Houghton Mifflin, 1991. (0-395-51136-4) $22.45. « Time: ca. late 1930s-1970.

Sean Dillon drops out of the seminary and enrolls in law school, working in a Chicago stockyard to pay his way. He discovers a murdered man and seeks justice for the victim, making his life's work the FBI and military intelligence. Carroll explores Washington politics, the growth of intelligence activities during and following World War II, and the controversy of American involvement in the Vietnam War.

864. Davenport, Marcia. **The Valley of Decision**. Scribner, 1942. Repr. Bentley, 1979. (0-8376-0427-3) Lib Bdg $18.00. University of Pittsburgh Press, 1989. (0-8229-5805-8) Pb $15.95. « Time: 1873-1940s.

This is a multigenerational story of a Pennsylvania steel manufacturer's family who sees the rise of the steel industry and changes in social attitudes from the panic of 1873 to the early days of World War II. Mary Rafferty, an inexperienced Irish servant, comes to the home of the Scott family to work. Over the years, Mary becomes increasingly important to the family. For mature readers.

865. Erdrich, Louise. **Love Medicine**. Holt, 1984. Several editions available. « Time: 1934-1984.

In 14 chapters spanning 50 years in the lives of two families, seven narrators on a Chippewa reservation tell of their relationships with a deceased woman. The Native American experience in modern times are revealed in this novel that shows how the love of one woman holds the families together.

866. Fairbairn, Ann. **Five Smooth Stones**. Crown, 1966. Repr. Buccaneer Books, 1991. (0-89966-805-4) Lib Bdg $46.95. Bantam, 1985. (0-553-25203-8) Pb $4.95. « Time: 1930s-1960s.

As a Black child growing up in New Orleans, David Champlin is strongly influenced by his loving, religious grandfather and a Danish scholar. He becomes an attorney, is appointed to a diplomatic post, and achieves a measure of success. Then a racist incident causes the death of a childhood friend. In his grief, David joins the fight for equality. The title of this lengthy work alludes to the David and Goliath story.

867. Faulkner, William. **Absalom, Absalom!** Random House, 1936. Several editions available. « Time: ca. 1850-1910.

The "grand design" of Thomas Sutpen, son of poor West Virginia whites, is to found a wealthy family and be accepted as a Southern aristocrat. He establishes himself in Mississippi and rises to prominence, becoming a colonel of a Confederate regiment. After the war, he finds his daughter's life and his plantation in ruins. His attempt to have another son ends in murder, and his only descendant is a mixed-breed mentally handicapped child. This is a strange story with long and convoluted paragraphs. The appended chronology and brief biographies of primary characters provide clarification.

868. Ferber, Edna. **Cimmaron**. Doubleday, 1930. Amereon, n.d. (0-88411-548-8) $24.95. Repr. Lightyear, 1992. (0-89968-279-0) Lib Bdg $21.95. « Time: 1889-1920s.

This mix of fact and fiction concerns the development of Oklahoma, from the official opening of the territory to settlers to the 1920s. Action centers on two hardy pioneers: the restless Yancey Cravat and Sabra, his practical wife. Ferber's novel tells the story of the dislocation of the Osage Indians and the discovery of oil on land previously considered useless.

869. Ferber, Edna. **Ice Palace**. Doubleday, 1958. Repr. Lightyear, 1992. (0-89968-278-2) $21.95. « Time: 1850s-1950.

Ferber focuses on the romance of Christine Storm to tell about Alaska's history and how statehood would protect its rich resources from the greedy. Christine is of mixed Norwegian, Inuit, and American background. She loves Alaska but must choose between a prosperous politician from Oregon and a part-Eskimo pilot.

870. Fleischman, Paul. **The Borning Room**. HarperCollins, 1991. Several editions available. « Time: 1851-1918.

In 1918, Georgina Caroline Lott, who was born in the family's "borning room" in 1851, tells the story of four generations of her Ohio farm family. Her reminiscences include finding a runaway slave, suffragettes, new farm technologies, and the births, marriages, illnesses, and deaths of loved ones. Georgina's story covers the transformations brought about by political and social change and provides a rich picture of family and farm life.

871. Gaines, Ernest J. **The Autobiography of Miss Jane Pittman**. Dial, 1971. Bantam, 1982. (0-553-26357-9) Pb $4.50. « Time: 1850s-1960s.

Jane Pittman was born a slave and lived to see the civil rights movement. This fictional autobiography tells the story of a people. Jane is a master storyteller; her account is filled with humor, pathos, satire, fear, courage, and social commentary. Rich and balanced characterizations make this outstanding work unforgettable.

872. Garber, Eugene K. **The Historian: Six Fantasies of the American Experience**. Milkweed Editions, 1993. (0-915943-57-3) $21.95. « Time: 1807-1912.

In Garber's award-winning historical fantasy, a historian and his cousin move back and forth through events of the nineteenth century, seeking answers to questions about the principal forces that move historic events. They also seek the quintessential American woman. Philosophical questions and outlandish adventures are interwoven in an unusual yarn for sophisticated readers.

873. Gold, Herbert. **Fathers**. Random House, 1967. D. I. Fine, 1991. (1-55611-314-5) $12.95. « Time: 1930s-1960s.

This novelized memoir is a record of the persecution of Jews in Czarist Russia, the flight of Gold's father to the United States, his struggles against poverty, and his eventual success. Action is set in New York's Lower East Side and Cleveland as the family struggles with the Depression, anti-Semitic persecution, and the normal difficulties of immigrants. Within that account is the story of the difficult relations between generations.

874. Gordon, Caroline. **Penhally**. Scribner, 1931. J. S. Sanders, 1991. (1-879941-03-1) Pb $10.95. « Time: ca. 1826-1930.

Penhally is a Kentucky manor. The interwoven stories of the generations that lived there for a century are told with vigor.

875. Gordon, Noah. **Shaman**. NAL-Dutton, 1992. (0-525-93554-1) $23.00. NAL-Dutton, 1993. (0-451-17701-0) Pb $5.99. « Time: 1839-1860s.

The political writings of physician Rob J. Cole force him to flee Scotland. In Boston he becomes the protégé of Oliver Wendell Holmes, but the frontier lures him. He establishes a flourishing practice in Illinois, basing much of his work on techniques learned from Makwa-ikwa, a native Blackhawk healer. Some resent his use of her wisdom, and her murder reveals racial and religious prejudices. Following Rob's death, the tribulations of his life are revealed to his son, Shaman, also a physician, who fights for admission to medical school despite his deafness. Their story reveals the realities of medical practice on the frontier and the deplorable conditions of medicine during the Civil War.

876. Greenberg, Joanne. **No Reck'ning Made**. Holt, 1993. (0-8050-2579-0) $23.00. « Time: ca. 1900-1970s.

Starting with her poverty-stricken youth in rural Colorado just after the turn of the century, this story follows the life of Clara Coleman. She works in a factory during World War II and becomes a teacher and school principal in a small mountain town. Through her efforts with the underprivileged, the reader sees the social divisions of the changing community. When her daughter is arrested because of antiwar activities during the Vietnam War, the national anguish of the time is personalized. Through this story of an ordinary woman, the reader sees the sweep of twentieth-century U.S. history.

877. Griswold, Francis. **Sea Island Lady**. Morrow, 1939. Beaufort Book, n.d. (0-685-06833-1) $19.95. « Time: 1860s-1920s.

Emily Moffett is a Yankee. Her first husband is a carpetbagger, her second a plantation owner. She slowly becomes fond of Southern ways and struggles to help build a new society in South Carolina after the Civil War. A hurricane, the Spanish-American War, and World War I are all part of the action in this lengthy but absorbing novel.

878.  Harris, Marilyn. **Lost and Found**. Crown, 1991. (0-517-58333-X) $19.95. Ballantine, 1992. (0-345-37462-2) Pb $5.99. « Time: 1930-1965.

Two children who were orphaned early in the Depression are rescued by Martha, a loving woman who directs a soup kitchen in Texas. Through a mishap, the younger child, Belle, is separated from her brother and Martha; she grows up in California. Belle is befriended by a Japanese family which is interned during the war; she also becomes involved in the racial torment surrounding school integration. Her brother serves in the navy and then goes to college. A happy ending brings the family together again in this informative and uplifting work that features rich characterizations and humor.

879.  Highland, Monica. **Lotus Land**. Coward, McCann & Geoghegan, 1983. McGraw-Hill, 1985. (0-07-028791-0) Pb text ed. $5.95. 1986. (0-07-028793-7) Pb $4.95. « Time: ca. 1880-1945.

Sung Wing On survives a plague in China and flees to Los Angeles. Maria Ortiz, driven from her home in Mexico because she is pregnant with the child of an Anglo, and Baltimore socialite Clifford Creighton also sees Los Angeles as a place to try to make their fortunes. The three meet in the 1880s. Over the next decades their families interact, and they are all involved in the growth of a flourishing city that knows its share of difficulties. This lively story is filled with tidbits of history and strong characters.

880.  Hughes, Rupert. **The Giant Wakes: A Novel About Samuel Gompers**. Borden, 1950. (0-87505-132-4) $5.95. « Time: 1870s-1920s.

Gompers was the first president of the American Federation of Labor (AFL) and served in that position from 1886 to 1924. This romantic novelized biography is informative concerning the growth of the labor movement.

881.  Jakes, John. **California Gold**. Random House, 1989. (0-394-56106-6) $19.95. Ballantine, 1990. (0-345-36943-2) Pb $5.95. « Time: 1886-1921.

In this rags-to-riches story, Mack Chance leaves his work in an Appalachian coal mine and arrives in California penniless. He soon amasses a fortune through investments in oil, real estate, oranges, and movie-making. He survives the 1906 earthquake, labor disputes, a train wreck, and various romances; he meets and befriends such persons as William Randolph Hearst, Leland Stanford, Mack Sennett, Jack London, and D. W. Griffith. This colorful, entertaining story is informative about life in California at the turn of the century.

882.  Jones, Douglas C. **This Savage Race**. Holt, 1993. (0-8050-2243-0) $23.00. « Time: 1808-1865.

Jones portrays the settlement of the Ozarks in this epic that chronicles the adventures of the Fawley family from the close of the Revolution through the Civil War. They settle first on the banks of the Mississippi but suffer great loss in the New Madrid earthquake of 1811. They then settle in northern Arkansas, where one son develops a fine farm while the other chooses the life of a wilderness man. Outstanding descriptions of the flora and fauna and of the customs of Cherokee and Osage Indians characterize this fine work.

883. Lafferty, R. A. **Okla Hannali**. Doubleday, 1972. University of Oklahoma Press, 1991. (0-8061-2349-4) Pb $9.95. « Time: ca. 1800-1890s.

The nineteenth-century experiences of the Choctaw people are revealed in Lafferty's novel about Hannali Innominee, a member of the Okla Hannali clan. He participates in the Great Removal from the southeast in the early 1830s, loses his home during the bitter territorial wars of the late 1860s, and sees the erosion of Choctaw culture at the end of the century. Told in the storytelling style of Native Americans, this work reflects the Choctaw culture and philosophy.

884. Lee, Helen Elaine. **The Serpent's Gift**. Athenaeum, 1994. (0-689-12193-8) $21.00. « Time: 1910-1990s.

Tracing several generations of two intermingled Southern Black families, Lee tells a powerful story of survival. Members of the families handle the events of the times in their own ways, some retreating in fear, others finding strength through their interpersonal connections. The narrative, which features storyteller LaRue Smalls, is lyrical, coherent, and richly varied. Suitable for mature secondary students.

885. Lewis, Janet. **The Invasion: A Narrative of Events Concerning the Johnston Family of St. Mary's**. Harcourt, 1932. Swallow, 1964. (0-8040-0166-9) $15.00. (0-8040-0167-7) Pb $9.00. « Time: 1770s-early 1900s.

Shortly after the Revolutionary War, John Johnston came from Ireland and settled in the wilderness area that was to become Michigan. Here he married the daughter of an Ojibway chief. This novel chronicles their descendants into the twentieth century.

886. Lockridge, Ross, Jr. **Raintree County**. Houghton, 1948. Repr. Buccaneer Books, 1991. (0-89966-865-8) Lib Bdg $49.95. Viking, 1994. (0-14-023666-X) Pb $16.95. « Time: 1840s-1892.

Schoolteacher Johnny Shawnessy meets a number of old boyhood friends (one now a U.S. Senator, one a financier) at a community Fourth of July picnic in 1892. He reminisces about his boyhood days in Indiana, his experiences in the Civil War, his political life, and his marriages. The flashbacks of this lengthy saga deal with personal events of Shawnessy's life and the crucial public events of the day, providing a memorable sweep of nineteenth-century life in the Midwest.

887. Martin, William. **Back Bay**. Crown, 1980. Warner, 1992. (0-446-36316-2) Pb $5.99. « Time: 1775-1980.

A gold and silver tea set that Paul Revere made for George Washington was stolen from the White House in 1814 and plays a part in the history of the fictional Pratt family. Now, in the mid-twentieth century, only someone who can decipher obscure clues in a diary can find the tea set again. This mystery includes a lively account of family and political history. Suitable for mature readers.

888. Martin, William. **Cape Cod**. Warner, 1991. (0-446-51510-8) $21.95. 1992. (0-446-36317-0) Pb $5.95. « Time: 1600s-1900s.

The ship's log of the Mayflower contains information about a possible murder. As a result, a feud erupts between the Bigelows and the Hilyards that continues for three centuries. The two families struggle to control Massachusetts property and to gain political and economic power. Some members of the family move south and west, and between them they are involved in everything that affects the nation. This lengthy novel provides an accurate and entertaining overview of our history and culture. Suitable for mature readers.

889. McNamee, Thomas. **A Story of Deep Delight**. Viking, 1990, 1992. (0-14-010443-7) Pb $11.00. « Time: 1811-1970s.

In three parts McNamee tells the story of the development of the area near Memphis, Tennessee. Part I tells of the Chickasaw meeting with white society and the tragic results of the acquisitive habits of the new settlers. Part II shows the way in which lands (once sacred to Native Americans) became plantations worked by Black slaves, and how the practice of slavery led to the Civil War. Part III concerns the lives of descendants of the earlier inhabitants of the area and the way that bigotry has influenced their lives. This saga shows Southern history in a microcosm.

890. Michener, James A. **Alaska**. Random House, 1988. Several editions available. « Time: Prehistory-World War II.

Michener clarifies the separation of fact and fiction in an introduction to this lengthy account of the growth of Alaska. Along the way, the reader meets some memorable characters and is caught up in the beauty of a land so rich in resources that it became the target of greedy developers.

891. Michener, James A. **Centennial**. Random House, 1974. Several editions available. « Time: Prehistory-1970s.

In this very lengthy novel about Colorado, Michener traces the formation of the mountains, the first Native Americans, the first white hunters and trappers, and all that followed—settlers, gold and silver strikes, the railroad, the coming of cattle and sheep, and natural, economic, political, and social events.

892. Michener, James A. **Chesapeake**. Random House, 1978. (0-394-50079-2) $45.00. Fawcett, 1986. (0-449-21158-4) Pb $6.95. « Time: Seventeenth-twentieth centuries.

Three immigrant families (headed by a persecuted Catholic nobleman from England, a criminal, and a Quaker banished from Massachusetts) settle on Maryland's eastern shore. They and their descendants interact with Native Americans, African Americans, and other immigrants. The reader of this lengthy novel will learn about the major events, personalities, flora, and fauna of the Chesapeake area, and its social, political, economic, and environmental development. Action ranges from the earliest settlements through Watergate.

893. Michener, James A. **Hawaii**. Random House, 1959. Several editions available. « Time: Prehistory to mid-twentieth century.

Michener tells this very lengthy saga in four parts. The first concerns the original settlers of Hawaii, who arrived from Polynesia 11 centuries ago. Their story is followed by that of a group of American missionaries and traders, who come to convert the heathen and make money in trade. Through the story of an American, Abner Hale, the reader sees both the good and bad of these ethnocentric visionaries. The last two parts tell of the migrations of Chinese and Japanese settlers. Throughout these stories is shown the development of fruit plantations, shipping empires, and local rivalries. Suitable for mature readers.

894.   Michener, James A. **Legacy**. Random House, 1988. Several editions available. « Time: 1770s-1980s.

Members of the Starr family fought in the Revolution, were involved in drafting the Constitution, and argued over slavery and women's suffrage. Now Norman Starr, a West Point graduate, is involved in the Iran-Contra affair and is about to face a Senate investigation for unconstitutional activity. As his lawyer prepares Starr's case, the development of the Constitution and its effect on our lives is traced.

895.   Michener, James A. **Texas**. Random House, 1985. Several editions available. « Time: 1527-1980s.

In telling the story of the Spanish and American exploration and settling of Texas, Michener presents a sympathetic analysis of events that are still in development. Every colorful character and significant development is included in this very lengthy saga.

896.   Myers, Walter Dean. **The Glory Field**. Scholastic, 1994. (0-590-45897-3) $14.95. « Time: 1750s-late twentieth century.

Myers follows the experiences of the Lewis family for more than 250 years as the descendants of an African slave move away from, and return to, the small plot of South Carolina that they call the Glory Field.

897.   Myrer, Anton. **A Green Desire: A Novel**. Putnam, 1982. Avon, 1983. (0-380-61580-0) Pb $3.95. « Time: ca. 1910-1940s.

Family circumstances cause two brothers to be separated in childhood. Chapin, the elder, is raised by a wealthy aunt; Tipton remains with his impoverished mother. Both young men rise to prominence in business, and both fall in love with the spirited daughter of a Portuguese fisherman. Myrer presents an accurate picture of Massachusetts social life from World War I through the 1920s, the Depression, and World War II.

898.   Myrer, Anton. **Once an Eagle**. Holt, 1968. Repr. Buccaneer Books, 1991. (0-89966-789-9) Lib Bdg. $48.95. « Time: ca. 1916-1970.

Sam Damon begins his military career as a part of the army that tries to control the raids of Pancho Villa from Mexico into the United States. Through subsequent military ventures he rises from private to general, and the reader is provided with a fine, realistic picture of military life and leadership. Excellent battle scenes and revelations of political realities characterize this lengthy novel. Among the real-life characters are generals Pershing and MacArthur.

899.   Page, Elizabeth. **Tree of Liberty**. Farrar, 1939. Repr. Buccaneer Books, 1990. (0-89966-658-2) Lib Bdg $57.95. « Time: 1754-1806.

This lengthy novel follows the lives and adventures of Matthew and Jane Howard and their children and grandchildren as the family moves from the Eastern Seaboard to the Western Plains frontier. The time span is from the political unrest that preceded the Revolution into Thomas Jefferson's second term as president. Matthew is a natural frontiersman, while Jane was raised as an aristocrat. One of their sons follows the politics of Jefferson; the other champions Hamilton. The lives of other siblings exemplify the many ways in which citizens of the new nation followed their natural inclinations. Many historical figures, including Jefferson, appear in a story based on excellent research.

900.   Power, Susan. **The Grass Dancer**. Putnam, 1994. (0-399-13911-7) $22.95. « Time: 1864-1982.

Power's rich account of Sioux history and legend begins with the story of Red Dress, who sees the hypocrisy of white culture, thwarts the efforts of a priest to convert her tribe, and is murdered. Subsequent generations, haunted by her legend, must deal with life on the reservation. The intermingled episodic stories of myth and family life will be enjoyed by mature readers.

901.   Price, Eugenia. **Margaret's Story**. Lippincott, 1980. Bantam, 1984. (0-553-26559-8) Pb $4.99. Thorndike, 1993. (1-56054-468-6) Large type ed. $20.95. « Time: ca. 1830-1878.

Based on the experiences of actual families, this is the third in the author's trilogy about northern Florida. The rich history of the Florida-Georgia coastline is revealed in this fictionalized biography of Margaret Seton, who married widowed Lewis Fleming. They build their lives around raising their 10 children and serving the Northern tourist trade. With the coming of the Civil War, they see sons fight on both sides of the war and the destruction of their home. Following the war, they rebuild their home and continue to live according to Lewis's optimistic approach to life, based on firm religious faith. This work was published simultaneously with *Diary of a Novel,* in which Price tells about the research that goes into a novel such as this. Sequel to *Maria.*

902.   Roberts, Carey and Rebecca Seely. **Tidewater Dynasty: The Lees of Stratford Hall**. Harcourt Brace, 1981. (0-15-190294-1) $19.95. Harcourt Brace, 1983. (0-15-690336-9) Pb $6.95. « Time: 1718-early 1800s.

This is the story of the earliest generations of the famous Lee family of Virginia, including Thomas, who settled there; his two sons, who were signers of the Declaration of Independence; and their cousin "Light-Horse Harry," a Revolutionary War hero and the father of Robert E. Lee. The story concludes with Robert E. Lee considering the family's past and his own role in the upcoming Civil War. Many notable persons, including Washington and Franklin, play a part in the story of the Lee family.

903.   Sandburg, Carl. **Remembrance Rock**. Harcourt Brace, 1948. (0-15-176799-8) $15.00. 1991. (0-15-676390-7) Pb $19.95. « Time: 1600-1860s.

In a lengthy patriotic novel, Sandburg praises the sacrifices made by our forebears who settled Plymouth and fought in the Revolutionary and the Civil Wars. The novel is rich in its evocation of local customs and speech and examines not only how things were but *why* they were. The length of the novel makes it suitable for mature readers.

904.   Santmyer, Helen H. **. . . And Ladies of the Club**. Ohio State University Press, 1982. (0-8142-0323-X) $57.50. Berkley, 1988. (0-425-10243-2) Pb $7.95. « Time: 1868-1932.

In refutation of Sinclair Lewis's bleak picture of small town life (*Main Street*), Santmyer spent 50 years writing her account of life in an Ohio town. Action focuses on Anne Alexander Gordon and her physician husband, haunted by the horrors he saw during the Civil War, and on Sally Cochran Rausch and her banker husband. These women are two of the members of the Waynesboro Women's Club, which was founded to provide intellectual stimulation for young matrons and which provides the link for their lives and the novel. At the beginning of this lengthy work, Andrew Johnson is president; at its conclusion the president is Franklin Roosevelt. The story chronicles the social, political, and economic changes during that period. Because of its length (more than 1,000 pages) this work will require a patient reader. That reader will be rewarded by a rich account of the lives of middle-class WASPs from 1868 to 1932.

905.  Schumann, Mary. **Strife Before Dawn**. Dial, 1939. Repr. Reprint Service, 1993. (0-7812-5829-4) Lib Bdg $89.00. « Time: 1764-1782.
   In a well-paced and colorful romance, Schumann tells the story of Keith Maitland, a Quaker pioneer whose wife, Hope, is kidnapped by a Shawnee brave. Hope, believing Keith to be dead, marries the Shawnee and has a son. Before Keith finds her again, he falls in love with Jacqueline, a beauty from Virginia. The complexities of their story provide a good basis for authentic descriptions of colonial life and events of the Revolutionary War.

906.  Settle, Mary Lee. **Choices**. Doubleday, 1995. (0-385-47699-X) $21.95. « Time: 1931-1960s.
   Melinda Kregg Dunston grew up in high society in Virginia, but as a young woman she chooses to spend her life helping others. In the 1930s she works to help the coal miners of Kentucky. As a result of that experience, she becomes a social and political activist, is involved in Spain's civil war, is in London during the Blitz, and in Mississippi during the civil rights movement (1960s).

907.  Shreve, Susan Richards. **Daughters of the New World**. Doubleday, 1992. Ivy Books, 1994. (0-8041-1123-5) Pb $5.99. « Time: 1890-1960s.
   Anna, servant to a wealthy physician in Washington, D.C., marries his son. Their union is unacceptable to the family and to society, so they move to Wisconsin, where they work with the Chippewas on the Bad River Reservation. Anna's letters preserve the essence of their experience. Their daughter Amanda captures her life experiences through photography. Disguised as a man, she travels to Europe during World War I to record for posterity what is happening there. Amanda and her daughter, Sara, also travel through the Dust Bowl during the Depression and document the effects of poverty. Sara's daughter Eleanor records the events of the 1960s. Through the lives of these strong and unconventional women, Shreve provides an imaginative episodic overview of twentieth-century America.

908.  Skimin, Robert. **Apache Autumn: A Novel of the Apache Nation**. St. Martin's Press, 1992. (0-312-08697-0) $22.95. « Time: 1821-1892.
   Seventeen-year-old Carlotta is abducted from her New Mexico home and forced to marry the Apache chief, Lazaro. After the birth of her son Andres, Carlotta flees with the child to New Mexico and eventually marries an American army officer. When Andres learns of his heritage, he seeks his Apache father. Through his eyes, the reader sees the forced removal of the Apache from their ancient homeland and the tragic events that led to their incarceration at Fort Sill, Oklahoma. A number of historical characters appear in this fact-based work, including Silsoose, the great shaman of Apache lore.

909.  Stegner, Wallace. **Big Rock Candy Mountain**. Duell, 1943. University of Nebraska Press, 1983. (0-8032-9144-2) Pb $12.95. Viking, 1991. (0-14-013939-7) Pb $11.00. « Time: 1906-1942.

Bo Mason, his wife Elsa, and their two boys live a wandering life. They constantly seek Bo's fortune in many ways—gambling, bootlegging, real estate, and other entrepreneurial activities—and are always convinced that success is to be found in the next place. This enjoyable work is set in the far western states and Alaska.

910.  Steinbeck, John. **East of Eden**. Viking, 1952. Several editions available. « Time: 1860-1920.

Based on the lives of Steinbeck's family, the lengthy *East of Eden* realistically chronicles a California family and provides uplifting, sordid, gentle, and brutal details of small-town life over a span of 60 years.

911.  Vidal, Gore. **Washington, D.C.** Little, Brown, 1967. Ballantine, 1986. (0-345-34236-4) Pb $5.99. « Time: 1937-1950.

Opportunism, betrayal, and lust are all used as weapons by those seeking political and economic power in Washington from the time of Roosevelt's New Deal to the McCarthy years. Action centers on Clay Overbury, who manipulates events to bring about his election to the Senate.

912.  Walker, Margaret. **Jubilee**. Houghton, 1966. Bantam, 1975. (0-553-25791-9) Pb $4.95. 1984. (0-553-27383-3) Pb $5.95. « Time: 1840s-1860s.

The humiliations of slavery and the different but equally great challenges of freedom are seen in the experiences of Vyry. Born a slave serving in the home of her white father, Vyry has little hope for freedom. As the Civil War progresses, she begins to see possibilities, but after the war, the activities of the Ku Klux Klan make her dreams seem remote. Still, she maintains her spirit. Walker's award-winning novel was one of the first to tell about slavery and the Reconstruction period from the African-American point of view. It is based on the life of Walker's great-grandmother.

913.  Warren, Robert Penn. **Band of Angels**. Random House, 1946. Louisiana State University Press, 1994. (0-8071-1946-6) Pb $12.95. « Time: 1844-1888.

Amanda is educated at Oberlin School and lives a life of privilege, cared for by a Black nurse on her father's Kentucky plantation. At the age of 16 she is called home because of her father's death. She learns she was born of a slave and is to be sold into slavery to pay her father's debts. The story follows Amanda's life through the Civil War (which she experiences in New Orleans) and her marriage, living first in St. Louis and then in small towns in Kansas.

914.  Windle, Janice Woods. **True Women**. Putnam, 1994. (0-399-13813-7) $22.95. « Time: ca. 1840-mid 1900s.

The author's search for validation of incredible family tales related to the Texas war for independence, the Civil War, and Indian raids led to the examination of thousands of documents and many interviews. The result is an engrossing account of survival featuring the white, Black, and Native American women of her family.

915.   Woods, Stuart. **Chiefs**. Norton, 1981. (0-393-01461-4) $14.95. Avon, 1987 (0-380-70347-5) Pb $5.99. « Time: 1920s-early 1960s.

Over 40 years, a number of white boys have disappeared or been murdered in the small town of Delano, Georgia. Three police chiefs have struggled with the problem—a farmer, a racist, and a Black man. Through this story, Woods explores the politics of a Southern town and shows changing racial and social attitudes.

916.   Zaroulis, Nancy. **Massachusetts**. Fawcett, 1991. (0-449-90586-1) $19.95. « Time: Seventeenth-twentieth centuries.

Through the story of the Revell family, Zaroulis tells the history of Massachusetts from the Mayflower to 1990. The lengthy but easy-to-read novel includes the first Thanksgiving, the Salem Witch Trials, the Boston Tea Party, the development of the Triangular Trade and China trade systems, industrialization and its impact on the employment of women, the abolition movement, women's suffrage, the Sacco and Vanzetti trial, and other important economic, political, and social events.

# Chapter 10

# Additional Titles

In this work, the primary source for locating titles pertaining to the various states and the District of Columbia is the subject index. In addition to the name of the state, the most common subject headings for works about life in a state are "Frontier and Pioneer Life—(state name)" and "Social Life and Customs—(state name)."

For the most part, titles listed in the chronological chapters were identified through major bibliographies that have received national distribution. Some of the titles listed in this chapter also appeared in major bibliographies, but in general they were identified by their inclusion in bibliographies received from the states or from similar sources. As stated in the introduction, several agencies in every state were contacted by various means, including the Internet, for suggestions of appropriate titles about that state. Agencies and individuals in many states responded with helpful and extensive lists; some states did not respond at all. Naturally, more books are written about some states than about others. This fact, combined with the fact that this work includes only in-print titles, results in regrettably uneven coverage across the states.

The time of the setting and the subjects of the following titles that could be identified through normal review sources are included. As is the case with other titles in this work, all were listed in *Books in Print* 1993-1994, *Books in Print* 1994-1995, or *Forthcoming Books* 1994 and 1995.

## *ALABAMA*

917.   Stribling, T. S. **The Unfinished Cathedral**. Doubleday, 1934. University of Alabama Press, 1986. (0-8173-0252-2) $27.50. (0-8173-0253-0) $14.95. Sequel to *The Forge* and *The Store*. « Time: 1920s–early 1930s. Subject: ∞ Social Life and Customs—Alabama.

## *ALASKA*

918.   Beach, Rex Ellingwood. **Silver Horde**. Harper, 1909. Buccaneer Books, 1975. (0-89966-013-4) Lib Bdg $17.25. « Time: 1890s. Subject: ∞ Frontier and Pioneer Life—Alaska.

919. Delis, Leftare P. **The Inside Passage**. Peanut Butter Publishers, 1994. (0-89716-556-X) Pb $12.95. « Time: ca. 1945. Subject: ∞ Social Life and Customs—Alaska.

920. Doig, Ivan. **Sea Runners**. Athenaeum, 1982. Viking, 1983. (0-14-006780-9) Pb $9.00. Peter Smith, 1992. (0-8446-6538-X) $19.50. « Time: 1853. Subject: ∞ Frontier and Pioneer Life—Alaska.

921. Garland, Hamlin. **Trail of the Gold Seekers**. Macmillan, 1899. Repr. Reprint Services, 1988. (0-7812-1227-8) Lib Bdg $59.00. « Time: 1890s. Subject: ∞ Frontier and Pioneer Life—Alaska.

922. L'Amour, Louis. **Sitka**. Hawthorne, 1957. Bantam, 1984. (0-553-27881-9) Pb $4.50. 1986. (0-553-26119-3) Pb $3.50. « Time: 1890s. Subject: ∞ Frontier and Pioneer Life—Alaska.

923. London, Jack. **Smoke Bellew**. Mills and Boon, 1900. Repr. Buccaneer Books, 1992. (0-89966-952-2) Lib Bdg $19.95. Dover, 1992. (0-486-27364-4) Unabridged text ed. Pb $7.95. « Time: 1890s. Subject: ∞ Frontier and Pioneer Life—Alaska.

924. Muir, John. **Stickeen**. Houghton, 1909. Several editions available. « Time: 1880. Subject: ∞ Explorers and Exploration. ∞ Frontier and Pioneer Life—Alaska. ∞ Muir, John.

925. Robins, Elizabeth. **Magnetic North**. Heinemann, 1904. Repr. Irvington, n.d. (0-8398-1760-6) Lib Bdg $19.50. « Time: 1890s. Subject: ∞ Frontier and Pioneer Life—Alaska.

## *ARIZONA*

926. Burroway, Janet. **Cutting Stone**. Houghton, 1992. (0-395-59300-X) $21.45. Windsor Publishing Corp., 1993. (1-55817-757-4) Pb $4.50. « Time: 1913. Subject: ∞ Frontier and Pioneer Life—Arizona. ∞ Villa, Francisco (Pancho).

927. Fenady, Andrew J. **Claws of the Eagle**. Walker, 1984. Windsor Publishing Corp., 1990. (1-55817-442-7) Pb $3.95. « Time: 1880s. Subject: ∞ Frontier and Pioneer Life—Arizona. ∞ Geronimo. ∞ Horn, Tom. ∞ Indians of North America—Apache.

928. O'Dell, Scott. **Sing Down the Moon**. Houghton, 1970. Several editions available. « Time: 1864. Subject: ∞ Frontier and Pioneer Life—Arizona. ∞ Indians of North America—Navajo.

929. Seton, Anya. **Foxfire**. Houghton, 1950. Fawcett, 1979. (0-449-24017-7) Pb $1.95. « Time: 1930s. Subject: ∞ Depression. ∞ Social Life and Customs—Arizona.

# ARKANSAS

930. Giles, Janice Holt. **Savanna**. Houghton, 1962. Repr. Amereon, 1976. (0-8488-0502-X) $22.95. « Time: 1824. Subject: ∞ Frontier and Pioneer Life—Arkansas. ∞ Women—Social Conditions—1783-1860.

931. Harington, Donald. **The Architecture of the Arkansas Ozarks: A Novel**. Little, Brown, 1975. Harcourt Brace, 1987. (0-15-607880-5) Pb $7.95. « Time: Early 1800s-mid-1900s. Subject: ∞ Frontier and Pioneer Life—Arkansas. ∞ Social Life and Customs—Arkansas.

932. Medearis, Mary. **Big Doc's Girl**. Lippincott, 1942. August House, 1985. (0-87483-105-9) Pb $7.95. « Time: Early 1900s. Subject: ∞ Social Life and Customs—Arkansas.

933. Rhodes, Judy Carole. **Hunter's Heart**. Macmillan, 1993. (0-02-773935-X) $14.95. « Time: 1950s. Subject: ∞ Social Life and Customs—Arkansas.

# CALIFORNIA

934. Briskin, Jacqueline. **Paloverde**. McGraw-Hill, 1978. Warner, 1989 (0-446-35004-4) Pb $5.95. « Time: 1880s–1920s. Subject: ∞ Oil workers and Oil Industry. ∞ Motion Picture Industry.

935. Corle, Edwin. **Fig Tree John**. Liveright, 1971. (0-87140-518-0) $7.95. (0-87140-242-4) Pb $2.95. « Time: 1906. Subject: ∞ Frontier and Pioneer Life—California. ∞ Indians of North America—Apache.

936. De Blasis, Celeste. **The Proud Breed**. Coward, 1978. Bantam, 1985. (0-553-27196-2) Pb $5.95. (0-553-25379-4) Pb $4.95. « Time: Mid-nineteenth century. Subject: ∞ Frontier and Pioneer Life—California.

937. Donahue, Marilyn Cram. **Valley in Between**. Walker, 1987. (0-8027-6731-1) $14.95. (0-8027-6733-8) Lib Bdg Pb $15.85. « Time: 1857-1861. Subject: ∞ Frontier and Pioneer Life—California.

938. Epstein, Leslie. **Pinto and Sons**. Houghton Mifflin, 1990. (0-395-54704-0) $19.45. Norton, 1992. (0-393-30846-4) Pb $9.95. « Time: 1840s. Subject: ∞ Frontier and Pioneer Life—California. ∞ Gold Rush. ∞ Indians of North America—Modoc.

939. L'Amour, Louis. **The Californios**. Bantam, 1985. (0-553-25322-0) Pb $3.99. « Time: 1840s. Subject: ∞ Business and Finance. ∞ Social Life and Customs—California.

940. L'Amour, Louis. **The Lonesome Gods**. Bantam, 1984. (0-553-27518-6) Pb $5.50. « Time: 1840s. Subject: ∞ Frontier and Pioneer Life—California.

941. Li, Chin Yang. **The Flower Drum Song**. Farrar, 1957. H. Leonard, 1981. (0-88188-077-9) $8.95. « Time: 1950s. Subject: ∞ Chinese Americans. ∞ Social Life and Customs—California.

942. Neider, Charles. **The Authentic Death of Hendry Jones**. Harper, 1956. University of Nevada Press, 1993. (0-87417-206-3) Pb $10.95. « Time: 1880s. Subject: ∞ Crime and Criminals. ∞ Frontier and Pioneer Life—California.

943. Stewart, Fred M. **The Glitter and the Gold**. New American Library, 1989. NAL-Dutton, 1990. (0-451-16709-0) Pb $5.95. « Time: ca. 1840s-1980. Subject: ∞ Social Life and Customs—California.

944. Tan, Amy. **The Joy Luck Club**. Putman, 1989. Several editions available. « Time: 1949-1989. Subject: ∞ Immigrants, Chinese. ∞ Social Life and Customs—California.

# COLORADO

945. Harmon, Susan. **Colorado Ransom**. Walker, 1991. (0-8027-4125-8) $19.95. Repr. Thorndike, 1992. (1-56054-403-1) Large type ed. Lib Bdg $14.95. « Time: 1870s. Subject: ∞ Frontier and Pioneer Life—Colorado. ∞ Miners and Mining.

946. Haruf, Kent. **Tie That Binds**. Holt, 1984, 1991. (0-8050-1869-7) Pb. $9.95. « Time: Early 1900s. Subject: ∞ Social Life and Customs—Colorado. ∞ Women—Social Conditions—1900-1939.

# CONNECTICUT

947. Collier, James Lincoln. **The Clock**. Delacorte, 1992. (0-385-30037-9) Pb $15.00. « Time: 1810. Subject: ∞ Laborers and Labor Unions. ∞ Mills and Mill Work. ∞ Women—Social Conditions—1783-1860.

948. Tharp, Louise Hall. **Tory Hole**. Crowell, 1940. DCA, 1976. (0-686-16261-7) Pb $7.50. « Time: 1780. Subject: ∞ Espionage. ∞ Social Life and Customs—Connecticut.

949. Tryon, Thomas. **In the Fire of Spring**. Knopf, 1991. Ivy Books, 1994. (0-8041-1302-5) Pb $6.99. Sequel to *The Wings of the Morning*. « Time: 1840s. Subject: ∞ Abolitionists. ∞ Racism.

950. Tryon, Thomas. **The Wings of the Morning**. Knopf, 1990. Fawcett, 1992. (0-449-22056-7) Pb $5.99. Followed by *In the Fire of Spring*. « Time: 1820s-1830s. Subject: ∞ Social Life and Customs—Connecticut. ∞ Women—Social Conditions—1783-1860.

# FLORIDA

951.   Hemingway, Ernest. **To Have and Have Not**. Scribner, 1937. Several editions available. « Time: 1930s. Subject: ∞ Crime and Criminals. ∞ Depression. ∞ Laborers and Labor Unions. ∞ Social Life and Customs—Florida.

952.   Hurston, Zora Neale. **Their Eyes Were Watching God**. Lippincott, 1937. Several editions available. « Time: 1930s. Subject: ∞ African Americans. ∞ Depression. ∞ Social Life and Customs—Florida. ∞ Women—Social Conditions—1900-1939.

953.   Matthiessen, Peter. **Killing Mister Watson**. Random House, 1990. Several editions available. « Time: 1890-1910. Subject: ∞ Crime and Criminals. ∞ Racism. ∞ Social Life and Customs—Florida. ∞ Watson, Edgar J.

954.   Peck, Robert Newton. **Hallapoosa**. Walker, 1988. (0-8027-1016-6) $16.95. « Time: 1930s. Subject: ∞ Depression. ∞ Social Life and Customs—Florida.

955.   Smith, Patrick. **Angel City**. Valkyrie Publishing, 1978. (0-912760-71-0) $23.00. « Time: ca. 1970. Subject: ∞ Laborers and Labor Unions. ∞ Social Life and Customs—Florida.

956.   Smith, Patrick. **Forever Island**. Norton, 1973. Repr. Pineapple Press, 1987. (0-910923-42-6) $17.95. « Time: ca. 1970. Subject: ∞ Indians of North America— Seminole. ∞ Social Life and Customs—Florida.

# GEORGIA

957.   Hodge, Jane Aiken. **Savannah Purchase**. Doubleday, 1971. Fawcett, 1979. (0-449-24097-5) Pb $1.95. « Time: ca. 1820. Subject: ∞ Social Life and Customs— Georgia.

# HAWAII

958.   Abe, Keith S. **Hawaii Aloha**. Topgallant, 1986. (0-914916-76-9) « Time: Mid-1800s-1917. Subject: ∞ Liliuokalani, Lydia Kamekeha. ∞ Hawaii. ∞ Social Life and Customs—Hawaii. ∞ Women—Biography.

959.   Judd, Walter F. **Let Us Go: The Narrative of Kamehameha II, King of the Hawaiian Islands, 1819-1824**. Topgallant, 1976. (0-914916-16-5) Text ed. $4.95. (0-914916-17-3) Pb $1.50. « Time: Early 1800s. Subject: ∞ Kamehameha II. ∞ Social Life and Customs—Hawaii.

# *IDAHO*

960.   Davis, Nelle Portry. **Stump Ranch Pioneer**. Dodd, 1942. University of Idaho Press, 1990. (0-89301-141-X) Pb $14.95. « Time: 1930s. Subject: ∞ Depression. ∞ Farm and Ranch Life. ∞ Social Life and Customs—Idaho.

961.   Grey, Zane. **Thunder Mountain**. Harper, 1935. Repr. Chivers North American, 1990. (0-86220-940-4) Text ed. $12.95. Harper, 1991. (0-06-100216-X) Pb $3.99. « Time: 1860s. Subject: ∞ Frontier and Pioneer Life—Idaho. ∞ Gold Rush.

962.   Stegner, Wallace. **Angle of Repose**. Doubleday, 1971. Viking, 1992. (0-14-016930-X) Pb $12.00. « Time: 1870s. Subject: ∞ Frontier and Pioneer Life—Idaho. ∞ Miners and Mining.

# *ILLINOIS*

963.   Campbell, Bebe Moore. **Your Blues Ain't Like Mine**. Putnam, 1992. (0-399-13746-7) $22.95. Ballantine, 1993. (0-345-38395-8) Pb $12.00. « Time: 1955. Subject: ∞ African Americans. ∞ Racism. ∞ Social Life and Customs—Illinois.

964.   Cooke, Grace MacGowan. **The Grapple: A Story of the Illinois Coal Region**. Page, 1905. Repr. AMS Press, n.d. (0-404-58415-2) $34.50. « Time: ca. 1890. Subject: ∞ Laborers and Labor Unions. ∞ Social Life and Customs—Illinois.

965.   Dos Passos, John. **Chosen Country**. Houghton, 1951. Amereon, n.d. (0-685-10848-1) $27.95. « Time: 1848-1930. Subject: ∞ Social Life and Customs—Illinois.

966.   Farrell, James T. **Father and Son**. Vanguard, 1940. Ayer, 1976. (0-405-09335-7) $38.50. Sequel to *A World I Never Made* and *No Star Is Lost*. « Time: 1920s. Subject: ∞ Irish Americans. ∞ Social Life and Customs—Illinois.

967.   Maxwell, William. **They Came Like Swallows**. Harper, 1937. Godine, 1988. (0-87923-677-9) Pb $9.95. « Time: ca. 1918. Subject: ∞ Social Life and Customs—Illinois.

968.   Maxwell, William. **Time Will Darken It**. Harper, 1948. Godine, 1983. (0-87923-448-2) Pb $11.95. « Time: 1912. Subject: ∞ Social Life and Customs—Illinois.

969.   Peck, Richard. **The Ghost Belonged to Me**. Viking, 1975. Several editions available. « Time: ca. 1900. Subject: ∞ Social Life and Customs—Illinois.

970.   Powers, John. **The Last Catholic in America**. Saturday Review Press, 1973. Repr. Bentley, 1981. (0-8376-0439-7) Lib Bdg $18.00. NAL-Dutton, 1993. (0-451-17614-6) Pb $4.99. « Time: 1950s. Subject: ∞ Religion. ∞ Social Life and Customs—Illinois.

971. Tucker, Wilson. **The Lincoln Hunters**. Rinehart, 1958. Baen Books, 1992. (0-671-72108-9) Pb $3.99. « Time: 1856. Subject: ∞ Lincoln, Abraham. ∞ Social Life and Customs—Illinois.

972. Wilder, Thornton. **The Eighth Day**. Harper, 1967. Carroll & Graf, 1987. (0-88184-339-3) Pb $4.95. Amereon, n.d. (0-8488-0669-7) $24.95. « Time: ca. 1910. Subject: ∞ Social Life and Customs—Illinois.

# INDIANA

973. Lasky, Kathryn. **Pageant**. Macmillan, 1986. (0-02-751720-9) $14.95. Dell, 1988. (0-440-20161-6) Pb $3.95. « Time: 1960-1963. Subject: ∞ Social Life and Customs—Indiana.

974. Long, Eleanor Rice. **Wilderness to Washington: An 1811 Journey on Horseback**. Reflections Press, 1981. Guild Press of Indiana, 1981. (0-89917-324-1) Pb $7.95. « Time: 1811. Subject: ∞ Frontier and Pioneer Life—Indiana. ∞ Jennings, Ann Gilmore. ∞ Jennings, Jonathan.

975. Shepherd, Jean. **In God We Trust: All Others Pay Cash**. Doubleday, 1966, 1991. (0-385-02174-7) Pb $10.00. « Time: 1930s. Subject: ∞ Depression. ∞ Social Life and Customs—Indiana.

976. Tarkington, Booth. **The Gentleman from Indiana**. Doubleday, 1899. Repr. AMS Press, n.d. (0-404-06338-1) $17.50. Repr. Scholarly, 1971. (0-403-00483-7) $49.00. « Time: Late 1800s. Subject: ∞ Politics and Government. ∞ Social Life and Customs—Indiana.

# IOWA

977. Aldrich, Bess Streeter. **Miss Bishop**. Appleton-Century, 1933. Repr. Amereon, 1975. (0-88411-255-1) Lib Bdg $22.95. University of Nebraska Press, 1986. (0-8032-5909-3) Pb $11.95. « Time: 1880s-1930s. Subject: ∞ Social Life and Customs—Iowa.

978. Harrison, Nick, and Kenneth Sollitt. **These Years of Promise**. Sunrise Books, 1988. (0-940652-05-6) Pb $6.95. Sequel to *Our Changing Lives*. « Time: 1896-1900. Subject: ∞ Social Life and Customs—Iowa. ∞ Women—Social Conditions—1866-1899.

979. Sollitt, Kenneth. **Our Changing Lives**. Sunrise Books, 1986. (0-940652-04-8) Pb $6.95. « Time: ca. 1900. Subject: ∞ Social Life and Customs—Iowa.

980. Sollitt, Kenneth. **This Rough New Land**. Sunrise Books, 1985. (0-940652-03-X) Rev. ed. Pb $6.95. Original Title: *Remember the Days*. « Time: 1890s. Subject: ∞ Social Life and Customs—Iowa.

# KANSAS

981. Brown, Irene Bennett. **Morning Glory Afternoon**. Blue Heron Publishing, 1982, 1991. (0-936085-20-7) Pb $8.95. « Time: 1924. Subject. ∞ Ku Klux Klan. ∞ Racism. ∞ Social Life and Customs—Kansas.

982. Day, Robert. **The Last Cattle Drive**. Putnam, 1977. University Press of Kansas, 1983. (0-7006-0243-7) $14.95. (0-7006-0344-1) Pb $7.95. « Time: 1976. Subject: ∞ Cattle Drives.

983. Howe, Edgar Watson. **The Story of a Country Town**. Howe, 1883. Repr. Reprint Service, 1988. (0-7812-1286-3) Lib Bdg $59.00. North Carolina University Press, 1962. (0-8084-0287-0) Pb $12.95. « Time: Late 1800s. Subject: ∞ Social Life and Customs—Kansas.

984. Ise, John. **Sod and Stubble: The Story of a Kansas Homestead**. Wilson-Erikson, 1936. University of Nebraska Press, 1967. (0-8032-5098-3) Pb $10.95. « Time: Late 1800s. Subject: ∞ Farm and Ranch Life. ∞ Frontier and Pioneer Life—Kansas.

985. Jones, Kathy. **Wild Western Desire**. Kensington, 1993. Zebra, 1993. (0-8127-4028-8) Pb $4.50. « Time: 1880s. Subject: ∞ Frontier and Pioneer Life—Kansas. ∞ Masterson, William Barclay. ∞ Earp, Wyatt.

986. Lindsay, Mela Meisner. **Shukar Balan: The White Lamb**. American Historical Society of Germans from Russia, 1976. (0-914222-02-3) $16.00. « Time: 1910s. Subject: ∞ Immigrants, Russian. ∞ Russian Americans. ∞ Social Life and Customs—Kansas.

987. Vogt, Esther. **Turkey Red**. Cook, 1975. Kindred Press, 1987. (0-919797-62-8) Pb $4.95. « Time: 1870s. Subject: ∞ Farm and Ranch Life. ∞ Frontier and Pioneer Life—Kansas. ∞ Religion.

988. Woodrell, Daniel. **Woe to Live On**. Holt, 1987. Tor, 1989. (0-8125-8979-3) Pb $3.50. « Time: 1860s. Subject: ∞ Frontier and Pioneer Life—Kansas. ∞ Soldiers.

# KENTUCKY

989. Arnow, Harriette Simpson. **Flowering of the Cumberland**. Macmillan, 1963. University Press of Kentucky, 1984. (0-8131-0147-6) Pb $13.00. « Time: 1780-1803. Subject: ∞ Frontier and Pioneer Life—Kentucky.

990. Cannon, Bettie Waddell. **A Bellsong for Sarah Raines**. Macmillan, 1987. (0-684-18839-2) $14.95. « Time: 1930s. Subject: ∞ Depression. ∞ Social Life and Customs—Kentucky.

991. Cochran, Louis. **Raccoon John Smith: A Novel Based on the Life of the Famous Pioneer Kentucky Preacher**. Duell, 1963. College Press, 1985. (0-89900-277-3) Text ed. Pb $10.95. « Time: 1801-1830s. Subject: ∞ Smith, John (1784-1868). ∞ Religion. ∞ Social Life and Customs—Kentucky.

992. Eckert, Allan W. **The Court Martial of Daniel Boone**. Little, Brown, 1973. Bantam, 1987. (0-553-26283-1) Pb $4.99. « Time: 1770s. Subject: ∞ Boone, Daniel. ∞ Frontier and Pioneer Life—Kentucky.

993. Fox, John, Jr. **Trail of the Lonesome Pine**. Scribner, 1908. University Press of Kentucky, 1984. (0-8131-0156-5) Pb $16.00. « Time: ca. 1900. Subject: ∞ Social Life and Customs—Kentucky.

994. Giles, Janice Holt. **Enduring Hills**. Westminster, 1950. University Press of Kentucky, 1988. (0-8131-1673-2) $28.00. (0-8131-0185-9) Pb $15.00. « Time: 1941-1950. Subject: ∞ Social Life and Customs—Kentucky.

995. Giles, Janice Holt. **Tara's Healing**. Westminster, 1951. University Press of Kentucky, 1995. (0-8131-1886-7) $28.00. (0-8131-0832-2) Pb $15.00. « Time: 1945-1950. Subject: ∞ Social Life and Customs—Kentucky.

996. Gordon, Caroline. **Green Centuries**. Scribner, 1941. Sanders, 1992. (1-879941-05-8) Pb $10.95. « Time: 1770s. Subject: ∞ Boone, Daniel. ∞ Frontier and Pioneer Life—Kentucky.

997. Harper, Karen. **Circle of Gold**. NAL-Dutton, 1992. (0-525-93453-7) $20.00. NAL-Dutton, 1993. (0-451-40381-9) Pb $5.99. « Time: Early 1800s. Subject: ∞ Frontier and Pioneer Life—Kentucky. ∞ Religion.

998. Mason, Bobbie Ann. **Feather Crowns: A Novel**. HarperCollins, 1993. (0-06-016780-7) $23.00. « Time: ca. 1900. Subject: ∞ Social Life and Customs—Kentucky.

999. Stuart, Jesse. **Hie to the Hunters**. Whittlesey, 1950. Jesse Stuart Foundation, 1988. (0-945084-06-4) $20.00. « Time: 1950s. Subject: ∞ Social Life and Customs—Kentucky.

1000. Stuart, Jesse. **Taps for Private Tussie**. Dutton, 1943. Repr. Jesse Stuart Foundation, 1992. (0-945084-24-2) $20.00. « Time: 1941-1945. Subject: ∞ Social Life and Customs—Kentucky.

1001. Warren, Robert Penn. **World Enough and Time**. Random House, 1950. J. S. Sanders, 1993. (1-879941-23-6) Pb $11.95. « Time: 1820s. Subject: ∞ Politics and Government. ∞ Social Life and Customs—Kentucky.

# *LOUISIANA*

1002. Gaines, Ernest J. **In My Father's House**. Knopf, 1978. Random House, 1992. (0-679-72791-4) Pb $10.00. « Time: ca. 1970. Subject: ∞ Racism. ∞ Social Life and Customs—Louisiana.

1003. Gaines, Ernest J. **A Lesson Before Dying**. Knopf, 1993. (0-679-41477-0) $21.00. « Time: 1948. Subject: ∞ Racism. ∞ Social Life and Customs—Louisiana.

1004. Ripley, Alexandra. **New Orleans Legacy**. Macmillan, 1987. Warner, 1988. (0-446-34210-6) Pb $5.99. « Time: ca. 1850s. Subject: ∞ Social Life and Customs—Louisiana.

## MAINE

1005. Siddons, Anne Rivers. **Colony**. HarperCollins, 1992. Several editions available. « Time: 1920s-1990. Subject: ∞ Social Life and Customs—Maine.

## MASSACHUSETTS

1006. Bromfield, Louis. **Early Autumn**. Stokes, 1926. Repr. Amereon, n.d. (0-88411-508-9) Lib Bdg $19.95. Pulitzer prize winner, 1927. « Time: Early 1900s. Subject: ∞ Social Life and Customs—Massachusetts.

1007. Fleischman, Paul. **Saturnalia**. HarperCollins, 1990. Several editions available. « Time: 1681. Subject: ∞ Apprentices. ∞ Indians of North America—Narragansett. ∞ Social Life and Customs—Massachusetts.

1008. Hawthorne, Nathaniel. **The House of Seven Gables**. Ticknor, 1851. Several editions available. « Time: 1850. Subject: ∞ Social Life and Customs—Massachusetts.

1009. Howells, William Dean. **The Rise of Silas Lapham**. Ticknor, 1885. Several editions available. « Time: Mid-1800s. Subject: ∞ Social Life and Customs—Massachusetts.

1010. Marquand, John. **The Late George Apley: A Novel in the Form of a Memoir**. Little, Brown, 1937. (0-685-03075-X) $18.95. « Time: Late 1800s. Subject: ∞ Social Life and Customs—Massachusetts.

1011. O'Connor, Edwin. **The Last Hurrah**. Little, Brown, 1956, 1985. (0-316-62659-7) Pb $9.95. « Time: Early 1900s. Subject: ∞ Irish Americans. ∞ Politics and Government. ∞ Social Life and Customs—Massachusetts.

1012. Seton, Anya. **The Winthrop Woman**. Houghton, 1958. Fawcett, 1986. (0-449-21006-5) Pb $4.50. « Time: 1660s. Subject: ∞ Frontier and Pioneer Life—Massachusetts. ∞ Winthrop, Elizabeth. ∞ Women—Biography. ∞ Women—Social Conditions—1492-1775.

## MICHIGAN

1013. Arnow, Harriette Simpson. **The Dollmaker**. Macmillan, 1954. Avon, 1976. (0-380-00947-1) Pb $5.95. « Time: 1941-1945. Subject: ∞ Kentucky. ∞ Social Life and Customs—Kentucky. ∞ Social Life and Customs—Michigan.

1014.   Boyle, T. C. **The Road to Wellville**. Viking, 1993. (0-670-84334-2) $22.50. « Time: 1907. Subject: ∞ Business and Finance. ∞ Kellogg, John H. ∞ Social Life and Customs—Michigan.

1015.   Catherwood, Mary Harwell. **Romance of Dollard**. Century, 1889. Repr. Ayer, n.d. (0-8369-7024-1) $18.00. « Time: ca. 1660. Subject: ∞ Frontier and Pioneer Life—Michigan. ∞ Indians of North America—Huron.

1016.   Curwood, James Oliver. **Courage of Captain Plum**. Bobbs, 1908. Repr. AMS Press, n.d. (0-404-01895-5) $18.00. « Time: Late 1850s. Subject: ∞ Religion.

1017.   Gringhuis, Dirk. **The Young Voyageur: Trade and Treachery at the Michilimackinac**. McGraw, 1955. Mackinac Island, 1969. (0-911872-34-5) Pb $6.00. « Time: 1760s. Subject: ∞ Frontier and Pioneer Life—Michigan. ∞ Fur Trappers and Trade. ∞ Indians of North America—Chippewa.

1018.   Harrison, Jim. **Farmer**. Viking, 1976. Doubleday, 1980. (0-385-28228-1) Pb $9.95. Delacorte, 1989. (0-440-55017-3) Pb $7.95. « Time: 1950s. Subject: ∞ Social Life and Customs—Michigan.

1019.   Hedrick, Ulysses P. **Land of the Crooked Tree**. Oxford, 1948. Wayne State University Press, 1986. (0-8143-1833-9) $24.95. (0-8143-1834-7) Pb $13.95. « Time: 1874. Subject: ∞ Frontier and Pioneer Life—Michigan. ∞ Indians of North America—Ottawa.

1020.   Hemming, Robert J. **Gales of November: Sinking of the *Edmund Fitzgerald***. Contemporary, 1984. (0-8092-5384-4) Pb $12.95. « Time: 1975. Subject: ∞ Ships and Shipping. ∞ Social Life and Customs—Michigan.

1021.   Hemming, Robert J. **Ships Gone Missing: The Great Lakes Storm of 1913**. Contemporary, 1992. (0-8092-3909-4) $19.95. (0-8092-3715-6) Pb $11.95. « Time: 1913. Subject: ∞ Ships and Shipping. ∞ Social Life and Customs—Michigan.

1022.   Kirkland, Caroline M. **Forest Life**. C. S. Francis, 1842. Repr. Irvington, n.d. (0-8398-1056-3) Lib Bdg $19.50. Irvington, 1987. (0-8290-2112-4) Text ed. Pb $6.95. « Time: Late 1830s. Subject: ∞ Frontier and Pioneer Life—Michigan.

1023.   Love, Edmund G. **A Small Bequest**. Doubleday, 1973. Wayne State University Press, 1987. (0-8143-1925-4) $28.50. (0-8143-1926-2) Pb $13.95. « Time: 1934. Subject: ∞ Social Life and Customs—Michigan.

1024.   Morris, Bill. **Motor City**. Knopf, 1992. Pocket Books, 1993. (0-671-86813-6) Pb $10.00. « Time: 1954. Subject: ∞ Laborers and Labor Unions. ∞ Social Life and Customs—Michigan.

# MINNESOTA

1025. Lund, Duane R. **White Indian Boy**. Adventure, 1981. (0-934860-17-3) $7.95. « Time: Early 1800s. Subject: ∞ Frontier and Pioneer Life—Minnesota. ∞ Indians of North America—Captivities. ∞ Tanner, John.

1026. Lund, Duane R. **Youngest Voyageur**. Adventure, 1985. (0-934860-41-6) $7.95. « Time: 1790s. Subject: ∞ Frontier and Pioneer Life—Minnesota. ∞ Fur Trappers and Trade.

1027. Moberg, Vilhelm. **The Emigrants**. Simon & Schuster, 1951. Repr. Buccaneer Books, 1994. (1-56849-312-6) Lib Bdg $29.95. « Time: 1850. Subject: ∞ Immigrants, Swedish. ∞ Social Life and Customs—Minnesota.

1028. Moberg, Vilhelm. **Unto a Good Land**. Simon & Schuster, 1954. Repr. Buccaneer Books, 1994. (1-56849-313-4) Lib Bdg $29.95. « Time: 1850. Subject: ∞ Immigrants, Swedish. ∞ Social Life and Customs—Minnesota.

1029. Spencer, LaVyrle. **November of the Heart**. Putnam, 1993. Several editions available. « Time: Late 1800s. ∞ Social Life and Customs—Minnesota.

# MISSISSIPPI

1030. Faulkner, William. **Intruder in the Dust**. Random House, 1948. Several editions available. « Time: 1940s. Subject: ∞ Racism. ∞ Social Life and Customs—Mississippi.

1031. Killens, John Oliver. **'Sippi**. Trident, 1967. Thunders Mouth, 1988. (0-938410-55-5) Pb $9.95. « Time: 1960s. Subject: ∞ African American. ∞ Civil Rights. ∞ Racism. ∞ Social Life and Customs—Mississippi.

1032. Nordan, Lewis. **Wolf Whistle: A Novel**. Algonquin, 1993. (1-56512-028-0) $16.95. « Time: 1955. Subject: ∞ African Americans. ∞ Racism. ∞ Social Life and Customs—Mississippi.

# MISSOURI

1033. Conroy, Jack. **The Disinherited: A Novel of the 1930s**. Covici, 1933. Repr. Bentley, 1979. (0-8376-0426-5) Lib Bdg $18.00. University of Missouri Press, 1991. (0-8262-0770-7) Text ed. Pb $15.95. « Time: 1920s-early 1930s. Subject: ∞ Laborers and Labor Unions. ∞ Social Life and Customs—Missouri.

1034. Wooldridge, Rhoda. **Hannah's Mill**. Independence Press, 1984. (0-8309-0386-0) Pb $8.00. Sequel to *Hannah's House*. « Time: Mid-nineteenth century. Subject: ∞ Frontier and Pioneer Life—Missouri.

# MONTANA

1035.   Doig, Ivan. **Dancing at the Rascal Fair**. Harper & Row, 1988. (0-06-097181-9) Pb $11.00. « Time: 1889-1920. Subject: ∞ Frontier and Pioneer Life—Montana.

1036.   Doig, Ivan. **English Creek**. Athenaeum, 1984. Peter Smith, 1992. (0-8446-6608-4) $19.50. Viking, 1985. (0-14-008442-8) Pb $9.00. « Time: 1939. Subject: ∞ Frontier and Pioneer Life—Montana.

1037.   Dorris, Michael. **A Yellow Raft in Blue Water**. Holt, 1987. (0-8050-0045-3) $16.95. Warner, 1993. (0-446-38787-8) Pb $9.99. « Time: 1960s. Subject: ∞ Indians of North America. ∞ Social Life and Customs—Montana. ∞ Women—Social Conditions—1946-1994.

1038.   James, Will. **Sand**. Scribner, 1929. Repr. Buccaneer Books, 1993. (1-56849-237-5) Lib Bdg $18.95. « Time: ca. 1900. Subject: ∞ Frontier and Pioneer Life—Montana.

1039.   Lasky, Kathryn. **The Bone Wars**. Morrow, 1988. (0-688-07433-2) $12.95. Puffin, 1989. (0-14-034168-4) Pb $5.99. « Time: 1870s. Subject: ∞ Frontier and Pioneer Life—Montana. ∞ Paleontology.

1040.   Watson, Larry. **Montana 1948**. Milkweed, 1993. (0-915943-13-1) $17.95. Sequel to *Justice*. « Time: 1948. Subject: ∞ Racism. ∞ Social Life and Customs—Montana.

# NEBRASKA

1041.   Aldrich, Bess Streeter. **Rim of the Prairie**. Appleton, 1926. Repr. Amereon, nd. (0-88411-259-4) Lib Bdg $23.95. University of Nebraska Press, 1966. (0-8032-5002-9) Pb $10.95. « Time: 1920s. Subject: ∞ Frontier and Pioneer Life—Nebraska.

1042.   Aldrich, Bess Streeter. **A White Bird Flying**. Appleton, 1931. Repr. Amereon, 1975. (0-88411-253-5) Lib Bdg $22.95. University of Nebraska Press, 1988. (0-8032-5915-8) Pb $7.50. Sequel to *A Lantern in Her Hand*. « Time: 1920s. Subject: ∞ Social Life and Customs—Nebraska.

1043.   Morris, Wright. **Ceremony in Lonetree**. Athenaeum, 1960. University of Nebraska Press, 1973. (0-8032-5782-1) Pb $9.95. « Time: Late nineteenth century-mid-twentieth century. Subject: ∞ Social Life and Customs—Nebraska.

1044.   Morris, Wright. **Plains Song**. Harper & Row, 1980. Godine, 1991. (0-87923-835-6) Pb $10.95. « Time: 1910s-1970s. Subject: ∞ Social Life and Customs—Nebraska. ∞ Women—Social Conditions—1900-1939.

1045.   Neihardt, John G. **When the Tree Flowered: The Story of Eagle Voice, a Sioux Indian**. Macmillan, 1951. University of Nebraska Press, 1991. (0-8032-8363-6) Pb $8.95. « Time: ca. 1860-1900. Subject: ∞ Eagle Voice. ∞ Frontier and Pioneer Life—Nebraska. ∞ Indians of North America—Sioux.

1046.   Thomas, Dorothy. **The Home Place**. Knopf, 1936. University of Nebraska Press, 1966. (0-8032-5197-1) Pb $4.50. « Time: 1930s. Subject: ∞ Depression. ∞ Social Life and Customs—Nebraska.

1047.   Thomas, Dorothy. **Ma Jeeter's Girls**. Knopf, 1933. University of Nebraska Press, 1986. (0-8032-9405-0) Pb $6.95. « Time: 1920s. Subject: ∞ Social Life and Customs—Nebraska.

# NEVADA

1048.   Bailey, Paul. **Ghost Dance Messiah: The Jack Wilson Story**. Westernlore, 1970. (0-87026-025-1) $24.95. « Time: 1980s. Subject: ∞ Indians of North America—Paiute. ∞ Social Life and Customs—Nevada.

1049.   Bergon, Frank. **Shoshone Mike**. Viking, 1987, 1989. (0-14-009876-3) Pb $7.95. « Time: 1911. Subject: ∞ Immigrants, Basque. ∞ Indians of North America—Shoshone. ∞ Social Life and Customs—Nevada.

1050.   Grey, Zane. **Boulder Dam**. HarperCollins, 1963, 1990. (0-06-100111-2) Pb $3.99. « Time: 1930s. Subject: ∞ Depression. ∞ Hoover Dam. ∞ Laborers and Labor Unions. ∞ Social Life and Customs—Nevada. ∞ Water Supply.

1051.   Laxalt, Robert. **The Basque Hotel**. University of Nevada Press, 1989, 1993. (0-87417-216-0) Pb $10.95. « Time: 1930s. Subject: ∞ Depression. ∞ Social Life and Customs—Nevada.

1052.   Maclean, Alistair. **Breakheart Pass**. Doubleday, 1974. G. K. Hall, 1990. (0-8161-4982-8) Pb $12.95. « Time: Late 1860s. Subject: ∞ Frontier and Pioneer Life—Nevada.

# NEW HAMPSHIRE

1053.   Shute, Henry A. **The Real Diary of a Real Boy**. R. R. Smith, 1967. Repr. Buccaneer Books, 1990. (0-89966-687-6) Lib Bdg $21.95. « Time: Late 1860s. Subject: ∞ Social Life and Customs—New Hampshire.

1054.   Stegner, Wallace. **Second Growth**. Houghton, 1947. University of Nebraska Press, 1985. (0-8032-4162-3) $25.00. (0-8032-9157-4) Pb $9.95. « Time: 1940s. Subject: ∞ Social Life and Customs—New Hampshire.

1055.   Williams, Thomas. **Town Burning**. Macmillan, 1959. Doubleday, 1988. (0-385-24250-6) Pb $8.95. « Time: 1950s. Subject: ∞ Social Life and Customs—New Hampshire.

1056. Williams, Thomas. **Whipple's Castle**. Random House, 1969. Doubleday, 1988. (0-385-24249-2) Pb $9.95. « Time: Late 1930s-early 1950s. Subject: ∞ Social Life and Customs—New Hampshire.

1057. Yates, Elizabeth. **Hue and Cry**. Coward-McCann, 1953. Bob Jones University Press, 1991. (0-89084-536-0) Pb $4.95. « Time: 1836-1837. Subject: ∞ Farm and Ranch Life. ∞ Social Life and Customs—New Hampshire.

# *NEW MEXICO*

1058. Anaya, Rudolfo A. **Bless Me, Ultima**. Quinto Sol, 1972. Several editions available. « Time: 1940s. Subject: ∞ Medicine. ∞ Social Life and Customs—New Mexico.

1059. Bohnaker, Joseph S. **Of Arms I Sing**. Sunstone Press, 1989. (0-86534-136-2) Pb $10.95. « Time: 1598. Subject: ∞ Frontier and Pioneer Life—New Mexico. ∞ Orate, Juan de.

1060. Bradford, Richard. **Red Sky at Morning**. Harper & Row, 1986. (0-06-091361-4) Pb $11.00. Repr. Borgo Press, 1991. (0-8095-9095-6) Lib Bdg $23.00. « Time: 1940. Subject: ∞ Social Life and Customs—New Mexico.

1061. Chavez, Fray Angelico. **The Lady from Toledo**. Academy Guild Press, 1960. Friends of the Palace Press, 1993. (0-941108-03-1) Pb $9.95. « Time: ca. 1680. Subject: ∞ Frontier and Pioneer Life—New Mexico. ∞ Politics and Government. ∞ Religion.

1062. Cleaveland, Agnes Morley. **No Life for a Lady**. Houghton, 1941. University of Nebraska Press, 1977. (0-8032-5868-2) Pb $9.95. « Time: 1880s-1890s. Subject: ∞ Frontier and Pioneer Life—New Mexico.

1063. Fergusson, Harvey. **Wolf Song**. Knopf, 1927. University of Nebraska Press, 1981. (0-8032-6855-6) Pb $8.95. « Time: Late 1880s. Subject: ∞ Frontier and Pioneer Life—New Mexico.

1064. Horgan, Paul. **Far from Cibola**. Farrar, 1936. Repr. Ayer, n.d. (0-8369-4083-0) $12.00. « Time: 1930s. Subject: ∞ Depression. ∞ Social Life and Customs—New Mexico.

1065. LaFarge, Oliver. **Laughing Boy**. Houghton, 1929. Several editions available. Pulitzer prize winner. « Time: ca. 1900. Subject: ∞ Frontier and Pioneer Life—New Mexico. ∞ Indians of North America—Navajo.

1066. McCulloch, Frank. **Eagle in the Sky**. Sunstone Press, 1975. (0-913270-74-1) Pb $4.95. « Time: 1830s. Subject: ∞ Frontier and Pioneer Life—New Mexico. ∞ Indians of North America—Pueblo Nation. ∞ Pérez, Albino. ∞ Politics and Government. ∞ Pueblo Revolt of 1837.

1067. Momaday, N. Scott. **House Made of Dawn**. Harper & Row, 1968, 1989. (0-06-091633-8) Pb $12.00. Pulitzer prize winner. « Time: 1940s-1950s. Subject: ∞ Indians of North America—Pueblo Nation. ∞ Social Life and Customs—New Mexico.

1068. Nichols, John. **The Milagro Beanfield War**. Holt, 1974, 1993. (0-8050-2805-6) Anniversary ed. $27.50. Ballantine, 1987. (0-345-34446-4) Pb $5.95. « Time: 1970s. Subject: ∞ Mexican Americans. ∞ Racism. ∞ Social Life and Customs—New Mexico. ∞ Water Supply.

1069. O'Meara, Walter. **The Spanish Bride**. Putnam, 1954. Friends of the Palace Press, 1990. (0-941108-02-3) Pb $12.95. « Time: Early 1700s. Subject: ∞ Religion. ∞ Social Life and Customs—New Mexico.

1070. Richter, Conrad. **The Sea of Grass**. Grosset, 1936. Knopf, 1937. (0-394-44397-7) $13.95. Ohio University Press, 1992. (0-8214-1026-1) Pb $9.95. « Time: 1885-1910. Subject: ∞ Frontier and Pioneer Life—New Mexico.

1071. Savage, Les, Jr. **The Royal City**. Hanover House, 1956. Museum of New Mexico Press, 1989. (0-685-45629-3) Pb $9.95. Friends of the Palace Press, 1988. (0-941108-01-5) Pb $0.40. « Time: 1680. Subject: ∞ Indians of North America—Pueblo Nation. ∞ Politics and Government. ∞ Social Life and Customs—New Mexico.

1072. Sinclair, John L. **In Time of Harvest**. Macmillan, 1943. Several editions available. « Time: 1919-1930. Subject: ∞ Social Life and Customs—New Mexico.

1073. Stevenson, Paul R. **Cross a Wide River**. Sunstone Press, 1989. (0-86534-117-6) Pb $13.95. « Time: 1850s-Early 1900s. Subject: ∞ Slaves and Slavery. ∞ Social Life and Customs—New Mexico.

1074. Swisher, Robert K. **The Land**. Sunstone Press, 1987. (0-86534-095-1) Pb $12.95. « Time: 1500s–mid-1900s. Subject: ∞ Politics and Government. ∞ Social Life and Customs—New Mexico.

1075. Waters, Frank. **The Man Who Killed the Deer**. Swallow, 1942. (0-8040-0194-4) Pb $8.95. Pocket Books, 1984. (0-671-55502-2) Pb $4.99. « Time: Early 1900s. Subject: ∞ Indians of North America—Pueblo Nation. ∞ Social Life and Customs—New Mexico.

1076. Waters, Frank. **People of the Valley**. Farrar, 1941. Swallow, 1941. (0-8040-0243-6) Pb $8.95. « Time: Early 1900s. Subject: ∞ Indians of North America—Pueblo Nation. ∞ Social Life and Customs—New Mexico. ∞ Water Supply.

1077. Waters, Frank. **Woman at Otowi Crossing**. Swallow, 1966, 1987. (0-8040-0893-0) Pb $9.95. « Time: 1940s. Subject: ∞ Military History—1939-1945. ∞ Social Life and Customs—New Mexico.

1078. Zollinger, Norman. **Riders to Cibola**. Museum of New Mexico Press, 1977. Bantam, 1989. (0-553-27759-6) Pb $3.95. « Time: 1930s-1940s. Subject: ∞ Mexican Americans. ∞ Racism. ∞ Social Life and Customs—New Mexico.

# *NEW YORK*

1079. Abu-Jaber, Diana. **Arabian Jazz**. Harcourt Brace, 1993. (0-15-107862-9) $21.95. « Time: ca. 1990. Subject: ∞ Arab Americans. ∞ Racism. ∞ Social Life and Customs—New York.

1080. Asch, Sholem. **East River**. Putnam, 1946. Carroll & Graf, 1986. (0-88184-280-X) Pb $4.50. « Time: Early 1900s. Subject: ∞ Jewish Americans. ∞ Social Life and Customs—New York.

1081. Carr, Caleb. **The Alienist**. Random House, 1994. (0-679-41779-6) $22.00. « Time: 1896. Subject: ∞ Morgan, John Pierpont, Sr. ∞ Roosevelt, Theodore. ∞ Social Life and Customs—New York.

1082. Courter, Gay. **The Midwife**. Houghton Mifflin, 1981. NAL-Dutton, 1985. (0-451-15623-4) Pb $5.99. « Time: 1904-1910. Subject: ∞ Immigrants. ∞ Jewish Americans. ∞ Medicine. ∞ Social Life and Customs—New York.

1083. Doctorow, E. L. **Billy Bathgate**. Random House, 1989. Several editions available. « Time: 1930s. Subject: ∞ Crime and Criminals. ∞ Depression. ∞ Schultz, Dutch. ∞ Social Life and Customs—New York.

1084. Doctorow, E. L. **The Waterworks**. Random House, 1994. (0-394-58754-5) $23.00. « Time: 1870s. Subject: ∞ Social Life and Customs—New York.

1085. Kennedy, William P. **Ironweed**. Viking, 1983, 1984. (0-14-007020-6) Pb $7.95. 1988. (0-14-008103-8) Pb $4.50. « Time: 1920s-1930s. Subject: ∞ Depression. ∞ Social Life and Customs—New York.

1086. Potok, Chaim. **The Chosen**. Simon & Schuster, 1967. Several editions available. « Time: Late 1940s-1950s. Subject: ∞ Jewish Americans. ∞ Social Life and Customs—New York.

1087. Potok, Chaim. **In the Beginning**. Knopf, 1975. Fawcett, 1986. (0-449-20911-3) Pb $5.95. « Time: 1930s-1940s. Subject: ∞ Jewish Americans. ∞ Social Life and Customs—New York.

1088. Schulberg, Budd. **Waterfront: A Novel**. Random House, 1955. Repr. Bentley, 1979. (0-8376-0434-6) Lib Bdg $20.00. Fine, n.d. (1-55611-028-6) Pb $8.95. « Time: ca. 1950. Subject: ∞ Laborers and Labor Unions. ∞ Social Life and Customs—New York.

1089. Wouk, Herman. **City Boy: The Adventures of Herbie Bookbinder**. Simon, 1948. Little, Brown, 1992. (0-316-95511-6) Pb $14.95. « Time: 1920s. Subject: ∞ Social Life and Customs—New York.

# NORTH CAROLINA

1090. Gurganus, Allan. **The Oldest Living Confederate Widow Tells All**. Knopf, 1989. (0-394-54537-0) $21.95. Ivy Books, 1992. (0-8041-0643-6) Pb $6.99. « Time: ca. 1860-1970. Subject: ∞ Social Life and Customs—North Carolina. ∞ Soldiers.

# NORTH DAKOTA

1091. Davis, Kathryn. **The Dakotas: At the Wind's Edge**. Pinnacle, 1983. Windsor Publishing Corp., 1990. (1-55817-330-7) Pb $3.95. « Time: Late 1800s. Subject: ∞ Frontier and Pioneer Life—North Dakota.

1092. Davis, Kathryn. **The Dakotas: The Endless Sky**. Pinnacle, 1984. Windsor Publishing Corp., 1990. (1-55817-352-8) Pb $3.95. « Time: Late 1800s. Subject: ∞ Frontier and Pioneer Life—North Dakota.

1093. Erdrich, Louise. **The Beet Queen**. Holt, 1986. Several editions available. « Time: 1930-1940s. Subject: ∞ Social Life and Customs—North Dakota.

1094. Erdrich, Louise. **Bingo Palace**. HarperCollins, 1994. (0-06-017080-8) $23.00. Wheeler, 1994. (1-56895-073-X) $25.95. « Time: 1980s. Subject: ∞ Indians of North America—Chippewa. ∞ Social Life and Customs—North Dakota.

1095. Spencer, LaVyrle. **Years**. Jove, 1986. Several editions available. « Time: 1917. Subject: ∞ Social Life and Customs—North Dakota.

1096. Woiwode, Larry. **Beyond the Bedroom Wall: A Family Album**. Farrar, 1975. Viking, 1989 (0-15-012186-2) Pb $8.95. « Time: 1930s-1970s. Subject: ∞ Social Life and Customs—North Dakota.

# OHIO

1097. Bromfield, Louis. **Green Bay Tree**. Stokes, 1924. Amereon, n.d. (0-8488-0689-1) $17.95. Repr. Reprint Service, 1993. (0-7812-5343-8) Lib Bdg $89.00. « Time: Early 1900s-1915. Subject: ∞ Social Life and Customs—Ohio.

1098. Havighurst, Walter. **Quiet Shore**. Macmillan, 1937. Repr. Reprint Service, 1993. (0-7812-5372-1) Lib Bdg $89.00. « Time: 1860s-1930s. Subject: ∞ Depression. ∞ Social Life and Customs—Ohio.

1099. McKenney, Ruth. **Industrial Valley**. Harcourt, 1939. ILR Press, 1992. (0-87546-183-2) Pb $16.95. Repr. Reprint Service, 1993. (0-7812-5389-6) Lib Bdg $89.00. « Time: 1932-1936. Subject: ∞ Laborers and Labor Unions. ∞ Social Life and Customs—Ohio.

1100. Sanders, Scott R. **Bad Man Ballad**. Bradbury, 1986. (0-02-778230-1) $13.95. « Time: 1812. Subject: ∞ Frontier and Pioneer Life—Ohio. ∞ Racism.

# OKLAHOMA

1101. Sample, Zola. **Cherokee Strip Fever**. Metro Press, 1976. Evans, 1984. (0-934188-13-0) $14.95. « Time: 1893. Subject: ∞ Frontier and Pioneer Life—Oklahoma.

# OREGON

1102. Haig-Brown, Roderick. **Timber: A Novel of Pacific Northwest Loggers**. Morrow, 1942. Oregon State University Press, 1993. (0-87071-514-3) Text ed. $27.95. (0-78071-515-1) Pb $15.95. « Time: ca. 1940. Subject: ∞ Lumber and Lumbering. ∞ Social Life and Customs—Oregon.

1103. Jones, Nard. **Oregon Detour**. Brewer, 1930. Oregon State University Press, 1990. (0-87071-500-3) Text ed. $24.95. (0-87071-501-1) Pb $13.95. « Time: Early twentieth century. Subject: ∞ Social Life and Customs—Oregon.

# PENNSYLVANIA

1104. Caldwell, Janet Taylor. **Balance Wheel**. Scribner, 1951. Repr. Amereon, 1974. (0-88411-153-9) Lib Bdg $28.95. « Time: 1913-1939. Subject: ∞ Immigrants, German.

1105. Collier, James Lincoln. **The Bloody Country**. Four Winds, 1976. Scholastic, 1985. (0-590-43126-9) Pb $3.25. « Time: Late 1700s. Subject: ∞ Frontier and Pioneer Life—Pennsylvania. ∞ Indians of North America—Paugussett.

1106. Turnbull, Agnes. **Remember the End**. Macmillan, 1938. Repr. Reprint Service, 1993. (0-7812-5846-4) Lib Bdg $89.00. « Time: 1890-1915. Subject: ∞ Business and Finance. ∞ Miners and Mining. ∞ Social Life and Customs—Pennsylvania.

1107. Turnbull, Agnes. **The Richlands**. Houghton, 1974. Amereon, n.d. (0-89190-477-8) $20.95. « Time: ca. 1900. Subject: ∞ Social Life and Customs—Pennsylvania.

1108. Turnbull, Agnes. **Rolling Years**. Macmillan, 1936. Repr. Reprint Service, 1993. (0-7812-5845-6) Lib Bdg $89.00. « Time: 1870-1910. Subject: ∞ Social Life and Customs—Pennsylvania.

1109.   Wells, Lawrence. **Let the Band Play Dixie**. Doubleday, 1987. Repr. Yokna-patowpha, 1989. (0-916242-61-7) $17.95. « Time: 1898. Subject: ∞ Du Bois, W. E. B. ∞ Football. ∞ Heisman, John. ∞ Longstreet, James. ∞ Sickles, Daniel Edgar. ∞ Social Life and Customs—Pennsylvania. ∞ Stagg, Alonzo.

## SOUTH CAROLINA

1110.   Conroy, Pat. **The Lords of Discipline**. Houghton Mifflin, 1980. Old New York Book Shop, 1980. (0-937036-01-3) $25.00. Bantam, 1986. (0-553-27136-9) Pb $5.99. « Time: Late 1960s. Subject: ∞ Racism. ∞ Social Life and Customs—South Carolina. ∞ Soldiers.

1111.   Rhyne, Nancy. **Alice Flagg: The Ghost of the Hermitage**. Pelican, 1990. (0-88289-760-8) $19.95. « Time: 1800s. Subject: ∞ Flagg, Alice Berlin. ∞ Social Life and Customs—South Carolina. ∞ Women—Biography.

## SOUTH DAKOTA

1112.   Adams, Harold. **The Man Who Was Taller Than God**. Walker, 1992. (0-8027-1239-8) $18.95. « Time: 1930s. Subject: ∞ Depression. ∞ Social Life and Customs—South Dakota.

1113.   Benchley, Nathaniel. **Only Earth and Sky Last Forever**. Harper & Row, 1974. (0-06-440049-2) Pb $4.95. Peter Smith, 1992. (0-8446-6583-5) $17.25. « Time: 1874-1876. Subject: ∞ Crazy Horse. ∞ Frontier and Pioneer Life—South Dakota. ∞ Indians of North America—Sioux.

1114.   Deloria, Ella Cara. **Waterlily**. University of Nebraska Press, 1988. (0-8032-6579-4) Pb $9.95. (0-8032-4739-7) $27.50. « Time: Nineteenth century. Subject: ∞ Frontier and Pioneer Life—South Dakota. ∞ Indians of North America—Sioux.

1115.   Dexter, Pete. **Deadwood**. Random House, 1986. Several editions available. « Time: 1876. Subject: ∞ Burk, Martha Jane Cannary. ∞ Frontier and Pioneer Life—South Dakota. ∞ Hickok, James Butler.

1116.   Jones, Thelma. **Skinny Angel**. McGraw-Hill, 1946. Ross, n.d. (0-87018-035-5) $6.95. « Time: Early 1900s. Subject: ∞ Social Life and Customs—South Dakota.

1117.   Manfred, Frederick F. **The Golden Bowl**. Grosset & Dunlap, 1944. South Dakota Humanities Foundation, 1992. (0-9632157-0-1) Pb $9.95. « Time: 1930s. Subject: ∞ Depression. ∞ Social Life and Customs—South Dakota.

1118.   Manfred, Frederick F. **King of Spades**. Trident, 1966. University of Nebraska Press, 1983. (0-8032-8121-8) Pb $7.95. « Time: 1786. Subject: ∞ Frontier and Pioneer Life—South Dakota.

1119. Manfred, Frederick F. **Scarlet Plume**. Trident, 1964. University of Nebraska Press, 1983. (0-8032-8120-X) Pb $12.95. « Time: 1862. Subject: ∞ Frontier and Pioneer Life—South Dakota. ∞ Indians of North America—Sioux.

1120. Micheaux, Oscar. **Conquest: The Story of a Negro Pioneer, by the Pioneer**. Woodruff, 1913. Several editions available. « Time: ca. 1900. Subject: ∞ African Americans. ∞ Frontier and Pioneer Life—South Dakota.

1121. Micheaux, Oscar. **The Homesteader**. McGrath, 1917. University of Nebraska Press, (0-8032-8208-7) Pb $12.95. « Time: ca. 1910. Subject: ∞ African Americans. ∞ Frontier and Pioneer Life—South Dakota.

1122. Micheaux, Oscar. **The Wind from Nowhere**. Book Supply, 1941. Repr. Ayer, n.d. (0-8369-9109-5) $20.00. « Time: ca. 1910. Subject: ∞ African Americans. ∞ Frontier and Pioneer Life—South Dakota.

1123. Neihardt, John G. **Life's Lure**. Kennerley, 1914. University of Nebraska Press, 1991. (0-8032-3333-7) $45.00. « Time: 1880s. Subject: ∞ Frontier and Pioneer Life—South Dakota. ∞ Miners and Mining.

1124. O'Brien, Dan. **In the Center of the Nation**. Atlantic Monthly Press, 1991. Avon, 1992. (0-380-71702-6) Pb $10.00 « Time: 1970s. Subject: ∞ Farm and Ranch Life. ∞ Frontier and Pioneer Life—South Dakota.

1125. Smith, Stewart E. White. **The Claim Jumpers**. McClure, 1901. Amereon, n.d. (0-88411-828-2) Lib Bdg $20.95. « Time: Late 1800s. Subject: ∞ Frontier and Pioneer Life—South Dakota. ∞ Miners and Mining.

1126. Spencer, LaVyrle. **Forgiving**. Putnam, 1991. Several editions available. « Time: 1876. Subject: ∞ Frontier and Pioneer Life—South Dakota. ∞ Women—Social Conditions—1866-1899.

# *TENNESSEE*

1127. Alther, Lisa. **Original Sins**. Knopf, 1981. NAL-Dutton, 1982. (0-451-15517-3) Pb $5.99. 1985. (0-451-13966-6) Pb $4.95. « Time: 1960s-1970s. Subject: ∞ Civil Rights. ∞ Social Life and Customs—Tennessee.

1128. Miller, Jim Wayne. **Newfound: A Richard Jackson Book**. Orchard Books, 1989. (0-531-05845-X) $14.95. (0-531-08445-0) Lib Bdg Pb $14.99. « Time: ca. 1970. Subject: ∞ Social Life and Customs—Tennessee.

1129. Taylor, Peter. **Summons to Memphis**. Knopf, 1986. (0-394-41062-9) $15.95. Ballantine, 1987. (0-345-34660-2) Pb $4.95. « Time: 1930s. Subject: ∞ Depression. ∞ Social Life and Customs—Tennessee.

## *TEXAS*

1130.   Bunkley, Anita Richmond. **Black Gold**. NAL-Dutton, 1994. (0-525-93752-8) $21.95. Repr. G. K. Hall, 1994. (0-8161-7434-2) Large text ed. Lib Bdg $22.95. « Time: 1920s. Subject: ∞ African Americans. ∞ Oil Workers and Oil Industry. ∞ Social Life and Customs—Texas.

1131.   Davis, James F. **The Road to San Jacinto**. Bobbs, 1936. Repr. Reprint Service, 1993. (0-7812-5964-9) Lib Bdg $75.00. « Time: 1840s. Subject: ∞ Frontier and Pioneer Life—Texas. ∞ Houston, Sam.

1132.   Ferber, Edna. **Giant**. Doubleday, 1952. Several editions available. « Time: ca. 1950. Subject: ∞ Social Life and Customs—Texas.

1133.   Flynn, Robert. **North to Yesterday**. Knopf, 1967. Texas Christian University Press, 1985. (0-87565-014-7) $16.95. (0-87565-015-5) Pb $9.95. « Time: ca. 1890. Subject: ∞ Cowhands. ∞ Farm and Ranch Life. ∞ Frontier and Pioneer Life—Texas.

1134.   Humphrey, William. **The Ordways**. Knopf, 1965. Delacorte, 1989. (0-385-29734-3) Pb $9.95. Dell, 1989. (0-440-55046-7) Pb $9.95. « Time: Late nineteenth century. Subject: ∞ Social Life and Customs—Texas.

1135.   Jenkins, Dan. **Fast Copy**. Simon & Schuster, 1988. St. Martin's Press, 1989. (0-312-91767-8) Pb $5.95. « Time: 1930s. Subject: ∞ Business and Finance. ∞ Crime and Criminals. ∞ Depression. ∞ Social Life and Customs—Texas.

1136.   Lo, Steven C. **The Incorporation of Eric Chung**. Algonquin, 1989. (0-945575-18-1) $14.95. « Time: 1980s. Subject: ∞ Business and Finance. ∞ Chinese Americans. ∞ Immigrants, Chinese. ∞ Social Life and Customs—Texas.

1137.   McMurtry, Larry. **Texasville**. Simon & Schuster, 1987. Pocket Books, 1990. (0-671-73517-9) Pb $6.50. « Time: 1980s. Subject: ∞ Oil Workers and Oil Industry. ∞ Social Life and Customs—Texas.

1138.   Owens, William A. **Look to the River**. Athenaeum, 1963. Texas Christian University Press, 1988. (0-87565-026-0) Pb $11.95. « Time: 1910. Subject: ∞ Frontier and Pioneer Life—Texas.

1139.   Randle, Kevin J. **Spanish Gold**. Evans, 1990. (0-87131-615-3) $15.95. « Time: 1863. Subject: ∞ Frontier and Pioneer Life—Texas. ∞ Indians of North America—Apache.

1140.   Robson, Lucia St. Clair. **Walk in My Soul**. Ballantine, 1985. (0-345-30789-5) Pb $8.95. 1987. (0-345-34701-3) Pb $5.95. « Time: 1840s. Subject: ∞ Frontier and Pioneer Life—Texas. ∞ Houston, Sam.

1141.   Smith, C. W. **Thin Men of Haddam**. Grossman, 1974. Texas Christian University Press, 1990. (0-87565-078-3) Pb $15.95. « Time: 1970s. Subject: ∞ Mexican Americans. ∞ Racism. ∞ Social Life and Customs—Texas.

1142.   Woolley, Bryan. **Time and Place**. Dutton, 1977. Texas Christian University Press, 1985. (0-912646-98-5) $16.95 (0-912646-99-3) Pb $9.95. « Time: Early 1950s. Subject: ∞ Racism. ∞ Social Life and Customs—Texas.

## UTAH

1143.   Underwood, Phillip. **Ben Cooper, U.S. Marshal**. Walker, 1990. (0-8027-4109-6) $17.95. Repr. Thorndike, 1991. (1-56054-141-5) Large type ed. Lib Bdg $15.95. « Time: Late 1800s. Subject: ∞ Crime and Criminals. ∞ Frontier and Pioneer Life—Utah.

## VERMONT

1144.   Huntington, Lee Pennock. **Brothers in Arms**. Countryman Press, 1976, 1991. (0-88150-214-6) Pb $8.00. « Time: 1776-1783. Subject: ∞ American Loyalists. ∞ Soldiers.

1145.   Jackson, Edgar N. **Green Mountain Hero**. Lantern, 1961. New England Press, 1988. (0-933050-61-5) Pb $9.95. « Time: 1776-1783. Subject: ∞ Soldiers. ∞ Story, Ann. ∞ Story, Solomon.

1146.   Speare, Elizabeth. **Calico Captive**. Houghton, 1957. (0-395-07112-7) $13.45. Dell, 1973. (0-440-41156-4) Pb $3.99. « Time: 1750s. Subject: ∞ Frontier and Pioneer Life—Vermont.

## VIRGINIA

1147.   Adams, Richard. **Traveller**. Knopf, 1988. Dell, 1989. (0-440-20493-3) Pb $4.95. « Time: 1860s. Subject: ∞ Lee, Robert E. ∞ Social Life and Customs—Virginia. ∞ Soldiers.

1148.   Shreve, Susan Richards. **A Country of Strangers**. Simon & Schuster, 1989. Doubleday, 1990. (0-385-26775-4) Pb $9.95. « Time: 1940s. Subject: ∞ African Americans. ∞ Racism. ∞ Social Life and Customs—Virginia.

1149.   Smith, Lee. **Fair and Tender Ladies**. Putnam, 1988. Ballantine, 1989. (0-345-36208-X) Pb $4.95. 1993. (0-345-38399-0) Pb $10.00. « Time: 1900-1930s. Subject: ∞ Social Life and Customs—Virginia.

# WASHINGTON

1150.  Balch, Frederick H. **Bridge of the Gods**. Binford & Mort, 1890, 1985. (0-8323-0433-6) Pb $10.95. « Time: 1600s. Subject: ∞ Indians of North America—Willamette Valley.

1151.  Craven, Margaret. **Walk Gently This Good Earth**. Putnam, 1971. Dell, 1981. (0-440-39484-8) Pb $2.25. « Time: 1930s. Subject: ∞ Depression. ∞ Social Life and Customs—Washington.

1152.  Dillard, Annie. **The Living**. HarperCollins, 1992. Several editions available. « Time: ca. 1865-1899. Subject: ∞ Frontier and Pioneer Life—Washington. ∞ Social Life and Customs—Washington.

1153.  Wilbee, Brenda. **Sweetbriar**. Harvest House, 1983. (0-89081-336-1) Pb $6.99. « Time: 1851. Subject: ∞ Frontier and Pioneer Life—Washington.

1154.  Wilbee, Brenda. **Sweetbriar Bride**. Harvest House, 1986. (0-89081-482-1) Pb $6.99. « Time: 1850s. Subject: ∞ Frontier and Pioneer Life—Washington.

1155.  Wilbee, Brenda. **Sweetbriar Spring**. Harvest House, 1989. (0-89081-661-1) Pb $6.99. « Time: Late 1800s. Subject: ∞ Frontier and Pioneer Life—Washington.

1156.  Wood, Elizabeth L. **Many Horses**. Binford & Mort, 1953. (0-8323-0175-2) $7.95. « Time: Late 1800s. Subject: ∞ Frontier and Pioneer Life—Washington.

# WEST VIRGINIA

1157.  Grubb, Davis. **The Barefoot Man**. Simon & Schuster, 1971. Zebra, 1992. (0-8217-3653-1) Pb $9.00. « Time: 1930s. Subject: ∞ Depression. ∞ Laborers and Labor Unions. ∞ Social Life and Customs—West Virginia.

1158.  Phillips, Jayne Anne. **Machine Dreams**. Dutton, 1984. Pocket Books, 1992. (0-671-74235-3) Pb $10.00. « Time: 1930s-1960s. Subject: ∞ Social Life and Customs—West Virginia.

1159.  Settle, Mary Lee. **Killing Ground**. Farrar, 1982. (0-374-18109-8) Limited ed. $60.00. Macmillan, 1988. (0-684-18849-X) Pb $9.95. Fifth in the Beulah Quintet series. « Time: 1980. Subject: ∞ Social Life and Customs—West Virginia.

# WISCONSIN

1160.  Dopp, Peggy. **Tomorrow Is a River**. Phunn, 1977. (0-931762-00-6) $14.95. (0-931762-01-4) Pb $9.95. « Time: Early 1800s-1871. Subject: ∞ Frontier and Pioneer Life—Wisconsin.

1161. Ferber, Edna. **Come and Get It**. Doubleday, 1935. Prairie Oak Press, 1991. (1-879483-05-X) Pb $14.95. « Time: ca. 1880s-1920s. Subject: ∞ Frontier and Pioneer Life—Wisconsin. ∞ Lumber and Lumbering.

1162. Logan, Ben. **The Empty Meadow**. Stanton & Lee, 1983. Prairie Oak Press, 1991. (1-879483-03-3) Pb $12.95. « Time: 1930s. Subject: ∞ Depression. ∞ Social Life and Customs—Wisconsin.

1163. Logan, Ben. **The Land Remembers: The Story of a Farm and Its People**. Holt, 1975. NorthWord, 1975. (1-55971-014-4) Pb $11.95. 1992. (1-55971-184-1) Collector's ed. $29.95. « Time: 1920s-1930s. Subject: ∞ Depression. ∞ Farm and Ranch Life. ∞ Social Life and Customs—Wisconsin.

1164. Seno, William J. **Enemies: A Saga of the Great Lakes Wilderness**. Prairie Oak Press, 1993. (1-879483-10-6) Pb $12.95. « Time: Eighteenth century. Subject: ∞ Frontier and Pioneer Life—Wisconsin. ∞ Fur Trappers and Trade.

1165. Vukelich, George. **Fisherman's Beach**. St. Martin's Press, 1962. North Country Press, 1990. (0-944133-08-8) Pb $9.95. « Time: 1950s. Subject: ∞ Fishing and Fisheries. ∞ Social Life and Customs—Wisconsin.

# WYOMING

1166. Henry, Will. **I, Tom Horn**. Lippincott, 1975. Bantam, 1992. (0-553-29835-6) Pb $4.99. « Time: 1880s. Subject: ∞ Crime and Criminals. ∞ Frontier and Pioneer Life—Wyoming. ∞ Horn, Tom.

1167. L'Amour, Louis. **Bendigo Shafter**. Dutton, 1979. Bantam, 1983. (0-553-26446-X) Pb $5.50. « Time: Late 1860s. Subject: ∞ Frontier and Pioneer Life—Wyoming.

1168. Manfred, Frederick F. **Riders of Judgment**. Random House, 1957. University of Nebraska Press, 1982. (0-8032-8117-X) Pb $6.95. « Time: 1890s. Subject: ∞ Frontier and Pioneer Life—Wyoming.

# AUTHOR INDEX

Numbers refer to entry numbers not page numbers. For the reader's convenience entry number and dates correspond to the following order. Entries 1-61: 1492-1775, Entries 62-122: 1776-1783, Entries 123-304: 1783-1860, Entries 305-380: 1861-1899, Entries 381-533: 1866-1899, Entries 534-688: 1900-1939, Entries 689-759: 1939-1945, Entries 760-855: 1945-1995, Entries 856-916: Epic Novels, Entries 917-1168: Additional Titles.

Abbey, Edward
  *Fire on the Mountain*, 760
Abe, Keith S.
  *Hawaii Aloha*, 958
Abu-Jaber, Diana
  *Arabian Jazz*, 1079
Adams, Alice
  *Southern Exposure, A*, 634
Adams, Andy
  *Log of a Cowboy*, 432
Adams, Harold
  *Man Who Was Taller Than God, The*, 1112
Adams, Henry
  *Democracy*, 381
Adams, Richard
  *Traveller*, 1147
Adams, Samuel Hopkins
  *Canal Town*, 136
  *Revelry*, 594
  *Tenderloin*, 382
Adicks, Richard
  *Court for Owls, A*, 305
Agee, Jonis
  *Strange Angels*, 803
Aldrich, Bess Streeter
  *Lantern in Her Hand, A*, 231
  *Lieutenant's Lady*, 433
  *Miss Bishop*, 977
  *Rim of the Prairie*, 1041
  *Song of Years, A*, 208
  *Spring Came On Forever*, 856
  *White Bird Flying, A*, 1042

Alexander, Lawrence
  *Speak Softly*, 383
Algren, Nelson
  *Walk on the Wild Side, A*, 635
Allis, Marguerite
  *Not Without Peril*, 137
Alter, Judy
  *Jessie*, 123
Alther, Lisa
  *Original Sins*, 1127
Altsheler, J. A.
  *Border Watch*, 109
  *Eyes of the Woods*, 110
  *Forest Runners*, 111
  *Free Rangers*, 112
  *Guns of Bull Run*, 306
  *Guns of Shiloh*, 307
  *Keepers of the Trail*, 113
  *Riflemen of the Ohio*, 114
  *Rock of Chickamauga*, 308
  *Scouts of Stonewall*, 309
  *Scouts of the Valley*, 115
  *Shades of the Wilderness*, 310
  *Star of Gettysburg*, 311
  *Sword of Antietam*, 312
  *Texan Scouts*, 232
  *Texan Star*, 233
  *Texan Triumph*, 234
  *Tree of Appomattox*, 313
  *Young Trailers*, 116
Amos, James
  *Memorial, The*, 804
Anania, Michael
  *Red Menace*, 761

Anaya, Rudolfo A.
  *Bless Me, Ultima*, 1058
Anderson, Edward
  *Hungry Men*, 636
Andrews, Mary Raymond Shipman
  *Perfect Tribute*, 314
Appel, Allen
  *Till the End of Time*, 689
Armstrong, Jennifer
  *Ann of the Wild Rose Inn*, 62
  *Steal Away*, 138
Arnold, Elliott
  *Blood Brother*, 235
  *Commandos, The*, 714
  *Time of the Gringo*, 236
Arnow, Harriette Simpson
  *Dollmaker, The*, 1013
  *Flowering of the Cumberland*, 989
Asch, Nathan
  *Pay Day*, 595
Asch, Sholem
  *East River*, 1080
Atherton, Gertrude
  *Conqueror, The*, 139
Atherton, Sarah
  *Mark's Own*, 857

Bacheller, Irving
  *Eben Holden*, 140
Bailey, Anthony
  *Major André*, 63
Bailey, Paul
  *Ghost Dance Messiah*, 1048
Bakst, Harold
  *Prairie Widow*, 434
Balch, Frederick H.
  *Bridge of the Gods*, 1150
Baldwin, James
  *Go Tell It on the Mountain*, 637
Barreiro, Jose
  *Indian Chronicles, The*, 1
Barry, Lynda
  *Good Times Are Killing Me, The*, 805
Barth, John
  *Sot Weed Factor, The*, 11

Bass, Cynthia
  *Sherman's March*, 315
Beach, Edward
  *Dust on the Sea*, 734
  *Run Silent, Run Deep*, 735
Beach, Rex Ellingwood
  *Barrier*, 435
  *Silver Horde*, 918
  *Spoilers*, 436
Becnel, Rexanne
  *When Lightning Strikes*, 237
Beebe, Elswyth Thane (*See* Thane, Elswyth
  Beebe)
Bell, Thomas
  *Out of This Furnace*, 858
Benchley, Nathaniel
  *Only Earth and Sky Last Forever*, 1113
Benet, Stephen Vincent
  *Spanish Bayonet*, 64
Berger, Thomas
  *Little Big Man*, 437
Bergon, Frank
  *Shoshone Mike*, 1049
Bernhard, Virginia
  *Durable Fire, A*, 12
Berry, Don
  *Moontrap*, 290
  *To Build a Ship*, 291
  *Trask*, 292
Bigsby, Christopher
  *Hester*, 13
Binns, Archie
  *Land Is Bright, The*, 238
  *Mighty Mountain*, 293
Bisno, Beatrice
  *Tomorrow's Bread*, 384
Bissell, Richard Pike
  *High Water*, 762
  *Stretch on the River, A*, 763
Bittner, Rosanne
  *Thunder on the Plains*, 239
Bjorn, Thyra Ferre
  *Papa's Wife*, 385
Blake, James Carlos
  *Pistoleer, The*, 438

Blake, Michael
*Dances with Wolves*, 439
Blakely, Mike
*Shortgrass Song*, 859
Blevins, Win
*Stone Song*, 440
Bohnaker, Joseph S.
*Of Arms I Sing*, 1059
Bojer, Johan
*Emigrants, The*, 441
Bonner, Cindy
*Lily*, 442
*Looking After Lily*, 443
Bontemps, Arna
*Black Thunder*, 141
Borden, G. F.
*Seven Six One*, 715
Borland, Hal
*When the Legends Die*, 544
Boyd, Brendan
*Blue Ruin*, 545
Boyd, Thomas Alexander
*Shadow of the Long Knives*, 117
Boyle, T. C.
*Road to Wellville, The*, 1014
Brackett, Leigh
*Follow the Free Wind*, 240
Bradbury, Ray
*Dandelion Wine*, 596
Bradford, Richard
*Red Sky at Morning*, 1060
Bradley, David
*Chaneysville Incident*, 142
Brady, Joan
*Theory of War*, 444
Brewer, James O.
*No Bottom*, 386
*No Virtue*, 387
Brinig, Myron
*Wide Open Town*, 546
Briskin, Jacqueline
*Paloverde*, 934
Bristow, Gwen
*Deep Summer*, 143
*Handsome Road*, 316
*This Side of Glory*, 547
Brock, Darryl
*If I Never Get Back*, 388

Bromfield, Louis
*Early Autumn*, 1006
*Green Bay Tree*, 1097
*Mrs. Parkington*, 860
*Wild Is the River*, 317
Brooks, Gwendolyn
*Maude Martha*, 764
Broome, H. B.
*Dark Winter*, 445
Brown, Harry
*Walk in the Sun, A*, 716
Brown, Irene Bennett
*Morning Glory Afternoon*, 981
Brown, Rita Mae
*Dolley*, 144
*High Hearts*, 318
Brush, Katherine
*Don't Ever Leave Me*, 638
Bryant, Dorothy
*Ella Price's Journal*, 806
Bunkley, Anita Richmond
*Black Gold*, 1130
Bunting, Josiah
*Lionheads, The*, 807
Burke, Phyllis
*Atomic Candy*, 808
Burks, Brian
*Runs with Horses*, 446
Burnett, William Riley
*Little Caesar*, 597
Burns, Olive Ann
*Cold Sassy Tree*, 548
Burroughs, Edgar Rice
*Apache Devil*, 447
Burroway, Janet
*Cutting Stone*, 926
Butters, Dorothy. (*See* Gilman, Dorothy Butters)
Byrd, Max
*Jefferson*, 145
Byron, Gilbert
*Lord's Oysters, The*, 549

Caldwell, Janet Taylor
*Answer As a Man*, 550
*Balance Wheel*, 1104
*Captains and the Kings, The*, 861
*Eagles Gather*, 598

Caldwell, Janet Taylor (*continued*)
  *Never Victorious, Never Defeated*, 862
  *Testimony of Two Men*, 551
Callahan, North
  *Peggy*, 65
Campbell, Bebe Moore
  *Your Blues Ain't Like Mine*, 963
Cannon, Bettie Waddell
  *Bellsong for Sarah Raines, A*, 990
Cannon, LeGrand
  *Look to the Mountain*, 14
Capps, Benjamin
  *Sam Chance*, 448
  *Trail to Ogallala, The*, 449
  *White Man's Road*, 450
  *Woman of the People, A*, 241
Carlile, Clancy
  *Children of the Dust*, 451
Carr, Caleb
  *Alienist, The*, 1081
Carr, John Dickson
  *Papa La-Bas*, 146
Carroll, James
  *Memorial Bridge*, 863
Carter, Forrest
  *Gone to Texas*, 452
  *Watch for Me on the Mountain*, 453
Cary, Lorene
  *Price of a Child, The*, 147
Cather, Willa
  *Death Comes for the Archbishop*, 242
  *My Antonia*, 454
  *O Pioneers!*, 455
  *One of Ours*, 585
  *Sapphira and the Slave Girl*, 148
Catherwood, Mary Harwell
  *Romance of Dollard*, 1015
Catton, Bruce
  *Banners at Shenandoah*, 319
Charbonneau, Eileen
  *In the Time of the Wolves*, 149
Charbonneau, Louis
  *Trail*, 124
Charyn, Jerome
  *Darlin' Bill*, 456

Chase, Mary Ellen
  *Lovely Ambition, The*, 552
Chase-Riboud, Barbara
  *Echo of Lions*, 150
  *President's Daughter, The*, 151
  *Sally Hemmings*, 152
Chavez, Fray Angelico
  *Lady from Toledo, The*, 1061
Childress, Mark
  *V for Victor*, 694
Choi, Sook Nyul
  *Gathering of Pearls*, 765
Christilian, J. D.
  *Scarlet Women*, 389
Churchill, Winston
  *Richard Carvel*, 66
Clapp, Patricia
  *Tamarack Tree*, 320
  *Witches' Children*, 15
Clark, Walter Van Tilberg
  *Ox Bow Incident*, 457
Clavell, James
  *King Rat*, 736
Cleaveland, Agnes Morley
  *No Life for a Lady*, 1062
Clemens, Samuel
  *Adventures of Huckleberry Finn, The*, 153
  *Adventures of Tom Sawyer, The*, 154
  *Pudd'nhead Wilson*, 155
Cobb, William
  *Walk Through Fire, A*, 766
Cochran, Louis
  *Fool of God, The*, 156
  *Raccoon John Smith*, 991
Coldsmith, Don
  *Return of the Spanish*, 16
Coleman, Lonnie
  *Legacy of Beulah Land*, 390
Collier, James Lincoln
  *Bloody Country, The*, 1105
  *Clock, The*, 947
  *With Every Drop of Blood*, 321
Collins, Max Allan
  *Murder by the Numbers*, 639
  *True Detective*, 640

Comfort, Will
  *Apache*, 243
Conde, Maryse
  *I, Tituba, Black Witch of Salem*, 17
Conley, Robert J.
  *Mountain Windsong*, 244
  *Ned Christie's War*, 458
Connell, Evan S.
  *Mr. Bridge*, 641
  *Mrs. Bridge*, 642
Conroy, Jack
  *Disinherited, The*, 1033
Conroy, Pat
  *Lords of Discipline, The*, 1110
Conroy, Sarah Booth
  *Refinements of Love*, 391
Cook, Thomas H.
  *Streets of Fire*, 809
Cooke, Grace MacGowan
  *Grapple, The*, 964
Cooney, Caroline B.
  *Both Sides of Time*, 392
Coonts, Stephen
  *Flight of the Intruder*, 810
Cooper, J. California
  *Family*, 157
Cooper, James Fenimore
  *Deerslayer, The*, 18
  *Last of the Mohicans*, 19
  *Pathfinder, The*, 20
  *Pilot, The*, 67
  *Pioneers, The*, 158
  *Prairie, The*, 209
  *Red Rover, The*, 21
  *Spy, The*, 68
Corcoran, Barbara
  *Sky Is Falling, The*, 643
Corle, Edwin
  *Fig Tree John*, 935
Cormier, Robert
  *Tunes for Bears to Dance To*, 767
Cornwell, Bernard
  *Copperhead*, 322
  *Rebel*, 323
  *Redcoat*, 69
Costain, Thomas B.
  *High Towers*, 2
Cotton, Ralph
  *While Angels Dance*, 459

Courter, Gay
  *Midwife, The*, 1082
Covington, Dennis
  *Lasso the Moon*, 811
Coyle, Harold
  *Look Away*, 324
Cozzens, James Gould
  *Guard of Honor*, 710
Crane, Stephen
  *Red Badge of Courage*, 325
Craven, Margaret
  *Walk Gently This Good Earth*, 1151
Crew, Linda
  *Children of the River*, 812
Crook, Elizabeth
  *Promised Land*, 245
  *Raven's Bride, The*, 246
Cross, Ruth
  *Soldier of Good Fortune*, 3
Cummings, Betty Sue
  *Say These Names (Remember Them)*, 159
Cummings, Jack
  *Deserter Troop, The*, 460
  *Indian Fighter's Return, The*, 461
Curwood, James Oliver
  *Courage of Captain Plum*, 1016


Dailey, Janet
  *Legacies*, 326
  *Proud and the Free, The*, 160
  *Silver Wings, Santiago Blue*, 711
Dallas, Sandra
  *Persian Pickle Club, The*, 644
Dana, Richard Henry, Jr.
  *Two Years Before the Mast*, 294
Davenport, Marcia
  *Valley of Decision, The*, 864
David, Donald
  *Thirteen Miles from Suncrest*, 553
Davis, Harold Lenoir
  *Beulah Land*, 247
  *Honey in the Horn*, 554
  *Winds of Morning*, 599
Davis, James F.
  *Road to San Jacinto, The*, 1131
Davis, Kathryn
  *Dakotas: At the Wind's Edge*, 1091
  *Dakotas: The Endless Sky*, 1092

Davis, Nelle Portry
  *Stump Ranch Pioneer*, 960
Davis, Thulani
  *Nineteen Fifty Nine*, 768
Davis, William Stearns
  *Gilman of Redford*, 70
Day, Robert
  *Last Cattle Drive, The*, 982
De Blasis, Celeste
  *Proud Breed, The*, 936
  *Swan's Chance*, 161
De Mille, Nelson
  *Word of Honor*, 815
Deal, Bordon
  *Least One, The*, 645
DeForest, J. W.
  *Playing the Mischief*, 393
Degenhard, William
  *Regulators, The*, 162
DeHartog, Jan
  *Peculiar People, The*, 210
Deighton, Len
  *Goodbye Mickey Mouse*, 717
Del Vecchio, John M.
  *Thirteenth Valley, The*, 814
DeLillo, Don
  *Libra*, 813
Delis, Leftare P.
  *Inside Passage, The*, 919
Dell, Floyd
  *Diana Stair*, 163
Deloria, Ella Cara
  *Waterlily*, 1114
Denny, Robert
  *Night Run*, 718
Derleth, August W.
  *Bright Journey*, 211
  *Hills Stand Watch*, 212
Dexter, Pete
  *Deadwood*, 1115
Dillard, Annie
  *Living, The*, 1152
Dinneen, Joseph
  *Ward Eight*, 555

DiPerna, Paula
  *Discoveries of Mrs. Christopher
    Columbus, The*, 4
Doctorow, E. L.
  *Billy Bathgate*, 1083
  *Book of Daniel*, 816
  *Ragtime*, 556
  *Waterworks, The*, 1084
  *World's Fair*, 646
Doig, Ivan
  *Dancing at the Rascal Fair*, 1035
  *English Creek*, 1036
  *Sea Runners*, 920
Donahue, Marilyn Cram
  *Valley in Between*, 937
Donnell, Susan
  *Pocahontas*, 22
Dopp, Peggy
  *Tomorrow Is a River*, 1160
Dorris, Michael
  *Yellow Raft in Blue Water, A*, 1037
Dos Passos, John
  *Big Money, The*, 600
  *Chosen Country*, 965
  *Grand Design*, 647
  *1919*, 586
  *Three Soldiers*, 587
Dowdey, Clifford
  *Bugles Blow No More*, 327
Dreiser, Theodore
  *American Tragedy, An*, 557
  *Financier, The*, 394
  *Jennie Gerhardt*, 395
  *Sister Carrie*, 396
  *Titan, The*, 397
Drury, Allen
  *Toward What Bright Glory?*, 648
Dykeman, Wilma
  *Tall Woman, The*, 398

Early, Tom
  *Sons of Texas*, 248
Eastlake, William
  *Castle Keep*, 719

Eberhart, Mignon G.
  *Bayou Road*, 328
  *Family Fortune*, 329
Eckert, Allan W.
  *Court Martial of Daniel Boone, The*, 992
Edmonds, Janet
  *Rivers of Gold*, 462
Edmonds, Walter D.
  *Boyds of Black River, The*, 558
  *Drums Along the Mohawk*, 71
  *Rome Haul*, 164
Eggleston, Edward
  *Circuit Rider, The*, 213
  *Graysons, The*, 214
  *Hoosier School-Boy, The*, 215
  *Hoosier School-Master, The*, 216
Ehrlichman, John
  *China Card, The*, 817
Ell, Flynn J.
  *Dakota Scouts*, 463
Elliott, Edward E.
  *Devil and the Mathers, The*, 23
Ellis, William D.
  *Bounty Lands, The*, 217
Ellison, Ralph
  *Invisible Man*, 769
Endo, Shusaku
  *Sea and Poison, The*, 737
Epstein, Leslie
  *Pinto and Sons*, 938
Erdman, Loula
  *Edge of Time, The*, 464
Erdrich, Louise
  *Beet Queen, The*, 1093
  *Bingo Palace*, 1094
  *Love Medicine*, 865
Estes, Winston M.
  *Another Part of the House*, 649
Estleman, Loren D.
  *Bloody Season*, 465
  *Edsel*, 770
  *This Old Bill*, 466
  *Whiskey River*, 534
Eulo, Elena Yates
  *Southern Woman*, 330

Fackler, Elizabeth
  *Billy the Kid*, 467
Fairbairn, Ann
  *Five Smooth Stones*, 866
Falstein, Louis
  *Laughter on a Weekday*, 559
Fante, John
  *1933 Was a Bad Year*, 650
Farrell, James T.
  *Father and Son*, 966
Fast, Howard
  *April Morning*, 72
  *Citizen Tom Paine*, 73
  *Establishment, The*, 771
  *Proud and the Free, The*, 74
Faulkner, William
  *Absalom, Absalom!*, 867
  *Intruder in the Dust*, 1030
Fenady, Andrew J.
  *Claws of the Eagle*, 927
Ferber, Edna
  *Cimmaron*, 868
  *Come and Get It*, 1161
  *Giant*, 1132
  *Ice Palace*, 869
  *Saratoga Trunk*, 399
  *Show Boat*, 400
Fergus, Charles
  *Shadow Catcher*, 560
Fergusson, Harvey
  *Wolf Song*, 1063
Ferry, Charles
  *Raspberry One*, 738
Field, Rachel
  *All This and Heaven Too*, 165
Filene, Peter
  *Home and Away*, 772
Fisher, Vardis
  *Children of God*, 249
  *Mothers, The*, 250
  *Mountain Man*, 251
  *Tale of Valor*, 125
Fitzgerald, F. Scott
  *Beautiful and the Damned, The*, 601
  *Great Gatsby, The*, 602

Fleischman, Paul
  Borning Room, The, 870
  Bull Run, 331
  Saturnalia, 1007
Fleming, Thomas J.
  Over There, 588
  Spoils of War, The, 401
  Time and Tide, 739
Fletcher, Inglis
  Bennet's Welcome, 24
  Cormorant's Brood, 25
  Lusty Wind for Carolina, 26
  Men of Albemarle, 27
  Queen's Gift, The, 166
  Raleigh's Eden, 75
  Roanoke Hundred, 28
  Scotswoman, The, 76
  Toil of the Brave, 77
Flynn, Robert
  North to Yesterday, 1133
Follett, Ken
  Place Called Freedom, A, 29
Foote, Shelby
  Shiloh, 332
Forbes, Esther
  Johnny Tremain, 78
  Mirror for Witches, A, 30
Ford, Paul Leicester
  Janice Meredith, 79
Forester, C. S.
  Good Shepherd, The, 720
  To the Indies, 5
Forman, James D.
  Becca's Story, 333
Forrester, Sandra
  Sound the Jubilee, 334
Fox, John, Jr.
  Little Shepherd of Kingdom Come, 335
  Trail of the Lonesome Pine, 993
French, Albert
  Billy, 651
  Holly, 695
Frohlich, Newton
  1492, 6
Fuller, Iola
  Loon Feather, 218

Fulton, Len
  Grassman, The, 468

Gaines, Ernest J.
  Autobiography of Miss Jane Pittman,
    The, 871
  Gathering of Old Men, A, 818
  In My Father's House, 1002
  Lesson Before Dying, A, 1003
Garber, Eugene K.
  Historian, 872
Garfield, Brian
  Manifest Destiny, 469
Garland, Hamlin
  Little Norsk, or Old Pap's Flaxen, A, 470
  Main Travelled Roads, 471
  Trail-Makers of the Middle Border, 336
  Trail of the Gold Seekers, 921
Garland, Sherry
  Indio, 7
  Shadow of the Dragon, 819
Garwood, Julie
  For the Roses, 252
Gear, Kathleen O'Neal
  This Widowed Land, 31
Gerard, Phillip
  Cape Fear Rising, 402
Gerson, Noel B.
  Clear for Action!, 337
  Swamp Fox, Francis Marion, The,
    80
Giardina, Denise
  Storming Heaven, 603
Gibbons, Reginald
  Sweetbitter, 472
Giles, Janice Holt
  Believers, The, 167
  Enduring Hills, 994
  Hannah Fowler, 118
  Kentuckians, The, 119
  Land Beyond the Mountains, 168
  Plum Thicket, The, 473
  Savanna, 930
  Tara's Healing, 995

Gilman, Dorothy Butters
  *Bells of Freedom*, 81
  *Girl in Buckskin*, 32
Gipson, Fred
  *Old Yeller*, 474
Gobbell, John J.
  *Last Lieutenant, The*, 740
Gold, Herbert
  *Fathers*, 873
Goldreich, Gloria
  *That Year of Our War*, 696
  *West to Eden*, 535
Goodman, Mitchell
  *End of It, The*, 721
Goodrich, Marcus
  *Delilah*, 589
Gordon, Caroline
  *Green Centuries*, 996
  *Penhally*, 874
Gordon, Leo V.
  *Powderkeg*, 253
Gordon, Noah
  *Shaman*, 875
Gorman, Edward
  *Night of Shadows*, 475
Graham, Heather
  *Runaway*, 169
Green, Gerald
  *East and West*, 741
Green, Julian
  *Distant Lands, The*, 170
Greenberg, Joanne
  *No Reck'ning Made*, 876
Greene, Bette
  *Summer of My German Soldier*, 697
Grey, Zane
  *Betty Zane*, 82
  *Boulder Dam*, 1050
  *Desert of Wheat*, 590
  *Nevada*, 476
  *Riders of the Purple Sage*, 477
  *Thunder Mountain*, 961
  *U. P. Trail, The*, 478
  *Western Union*, 171
Griffin, W. E. B.
  *Aviators, The*, 820
  *Battleground*, 742
  *Call to Arms*, 712
  *Counterattack*, 743

*New Breed, The*, 821
Grimes, Roberta
  *My Thomas*, 83
Gringhuis, Dirk
  *Young Voyageur, The*, 1017
Griswold, Francis
  *Sea Island Lady*, 877
Grosser, Morton
  *Fabulous Fifty, The*, 604
Grubb, Davis
  *Barefoot Man, The*, 1157
Gurasich, Marj
  *House Divided*, 338
Gurganus, Allan
  *Oldest Living Confederate Widow
    Tells All, The*, 1090
Guthrie, A. B.
  *Big Sky, The*, 254
  *Way West, The*, 255
Guy, Rosa
  *Measure of Time*, 605
Gwaltney, Frances I.
  *Idols and Axle-Grease*, 652


Haig-Brown, Roderick
  *Timber*, 1102
Halacy, Dan
  *Empire in the Dust*, 479
Hall, Oakley
  *Bad Lands*, 480
  *Warlock*, 481
Halper, Albert
  *Chute, The*, 653
  *Foundry, The*, 606
Hansen, Ron
  *Assassination of Jesse James by the
    Coward Robert Ford*, 482
  *Desperadoes*, 483
Harington, Donald
  *Architecture of the Arkansas Ozarks,
    The*, 931
Harmon, Susan
  *Colorado Ransom*, 945
Harper, Karen
  *Circle of Gold*, 997
Harris, Julie
  *Longest Winter, The*, 607

Harris, Marilyn
  *American Eden*, 403
  *Lost and Found*, 878
Harrison, Jim
  *Farmer*, 1018
Harrison, Nick
  *These Years of Promise*, 978
Haruf, Kent
  *Tie That Binds*, 946
Havighurst, Walter
  *Quiet Shore*, 1098
Hawthorne, Nathaniel
  *Blithedale Romance, The*, 172
  *House of Seven Gables, The*, 1008
  *Scarlet Letter, The*, 33
Haycox, Ernest
  *Bugles in the Afternoon*, 484
  *Earthbreakers*, 295
Hazelgrove, William Elliott
  *Tobacco Sticks*, 773
Heath, William
  *Children Bob Moses Led, The*, 822
Hedrick, Ulysses P.
  *Land of the Crooked Tree*, 1019
Heggen, Thomas
  *Mister Roberts*, 744
Heidish, Marcy
  *Miracles*, 173
  *Witnesses*, 34
Heller, Joseph
  *Catch-22*, 722
Hemingway, Ernest
  *Farewell to Arms, A*, 591
  *To Have and Have Not*, 951
Hemming, Robert J.
  *Gales of November*, 1020
  *Ships Gone Mi sing*, 1021
Henry, Will
  *Alias Butch Cassidy*, 485
  *From Where the Sun Now Stands*,
    486
  *I, Tom Horn*, 1166
  *No Survivors*, 487
Herbst, Josephine
  *Executioner Waits, The*, 608

Hergesheimer, Joseph
  *Balisand*, 174
Herrick, William
  *Hermanos!*, 654
Herrin, Lamar
  *Unwritten Chronicles of Robert E. Lee*,
    339
Hersey, John
  *Bell for Adano, A*, 723
Higgins, Jack
  *Luciano's Luck*, 724
Highland, Monica
  *Lotus Land*, 879
Highwater, Jamake
  *Eyes of Darkness, The*, 488
Hillerman, Tony
  *Finding Moon*, 823
Hinojosa, Rolando
  *Useless Servants, The*, 774
Hobbs, Valerie
  *How Far Would You Have Gotten If...*, 775
Hobson, Laura Z.
  *Gentleman's Agreement*, 776
Hodge, Jane Aiken
  *Judas Flowering*, 84
  *Savannah Purchase*, 957
Hogan, Linda
  *Mean Spirit*, 609
Holland, Cecelia
  *Bear Flag, The*, 296
  *Pacific Street*, 297
Holland, Isabelle
  *Behind the Lines*, 340
Homewood, Harry
  *O God of Battles*, 691
  *Silent Sea*, 746
Honig, Donald
  *Plot to Kill Jackie Robinson, The*, 777
Hooker, Richard
  *MASH*, 778
Horgan, Paul
  *Distant Trumpet, A*, 489
  *Far from Cibola*, 1064
Hotchkiss, Bill
  *Ammahabas*, 256
  *Medicine Calf*, 257

Hotchner, A. E.
  *King of the Hill*, 655
Hotze, Sollace
  *Circle Unbroken, A*, 258
Hough, Emerson
  *Covered Wagon, The*, 259
  *54-40 or Fight*, 298
  *Heart's Desire*, 490
Houston, James
  *White Dawn*, 491
Howe, Edgar Watson
  *Story of a Country Town, The*, 983
Howells, William Dean
  *Hazard of New Fortunes, A*, 404
  *Rise of Silas Lapham, The*, 1009
Hoyt, Edwin P.
  *Last Stand, The*, 492
Hudson, Lois Phillips
  *Bones of Plenty, The*, 656
Huggett, William Turner
  *Body Count*, 824
Hughes, Langston
  *Not Without Laughter*, 561
Hughes, Rupert
  *Giant Wakes, The*, 880
Humphrey, William
  *No Resting Place*, 175
  *Ordways, The*, 1134
Hunt, Irene
  *Across Five Aprils*, 341
  *No Promises in the Wind*, 657
Huntington, Lee Pennock
  *Brothers in Arms*, 1144
Hurston, Zora Neale
  *Their Eyes Were Watching God*, 952

Ignatius, David
  *Agents of Innocence*, 825
Irwin, Hadley
  *Kim/Kimi*, 779
Ise, John
  *Sod and Stubble*, 984

Jackson, Edgar N.
  *Green Mountain Hero*, 1145
Jackson, Helen Hunt
  *Ramona*, 299

Jakes, John
  *California Gold*, 881
  *Heaven and Hell*, 405
  *Homeland*, 406
  *Love and War*, 342
  *North and South*, 176
James, Henry
  *Bostonians, The*, 407
  *Washington Square*, 177
James, Will
  *Sand*, 1038
Janus, Christopher G.
  *Miss 4th of July, Goodbye*, 562
Jen, Gish
  *Typical American*, 780
Jenkins, Dan
  *Fast Copy*, 1135
Johnston, Mary
  *To Have and To Hold*, 35
Johnston, Terry C.
  *Carry the Wind*, 300
  *Cry of the Hawk*, 493
  *Dance on the Wind*, 260
Jones, Adrienne
  *Long Time Passing*, 826
Jones, Douglas C.
  *Barefoot Brigade*, 343
  *Come Winter*, 494
  *Creek Called Wounded Knee, A*, 495
  *Elkhorn Tavern*, 344
  *Gone the Dreams and the Dancing*, 496
  *Remember Santiago*, 408
  *Roman*, 497
  *Search for Temperance Moon*, 498
  *This Savage Race*, 882
  *Weedy Rough*, 658
  *Winding Stair*, 499
Jones, James
  *From Here to Eternity*, 747
  *Thin Red Line, The*, 748
  *Whistle*, 713
Jones, Kathy
  *Wild Western Desire*, 985
Jones, Madison
  *Cry of Absence*, 781
Jones, Nard
  *Oregon Detour*, 1103
  *Swift Flows the River*, 301

Jones, Ted
  Grant's War, 345
  Hard Road to Gettysburg, 346
Jones, Thelma
  Skinny Angel, 1116
Jordan, Mildred A.
  One Red Rose Forever, 36
Judd, Walter F.
  Let Us Go, 959
Just, Ward S.
  Jack Gance, 782


Kantor, MacKinlay
  Andersonville, 347
Kassem, Lou
  Listen for Rachel, 348
Kay, Terry
  Year the Lights Came On, The, 783
Keehn, Sally M.
  I Am Regina, 37
Keith, Agnes Newton
  Beloved Exiles, 749
Keith, Harold
  Rifles for Watie, 349
Kelly, Jack
  Mad Dog, 659
  Unexpected Peace, The, 750
Kelton, Elmer
  Day the Cowboys Quit, The, 500
  Slaughter, 501
Kennedy, William P.
  Ironweed, 1085
Keras, Phyllis
  Hate Crime, The, 827
Kerr, M. E.
  Linger, 828
Kesey, Ken
  Sometimes a Great Notion, 784
Keyes, Frances Parkinson
  All That Glitters, 660
Kherdian, David
  Bridger, 261
Killens, John Oliver
  And Then We Heard the Thunder, 751
  'Sippi, 1031

  Youngblood, 536
King, Benjamin
  Bullet for Lincoln, 350
  Bullet for Stonewall, 351
King, Sara
  Irregular Moon, An, 829
Kingman, Lee
  Peter Pan Bag, 830
Kirkland, Caroline M.
  Forest Life, 1022
  New Home—Who'll Follow?, 219
Kirkland, Elithe
  Divine Average, 262
  Love Is a Wild Assault, 263
Kirkpatrick, Katherine
  Keeping the Good Light, 563
Kissinger, Rosemary K.
  Quanah Parker, 502
Kluge, P. F.
  Season for War, 503
Knowles, John
  Separate Peace, A, 698
Koller, Jackie French
  Primrose Way, The, 38
Krisher, Trudy
  Spite Fences, 785
Kunstler, James Howard
  Embarrassment of Riches, 264


LaFarge, Oliver
  Laughing Boy, 1065
Lafferty, R. A.
  Okla Hannali, 883
Lambdin, Dewey
  French Admiral, The, 85
  King's Coat, The, 86
L'Amour, Louis
  Bendigo Shafter, 1167
  Californios, The, 939
  Cherokee Trail, The, 504
  Comstock Lode, 265
  Lonesome Gods, The, 940
  Sackett's Land, 39
  Sitka, 922
  To the Far Blue Mountains, 40

Lancaster, Bruce
  *Blind Journey*, 87
  *Bride of a Thousand Cedars*, 352
  *For Us the Living*, 220
  *Guns of Burgoyne*, 88
  *Phantom Fortress*, 89
  *Scarlet Patch*, 353
  *Secret Road*, 90
  *Trumpet to Arms*, 91
Landis, Jill Marie
  *Jade*, 505
Lane, Rose Wilder
  *Free Land*, 506
  *Let the Hurricane Roar*, 507
Lasky, Kathryn
  *Beyond the Burning Time*, 41
  *Beyond the Divide*, 266
  *Bone Wars, The*, 1039
  *Pageant*, 973
Laughlin, Ruth
  *Wind Leaves No Shadow, The*, 267
Laurents, Arthur
  *Way We Were, The*, 786
Laxalt, Robert
  *Basque Hotel, The*, 1051
Lay, Beirne
  *Twelve O'Clock High*, 725
Lea, Tom
  *Wonderful Country, The*, 508
Lederer, Paul Joseph
  *Manitou's Daughter*, 42
Lee, C. Y. (*See* Li, Chin Yang)
Lee, Harper
  *To Kill a Mockingbird*, 661
Lee, Helen Elaine
  *Serpent's Gift, The*, 884
Leffland, Ella
  *Rumors of Peace*, 699
LeMay, Alan
  *Searchers, The*, 509
Lenski, Lois
  *Bound Girl of Cobble Hill*, 178
Levin, Meyer
  *Old Bunch, The*, 610
Levitin, Sonia
  *Annie's Promise*, 700
Lewis, Janet
  *Invasion*, 885

Lewis, Sinclair
  *Babbitt*, 611
  *Elmer Gantry*, 612
  *Main Street*, 537
Lewisohn, Ludwig
  *Island Within, The*, 409
Li, Chin Yang
  *Flower Drum Song, The*, 941
Lindsay, Mela Meisner
  *Shukar Balan*, 986
Liotta, P. H.
  *Diamond's Compass*, 831
Litvin, Martin
  *Impresario, The*, 564
Litwak, Leo
  *Waiting for the News*, 662
Lo, Steven C.
  *Incorporation of Eric Chung, The*, 1136
Lockridge, Ross, Jr.
  *Raintree County*, 886
Logan, Ben
  *Empty Meadow, The*, 1162
  *Land Remembers, The*, 1163
London, Jack
  *Smoke Bellew*, 923
Long, Eleanor Rice
  *Wilderness to Washington*, 974
Long, Jeff
  *Empire of Bones*, 268
Love, Edmund G.
  *Small Bequest, A*, 1023
Lund, Duane R.
  *White Indian Boy*, 1025
  *Youngest Voyageur*, 1026
Lynch, Daniel
  *Yellow*, 410
Lyons, Mary E.
  *Letters from a Slave Girl*, 179
Lytle, Andrew
  *At the Moon's Inn*, 8
  *Long Night*, 354

MacDonald, Robert S.
  *Catherine, The*, 355
MacInnes, Helen
  *I and My True Love*, 787
MacLean, Alistair
  *Breakheart Pass*, 1052

Mailer, Norman
  *Naked and the Dead, The*, 752
Major, Charles
  *Bears of Blue River*, 180
Mallon, Thomas
  *Henry and Clara*, 411
Manfred, Frederick F.
  *Golden Bowl, The*, 1117
  *King of Spades*, 1118
  *Lord Grizzley*, 269
  *Riders of Judgment*, 1168
  *Scarlet Plume*, 1119
Mark, Grace
  *Dream Seekers*, 412
Marks, Percy
  *Plastic Age*, 613
Marquand, John
  *Late George Apley, The*, 1010
Marshall, Catherine
  *Christy*, 565
  *Julie*, 566
Martin, William
  *Back Bay*, 887
  *Cape Cod*, 888
Mason, Bobbie Ann
  *Feather Crowns*, 998
  *In Country*, 832
Mason, F. Van Wyck. (*See* Van Wyck
  Mason, F.)
Matheson, Richard
  *Journal of the Gun Years*, 510
Matthiessen, Peter
  *Killing Mister Watson*, 953
  *Raditzer*, 753
Maxwell, William
  *Folded Leaf, The*, 614
  *They Came Like Swallows*, 967
  *Time Will Darken It*, 968
Mazer, Harry
  *Last Mission, The*, 726
McCord, Christian
  *Across the Shining Mountains*, 302
McCulloch, Frank
  *Eagle in the Sky*, 1066
McDonald, Julie
  *Amalie's Story*, 221

McIntyre, John Thomas
  *Ferment*, 663
McKenna, Richard
  *Sand Pebbles, The*, 615
McKenney, Ruth
  *Industrial Valley*, 1099
McMurtry, Larry
  *Anything for Billy*, 511
  *Buffalo Girls*, 512
  *Dead Man's Walk*, 270
  *Lonesome Dove*, 513
  *Streets of Laredo*, 514
  *Texasville*, 1137
McNamee, Thomas
  *Story of Deep Delight, A*, 889
McSorley, Edward
  *Our Own Kind*, 616
Medearis, Mary
  *Big Doc's Girl*, 932
Melville, Herman
  *Israel Potter*, 92
  *Moby Dick*, 126
Meriwether, Louise
  *Daddy Was a Numbers Runner*, 664
  *Fragments of the Ark*, 356
Merrick, Gordon
  *Strumpet Wind, The*, 727
Meyer, Carolyn
  *Where the Broken Heart Still Beats*, 271
Meyers, Maan
  *Dutchman, The*, 43
  *High Constable, The*, 181
  *Kingsbridge Plot, The*, 93
Micheaux, Oscar
  *Conquest*, 1120
  *Homesteader, The*, 1121
  *Wind from Nowhere, The*, 1122
Michener, James A.
  *Alaska*, 890
  *Bridges at Toko-Ri*, 788
  *Centennial*, 891
  *Chesapeake*, 892
  *Eagle and the Raven, The*, 272
  *Hawaii*, 893
  *Legacy*, 894

*Space*, 833
*Texas*, 895
Miller, Jim Wayne
*Newfound*, 1128
Mitchell, Margaret
*Gone with the Wind*, 357
Moberg, Vilhelm
*Emigrants, The*, 1027
*Unto a Good Land*, 1028
Momaday, N. Scott
*House Made of Dawn*, 1067
Monfredo, Miriam Grace
*Seneca Falls Inheritance*, 182
Moore, Ruth
*Spoonhandle*, 665
Moore, Yvette
*Freedom Songs*, 834
Morris, Bill
*Motor City*, 1024
Morris, Gilbert
*Yukon Queen, The*, 515
Morris, Wright
*Ceremony in Lonetree*, 1043
*Huge Season, The*, 617
*Plains Song*, 1044
Morrison, Toni
*Beloved*, 413
*Jazz*, 618
Morrow, Honore
*On to Oregon*, 273
Moss, Robert
*Firekeeper, The*, 44
Muir, John
*Stickeen*, 924
Mukherjee, Bharati
*Jasmine*, 835
Murray, Albert
*Train Whistle Guitar*, 619
Myers, Walter Dean
*Fallen Angels*, 836
*Glory Field, The*, 896
Myrdal, Jan
*Another World*, 666
Myrer, Anton
*Green Desire, A*, 897
*Once an Eagle*, 898

Namioka, Lensey
*April and the Dragon Lady*, 837
Nason, Tema
*Ethel*, 789
Neider, Charles
*Authentic Death of Hendry Jones, The*, 942
Neihardt, John G.
*Life's Lure*, 1123
*Splendid Wayfaring*, 127
*When the Tree Flowered*, 1045
Nelson, Theresa
*And One for All*, 838
Nichols, John
*Milagro Beanfield War, The*, 1068
Nixon, Joan L.
*High Trail to Danger*, 516
Nordan, Lewis
*Wolf Whistle*, 1032
Norris, Frank
*McTeague*, 517
*Octopus, The*, 518
*Pit, The*, 414

O'Brien, Dan
*In the Center of the Nation*, 1124
O'Connor, Edwin
*Last Hurrah, The*, 1011
O'Dell, Scott
*King's Fifth*, 9
*Sarah Bishop*, 94
*Serpent Never Sleeps, The*, 45
*Sing Down the Moon*, 928
*Streams to the River, River to the Sea*, 128
O'Meara, Walter
*Spanish Bride, The*, 1069
Ogilvie, Elisabeth
*Ebbing Tide*, 701
*Jennie Glenroy*, 183
*Storm Tide*, 702
Okimoto, Jean Davies
*Talent Night*, 839
Olds, Bruce
*Raising Holy Hell*, 274
Olsen, Tillie
*Yonnondio*, 667
Osborn, Karen
*Between Earth and Sky*, 519

Oughton, Jerrie
  *Music from a Place Called Half Moon*,
    790
Owen, Dean
  *Sam Houston Story, The*, 275
Owens, William A.
  *Fever in the Earth*, 567
  *Look to the River*, 1138


Page, Elizabeth
  *Tree of Liberty*, 899
Page, Thomas Nelson
  *Red Rock*, 415
Parini, Jay
  *Patch Boys, The*, 621
Parks, Gordon
  *Learning Tree, The*, 620
Partridge, Bellamy
  *Big Freeze, The*, 184
Paulsen, Gary
  *Canyons*, 520
  *Nightjohn*, 185
Peck, Richard
  *Ghost Belonged to Me, The*, 969
Peck, Robert Newton
  *Day No Pigs Would Die, A*, 622
  *Hallapoosa*, 954
  *Part of the Sky, A*, 668
Perez, N. A.
  *Slopes of War*, 358
Petry, Ann
  *Tituba of Salem Village*, 46
Phillippi, Wendell C.
  *Dear Ike*, 728
Phillips, Jayne Anne
  *Machine Dreams*, 1158
Piercy, Marge
  *Gone to Soldiers*, 690
  *Vida*, 840
Plain, Belva
  *Crescent City*, 359
Pope, E(lizabeth) M(arie)
  *Sherwood Ring*, 95
Porter, Gene Stratton. (*See* Stratton-Porter,
    Gene)

Portis, Charles
  *True Grit*, 521
Potok, Chaim
  *Chosen, The*, 1086
  *Davita's Harp*, 669
  *In the Beginning*, 1087
Powell, Dawn
  *Golden Spur, The*, 623
Power, Susan
  *Grass Dancer*, 900
Powers, John
  *Last Catholic in America, The*, 970
Poynter, Margaret
  *Time Too Swift, A*, 703
Pratt, Theodore
  *Barefoot Mailman, The*, 416
Price, Eugenia
  *Before the Darkness Falls*, 186
  *Beloved Invader, The*, 417
  *Lighthouse*, 187
  *Margaret's Story*, 901
  *Maria*, 188
  *New Moon Rising*, 189
  *Savannah*, 190
  *Stranger in Savannah*, 360
  *To See Your Face Again*, 191
  *Where Shadows Go*, 192
Proctor, George W.
  *Walks Without a Soul*, 276
Proffitt, Nicholas
  *Gardens of Stone*, 841
Puzo, Mario
  *Fortunate Pilgrim, The*, 538
Pye, Michael
  *Drowning Room, The*, 47


Qualey, Marsha
  *Come in from the Cold*, 842
Quick, Herbert
  *Vandemark's Folly*, 222


Randle, Kevin J.
  *Spanish Gold*, 1139

Receveur, Betty Layman
  Kentucky Home, 193
  Oh Kentucky!, 120
Rhodes, Judy Carole
  Hunter's Heart, 933
Rhyne, Nancy
  Alice Flagg, 1111
Rice, Anne O.
  Feast of All Saints, 194
Richter, Conrad
  Fields, The, 223
  Lady, The, 522
  Light in the Forest, The, 48
  Sea of Grass, The, 1070
  Town, The, 224
  Trees, The, 225
Riefe, Barbara
  For Love of Two Eagles, 49
  Woman Who Fell from the Sky, The, 50
Rinaldi, Ann
  Break with Charity, A, 51
  Broken Days, 195
  Fifth of March, The, 96
  Finishing Becca, 97
  In My Father's House, 361
  Last Silk Dress, 362
  Ride into Morning, A, 98
  Secret of Sarah Revere, The, 99
  Stitch in Time, A, 196
  Time Enough for Drums, 100
  Wolf by the Ears, 197
Ripley, Alexandra
  Charleston, 418
  New Orleans Legacy, 1004
Roberts, Carey
  Tidewater Dynasty, 902
Roberts, Elizabeth Madox
  Great Meadow, 121
Roberts, Kenneth L.
  Arundel, 101
  Boon Island, 52
  Captain Caution, 129
  Northwest Passage, 10
  Oliver Wiswell, 102
Roberts, Walter
  Royal Street, 198
Robinet, Harriette Gillen
  Mississippi Chariot, 670

Robins, Elizabeth
  Magnetic North, 925
Robson, Lucia St. Clair
  Light a Distant Fire, 199
  Mary's Land, 53
  Ride the Wind, 277
  Walk in My Soul, 1140
Roesch, E. P.
  Ashana, 303
Rolvaag, Ole
  Giants in the Earth, 523
  Peder Victorious, 524
Rose, Howard
  Pooles of Pismo Bay, The, 539
Ross, Alice
  Whistle Punk, 704
Roth-Hano, Renee
  Safe Harbors, 791
Rylant, Cynthia
  I Had Seen Castles, 691

Safire, William
  Freedom, 363
Salisbury, Graham
  Under the Blood-Red Sun, 754
Sample, Zola
  Cherokee Strip Fever, 1101
Sandburg, Carl
  Remembrance Rock, 903
Sanders, Dori
  Her Own Place, 705
Sanders, Leonard
  Star of Empire, 278
Sanders, Scott R.
  Bad Man Ballad, 110
Sandoz, Mari
  Miss Morissa, Doctor of the Gold Trail, 525
  Son of the Gamblin' Man, 526
Santmyer, Helen H.
  . . . And Ladies of the Club, 904
Saroyan, William
  Human Comedy, The, 706
Savage, Les, Jr.
  Royal City, The, 1071
Schaefer, Jack
  Company of Cowards, 364
  Monte Walsh, 568
  Shane, 527

Schroeder, Ralph E.
  *Glory from the Earth, A*, 624
Schulberg, Budd
  *Waterfront*, 1088
Schultz, Duane P.
  *Glory Enough for All*, 365
Schultz, James Willard
  *Quest of the Fish-Dog Skin*, 279
  *With the Indians in the Rockies*, 280
Schumann, Mary
  *Strife Before Dawn*, 905
Scott, Evelyn
  *Wave, The*, 366
Searls, Hank
  *Blood Song*, 281
Seifert, Shirley
  *Farewell, My General*, 367
  *Never No More*, 54
  *Three Lives of Elizabeth*, 130
  *Turquoise Trail, The*, 282
Seno, William J.
  *Enemies*, 1164
Seton, Anya
  *Devil Water*, 55
  *Foxfire*, 929
  *My Theodosia*, 131
  *Winthrop Woman, The*, 1012
Settle, Mary Lee
  *Choices*, 906
  *Killing Ground*, 1159
  *Know Nothing*, 200
  *Scapegoat, The*, 569
Shaara, Michael
  *Killer Angels, The*, 368
Shange, Ntozake
  *Betsy Brown*, 792
Shaw, Irwin
  *Troubled Air, The*, 793
  *Young Lions, The*, 729
Shepard, Jim
  *Paper Doll*, 730
Shepherd, Jean
  *In God We Trust*, 975
Sherman, Dan
  *Traitor, The*, 103

Shreve, Anita
  *Resistance*, 731
Shreve, Susan Richards
  *Country of Strangers, A*, 1148
  *Daughters of the New World*, 907
Shuken, Julia
  *In the House of My Pilgrimage*, 570
Shute, Henry A.
  *Real Diary of a Real Boy, The*, 1053
Siddons, Anne Rivers
  *Colony*, 1005
  *Heartbreak Hotel*, 794
Sidhwa, Bapsi
  *American Brat, An*, 843
Silko, Leslie Marmon
  *Ceremony*, 795
Simms, William Gilmore
  *Yemassee, The*, 56
Sinclair, Harold
  *American Years*, 226
Sinclair, Jo
  *Changelings, The*, 796
Sinclair, John L.
  *In Time of Harvest*, 1072
Sinclair, Upton
  *Boston*, 579
  *Dragon's Teeth*, 671
  *Jungle, The*, 571
  *King Coal*, 572
  *Oil!*, 626
Skimin, Robert
  *Apache Autumn*, 908
Slaughter, Frank G.
  *Sword and Scalpel*, 797
  *Warrior, The*, 201
Slone, Verna Mae
  *Rennie's Way*, 627
Smith, Betty
  *Tomorrow Will Be Better*, 628
  *Tree Grows in Brooklyn, A*, 573
Smith, C. W.
  *Thin Men of Haddam*, 1141
Smith, Lee
  *Fair and Tender Ladies*, 1149

---

Entries 1-61: 1492-1775, Entries 62-122: 1776-1783, Entries 123-304: 1783-1860, Entries 305-380: 1861-1899, Entries 381-533: 1866-1899, Entries 534-688: 1900-1939, Entries 689-759: 1939-1945, Entries 760-855: 1945-1995, Entries 856-916: Epic Novels, Entries 917-1168: Additional Titles.

Smith, Patrick
  *Angel City*, 955
  *Forever Island*, 956
Smith, Steven Phillip
  *American Boys*, 844
Smith, Stewart E. White
  *Claim Jumpers, The*, 1125
Sollitt, Kenneth
  *Our Changing Lives*, 979
  *These Years of Promise*, 978
  *This Rough New Land*, 980
Soto, Gary
  *Jesse*, 845
Speare, Elizabeth
  *Calico Captive*, 1146
Spencer, LaVyrle
  *Forgiving*, 1126
  *November of the Heart*, 1029
  *Years*, 1095
St. Clair Robson, Lucia (*See* Robson,
  Lucia St. Clair)
Stegner, Wallace
  *Angle of Repose*, 962
  *Big Rock Candy Mountain*, 909
  *Second Growth*, 1054
Stein, Harry
  *Hoopla*, 574
Steinbeck, John
  *Cannery Row*, 672
  *East of Eden*, 910
  *Grapes of Wrath, The*, 673
  *In Dubious Battle*, 674
  *Of Mice and Men*, 675
Steuber, William
  *Landlooker, The*, 419
Stevenson, Paul R.
  *Cross a Wide River*, 1073
Stewart, Fred M.
  *Glitter and the Gold, The*, 943
Stolz, Mary
  *Cezanne Pinto*, 202
Stone, Irving
  *Immortal Wife*, 132
  *Love Is Eternal*, 369
  *President's Lady, The*, 133
  *Those Who Love*, 104
Stowe, Harriet Beecher
  *Oldtown Folks*, 203
  *Uncle Tom's Cabin*, 204

Stratton-Porter, Gene
  *Freckles*, 575
  *Girl of the Limberlost*, 576
  *Harvester, The*, 577
  *Laddie*, 420
Stribling, T. S.
  *Forge, The*, 370
  *Store, The*, 421
  *Unfinished Cathedral, The*, 917
Strunk, Frank C.
  *Jordon's Showdown*, 676
Stuart, Jesse
  *Hie to the Hunters*, 999
  *Taps for Private Tussie*, 1000
Styron, William
  *Confessions of Nat Turner, The*, 205
  *Long March, The*, 798
Svee, Gary D.
  *Single Tree*, 528
Swarthout, Glendon
  *Eagle and the Iron Cross, The*, 707
Swisher, Robert K.
  *Land, The*, 1074

Taber, Gladys
  *Spring Harvest*, 578
Tan, Amy
  *Joy Luck Club*, 944
Tarkington, Booth
  *Gentleman from Indiana, The*, 976
  *Magnificent Ambersons, The*, 422
  *Penrod*, 579
Tate, Allen
  *Fathers*, 371
Tax, Meredith
  *Rivington Street*, 540
  *Union Square*, 541
Taylor, Mildred D.
  *Road to Memphis, The*, 708
  *Roll of Thunder, Hear My Cry*, 677
Taylor, Peter
  *Summons to Memphis*, 1129
Taylor, Robert Lewis
  *Travels of Jamie McPheeters, The*, 283
Taylor, Theodore
  *Bomb, The*, 755
  *Walking Up a Rainbow*, 284

Terris, Susan
*Nell's Quilt*, 423
Thane, Elswyth Beebe
*Dawn's Early Light*, 105
*Ever After*, 424
*Yankee Stranger*, 372
Tharp, Louise Hall
*Tory Hole*, 948
Thoene, Brock
*Legend of Storey County, The*, 227
Thom, James Alexander
*Follow the River*, 57
*From Sea to Shining Sea*, 285
*Panther in the Sky*, 228
Thomas, D. M.
*Flying in to Love*, 846
Thomas, Dorothy
*Home Place, The*, 1046
*Ma Jeeter's Girls*, 1047
Thompson, Maurice
*Alice of Old Vincennes*, 122
Tippett, Thomas
*Horse Shoe Bottoms*, 425
Toland, John
*Gods of War*, 756
*Occupation*, 757
Tourgee, Albion W.
*Fool's Errand, A*, 426
Townsend, George A.
*Katy of Catoctin*, 373
Tregaskis, Richard
*Stronger Than Fear*, 732
Trumbo, Dalton
*Johnny Got His Gun*, 592
Truscott, Lucian K.
*Army Blue*, 847
Tryon, Thomas
*In the Fire of Spring*, 949
*Wings of the Morning, The*, 950
Tucker, Augusta
*Miss Susie Slagle's*, 580
Tucker, Wilson
*Lincoln Hunters, The*, 971
Turnbull, Agnes
*Remember the End*, 1106
*Richlands, The*, 1107

*Rolling Years*, 1108
Turpin, Waters Edward
*O Canaan!*, 542
Twain, Mark (*See* Clemens, Samuel)

Underwood, Phillip
*Ben Cooper, U. S. Marshal*, 1143
Unger, Douglas
*Leaving the Land*, 799
Unsworth, Barry
*Sacred Hunger*, 58
Uris, Leon
*Battle Cry*, 758

Van Peebles, Melvin
*Panther*, 848
Van Raven, Pieter
*Time of Troubles, A*, 679
Van Wyck Mason, F.
*Rascals Heaven*, 59
*Sea Venture, The*, 60
*Young Titan, The*, 61
Vance, James
*Kings in Disguise*, 678
Verdelle, A. J.
*Good Negress, The*, 800
Vidal, Gore
*Burr*, 134
*1876*, 427
*Empire*, 428
*Hollywood*, 629
*Lincoln*, 374
*Washington, D.C.*, 911
Villars, Elizabeth
*Wars of the Heart*, 709
Vliet, R. G.
*Rockspring*, 286
Vogel, Joseph
*Man's Courage*, 680
Vogt, Esther
*Turkey Red*, 987
Voigt, Cynthia
*David and Jonathan*, 801
*Tree by Leaf*, 593

---

Vukelich, George
  *Fisherman's Beach*, 1165


Waldo, Anna Lee
  *Sacajawea*, 135
Walker, Alice
  *Color Purple*, 681
Walker, Charles Rumford
  *Bread and Fire*, 630
Walker, Margaret
  *Jubilee*, 912
Warren, Lella
  *Foundation Stone*, 206
Warren, Robert Penn
  *All the King's Men*, 682
  *Band of Angels*, 913
  *Night Rider*, 581
  *World Enough and Time*, 1001
Wartski, Maureen
  *Face in My Mirror, The*, 849
Waters, Frank
  *Man Who Killed the Deer, The*, 1075
  *People of the Valley*, 1076
  *Woman at Otowi Crossing*, 1077
Watson, Larry
  *Justice*, 543
  *Montana 1948*, 1040
Webb, James H.
  *Fields of Fire*, 850
  *Sense of Honor, A*, 851
Welch, James
  *Fools Crow*, 529
Wells, Lawrence
  *Let the Band Play Dixie*, 1109
Welty, Eudora
  *Delta Wedding*, 631
  *Losing Battles*, 683
West, Dorothy
  *Wedding, The*, 802
West, Jessamyn
  *Friendly Persuasion, The*, 229
  *Massacre at Fall Creek, The*, 230
Wharton, Edith
  *Age of Innocence*, 429
Wharton, William
  *Midnight Clear*, 733
Whipple, Maurine
  *Giant Joshua*, 287

White, Ellen Emerson
  *Road Home, The*, 852
White, Richard W.
  *Jordan Freeman Was My Friend*, 106
White, Stewart Edward
  *Long Rifle*, 288
  *Stampede*, 304
Whitney, Phyllis A.
  *Quicksilver Pool*, 375
  *Step to the Music*, 376
Wilbee, Brenda
  *Sweetbriar*, 1153
  *Sweetbriar Bride*, 1154
  *Sweetbriar Spring*, 1155
Wilder, Thornton
  *Eighth Day, The*, 972
Williams, Ben Ames
  *Come Spring*, 107
Williams, Jana
  *Scuttlebutt*, 853
Williams, Jeanne
  *Home Mountain*, 530
  *Longest Road, The*, 684
  *Unplowed Sky, The*, 632
Williams, Thomas
  *Town Burning*, 1055
  *Whipple's Castle*, 1056
Williamson, Penelope
  *Heart of the West*, 531
Willis, Connie
  *Lincoln's Dreams*, 377
Windle, Janice Woods
  *True Women*, 914
Woiwode, Larry
  *Beyond the Bedroom Wall*, 1096
Wolf, William J.
  *Benedict Arnold, A Novel*, 108
Wolfe, Thomas
  *You Can't Go Home Again*, 685
Wood, Elizabeth L.
  *Many Horses*, 1156
Wood, Jane Roberts
  *Place Called Sweet Shrub, A*, 582
Woodrell, Daniel
  *Woe to Live On*, 988
Woods, Stuart
  *Chiefs*, 915
Wooldridge, Rhoda
  *Hannah's Mill*, 1034

Woolley, Bryan
  *Sam Bass*, 532
  *Time and Place*, 1142
Wouk, Herman
  *Caine Mutiny, The*, 759
  *City Boy*, 1089
  *Inside, Outside*, 854
  *War and Remembrance*, 692
  *Winds of War, The*, 693
Wright, Richard
  *Native Son*, 686
Wright, Sarah E.
  *This Child's Gonna Live*, 687


Yamanaka, Lois-Ann
  *Wild Meat and the Bully Burgers*, 855
Yates, Elizabeth
  *Hue and Cry*, 1057
Yeager, Charles Gordon
  *Fightin' with Forrest*, 378
Yep, Laurence
  *Dragon's Gate*, 533
  *Star Fisher, The*, 633

Yerby, Frank
  *Foxes of Harrow, The*, 207
  *Serpent and the Staff, The*, 583
  *Vixens, The*, 430
Young, Stark
  *So Red the Rose*, 379
Yount, John
  *Hardcastle*, 688
Yount, Steven
  *Wandering Star*, 584

Zach, Cheryl
  *Hearts Divided*, 380
Zaroulis, Nancy
  *Last Waltz*, 431
  *Massachusetts*, 916
Zelazny, Roger
  *Wilderness*, 289
Zollinger, Norman
  *Riders to Cibola*, 1078

---

Entries 1-61: 1492-1775, Entries 62-122: 1776-1783, Entries 123-304: 1783-1860, Entries 305-380: 1861-1899, Entries 381-533: 1866-1899, Entries 534-688: 1900-1939, Entries 689-759: 1939-1945, Entries 760-855: 1945-1995, Entries 856-916: Epic Novels, Entries 917-1168: Additional Titles.

# TITLE INDEX

Numbers refer to entry numbers not page numbers. For the reader's convenience entry number and dates correspond to the following order. Entries 1-61: 1492-1775, Entries 62-122: 1776-1783, Entries 123-304: 1783-1860, Entries 305-380: 1861-1899, Entries 381-533: 1866-1899, Entries 534-688: 1900-1939, Entries 689-759: 1939-1945, Entries 760-855: 1945-1995, Entries 856-916: Epic Novels, Entries 917-1168: Additional Titles.

*Absalom, Absalom!* (Faulkner, William), 867

*Across Five Aprils* (Hunt, Irene), 341

*Across the Shining Mountains* (McCord, Christian), 302

*Adventures of Huckleberry Finn, The* (Clemens, Samuel), 153

*Adventures of Tom Sawyer, The* (Clemens, Samuel), 154

*Age of Innocence* (Wharton, Edith), 429

*Agents of Innocence* (Ignatius, David), 825

*Alaska* (Michener, James A.), 890

*Alias Butch Cassidy* (Henry, Will), 485

*Alice Flagg* (Rhyne, Nancy), 1111

*Alice of Old Vincennes* (Thompson, Maurice), 122

*Alienist, The* (Carr, Caleb), 1081

*All That Glitters* (Keyes, Frances Parkinson), 660

*All the King's Men* (Warren, Robert Penn), 682

*All This and Heaven Too* (Field, Rachel), 165

*Amalie's Story* (McDonald, Julie), 221

*American Boys* (Smith, Steven Phillip), 844

*American Brat, An* (Sidhwa, Bapsi), 843

*American Eden* (Harris, Marilyn), 403

*American Tragedy, An* (Dreiser, Theodore), 557

*American Years* (Sinclair, Harold), 226

*Ammahabas* (Hotchkiss, Bill), 256

*. . . And Ladies of the Club* (Santmyer, Helen H.), 904

*And One for All* (Nelson, Theresa), 838

*And Then We Heard the Thunder* (Killens, John Oliver), 751

*Andersonville* (Kantor, MacKinlay), 347

*Angel City* (Smith, Patrick), 955

*Angle of Repose* (Stegner, Wallace), 962

*Ann of the Wild Rose Inn* (Armstrong, Jennifer), 62

*Annie's Promise* (Levitin, Sonia), 700

*Another Part of the House* (Estes, Winston M.), 649

*Another World* (Myrdal, Jan), 666

*Answer As a Man* (Caldwell, Janet Taylor), 550

*Anything for Billy* (McMurtry, Larry), 511

*Apache* (Comfort, Will), 243

*Apache Autumn* (Skimin, Robert), 908

*Apache Devil* (Burroughs, Edgar Rice), 447

*April and the Dragon Lady* (Namioka, Lensey), 837

*April Morning* (Fast, Howard), 72

*Arabian Jazz* (Abu-Jaber, Diana), 1079

*Architecture of the Arkansas Ozarks* (Harington, Donald), 931

*Army Blue* (Truscott, Lucian K.), 847

*Arundel* (Roberts, Kenneth L.), 101

*Ashana* (Roesch, E. P.), 303

*Assassination of Jesse James by the . . .* (Hansen, Ron), 482

*At the Moon's Inn* (Lytle, Andrew), 8

*Atomic Candy* (Burke, Phyllis), 808

*Authentic Death of Hendry Jones, The* (Neider, Charles), 942

*Autobiography of Miss Jane Pittman, The* (Gaines, Ernest J.), 871

*Aviators, The* (Griffin, W. E. B.), 820

*Babbitt* (Lewis, Sinclair), 611

*Back Bay* (Martin, William), 887

*Bad Lands* (Hall, Oakley), 480

*Bad Man Ballad* (Sanders, Scott R.), 110

*Balance Wheel* (Caldwell, Janet Taylor), 1104

*Balisand* (Hergesheimer, Joseph), 174

*Band of Angels* (Warren, Robert Penn), 913

*Banners at Shenandoah* (Catton, Bruce), 319

*Barefoot Brigade* (Jones, Douglas C.), 343

*Barefoot Mailman, The* (Pratt, Theodore), 416

*Barefoot Man, The* (Grubb, Davis), 1157

*Barrier* (Beach, Rex Ellingwood), 435

*Basque Hotel, The* (Laxalt, Robert), 1051

*Battle Cry* (Uris, Leon), 758

*Battleground* (Griffin, W. E. B.), 742

*Bayou Road* (Eberhart, Mignon G.), 328

*Bear Flag, The* (Holland, Cecelia), 296

*Bears of Blue River* (Major, Charles), 180

*Beautiful and the Damned, The* (Fitzgerald, F. Scott), 601

*Becca's Story* (Forman, James D.), 333

*Beet Queen, The* (Erdrich, Louise), 1093

*Before the Darkness Falls* (Price, Eugenia), 186

*Behind the Lines* (Holland, Isabelle), 340

*Believers, The* (Giles, Janice Holt), 167

*Bell for Adano, A* (Hersey, John), 723

*Bells of Freedom* (Gilman, Dorothy Butters), 81

*Bellsong for Sarah Raines, A* (Cannon, Bettie Waddell), 990

*Beloved* (Morrison, Toni), 413

*Beloved Exiles* (Keith, Agnes Newton), 749

*Beloved Invader, The* (Price, Eugenia), 417

*Ben Cooper, U. S. Marshal* (Underwood, Phillip), 1143

*Bendigo Shafter* (L'Amour, Louis), 1167

*Benedict Arnold, A Novel* (Wolf, William J.), 108

*Bennet's Welcome* (Fletcher, Inglis), 24

*Betsy Brown* (Shange, Ntozake), 792

*Betty Zane* (Grey, Zane), 82

*Between Earth and Sky* (Osborn, Karen), 519

*Beulah Land* (Davis, Harold Lenoir), 247

*Beyond the Bedroom Wall* (Woiwode, Larry), 1096

*Beyond the Burning Time* (Lasky, Kathryn), 41

*Beyond the Divide* (Lasky, Kathryn), 266

*Big Doc's Girl* (Medearis, Mary), 932

*Big Freeze, The* (Partridge, Bellamy), 184

*Big Money, The* (Dos Passos, John), 600

*Big Rock Candy Mountain* (Stegner, Wallace), 909

*Big Sky, The* (Guthrie, A. B.), 254

*Billy* (French, Albert), 651

*Billy Bathgate* (Doctorow, E. L.), 1083

*Billy the Kid* (Fackler, Elizabeth), 467

*Bingo Palace* (Erdrich, Louise), 1094

*Black Gold* (Bunkley, Anita Richmond), 1130

*Black Thunder* (Bontemps, Arna), 141

*Bless Me, Ultima* (Anaya, Rudolfo A.), 1058

*Blind Journey* (Lancaster, Bruce), 87

*Blithedale Romance, The* (Hawthorne, Nathaniel), 172

*Blood Brother* (Arnold, Elliott), 235

*Blood Song* (Searls, Hank), 281

*Bloody Country, The* (Collier, James Lincoln), 1105

*Bloody Season* (Estleman, Loren D.), 465

*Blue Ruin* (Boyd, Brendan), 545

*Body Count* (Huggett, William Turner), 824

*Bomb, The* (Taylor, Theodore), 755

*Bone Wars, The* (Lasky, Kathryn), 1039

*Bones of Plenty, The* (Hudson, Lois Phillips), 656

*Book of Daniel* (Doctorow, E. L.), 816
*Boon Island* (Roberts, Kenneth L.), 52
*Border Watch* (Altsheler, J. A.), 109
*Borning Room, The* (Fleischman, Paul), 870
*Boston* (Sinclair, Upton), 579
*Bostonians, The* (James, Henry), 407
*Both Sides of Time* (Cooney, Caroline B.), 392
*Boulder Dam* (Grey, Zane), 1050
*Bound Girl of Cobble Hill* (Lenski, Lois), 178
*Bounty Lands, The* (Ellis, William D.), 217
*Boyds of Black River, The* (Edmonds, Walter D.), 558
*Bread and Fire* (Walker, Charles Rumford), 630
*Break with Charity, A* (Rinaldi, Ann), 51
*Breakheart Pass* (MacLean, Alistair), 1052
*Bride of a Thousand Cedars* (Lancaster, Bruce), 352
*Bridge of the Gods* (Balch, Frederick H.), 1150
*Bridger* (Kherdian, David), 261
*Bridges at Toko-Ri* (Michener, James A.), 788
*Bright Journey* (Derleth, August W.), 211
*Broken Days* (Rinaldi, Ann), 195
*Brothers in Arms* (Huntington, Lee Pennock), 1144
*Buffalo Girls* (McMurtry, Larry), 512
*Bugles Blow No More* (Dowdey, Clifford), 327
*Bugles in the Afternoon* (Haycox, Ernest), 484
*Bull Run* (Fleischman, Paul), 331
*Bullet for Lincoln* (King, Benjamin), 350
*Bullet for Stonewall* (King, Benjamin), 351
*Burr* (Vidal, Gore), 134

*Caine Mutiny, The* (Wouk, Herman), 759
*Calico Captive* (Speare, Elizabeth), 1146
*California Gold* (Jakes, John), 881
*Californios, The* (L'Amour, Louis), 939
*Call to Arms* (Griffin, W. E. B.), 712
*Canal Town* (Adams, Samuel Hopkins), 136
*Cannery Row* (Steinbeck, John), 672

*Canyons* (Paulsen, Gary), 520
*Cape Cod* (Martin, William), 888
*Cape Fear Rising* (Gerard, Phillip), 402
*Captain Caution* (Roberts, Kenneth L.), 129
*Captains and the Kings, The* (Caldwell, Janet Taylor), 861
*Carry the Wind* (Johnston, Terry C.), 300
*Castle Keep* (Eastlake, William), 719
*Catch-22* (Heller, Joseph), 722
*Catherine, The* (MacDonald, Robert S.), 355
*Centennial* (Michener, James A.), 891
*Ceremony* (Silko, Leslie Marmon), 795
*Ceremony in Lonetree* (Morris, Wright), 1043
*Cezanne Pinto* (Stolz, Mary), 202
*Chaneysville Incident* (Bradley, David), 142
*Changelings, The* (Sinclair, Jo), 796
*Charleston* (Ripley, Alexandra), 418
*Cherokee Strip Fever* (Sample, Zola), 1101
*Cherokee Trail, The* (L'Amour, Louis), 504
*Chesapeake* (Michener, James A.), 892
*Chiefs* (Woods, Stuart), 915
*Children Bob Moses Led, The* (Heath, William), 822
*Children of God* (Fisher, Vardis), 249
*Children of the Dust* (Carlile, Clancy), 451
*Children of the River* (Crew, Linda), 812
*China Card, The* (Ehrlichman, John), 817
*Choices* (Settle, Mary Lee), 906
*Chosen, The* (Potok, Chaim), 1086
*Chosen Country* (Dos Passos, John), 965
*Christy* (Marshall, Catherine), 565
*Chute, The* (Halper, Albert), 653
*Cimmaron* (Ferber, Edna), 868
*Circle of Gold* (Harper, Karen), 997
*Circle Unbroken, A* (Hotze, Sollace), 258
*Circuit Rider, The* (Eggleston, Edward), 213
*Citizen Tom Paine* (Fast, Howard), 73
*City Boy* (Wouk, Herman), 1089
*Claim Jumpers, The* (Smith, Stewart E. White), 1125
*Claws of the Eagle* (Fenady, Andrew J.), 927
*Clear for Action!* (Gerson, Noel B.), 337

*Clock, The* (Collier, James Lincoln), 947

*Cold Sassy Tree* (Burns, Olive Ann), 548

*Colony* (Siddons, Anne Rivers), 1005

*Color Purple* (Walker, Alice), 681

*Colorado Ransom* (Harmon, Susan), 945

*Come and Get It* (Ferber, Edna), 1161

*Come in from the Cold* (Qualey, Marsha), 842

*Come Spring* (Williams, Ben Ames), 107

*Come Winter* (Jones, Douglas C.), 494

*Commandos, The* (Arnold, Elliott), 714

*Company of Cowards* (Schaefer, Jack), 364

*Comstock Lode* (L'Amour, Louis), 265

*Confessions of Nat Turner, The* (Styron, William), 205

*Conqueror, The* (Atherton, Gertrude), 139

*Conquest* (Micheaux, Oscar), 1120

*Copperhead* (Cornwell, Bernard), 322

*Cormorant's Brood* (Fletcher, Inglis), 25

*Counterattack* (Griffin, W. E. B.), 743

*Country of Strangers, A* (Shreve, Susan Richards), 1148

*Courage of Captain Plum* (Curwood, James Oliver), 1016

*Court for Owls, A* (Adicks, Richard), 305

*Court Martial of Daniel Boone, The* (Eckert, Allan W.), 992

*Covered Wagon, The* (Hough, Emerson), 259

*Creek Called Wounded Knee, A* (Jones, Douglas C.), 495

*Crescent City* (Plain, Belva), 359

*Cross a Wide River* (Stevenson, Paul R.), 1073

*Cry of Absence* (Jones, Madison), 781

*Cry of the Hawk* (Johnston, Terry C.), 493

*Cutting Stone* (Burroway, Janet), 926


*Daddy Was a Numbers Runner* (Meriwether, Louise), 664

*Dakota Scouts* (Ell, Flynn J.), 463

*Dakotas: At the Wind's Edge* (Davis, Kathryn), 1091

*Dakotas: The Endless Sky* (Davis, Kathryn), 1092

*Dance on the Wind* (Johnston, Terry C.), 260

*Dances with Wolves* (Blake, Michael), 439

*Dancing at the Rascal Fair* (Doig, Ivan), 1035

*Dandelion Wine* (Bradbury, Ray), 596

*Dark Winter* (Broome, H. B.), 445

*Darlin' Bill* (Charyn, Jerome), 456

*Daughters of the New World* (Shreve, Susan Richards), 907

*David and Jonathan* (Voigt, Cynthia), 801

*Davita's Harp* (Potok, Chaim), 669

*Dawn's Early Light* (Thane, Elswyth Beebe), 105

*Day No Pigs Would Die, A* (Peck, Robert Newton), 622

*Day the Cowboys Quit, The* (Kelton, Elmer), 500

*Dead Man's Walk* (McMurtry, Larry), 270

*Deadwood* (Dexter, Pete), 1115

*Dear Ike* (Phillippi, Wendell C.), 728

*Death Comes for the Archbishop* (Cather, Willa), 242

*Deep Summer* (Bristow, Gwen), 143

*Deerslayer, The* (Cooper, James Fenimore), 18

*Delilah* (Goodrich, Marcus), 589

*Delta Wedding* (Welty, Eudora), 631

*Democracy* (Adams, Henry), 381

*Desert of Wheat* (Grey, Zane), 590

*Deserter Troop, The* (Cummings, Jack), 460

*Desperadoes* (Hansen, Ron), 483

*Devil and the Mathers, The* (Elliott, Edward E.), 23

*Devil Water* (Seton, Anya), 55

*Diamond's Compass* (Liotta, P. H.), 831

*Diana Stair* (Dell, Floyd), 163

*Discoveries of Mrs. Christopher Columbus, The* (DiPerna, Paula), 4

*Disinherited, The* (Conroy, Jack), 1033

*Distant Lands, The* (Green, Julian), 170

*Distant Trumpet, A* (Horgan, Paul), 489

*Divine Average* (Kirkland, Elithe), 262

*Dolley* (Brown, Rita Mae), 144
*Dollmaker, The* (Arnow, Harriette Simpson), 1013
*Don't Ever Leave Me* (Brush, Katherine), 638
*Dragon's Gate* (Yep, Laurence), 533
*Dragon's Teeth* (Sinclair, Upton), 671
*Dream Seekers* (Mark, Grace), 412
*Drowning Room, The* (Pye, Michael), 47
*Drums Along the Mohawk* (Edmonds, Walter D.), 71
*Durable Fire, A* (Bernhard, Virginia), 12
*Dust on the Sea* (Beach, Edward), 734
*Dutchman, The* (Meyers, Maan), 43

*Eagle and the Iron Cross, The* (Swarthout, Glendon), 707
*Eagle and the Raven, The* (Michener, James A.), 272
*Eagle in the Sky* (McCulloch, Frank), 1066
*Eagles Gather* (Caldwell, Janet Taylor), 598
*Early Autumn* (Bromfield, Louis), 1006
*Earthbreakers* (Haycox, Ernest), 295
*East and West* (Green, Gerald), 741
*East of Eden* (Steinbeck, John), 910
*East River* (Asch, Sholem), 1080
*Ebbing Tide* (Ogilvie, Elisabeth), 701
*Eben Holden* (Bacheller, Irving), 140
*Echo of Lions* (Chase-Riboud, Barbara), 150
*Edge of Time, The* (Erdman, Loula), 464
*Edsel* (Estleman, Loren D.), 770
*1876* (Vidal, Gore), 427
*Eighth Day, The* (Wilder, Thornton), 972
*Elkhorn Tavern* (Jones, Douglas C.), 344
*Ella Price's Journal* (Bryant, Dorothy), 806
*Elmer Gantry* (Lewis, Sinclair), 612
*Embarrassment of Riches* (Kunstler, James Howard), 264
*Emigrants, The* (Bojer, Johan), 441
*Emigrants, The* (Moberg, Vilhelm), 1027
*Empire* (Vidal, Gore), 428
*Empire in the Dust* (Halacy, Dan), 479
*Empire of Bones* (Long, Jeff), 268
*Empty Meadow, The* (Logan, Ben), 1162
*End of It, The* (Goodman, Mitchell), 721
*Enduring Hills* (Giles, Janice Holt), 994

*Enemies* (Seno, William J.), 1164
*English Creek* (Doig, Ivan), 1036
*Establishment, The* (Fast, Howard), 771
*Ethel* (Nason, Tema), 789
*Ever After* (Thane, Elswyth Beebe), 424
*Executioner Waits, The* (Herbst, Josephine), 608
*Eyes of Darkness, The* (Highwater, Jamake), 488
*Eyes of the Woods* (Altsheler, J. A.), 110

*Fabulous Fifty, The* (Grosser, Morton), 604
*Face in My Mirror, The* (Wartski, Maureen), 849
*Fair and Tender Ladies* (Smith, Lee), 1149
*Fallen Angels* (Myers, Walter Dean), 836
*Family* (Cooper, J. California), 157
*Family Fortune* (Eberhart, Mignon G.), 329
*Far from Cibola* (Horgan, Paul), 1064
*Farewell, My General* (Seifert, Shirley), 367
*Farewell to Arms, A* (Hemingway, Ernest), 591
*Farmer* (Harrison, Jim), 1018
*Fast Copy* (Jenkins, Dan), 1135
*Father and Son* (Farrell, James T.), 966
*Fathers* (Gold, Herbert), 873
*Fathers* (Tate, Allen), 371
*Feast of All Saints* (Rice, Anne O.), 194
*Feather Crowns* (Mason, Bobbie Ann), 998
*Ferment* (McIntyre, John Thomas), 663
*Fever in the Earth* (Owens, William A.), 567
*Fields, The* (Richter, Conrad), 223
*Fields of Fire* (Webb, James H.), 850
*Fifth of March, The* (Rinaldi, Ann), 96
*54-40 or Fight* (Hough, Emerson), 298
*Fig Tree John* (Corle, Edwin), 935
*Fightin' with Forrest* (Yeager, Charles Gordon), 378
*Financier, The* (Dreiser, Theodore), 394
*Finding Moon* (Hillerman, Tony), 823
*Finishing Becca* (Rinaldi, Ann), 97
*Fire on the Mountain* (Abbey, Edward), 760
*Firekeeper, The* (Moss, Robert), 44
*Fisherman's Beach* (Vukelich, George), 1165

*Five Smooth Stones* (Fairbairn, Ann), 866

*Flight of the Intruder* (Coonts, Stephen), 810

*Flower Drum Song, The* (Li, Chin Yang), 941

*Flowering of the Cumberland* (Arnow, Harriette Simpson), 989

*Flying in to Love* (Thomas, D. M.), 846

*Folded Leaf, The* (Maxwell, William), 614

*Follow the Free Wind* (Brackett, Leigh), 240

*Follow the River* (Thom, James Alexander), 57

*Fool of God, The* (Cochran, Louis), 156

*Fools Crow* (Welch, James), 529

*Fool's Errand, A* (Tourgee, Albion W.), 426

*For Love of Two Eagles* (Riefe, Barbara), 49

*For the Roses* (Garwood, Julie), 252

*For Us the Living* (Lancaster, Bruce), 220

*Forest Life* (Kirkland, Caroline M.), 1022

*Forest Runners* (Altsheler, J. A.), 111

*Forever Island* (Smith, Patrick), 956

*Forge, The* (Stribling, T. S.), 370

*Forgiving* (Spencer, LaVyrle), 1126

*Fortunate Pilgrim, The* (Puzo, Mario), 538

*Foundation Stone* (Warren, Lella), 206

*Foundry, The* (Halper, Albert), 606

*1492* (Frohlich, Newton), 6

*Foxes of Harrow, The* (Yerby, Frank), 207

*Foxfire* (Seton, Anya), 929

*Fragments of the Ark* (Meriwether, Louise), 356

*Freckles* (Stratton-Porter, Gene), 575

*Free Land* (Lane, Rose Wilder), 506

*Free Rangers* (Altsheler, J. A.), 112

*Freedom* (Safire, William), 363

*Freedom Songs* (Moore, Yvette), 834

*French Admiral, The* (Lambdin, Dewey), 85

*Friendly Persuasion, The* (West, Jessamyn), 229

*From Here to Eternity* (Jones, James), 747

*From Sea to Shining Sea* (Thom, James Alexander), 285

*From Where the Sun Now Stands* (Henry, Will), 486

*Gales of November* (Hemming, Robert J.), 1020

*Gardens of Stone* (Proffitt, Nicholas), 841

*Gathering of Old Men, A* (Gaines, Ernest J.), 818

*Gathering of Pearls* (Choi, Sook Nyul), 765

*Gentleman from Indiana, The* (Tarkington, Booth), 976

*Gentleman's Agreement* (Hobson, Laura Z.), 776

*Ghost Belonged to Me, The* (Peck, Richard), 969

*Ghost Dance Messiah* (Bailey, Paul), 1048

*Giant* (Ferber, Edna), 1132

*Giant Joshua* (Whipple, Maurine), 287

*Giant Wakes, The* (Hughes, Rupert), 880

*Giants in the Earth* (Rolvaag, Ole), 523

*Gilman of Redford* (Davis, William Stearns), 70

*Girl in Buckskin* (Gilman, Dorothy Butters), 32

*Girl of the Limberlost* (Stratton-Porter, Gene), 576

*Glitter and the Gold, The* (Stewart, Fred M.), 943

*Glory Enough for All* (Schultz, Duane P.), 365

*Glory Field, The* (Myers, Walter Dean), 896

*Glory from the Earth, A* (Schroeder, Ralph E.), 624

*Go Tell It on the Mountain* (Baldwin, James), 637

*Gods of War* (Toland, John), 756

*Golden Bowl, The* (Manfred, Frederick F.), 1117

*Golden Spur, The* (Powell, Dawn), 623

*Gone the Dreams and the Dancing* (Jones, Douglas C.), 496

*Gone to Soldiers* (Piercy, Marge), 690

*Gone to Texas* (Carter, Forrest), 452

*Gone with the Wind* (Mitchell, Margaret), 357

Good Negress, The (Verdelle, A. J.), 800
Good Shepherd, The (Forester, C. S.), 720
Good Times Are Killing Me, The (Barry, Lynda), 805
Goodbye Mickey Mouse (Deighton, Len), 717
Grand Design (Dos Passos, John), 647
Grant's War (Jones, Ted), 345
Grapes of Wrath, The (Steinbeck, John), 673
Grapple, The (Cooke, Grace MacGowan), 964
Grass Dancer (Power, Susan), 900
Grassman, The (Fulton, Len), 468
Graysons, The (Eggleston, Edward), 214
Great Gatsby, The (Fitzgerald, F. Scott), 602
Great Meadow (Roberts, Elizabeth Madox), 121
Green Bay Tree (Bromfield, Louis), 1097
Green Centuries (Gordon, Caroline), 996
Green Desire, A (Myrer, Anton), 897
Green Mountain Hero (Jackson, Edgar N.), 1145
Guard of Honor (Cozzens, James Gould), 710
Guns of Bull Run (Altsheler, J. A.), 306
Guns of Burgoyne (Lancaster, Bruce), 88
Guns of Shiloh (Altsheler, J. A.), 307

Hallapoosa (Peck, Robert Newton), 954
Handsome Road (Bristow, Gwen), 316
Hannah Fowler (Giles, Janice Holt), 118
Hannah's Mill (Wooldridge, Rhoda), 1034
Hard Road to Gettysburg (Jones, Ted), 346
Hardcastle (Yount, John), 688
Harvester, The (Stratton-Porter, Gene), 577
Hate Crime, The (Keras, Phyllis), 827
Hawaii (Michener, James A.), 893
Hawaii Aloha (Abe, Keith S.), 958
Hazard of New Fortunes, A (Howells, William Dean), 404
Heart of the West (Williamson, Penelope), 531
Heartbreak Hotel (Siddons, Anne Rivers), 794
Heart's Desire (Hough, Emerson), 490
Hearts Divided (Zach, Cheryl), 380

Heaven and Hell (Jakes, John), 405
Henry and Clara (Mallon, Thomas), 411
Her Own Place (Sanders, Dori), 705
Hermanos! (Herrick, William), 654
Hester (Bigsby, Christopher), 13
Hie to the Hunters (Stuart, Jesse), 999
High Constable, The (Meyers, Maan), 181
High Hearts (Brown, Rita Mae), 318
High Towers (Costain, Thomas B.), 2
High Trail to Danger (Nixon, Joan L.), 516
High Water (Bissell, Richard Pike), 762
Hills Stand Watch (Derleth, August W.), 212
Historian (Garber, Eugene K.), 872
Holly (French, Albert), 695
Hollywood (Vidal, Gore), 629
Home and Away (Filene, Peter), 772
Home Mountain (Williams, Jeanne), 530
Home Place, The (Thomas, Dorothy), 1046
Homeland (Jakes, John), 406
Homesteader, The (Micheaux, Oscar), 1121
Honey in the Horn (Davis, Harold Lenoir), 554
Hoopla (Stein, Harry), 574
Hoosier School-Boy, The (Eggleston, Edward), 215
Hoosier School-Master, The (Eggleston, Edward), 216
Horse Shoe Bottoms (Tippett, Thomas), 425
House Divided (Gurasich, Marj), 338
House Made of Dawn (Momaday, N. Scott), 1067
House of Seven Gables, The (Hawthorne, Nathaniel), 1008
How Far Would You Have Gotten If I Hadn't . . . (Hobbs, Valerie), 775
Hue and Cry (Yates, Elizabeth), 1057
Huge Season, The (Morris, Wright), 617
Human Comedy, The (Saroyan, William), 706
Hungry Men (Anderson, Edward), 636
Hunter's Heart (Rhodes, Judy Carole), 933

I Am Regina (Keehn, Sally M.), 37
I and My True Love (MacInnes, Helen), 787
I Had Seen Castles (Rylant, Cynthia), 691

*I, Tituba, Black Witch of Salem* (Conde, Maryse), 16

*I, Tom Horn* (Henry, Will), 1166

*Ice Palace* (Ferber, Edna), 869

*Idols and Axle-Grease* (Gwaltney, Frances I.), 652

*If I Never Get Back* (Brock, Darryl), 388

*Immortal Wife* (Stone, Irving), 132

*Impresario, The* (Litvin, Martin), 564

*In Country* (Mason, Bobbie Ann), 832

*In Dubious Battle* (Steinbeck, John), 674

*In God We Trust* (Shepherd, Jean), 975

*In My Father's House* (Gaines, Ernest J.), 1002

*In My Father's House* (Rinaldi, Ann), 361

*In the Beginning* (Potok, Chaim), 1087

*In the Center of the Nation* (O'Brien, Dan), 1124

*In the Fire of Spring* (Tryon, Thomas), 949

*In the House of My Pilgrimage* (Shuken, Julia), 570

*In the Time of the Wolves* (Charbonneau, Eileen), 149

*In Time of Harvest* (Sinclair, John L.), 1072

*Incorporation of Eric Chung, The* (Lo, Steven C.), 1136

*Indian Chronicles, The* (Barreiro, Jose), 1

*Indian Fighter's Return, The* (Cummings, Jack), 461

*Indio* (Garland, Sherry), 7

*Industrial Valley* (McKenney, Ruth), 1099

*Inside Passage, The* (Delis, Leftare P.), 919

*Inside, Outside* (Wouk, Herman), 854

*Intruder in the Dust* (Faulkner, William), 1030

*Invasion* (Lewis, Janet), 885

*Invisible Man* (Ellison, Ralph), 769

*Ironweed* (Kennedy, William P.), 1085

*Irregular Moon, An* (King, Sara), 829

*Island Within, The* (Lewisohn, Ludwig), 409

*Israel Potter* (Melville, Herman), 92

*Jack Gance* (Just, Ward S.), 782

*Jade* (Landis, Jill Marie), 505

*Janice Meredith* (Ford, Paul Leicester), 79

*Jasmine* (Mukherjee, Bharati), 835

*Jazz* (Morrison, Toni), 618

*Jefferson* (Byrd, Max), 145

*Jennie Gerhardt* (Dreiser, Theodore), 395

*Jennie Glenroy* (Ogilvie, Elisabeth), 183

*Jesse* (Soto, Gary), 845

*Jessie* (Alter, Judy), 123

*Johnny Got His Gun* (Trumbo, Dalton), 592

*Johnny Tremain* (Forbes, Esther), 78

*Jordan Freeman Was My Friend* (White, Richard W.), 106

*Jordon's Showdown* (Strunk, Frank C.), 676

*Journal of the Gun Years* (Matheson, Richard), 510

*Joy Luck Club* (Tan, Amy), 944

*Jubilee* (Walker, Margaret), 912

*Judas Flowering* (Hodge, Jane Aiken), 84

*Julie* (Marshall, Catherine), 566

*Jungle, The* (Sinclair, Upton), 571

*Justice* (Watson, Larry), 543

*Katy of Catoctin* (Townsend, George A.), 373

*Keepers of the Trail* (Altsheler, J. A.), 113

*Keeping the Good Light* (Kirkpatrick, Katherine), 563

*Kentuckians, The* (Giles, Janice Holt), 119

*Kentucky Home* (Receveur, Betty Layman), 193

*Killer Angels, The* (Shaara, Michael), 368

*Killing Ground* (Settle, Mary Lee), 1159

*Killing Mister Watson* (Matthiessen, Peter), 953

*Kim/Kimi* (Irwin, Hadley), 779

*King Coal* (Sinclair, Upton), 572

*King of Spades* (Manfred, Frederick F.), 1118

*King of the Hill* (Hotchner, A. E.), 655

*King Rat* (Clavell, James), 736

*King's Coat, The* (Lambdin, Dewey), 86

*King's Fifth* (O'Dell, Scott), 9

*Kings in Disguise* (Vance, James), 678

*Kingsbridge Plot, The* (Meyers, Maan), 93

*Know Nothing* (Settle, Mary Lee), 200

*Laddie* (Stratton-Porter, Gene), 420

*Lady, The* (Richter, Conrad), 522

*Lady from Toledo, The* (Chavez, Fray Angelico), 1061

*Land, The* (Swisher, Robert K.), 1074

*Land Beyond the Mountains* (Giles, Janice Holt), 168

*Land Is Bright, The* (Binns, Archie), 238

*Land of the Crooked Tree* (Hedrick, Ulysses P.), 1019

*Land Remembers, The* (Logan, Ben), 1163

*Landlooker, The* (Steuber, William), 419

*Lantern in Her Hand, A* (Aldrich, Bess Streeter), 231

*Lasso the Moon* (Covington, Dennis), 811

*Last Catholic in America, The* (Powers, John), 970

*Last Cattle Drive, The* (Day, Robert), 982

*Last Hurrah, The* (O'Connor, Edwin), 1011

*Last Lieutenant, The* (Gobbell, John J.), 740

*Last Mission, The* (Mazer, Harry), 726

*Last of the Mohicans* (Cooper, James Fenimore), 19

*Last Silk Dress* (Rinaldi, Ann), 362

*Last Stand, The* (Hoyt, Edwin P.), 492

*Last Waltz* (Zaroulis, Nancy), 431

*Late George Apley, The* (Marquand, John), 1010

*Laughing Boy* (LaFarge, Oliver), 1065

*Laughter on a Weekday* (Falstein, Louis), 559

*Learning Tree, The* (Parks, Gordon), 620

*Least One, The* (Deal, Bordon), 645

*Leaving the Land* (Unger, Douglas), 799

*Legacies* (Dailey, Janet), 326

*Legacy* (Michener, James A.), 894

*Legacy of Beulah Land* (Coleman, Lonnie), 390

*Legend of Storey County, The* (Thoene, Brock), 227

*Lesson Before Dying, A* (Gaines, Ernest J.), 1003

*Let the Band Play Dixie* (Wells, Lawrence), 1109

*Let the Hurricane Roar* (Lane, Rose Wilder), 507

*Let Us Go* (Judd, Walter F.), 959

*Letters from a Slave Girl* (Lyons, Mary E.), 179

*Libra* (DeLillo, Don), 813

*Lieutenant's Lady* (Aldrich, Bess Streeter), 433

*Life's Lure* (Neihardt, John G.), 1123

*Light a Distant Fire* (Robson, Lucia St. Clair), 199

*Light in the Forest, The* (Richter, Conrad), 48

*Lighthouse* (Price, Eugenia), 187

*Lily* (Bonner, Cindy), 442

*Lincoln* (Vidal, Gore), 374

*Lincoln Hunters, The* (Tucker, Wilson), 971

*Lincoln's Dreams* (Willis, Connie), 377

*Linger* (Kerr, M. E.), 828

*Lionheads, The* (Bunting, Josiah), 807

*Listen for Rachel* (Kassem, Lou), 348

*Little Big Man* (Berger, Thomas), 437

*Little Caesar* (Burnett, William Riley), 597

*Little Norsk, or Old Pap's Flaxen, A* (Garland, Hamlin), 470

*Little Shepherd of Kingdom Come* (Fox, John, Jr), 335

*Living, The* (Dillard, Annie), 1152

*Log of a Cowboy* (Adams, Andy), 432

*Lonesome Dove* (McMurtry, Larry), 513

*Lonesome Gods, The* (L'Amour, Louis), 940

*Long March, The* (Styron, William), 798

*Long Night* (Lytle, Andrew), 354

*Long Rifle* (White, Stewart Edward), 288

*Long Time Passing* (Jones, Adrienne), 826

*Longest Road, The* (Williams, Jeanne), 684

*Longest Winter, The* (Harris, Julie), 607

*Look Away* (Coyle, Harold), 324

*Look to the Mountain* (Cannon, LeGrand), 14

*Look to the River* (Owens, William A.), 1138

*Looking After Lily* (Bonner, Cindy), 443

*Loon Feather* (Fuller, Iola), 218

*Lord Grizzley* (Manfred, Frederick F.), 269

*Lords of Discipline, The* (Conroy, Pat), 1110

*Lord's Oysters, The* (Byron, Gilbert), 549
*Losing Battles* (Welty, Eudora), 683
*Lost and Found* (Harris, Marilyn), 878
*Lotus Land* (Highland, Monica), 879
*Love and War* (Jakes, John), 342
*Love Is a Wild Assault* (Kirkland, Elithe), 263
*Love Is Eternal* (Stone, Irving), 369
*Love Medicine* (Erdrich, Louise), 865
*Lovely Ambition, The* (Chase, Mary Ellen), 552
*Luciano's Luck* (Higgins, Jack), 724
*Lusty Wind for Carolina* (Fletcher, Inglis), 26

*Ma Jeeter's Girls* (Thomas, Dorothy), 1047
*Machine Dreams* (Phillips, Jayne Anne), 1158
*Mad Dog* (Kelly, Jack), 659
*Magnetic North* (Robins, Elizabeth), 925
*Magnificent Ambersons, The* (Tarkington, Booth), 422
*Main Street* (Lewis, Sinclair), 537
*Main Travelled Roads* (Garland, Hamlin), 471
*Major André* (Bailey, Anthony), 63
*Man Who Killed the Deer, The* (Waters, Frank), 1075
*Man Who Was Taller Than God, The* (Adams, Harold), 1112
*Man's Courage* (Vogel, Joseph), 680
*Manifest Destiny* (Garfield, Brian), 469
*Manitou's Daughter* (Lederer, Paul Joseph), 42
*Many Horses* (Wood, Elizabeth L.), 1156
*Margaret's Story* (Price, Eugenia), 901
*Maria* (Price, Eugenia), 188
*Mark's Own* (Atherton, Sarah), 857
*Mary's Land* (Robson, Lucia St. Clair), 53
*MASH* (Hooker, Richard), 778
*Massachusetts* (Zaroulis, Nancy), 916
*Massacre at Fall Creek, The* (West, Jessamyn), 230
*Maude Martha* (Brooks, Gwendolyn), 764

*McTeague* (Norris, Frank), 517
*Mean Spirit* (Hogan, Linda), 609
*Measure of Time* (Guy, Rosa), 605
*Medicine Calf* (Hotchkiss, Bill), 257
*Memorial, The* (Amos, James), 804
*Memorial Bridge* (Carroll, James), 863
*Men of Albemarle* (Fletcher, Inglis), 27
*Midnight Clear* (Wharton, William), 733
*Midwife, The* (Courter, Gay), 1082
*Mighty Mountain* (Binns, Archie), 293
*Milagro Beanfield War, The* (Nichols, John), 1068
*Miracles* (Heidish, Marcy), 173
*Mirror for Witches, A* (Forbes, Esther), 30
*Miss 4th of July, Goodbye* (Janus, Christopher G.), 562
*Miss Bishop* (Aldrich, Bess Streeter), 977
*Miss Morissa, Doctor of the Gold Trail* (Sandoz, Mari), 525
*Miss Susie Slagle's* (Tucker, Augusta), 580
*Mississippi Chariot* (Robinet, Harriette Gillen), 670
*Mister Roberts* (Heggen, Thomas), 744
*Moby Dick* (Melville, Herman), 126
*Montana 1948* (Watson, Larry), 1040
*Monte Walsh* (Schaefer, Jack), 568
*Moontrap* (Berry, Don), 290
*Morning Glory Afternoon* (Brown, Irene Bennett), 981
*Mothers, The* (Fisher, Vardis), 250
*Motor City* (Morris, Bill), 1024
*Mountain Man* (Fisher, Vardis), 251
*Mountain Windsong* (Conley, Robert J.), 244
*Mr. Bridge* (Connell, Evan S.), 641
*Mrs. Bridge* (Connell, Evan S.), 642
*Mrs. Parkington* (Bromfield, Louis), 860
*Murder by the Numbers* (Collins, Max Allan), 639
*Music from a Place Called Half Moon* (Oughton, Jerrie), 790
*My Antonia* (Cather, Willa), 454
*My Theodosia* (Seton, Anya), 131
*My Thomas* (Grimes, Roberta), 83

Entries 1-61: 1492-1775, Entries 62-122: 1776-1783, Entries 123-304: 1783-1860, Entries 305-380: 1861-1899, Entries 381-533: 1866-1899, Entries 534-688: 1900-1939, Entries 689-759: 1939-1945, Entries 760-855: 1945-1995, Entries 856-916: Epic Novels, Entries 917-1168: Additional Titles.

*Naked and the Dead, The* (Mailer, Norman), 752
*Native Son* (Wright, Richard), 686
*Ned Christie's War* (Conley, Robert J.), 458
*Nell's Quilt* (Terris, Susan), 423
*Nevada* (Grey, Zane), 476
*Never No More* (Seifert, Shirley), 54
*Never Victorious, Never Defeated* (Caldwell, Janet Taylor), 862
*New Breed, The* (Griffin, W. E. B.), 821
*New Home—Who'll Follow?* (Kirkland, Caroline M.), 219
*New Moon Rising* (Price, Eugenia), 189
*New Orleans Legacy* (Ripley, Alexandra), 1004
*Newfound* (Miller, Jim Wayne), 1128
*Night of Shadows* (Gorman, Edward), 475
*Night Rider* (Warren, Robert Penn), 581
*Night Run* (Denny, Robert), 718
*Nightjohn* (Paulsen, Gary), 185
*Nineteen Fifty Nine* (Davis, Thulani), 768
*1919* (Dos Passos, John), 586
*1933 Was a Bad Year* (Fante, John), 650
*No Bottom* (Brewer, James O.), 386
*No Life for a Lady* (Cleaveland, Agnes Morley), 1062
*No Promises in the Wind* (Hunt, Irene), 657
*No Reck'ning Made* (Greenberg, Joanne), 876
*No Resting Place* (Humphrey, William), 175
*No Survivors* (Henry, Will), 487
*No Virtue* (Brewer, James O.), 387
*North and South* (Jakes, John), 176
*North to Yesterday* (Flynn, Robert), 1133
*Northwest Passage* (Roberts, Kenneth L.), 10
*Not Without Laughter* (Hughes, Langston), 561
*Not Without Peril* (Allis, Marguerite), 137
*November of the Heart* (Spencer, LaVyrle), 1029

*O Canaan!* (Turpin, Waters Edward), 542
*O God of Battles* (Homewood, Harry), 691
*O Pioneers!* (Cather, Willa), 455
*Occupation* (Toland, John), 757
*Octopus, The* (Norris, Frank), 518

*Of Arms I Sing* (Bohnaker, Joseph S.), 1059
*Of Mice and Men* (Steinbeck, John), 675
*Oh Kentucky!* (Receveur, Betty Layman), 120
*Oil!* (Sinclair, Upton), 626
*Okla Hannali* (Lafferty, R. A.), 883
*Old Bunch, The* (Levin, Meyer), 610
*Old Yeller* (Gipson, Fred), 474
*Oldest Living Confederate Widow Tells All, The* (Gurganus, Allan), 1090
*Oldtown Folks* (Stowe, Harriet Beecher), 203
*Oliver Wiswell* (Roberts, Kenneth L.), 102
*On to Oregon* (Morrow, Honore), 273
*Once an Eagle* (Myrer, Anton), 898
*One of Ours* (Cather, Willa), 585
*One Red Rose Forever* (Jordan, Mildred A.), 36
*Only Earth and Sky Last Forever* (Benchley, Nathaniel), 1113
*Ordways, The* (Humphrey, Wlliam), 1134
*Oregon Detour* (Jones, Nard), 1103
*Original Sins* (Alther, Lisa), 1127
*Our Changing Lives* (Sollitt, Kenneth), 979
*Our Own Kind* (McSorley, Edward), 616
*Out of This Furnace* (Bell, Thomas), 858
*Over There* (Fleming, Thomas J.), 588
*Ox Bow Incident* (Clark, Walter Van Tilberg), 457

*Pacific Street* (Holland, Cecelia), 297
*Pageant* (Lasky, Kathryn), 973
*Paloverde* (Briskin, Jacqueline), 934
*Panther* (Van Peebles, Melvin), 848
*Panther in the Sky* (Thom, James Alexander), 228
*Papa La-Bas* (Carr, John Dickson), 146
*Paper Doll* (Shepard, Jim), 730
*Papa's Wife* (Bjorn, Thyra Ferre), 385
*Part of the Sky, A* (Peck, Robert Newton), 668
*Patch Boys, The* (Parini, Jay), 621
*Pathfinder, The* (Cooper, James Fenimore), 20
*Pay Day* (Asch, Nathan), 595
*Peculiar People, The* (DeHartog, Jan), 210
*Peder Victorious* (Rolvaag, Ole), 524
*Peggy* (Callahan, North), 65

*Penhally* (Gordon, Caroline), 874

*Penrod* (Tarkington, Booth), 579

*People of the Valley* (Waters, Frank), 1076

*Perfect Tribute* (Andrews, Mary R. S.), 314

*Persian Pickle Club, The* (Dallas, Sandra), 644

*Peter Pan Bag* (Kingman, Lee), 830

*Phantom Fortress* (Lancaster, Bruce), 89

*Pilot, The* (Cooper, James Fenimore), 67

*Pinto and Sons* (Epstein, Leslie), 938

*Pioneers, The* (Cooper, James Fenimore), 158

*Pistoleer, The* (Blake, James Carlos), 438

*Pit, The* (Norris, Frank), 414

*Place Called Freedom, A* (Follett, Ken), 29

*Place Called Sweet Shrub, A* (Wood, Jane Roberts), 582

*Plains Song* (Morris, Wright), 1044

*Plastic Age* (Marks, Percy), 613

*Playing the Mischief* (DeForest, J. W.), 393

*Plot to Kill Jackie Robinson, The* (Honig, Donald), 777

*Plum Thicket, The* (Giles, Janice Holt), 473

*Pocahontas* (Donnell, Susan), 22

*Pooles of Pismo Bay, The* (Rose, Howard), 539

*Powderkeg* (Gordon, Leo V.), 253

*Prairie, The* (Cooper, James Fenimore), 209

*Prairie Widow* (Bakst, Harold), 434

*President's Daughter, The* (Chase-Riboud, Barbara), 151

*President's Lady, The* (Stone, Irving), 133

*Price of a Child, The* (Cary, Lorene), 147

*Primrose Way, The* (Koller, Jackie French), 38

*Promised Land* (Crook, Elizabeth), 245

*Proud and the Free, The* (Dailey, Janet), 160

*Proud and the Free, The* (Fast, Howard), 74

*Proud Breed, The* (De Blasis, Celeste), 936

*Pudd'nhead Wilson* (Clemens, Samuel), 155

*Quanah Parker* (Kissinger, Rosemary K.), 502

*Queen's Gift, The* (Fletcher, Inglis), 166

*Quest of the Fish-Dog Skin* (Schultz, James Willard), 279

*Quicksilver Pool* (Whitney, Phyllis A.), 375

*Quiet Shore* (Havighurst, Walter), 1098

*Raccoon John Smith* (Cochran, Louis), 991

*Raditzer* (Matthiessen, Peter), 753

*Ragtime* (Doctorow, E. L.), 556

*Raintree County* (Lockridge, Ross, Jr.), 886

*Raising Holy Hell* (Olds, Bruce), 274

*Raleigh's Eden* (Fletcher, Inglis), 75

*Ramona* (Jackson, Helen Hunt), 299

*Rascals Heaven* (Van Wyck Mason, F.), 59

*Raspberry One* (Ferry, Charles), 738

*Raven's Bride, The* (Crook, Elizabeth), 246

*Real Diary of a Real Boy, The* (Shute, Henry A.), 1053

*Rebel* (Cornwell, Bernard), 323

*Red Badge of Courage* (Crane, Stephen), 325

*Red Menace* (Anania, Michael), 761

*Red Rock* (Page, Thomas Nelson), 415

*Red Rover, The* (Cooper, James Fenimore), 21

*Red Sky at Morning* (Bradford, Richard), 1060

*Redcoat* (Cornwell, Bernard), 69

*Refinements of Love* (Conroy, Sarah Booth), 391

*Regulators, The* (Degenhard, William), 162

*Remember Santiago* (Jones, Douglas C.), 408

*Remember the End* (Turnbull, Agnes), 1106

*Remembrance Rock* (Sandburg, Carl), 903

*Rennie's Way* (Slone, Verna Mae), 627

*Resistance* (Shreve, Anita), 731

*Return of the Spanish* (Coldsmith, Don), 16

*Revelry* (Adams, Samuel Hopkins), 594

*Richard Carvel* (Churchill, Winston), 66

*Richlands, The* (Turnbull, Agnes), 1107

*Ride into Morning, A* (Rinaldi, Ann), 98

*Ride the Wind* (Robson, Lucia St. Clair), 277

*Riders of Judgment* (Manfred, Frederick F.), 1168

*Riders of the Purple Sage* (Grey, Zane), 477

*Riders to Cibola* (Zollinger, Norman), 1078

*Riflemen of the Ohio* (Altsheler, J. A.), 114

*Rifles for Watie* (Keith, Harold), 349

*Rim of the Prairie* (Aldrich, Bess Streeter), 1041

*Rise of Silas Lapham, The* (Howells, William Dean), 1009

*Rivers of Gold* (Edmonds, Janet), 462

*Rivington Street* (Tax, Meredith), 540

*Road Home, The* (White, Ellen Emerson), 852

*Road to Memphis, The* (Taylor, Mildred D.), 708

*Road to San Jacinto, The* (Davis, James F.), 1131

*Road to Wellville, The* (Boyle, T. C.), 1014

*Roanoke Hundred* (Fletcher, Inglis), 28

*Rock of Chickamauga* (Altsheler, J. A.), 308

*Rockspring* (Vliet, R. G.), 286

*Roll of Thunder, Hear My Cry* (Taylor, Mildred D.), 677

*Rolling Years* (Turnbull, Agnes), 1108

*Roman* (Jones, Douglas C.), 497

*Romance of Dollard* (Catherwood, Mary Harwell), 1015

*Rome Haul* (Edmonds, Walter D.), 164

*Royal City, The* (Savage, Les, Jr.), 1071

*Royal Street* (Roberts, Walter), 198

*Rumors of Peace* (Leffland, Ella), 699

*Run Silent, Run Deep* (Beach, Edward), 735

*Runaway* (Graham, Heather), 169

*Runs with Horses* (Burks, Brian), 446

*Sacajawea* (Waldo, Anna Lee), 135

*Sackett's Land* (L'Amour, Louis), 39

*Sacred Hunger* (Unsworth, Barry), 58

*Safe Harbors* (Roth-Hano, Renee), 791

*Sally Hemmings* (Chase-Riboud, Barbara), 152

*Sam Bass* (Woolley, Bryan), 532

*Sam Chance* (Capps, Benjamin), 448

*Sam Houston Story, The* (Owen, Dean), 275

*Sand* (James, Will), 1038

*Sand Pebbles, The* (McKenna, Richard), 615

*Sapphira and the Slave Girl* (Cather, Willa), 148

*Sarah Bishop* (O'Dell, Scott), 94

*Saratoga Trunk* (Ferber, Edna), 399

*Saturnalia* (Fleischman, Paul), 1007

*Savanna* (Giles, Janice Holt), 930

*Savannah* (Price, Eugenia), 190

*Savannah Purchase* (Hodge, Jane Aiken), 957

*Say These Names (Remember Them)* (Cummings, Betty Sue), 159

*Scapegoat, The* (Settle, Mary Lee), 569

*Scarlet Letter, The* (Hawthorne, Nathaniel), 33

*Scarlet Patch* (Lancaster, Bruce), 353

*Scarlet Plume* (Manfred, Frederick F.), 1119

*Scarlet Women* (Christilian, J. D.), 389

*Scotswoman, The* (Fletcher, Inglis), 76

*Scouts of Stonewall* (Altsheler, J. A.), 309

*Scouts of the Valley* (Altsheler, J. A.), 115

*Scuttlebutt* (Williams, Jana), 853

*Sea and Poison, The* (Endo, Shusaku), 737

*Sea Island Lady* (Griswold, Francis), 877

*Sea of Grass, The* (Richter, Conrad), 1070

*Sea Runners* (Doig, Ivan), 920

*Sea Venture, The* (Van Wyck Mason, F.), 60

*Search for Temperance Moon* (Jones, Douglas C.), 498

*Searchers, The* (LeMay, Alan), 509

*Season for War* (Kluge, P. F.), 503

*Second Growth* (Stegner, Wallace), 1054

*Secret of Sarah Revere, The* (Rinaldi, Ann), 99

*Secret Road* (Lancaster, Bruce), 90

*Seneca Falls Inheritance* (Monfredo, Miriam Grace), 182

*Sense of Honor, A* (Webb, James H.), 851

*Separate Peace, A* (Knowles, John), 698

*Serpent and the Staff, The* (Yerby, Frank), 583

*Serpent Never Sleeps, The* (O'Dell, Scott), 45

*Serpent's Gift, The* (Lee, Helen Elaine), 884

*Seven Six One* (Borden, G. F.), 715

*Shades of the Wilderness* (Altsheler, J. A.), 310

*Shadow Catcher* (Fergus, Charles), 560

*Shadow of the Dragon* (Garland, Sherry), 819

*Shadow of the Long Knives* (Boyd, Thomas Alexander), 117

*Shaman* (Gordon, Noah), 875

*Shane* (Schaefer, Jack), 527

*Sherman's March* (Bass, Cynthia), 315

*Sherwood Ring* (Pope, Elizabeth Marie), 95

*Shiloh* (Foote, Shelby), 332

*Ships Gone Missing* (Hemming, Robert J.), 1021

*Shortgrass Song* (Blakely, Mike), 859

*Shoshone Mike* (Bergon, Frank), 1049

*Show Boat* (Ferber, Edna), 400

*Shukar Balan* (Lindsay, Mela Meisner), 986

*Silent Sea* (Homewood, Harry), 746

*Silver Horde* (Beach, Rex Ellingwood), 918

*Silver Wings, Santiago Blue* (Dailey, Janet), 711

*Sing Down the Moon* (O'Dell, Scott), 928

*Single Tree* (Svee, Gary D.), 528

*'Sippi* (Killens, John Oliver), 1031

*Sister Carrie* (Dreiser, Theodore), 396

*Sitka* (L'Amour, Louis), 922

*Skinny Angel* (Jones, Thelma), 1116

*Sky Is Falling, The* (Corcoran, Barbara), 643

*Slaughter* (Kelton, Elmer), 501

*Slopes of War* (Perez, N. A.), 358

*Small Bequest, A* (Love, Edmund G.), 1023

*Smoke Bellew* (London, Jack), 923

*So Red the Rose* (Young, Stark), 379

*Sod and Stubble* (Ise, John), 984

*Soldier of Good Fortune* (Cross, Ruth), 3

*Sometimes a Great Notion* (Kesey, Ken), 784

*Son of the Gamblin' Man* (Sandoz, Mari), 526

*Song of Years, A* (Aldrich, Bess Streeter), 208

*Sons of Texas* (Early, Tom), 248

*Sot Weed Factor, The* (Barth, John), 11

*Sound the Jubilee* (Forrester, Sandra), 334

*Southern Exposure, A* (Adams, Alice), 634

*Southern Woman* (Eulo, Elena Yates), 330

*Space* (Michener, James A), 833

*Spanish Bayonet* (Benet, Stephen Vincent), 64

*Spanish Bride, The* (O'Meara, Walter), 1069

*Spanish Gold* (Randle, Kevin J.), 1139

*Speak Softly* (Alexander, Lawrence), 383

*Spite Fences* (Krisher, Trudy), 785

*Splendid Wayfaring* (Neihardt, John G.), 127

*Spoilers* (Beach, Rex Ellington), 436

*Spoils of War, The* (Fleming, Thomas J.), 401

*Spoonhandle* (Moore, Ruth), 665

*Spring Came On Forever* (Aldrich, Bess Streeter), 856

*Spring Harvest* (Taber, Gladys), 578

*Spy, The* (Cooper, James Fenimore), 68

*Stampede* (White, Stewart Edward), 304

*Star Fisher, The* (Yep, Laurence), 633

*Star of Empire* (Sanders, Leonard), 278

*Star of Gettysburg* (Altsheler, J. A.), 311

*Steal Away* (Armstrong, Jennifer), 138

*Step to the Music* (Whitney, Phyllis A.), 376

*Stickeen* (Muir, John), 924

*Stitch in Time, A* (Rinaldi, Ann), 196

*Stone Song* (Blevins, Win), 440

*Store, The* (Stribling, T. S.), 421

*Storm Tide* (Ogilvie, Elisabeth), 702

*Storming Heaven* (Giardina, Denise), 603

*Story of a Country Town, The* (Howe, Edgar Watson), 983

*Story of Deep Delight, A* (McNamee, Thomas), 889

*Strange Angels* (Agee, Jonis), 803

*Stranger in Savannah* (Price, Eugenia), 360

*Streams to the River, River to the Sea* (O'Dell, Scott), 128

Entries 1-61: 1492-1775, Entries 62-122: 1776-1783, Entries 123-304: 1783-1860, Entries 305-380: 1861-1899, Entries 381-533: 1866-1899, Entries 534-688: 1900-1939, Entries 689-759: 1939-1945, Entries 760-855: 1945-1995, Entries 856-916: Epic Novels, Entries 917-1168: Additional Titles.

*Streets of Fire* (Cook, Thomas H.), 809

*Streets of Laredo* (McMurtry, Larry), 514

*Stretch on the River, A* (Bissell, Richard Pike), 763

*Strife Before Dawn* (Schumann, Mary), 905

*Stronger Than Fear* (Tregaskis, Richard), 732

*Strumpet Wind, The* (Merrick, Gordon), 727

*Stump Ranch Pioneer* (Davis, Nelle Portry), 960

*Summer of My German Soldier* (Greene, Bette), 697

*Summons to Memphis* (Taylor, Peter), 1129

*Swamp Fox, Francis Marion, The* (Gerson, Noel B.), 80

*Swan's Chance* (De Blasis, Celeste), 161

*Sweetbitter* (Gibbons, Reginald), 472

*Sweetbriar* (Wilbee, Brenda), 1153

*Sweetbriar Bride* (Wilbee, Brenda), 1154

*Sweetbriar Spring* (Wilbee, Brenda), 1155

*Swift Flows the River* (Jones, Nard), 301

*Sword and Scalpel* (Slaughter, Frank G.), 797

*Sword of Antietam* (Altsheler, J. A.), 312


*Tale of Valor* (Fisher, Vardis), 125

*Talent Night* (Okimoto, Jean Davies), 839

*Tall Woman, The* (Dykeman, Wilma), 398

*Tamarack Tree* (Clapp, Patricia), 320

*Taps for Private Tussie* (Stuart, Jesse), 1000

*Tara's Healing* (Giles, Janice Holt), 995

*Tenderloin* (Adams, Samuel Hopkins), 382

*Testimony of Two Men* (Caldwell, Janet Taylor), 551

*Texan Scouts* (Altsheler, J. A.), 232

*Texan Star* (Altsheler, J. A.), 233

*Texan Triumph* (Altsheler, J. A.), 234

*Texas* (Michener, James A.), 895

*Texasville* (McMurtry, Larry), 1137

*That Year of Our War* (Goldreich, Gloria), 696

*Their Eyes Were Watching God* (Hurston, Zora Neale), 952

*Theory of War* (Brady, Joan), 444

*These Years of Promise* (Harrison, Nick; Sollitt, Kenneth), 978

*They Came Like Swallows* (Maxwell, William), 967

*Thin Men of Haddam* (Smith, C. W.), 1141

*Thin Red Line, The* (Jones, James), 748

*Thirteen Miles from Suncrest* (David, Donald), 553

*Thirteenth Valley, The* (Del Vecchio, John M.), 814

*This Child's Gonna Live* (Wright, Sarah E.), 687

*This Old Bill* (Estleman, Loren D.), 466

*This Rough New Land* (Sollitt, Kenneth), 980

*This Savage Race* (Jones, Douglas C.), 882

*This Side of Glory* (Bristow, Gwen), 547

*This Widowed Land* (Gear, Kathleen O'Neal), 31

*Those Who Love* (Stone, Irving), 104

*Three Lives of Elizabeth* (Seifert, Shirley), 130

*Three Soldiers* (Dos Passos, John), 587

*Thunder Mountain* (Grey, Zane), 961

*Thunder on the Plains* (Bittner, Rosanne), 239

*Tidewater Dynasty* (Roberts, Carey), 902

*Tie That Binds* (Haruf, Kent), 946

*Till the End of Time* (Appel, Allen), 689

*Timber* (Haig-Brown, Roderick), 1102

*Time and Place* (Woolley, Bryan), 1142

*Time and Tide* (Fleming, Thomas J.), 739

*Time Enough for Drums* (Rinaldi, Ann), 100

*Time of the Gringo* (Arnold, Elliott), 236

*Time of Troubles, A* (Van Raven, Pieter), 679

*Time Too Swift, A* (Poynter, Margaret), 703

*Time Will Darken It* (Maxwell, William), 968

*Titan, The* (Dreiser, Theodore), 397

*Tituba of Salem Village* (Petry, Ann), 46

*To Build a Ship* (Berry, Don), 291

*To Have and Have Not* (Hemingway, Ernest), 951

*To Have and To Hold* (Johnston, Mary), 35

*To Kill a Mockingbird* (Lee, Harper), 661

*To See Your Face Again* (Price, Eugenia), 191

*To the Far Blue Mountains* (L'Amour, Louis), 40

*To the Indies* (Forester, C. S.), 5

*Tobacco Sticks* (Hazelgrove, William Elliott), 773

*Toil of the Brave* (Fletcher, Inglis), 77

*Tomorrow Is a River* (Dopp, Peggy), 1160

*Tomorrow Will Be Better* (Smith, Betty), 628

*Tomorrow's Bread* (Bisno, Beatrice), 384

*Tory Hole* (Tharp, Louise Hall), 948

*Toward What Bright Glory?* (Drury, Allen), 648

*Town, The* (Richter, Conrad), 224

*Town Burning* (Williams, Thomas), 1055

*Trail* (Charbonneau, Louis), 124

*Trail of the Gold Seekers* (Garland, Hamlin), 921

*Trail of the Lonesome Pine* (Fox, John, Jr.), 993

*Trail to Ogallala, The* (Capps, Benjamin), 449

*Trail-Makers of the Middle Border* (Garland, Hamlin), 336

*Train Whistle Guitar* (Murray, Albert), 619

*Traitor, The* (Sherman, Dan), 103

*Trask* (Berry, Don), 292

*Traveller* (Adams, Richard), 1147

*Travels of Jamie McPheeters, The* (Taylor, Robert Lewis), 283

*Tree by Leaf* (Voigt, Cynthia), 593

*Tree Grows in Brooklyn, A* (Smith, Betty), 573

*Tree of Appomattox* (Altsheler, J. A.), 313

*Tree of Liberty* (Page, Elizabeth), 899

*Trees, The* (Richter, Conrad), 225

*Troubled Air, The* (Shaw, Irwin), 793

*True Detective* (Collins, Max Allan), 640

*True Grit* (Portis, Charles), 521

*True Women* (Windle, Janice Woods), 914

*Trumpet to Arms* (Lancaster, Bruce), 91

*Tunes for Bears to Dance To* (Cormier, Robert), 767

*Turkey Red* (Vogt, Esther), 987

*Turquoise Trail, The* (Seifert, Shirley), 282

*Twelve O'Clock High* (Lay, Beirne), 725

*Two Years Before the Mast* (Dana, Richard Henry, Jr.), 294

*Typical American* (Jen, Gish), 780

*U. P. Trail, The* (Grey, Zane), 478

*Uncle Tom's Cabin* (Stowe, Harriet Beecher), 204

*Under the Blood-Red Sun* (Salisbury, Graham), 754

*Unexpected Peace, The* (Kelly, Jack), 750

*Unfinished Cathedral, The* (Stribling, T. S.), 917

*Union Square* (Tax, Meredith), 541

*Unplowed Sky, The* (Williams, Jeanne), 632

*Unto a Good Land* (Moberg, Vilhelm), 1028

*Unwritten Chronicles of Robert E. Lee* (Herrin, Lamar), 339

*Useless Servants, The* (Hinojosa, Rolando), 774

*V for Victor* (Childress, Mark), 694

*Valley in Between* (Donahue, Marilyn Cram), 937

*Valley of Decision, The* (Davenport, Marcia), 864

*Vandemark's Folly* (Quick, Herbert), 222

*Vida* (Piercy, Marge), 840

*Vixens, The* (Yerby, Frank), 430

*Waiting for the News* (Litwak, Leo), 662

*Walk Gently This Good Earth* (Craven, Margaret), 1151

*Walk in My Soul* (Robson, Lucia St. Clair), 1140

*Walk in the Sun, A* (Brown, Harry), 716

*Walk on the Wild Side, A* (Algren, Nelson), 635

*Walk Through Fire, A* (Cobb, William), 766

*Walking Up a Rainbow* (Taylor, Theodore), 284

*Walks Without a Soul* (Proctor, George W.), 276

*Wandering Star* (Yount, Steven), 584

*War and Remembrance* (Wouk, Herman), 692

*Ward Eight* (Dinneen, Joseph), 555

*Warlock* (Hall, Oakley), 481

*Warrior, The* (Slaughter, Frank G.), 201

*Wars of the Heart* (Villars, Elizabeth), 709

*Washington, D.C.* (Vidal, Gore), 911

*Washington Square* (James, Henry), 177

*Watch for Me on the Mountain* (Carter, Forrest), 453

*Waterfront* (Schulberg, Budd), 1088

*Waterlily* (Deloria, Ella Cara), 1114

*Waterworks, The* (Doctorow, E. L.), 1084

*Wave, The* (Scott, Evelyn), 366

*Way We Were, The* (Laurents, Arthur), 786

*Way West, The* (Guthrie, A. B.), 255

*Wedding, The* (West, Dorothy), 802

*Weedy Rough* (Jones, Douglas C.), 658

*West to Eden* (Goldreich, Gloria), 535

*Western Union* (Grey, Zane), 171

*When Lightning Strikes* (Becnel, Rexanne), 237

*When the Legends Die* (Borland, Hal), 544

*When the Tree Flowered* (Neihardt, John G.), 1045

*Where Shadows Go* (Price, Eugenia), 192

*Where the Broken Heart Still Beats* (Meyer, Carolyn), 271

*While Angels Dance* (Cotton, Ralph), 459

*Whipple's Castle* (Williams, Thomas), 1056

*Whiskey River* (Estleman, Loren D.), 534

*Whistle* (Jones, James), 713

*Whistle Punk* (Ross, Alice), 704

*White Bird Flying, A* (Aldrich, Bess Streeter), 1042

*White Dawn* (Houston, James), 491

*White Indian Boy* (Lund, Duane R.), 1025

*White Man's Road* (Capps, Benjamin), 450

*Wide Open Town* (Brinig, Myron), 546

*Wild Is the River* (Bromfield, Louis), 317

*Wild Meat and the Bully Burgers* (Yamanaka, Lois-Ann), 855

*Wild Western Desire* (Jones, Kathy), 985

*Wilderness* (Zelazny, Roger), 289

*Wilderness to Washington* (Long, Eleanor Rice), 974

*Wind from Nowhere, The* (Micheaux, Oscar), 1122

*Wind Leaves No Shadow, The* (Laughlin, Ruth), 267

*Winding Stair* (Jones, Douglas C.), 499

*Winds of Morning* (Davis, Harold Lenoir), 599

*Winds of War, The* (Wouk, Herman), 693

*Wings of the Morning, The* (Tryon, Thomas), 950

*Winthrop Woman, The* (Seton, Anya), 1012

*Witches' Children* (Clapp, Patricia), 15

*With Every Drop of Blood* (Collier, James Lincoln), 321

*With the Indians in the Rockies* (Schultz, James Willard), 280

*Witnesses* (Heidish, Marcy), 34

*Woe to Live On* (Woodrell, Daniel), 988

*Wolf by the Ears* (Rinaldi, Ann), 197

*Wolf Song* (Fergusson, Harvey), 1063

*Wolf Whistle* (Nordan, Lewis), 1032

*Woman at Otowi Crossing* (Waters, Frank), 1077

*Woman of the People, A* (Capps, Benjamin), 241

*Woman Who Fell from the Sky, The* (Riefe, Barbara), 50

*Wonderful Country, The* (Lea, Tom), 508

*Word of Honor* (De Mille, Nelson), 815

*World Enough and Time* (Warren, Robert Penn), 1001

*World's Fair* (Doctorow, E. L.), 646

*Yankee Stranger* (Thane, Elswyth Beebe), 372

*Year the Lights Came On, The* (Kay, Terry), 783

*Years* (Spencer, LaVyrle), 1095

*Yellow* (Lynch, Daniel), 410

*Yellow Raft in Blue Water, A* (Dorris, Michael), 1037

*Yemassee, The* (Simms, William Gilmore), 56

*Yonnondio* (Olsen, Tillie), 667

*You Can't Go Home Again* (Wolfe, Thomas), 685

*Young Lions, The* (Shaw, Irwin), 729

*Young Titan, The* (Van Wyck Mason, F.), 61

*Young Trailers* (Altsheler, J. A.), 116

*Young Voyageur, The* (Gringhuis, Dirk), 1017

*Youngblood* (Killens, John Oliver), 536

*Youngest Voyageur* (Lund, Duane R.), 1026

*Your Blues Ain't Like Mine* (Campbell, Bebe Moore), 963

*Yukon Queen, The* (Morris, Gilbert), 515

# SUBJECT INDEX

Numbers refer to entry numbers not page numbers. For the reader's convenience entry number and dates correspond to the following order. Entries 1-61: 1492-1775, Entries 62-122: 1776-1783, Entries 123-304: 1783-1860, Entries 305-380: 1861-1899, Entries 381-533: 1866-1899, Entries 534-688: 1900-1939, Entries 689-759: 1939-1945, Entries 760-855: 1945-1995, Entries 856-916: Epic Novels, Entries 917-1168: Additional Titles.

**Abolitionists**
Diana Stair, 163
In the Fire of Spring, 949
Price of a Child, The, 147

**Adams, Abigail**
Fifth of March, The, 96
Those Who Love, 104

**Adams, Henry**
Refinements of Love, 391

**Adams, John Quincy**
Echo of Lions, 150

**Adams, John**
Fifth of March, The, 96
Those Who Love, 104

**Adams, Marian (Clover)**
Refinements of Love, 391

**Adams, Samuel**
Gilman of Redford, 70

**Addams, Jane**
Dream Seekers, 412
Homeland, 406

**African Americans.** (*See also* Racism; Slaves and Slavery)
Ammahabas, 256
And Then We Heard the Thunder, 751
Autobiography of Miss Jane Pittman, The, 871
Beloved, 413
Black Gold, 1130
Betsy Brown, 792
Changelings, The, 796
Color Purple, 681
Conquest, 1120
Country of Strangers, A, 1148

Five Smooth Stones, 866
Follow the Free Wind, 240
Fragments of the Ark, 356
Gathering of Old Men, A, 818
Glory Enough for All, 365
Glory Field, The, 896
Go Tell It on the Mountain, 637
Good Negress, The, 800
Her Own Place, 705
Invisible Man, 769
Irregular Moon, An, 829
Jazz, 618
Jordan Freeman Was My Friend, 106
Jubilee, 912
Learning Tree, The, 620
Legend of Storey County, The, 227
Maude Martha, 764
Measure of Time, 605
Medicine Calf, 257
Mississippi Chariot, 670
Nineteen Fifty Nine, 768
Not Without Laughter, 561
O Canaan!, 542
Panther, 848
Road to Memphis, The, 708
Roll of Thunder, Hear My Cry, 677
Serpent's Gift, The, 884
Seven Six One, 715
Shortgrass Song, 859
'Sippi, 1031
Story of Deep Delight, A, 889
Their Eyes Were Watching God, 952
This Child's Gonna Live, 687
Train Whistle Guitar, 619

**African Americans** (*continued*)
  Walk Through Fire, A, 766
  Wedding, The, 802
  With Every Drop of Blood, 321
  Wind from Nowhere, The, 1122
  Wolf Whistle, 1032
  Your Blues Ain't Like Mine, 963
**Airplane Pilots.** (*See* Aviators)
**Alabama**
  American Eden, 403
  Fightin' with Forrest, 378
  Forge, The, 370
  Foundation Stone, 206
  Heartbreak Hotel, 794
  Long Night, 354
  Store, The, 421
  Streets of Fire, 809
  To Kill a Mockingbird, 661
  Train Whistle Guitar, 619
  Unfinished Cathedral, The, 917
  V for Victor, 694
  Walk Through Fire, A, 766
**Alaska**
  Alaska, 890
  Ashana, 303
  Barrier, 435
  Big Rock Candy Mountain, 909
  Ice Palace, 869
  Longest Winter, The, 607
  Magnetic North, 925
  Rivers of Gold, 462
  Sea Runners, 920
  Silver Horde, 918
  Sitka, 922
  Smoke Bellew, 923
  Spoilers, 436
  Stickeen, 924
  Trail of the Gold Seekers, 921
  White Dawn, 491
  Yukon Queen, The, 515
**American Loyalists**
  Brothers in Arms, 1144
  Judas Flowering, 84
  Oliver Wiswell, 102
  Time Enough for Drums, 100

**Ames, Harriet Ann**
  Love Is a Wild Assault, 263
**André, John**
  Benedict Arnold, A Novel, 108
  Major André, 63
  Secret Road, 90
**Antietam, Battle of**
  Barefoot Brigade, 343
**Anti-Semitism.** (*See* Racism)
**Apprentices.** (*See also* Indentured
  Servants)
  Bells of Freedom, 81
  Saturnalia, 1007
**Arab Americans**
  Arabian Jazz, 1079
**Arizona**
  Blood Brother, 235
  Claws of the Eagle, 927
  Cutting Stone, 926
  Distant Trumpet, A, 489
  Deserter Troop, The, 460
  Eagle and the Iron Cross, The, 707
  Foxfire, 929
  Home Mountain, 530
  Nevada, 476
  Sing Down the Moon, 928
  Warlock, 481
  West to Eden, 535
**Arkansas**
  Architecture of the Arkansas Ozarks, 931
  Big Doc's Girl, 932
  Come Winter, 494
  Elkhorn Tavern, 344
  Hunter's Heart, 933
  Idols and Axle-Grease, 652
  Place Called Sweet Shrub, A, 582
  Plum Thicket, The, 473
  Savanna, 930
  Search for Temperance Moon, 498
  This Savage Race, 882
  True Grit, 521
  Weedy Rough, 658
  Winding Stair, 499
**Armijo, Manuel**
  Time of the Gringo, 236

---

Entries 1-61: 1492-1775, Entries 62-122: 1776-1783, Entries 123-304: 1783-1860, Entries 305-380: 1861-1899, Entries 381-533: 1866-1899, Entries 534-688: 1900-1939, Entries 689-759: 1939-1945, Entries 760-855: 1945-1995, Entries 856-916: Epic Novels, Entries 917-1168: Additional Titles.

**Arnold, Benedict**
  Arundel, 101
  Benedict Arnold, A Novel, 108
  Finishing Becca, 97
  Major André, 63
  Peggy, 65
  Secret Road, 90
**Articles of Confederation.** (*See* Politics
  and Government—1783-1860)
**Ashley, William Henry**
  Three Lives of Elizabeth, 130
**Atomic Bomb**
  Bomb, The, 755
**Authors and Literature**
  Blithedale Romance, The, 172
**Automobile Industry and Trade**
  Edsel, 770
**Autrim, Henry.** (*See* Bonney, William H.)
**Aviators**
  Aviators, The, 820
  Bridges at Toko-Ri, 788
  Catch-22, 722
  Flight of the Intruder, 810
  Goodbye Mickey Mouse, 717
  Guard of Honor, 710
  Last Mission, The, 726
  Night Run, 718
  O God of Battles, 691
  Paper Doll, 730
  Raspberry One, 738
  Resistance, 731
  Silver Wings, Santiago Blue, 711
  Twelve O'Clock High, 725

**Baca, Elfego**
  Dark Winter, 445
**Barton, Clara**
  Remember Santiago, 408
**Baseball**
  Blue Ruin, 545
  Hoopla, 574
  If I Never Get Back, 388
**Bass, Sam**
  Sam Bass, 532
**Bean, Roy**
  Streets of Laredo, 514
**Beckwourth, James P.**
  Ammahabas, 256

  Follow the Free Wind, 240
  Medicine Calf, 257
**Beecher Island, Battle of**
  Roman, 497
**Bierce, Ambrose**
  Yellow, 410
**Billy the Kid.** (*See* Bonney, William H.)
**Bishop, Sarah**
  Sarah Bishop, 94
**Blackburn, Salome**
  Darlin' Bill, 456
**Blacks.** (*See* African Americans)
**Bonney, William H.**
  Anything for Billy, 511
  Billy the Kid, 467
**Boone, Daniel**
  Court Martial of Daniel Boone, The, 992
  Green Centuries, 996
  Kentuckians, The, 119
  Never No More, 54
  Oh Kentucky!, 120
  Riflemen of the Ohio, 114
**Boone, Rebecca**
  Never No More, 54
**Booth, John Wilkes**
  Bullet for Lincoln, 350
  Court for Owls, A, 305
  Katy of Catoctin, 373
**Bowie, James**
  Texan Scouts, 232
**Bridger, Jim**
  Bridger, 261
  Carry the Wind, 300
**Brown, John**
  Katy of Catoctin, 373
  Raising Holy Hell, 274
**Buchanan, James**
  Powderkeg, 253
**Buffalo**
  Slaughter, 501
**Buford, John**
  Killer Angels, The, 368
**Bull Run, Battle of**
  Bull Run, 331
  Guns of Bull Run, 306
  Hearts Divided, 380
**Burk, Martha Jane Cannary**
  Buffalo Girls, 512
  Little Big Man, 437

**Burr, Aaron**
  Burr, 134
  Conqueror, The, 139
  My Theodosia, 131
**Burr, Theodosia**
  My Theodosia, 131
**Business and Finance**
  Babbitt, 611
  Big Rock Candy Mountain, 909
  Californios, The, 939
  Day the Cowboys Quit, The, 500
  Eagles Gather, 598
  Fast Copy, 1135
  Financier, The, 394
  Incorporation of Eric Chung, The, 1136
  Julie, 566
  Never Victorious, Never Defeated, 862
  Octopus, The, 518
  Pit, The, 414
  Remember the End, 1106
  Titan, The, 397
  Saratoga Trunk, 399
  Storming Heaven, 603
  Sacred Hunger, 58
**Butler, Benjamin F.**
  Wild Is the River, 317


**Calamity Jane.** (*See* Burk, Martha Jane
    Cannary)
**Calhoun, John C.**
  54-40 or Fight, 298
**California**
  Annie's Promise, 700
  Authentic Death of Hendry Jones,
    The, 942
  Californios, The, 939
  Cannery Row, 672
  Ella Price's Journal, 806
  East of Eden, 910
  Establishment, The, 771
  Fig Tree John, 935
  Flower Drum Song, The, 941
  Glitter and the Gold, The, 943
  Grapes of Wrath, The, 673

  How Far Would You Have Gotten If I
    Hadn't . . . , 775
  Human Comedy, The, 706
  In Dubious Battle, 674
  In the House of My Pilgrimage, 570
  Jade, 505
  Jesse, 845
  Joy Luck Club, 944
  Kim/Kimi, 779
  Lonesome Gods, The, 940
  Long Time Passing, 826
  Lost and Found, 878
  Lotus Land, 879
  McTeague, 517
  Octopus, The, 518
  Of Mice and Men, 675
  Oil!, 626
  Pacific Street, 297
  Paloverde, 934
  Panther, 848
  Pinto and Sons, 938
  Proud Breed, The, 936
  Ramona, 299
  Rumors of Peace, 699
  Stampede, 304
  Time of Troubles, A, 679
  Time Too Swift, A, 703
  Toward What Bright Glory?, 648
  Two Years Before the Mast, 294
  Valley in Between, 937
  Wars of the Heart, 709
  Way We Were, The, 786
**Cambodian Americans**
  Children of the River, 812
**Campbell, Alexander**
  Fool of God, The, 156
**Canals**
  Canal Town, 136
  Rome Haul, 164
  Vandemark's Folly, 222
**Captivities.** (*See* Indians of North
    America—Captivities)
**Carrick, Johnny**
  Theory of War, 444
**Carson, Kit**
  Bear Flag, The, 296

Death Comes for the Archbishop, 242
This Old Bill, 466
**Cassidy, Butch**
Alias Butch Cassidy, 485
**Cattle Drives**
Last Cattle Drive, The, 982
Log of a Cowboy, 432
Lonesome Dove, 513
Trail to Ogallala, The, 449
**Cattle Ranching.** (*See* Cattle Drives;
Cowhands; Farm and Ranch Life)
**Cermak, Anton**
True Detective, 640
**Chancellorsville, Battle of**
Red Badge of Courage, 325
**Children Slaves.** (*See* Slaves and Slavery)
**Chinese Americans**
April and the Dragon Lady, 837
Flower Drum Song, The, 941
Jade, 505
Star Fisher, The, 633
Typical American, 780
**Christie, Ned**
Ned Christie's War, 458
**Cinque, Joseph**
Echo of Lions, 150
**Civil Rights.** (Used for works dealing
with the Civil Rights Movement.
*See also* African Americans;
Jewish Americans; Racism; etc.)
Betsy Brown, 792
Cry of Absence, 781
Freedom Songs, 834
Nineteen Fifty Nine, 768
Original Sins, 1127
Streets of Fire, 809
Walk Through Fire, A, 766
**Civil War.** (*See* Military History—1861-
1865; Soldiers—1861-1865; etc.)
**Clark, George Rogers**
Border Watch, 109
From Sea to Shining Sea, 285
Streams to the River, River to the Sea,
128
**Clark, William**
From Sea to Shining Sea, 285
Tale of Valor, 125
Trail, 124

**Clay, Henry**
Fool of God, The, 156
**Clayton, John Buell**
No Survivors, 487
**Clemens, Samuel**
1876, 427
If I Never Get Back, 388
**Cleveland, Grover**
Refinements of Love, 391
**Cochise**
Blood Brother, 235
**Cody, William F.**
Buffalo Girls, 512
This Old Bill, 466
**College Students**
Folded Leaf, The, 614
Long Time Passing, 826
Plastic Age, 613
Toward What Bright Glory?, 648
**Colon, Diego**
Indian Chronicles, The, 1
**Colorado**
American Brat, An, 843
Centennial, 891
Cherokee Trail, The, 504
Colorado Ransom, 945
High Trail to Danger, 516
King Coal, 572
Monte Walsh, 568
1933 Was a Bad Year, 650
No Reck'ning Made, 876
Shortgrass Song, 859
Tie That Binds, 946
When the Legends Die, 544
**Colorado, Mangus.** (See Mangus
Colorado)
**Colter, John**
Wilderness, 289
**Columbia River**
Swift Flows the River, 301
**Columbus, Christopher**
Discoveries of Mrs. Christopher
Columbus, The, 4
1492, 6
Indian Chronicles, The, 1
To the Indies, 5
**Columbus, Felipa M.**
Discoveries of Mrs. Christopher
Columbus, The, 4

**Congo**
New Breed, The, 821
**Connecticut**
Bound Girl of Cobble Hill, 178
Clock, The, 947
In the Fire of Spring, 949
Jordan Freeman Was My Friend, 106
Tory Hole, 948
Wings of the Morning, The, 950
**Constitution.** (*See* Politics and
Government—1783-1860)
**Cooper, James Fenimore**
Big Freeze, The, 184
**Cornwallis, Charles**
Raleigh's Eden, 75
**Coronado, Francisco**
King's Fifth, 9
**Cowhands**
Log of a Cowboy, 432
North to Yesterday, 1133
Trail to Ogallala, The, 449
**Cozad, John**
Son of the Gamblin' Man, 526
**Crazy Horse**
No Survivors, 487
Only Earth and Sky Last Forever, 1113
Stone Song, 440
**Crime and Criminals.** (*See* also
Gunfighters)
Authentic Death of Hendry Jones, The,
942
Ben Cooper, U.S. Marshal, 1143
Blue Ruin, 545
Children of the Dust, 451
Deserter Troop, The, 460
Gone to Texas, 452
Journal of the Gun Years, 510
Killing Mister Watson, 953
Little Caesar, 597
Mad Dog, 659
Native Son, 686
Ox Bow Incident, 457
Streets of Laredo, 514
To Have and Have Not, 951
While Angels Dance, 459
Whiskey River, 534

**Crittenden, John Jordan**
Three Lives of Elizabeth, 130
**Crockett, Davy**
Texan Scouts, 232
**Custer, George A.**
Bugles in the Afternoon, 484
Creek Called Wounded Knee, A, 495
Last Stand, The, 492
Little Big Man, 437

**Dalton, Emmett**
Desperadoes, 483
**Darrow, Clarence**
Dream Seekers, 412
**Davis, Richard Harding**
Yellow, 410
**De Soto, Hernando**
At the Moon's Inn, 8
**Depression (1929-1939)**
Another Part of the House, 649
Barefoot Man, The, 1157
Basque Hotel, The, 1051
Bellsong for Sarah Raines, A, 990
Billy Bathgate, 1083
Bones of Plenty, The, 656
Boulder Dam, 1050
Empty Meadow, The, 1162
Far from Cibola, 1064
Fast Copy, 1135
Foxfire, 929
Golden Bowl, The, 1117
Grapes of Wrath, The, 673
Hallapoosa, 954
Home Place, The, 1046
Hungry Men, 636
Idols and Axle-Grease, 652
In God We Trust, 975
Ironweed, 1085
King of the Hill, 655
Kings in Disguise, 678
Land Remembers, The, 1163
Least One, The, 645
Longest Road, The, 684
Man Who Was Taller Than God, The, 1112
Man's Courage, 680

1933 Was a Bad Year, 650
No Promises in the Wind, 657
Quiet Shore, 1098
Sky Is Falling, The, 643
Stump Ranch Pioneer, 960
Summons to Memphis, 1129
Time of Troubles, A, 679
Walk Gently This Good Earth, 1151
Walk on the Wild Side, A, 635
Weedy Rough, 658
World's Fair, 646
Yonnondio, 667
**Desportes, Henriette**
All This and Heaven Too, 165
**Dillinger, John**
Mad Dog, 659
**Dodge, Anson**
Beloved Invader, The, 417
**Donner Party.** (*See* Overland Journeys)
**Dousman, Hercules**
Bright Journey, 211
**Draft Riots, 1863**
Behind the Lines, 340
**Du Bois, W. E. B.**
Let the Band Play Dixie, 1109


**Eagle Voice**
When the Tree Flowered, 1045
**Earp, Wyatt**
Bloody Season, 465
**Eastman, Charles Alexander**
Eyes of Darkness, The, 488
**Einstein, Albert**
Till the End of Time, 689
**Eisenhower, Dwight D.**
Dear Ike, 728
Space, 833
**Elkhorn Tavern, Battle of**
Elkhorn Tavern, 344
**Eskimos.** (*See* Indians of North
America—Inuit)
**Espionage**
Agents of Innocence, 825
Bullet for Stonewall, 351
Call to Arms, 712
Commandos, The, 714
Copperhead, 322
Finishing Becca, 97

Hard Road to Gettysburg, 346
I and My True Love, 787
Last Lieutenant, The, 740
Luciano's Luck, 724
Memorial Bridge, 863
Peggy, 65
Phantom Fortress, 89
Rifles for Watie, 349
Secret Road, 90
Spy, The, 68
Strumpet Wind, The, 727
Tory Hole, 948
Traitor, The, 103
Troubled Air, The, 793
V for Victor, 694
Yankee Stranger, 372
**Explorers and Exploration**
At the Moon's Inn, 8
Discoveries of Mrs. Christopher
Columbus, The, 4
Embarrassment of Riches, 264
1492, 6
From Sea to Shining Sea, 285
High Towers, 2
Indian Chronicles, The, 1
King's Fifth, 9
Northwest Passage, 10
Soldier of Good Fortune, 3
Splendid Wayfaring, 127
Stickeen, 924
Streams to the River, River to the Sea,
128
Tale of Valor, 125
To the Indies, 5
Trail, 124


**Farm and Ranch Life**
Bones of Plenty, The, 656
Borning Room, The, 870
Day No Pigs Would Die, A, 622
Edge of Time, The, 464
Free Land, 506
Giants in the Earth, 523
Glory from the Earth, A, 624
Home Mountain, 530
Honey in the Horn, 554
Hue and Cry, 1057
In the Center of the Nation, 1124

**Farm and Ranch Life** (*continued*)
Laddie, 420
Land Remembers, The, 1163
Leaving the Land, 799
Little Norsk, or Old Pap's Flaxen, A, 470
Main Travelled Roads, 471
Manifest Destiny, 469
North to Yesterday, 1133
O Pioneers!, 455
Old Yeller, 474
Part of the Sky, A, 668
Peder Victorious, 524
Roll of Thunder, Hear My Cry, 677
Shane, 527
Sod and Stubble, 984
Strange Angels, 803
Stump Ranch Pioneer, 960
Thirteen Miles from Suncrest, 553
Turkey Red, 987
Unplowed Sky, The, 632
Vandemark's Folly, 222
Winds of Morning, 599
**Farragut, David**
Clear for Action!, 337
**Finance.** (*See* Business and Finance)
**Fires, Illinois**
Landlooker, The, 419
**Fishing and Fisheries**
Fisherman's Beach, 1165
Lord's Oysters, The, 549
Moby Dick, 126
**Flagg, Alice Berlin**
Alice Flagg, 1111
**Florida**
Angel City, 955
Barefoot Mailman, The, 416
Forever Island, 956
Hallapoosa, 954
Killing Mister Watson, 953
Light a Distant Fire, 199
Margaret's Story, 901
Maria, 188
Runaway, 169
Sacred Hunger, 58
Say These Names (Remember Them),
159

Spanish Bayonet, 64
Their Eyes Were Watching God, 952
To Have and Have Not, 951
Warrior, The, 201
**Football**
Let the Band Play Dixie, 1109
**Foreign Policy**
Diamond's Compass, 831
**Forrest, Nathan Bedford**
Fightin' with Forrest, 378
**Franklin, Benjamin**
Blind Journey, 87
Citizen Tom Paine, 73
Israel Potter, 92
**Fremont, Jessie**
Immortal Wife, 132
Jessie, 123
**Fremont, John**
Bear Flag, The, 296
Immortal Wife, 132
Jessie, 123
**French and Indian War, 1755-1763**
Firekeeper, The, 44
Last of the Mohicans, 19
Pathfinder, The, 20
Young Titan, The, 61

*Note: Novels of Frontier and Pioneer
Life that have a clear geographic
setting are listed as Frontier and
Pioneer Life with the geographic
subdivision, e.g., Frontier and
Pioneer Life—Alaska. Others
are listed under Frontier and
Pioneer Life with the time period
as a subdivision, e.g., Frontier
and Pioneer Life—1776-1783.
See also Fur Trappers and Trade;
Overland Journeys; etc.*

**Frontier and Pioneer Life—1492-1775**
Girl in Buckskin, 32
I Am Regina, 37
Light in the Forest, The, 48
Never No More, 54
Primrose Way, The, 38
Return of the Spanish, 16

Sackett's Land, 39
Strife Before Dawn, 905
To the Far Blue Mountains, 40
Young Titan, The, 61
**Frontier and Pioneer Life—1776-1783**
Border Watch, 109
**Frontier and Pioneer Life—1783-1860**
Beulah Land, 247
Dance on the Wind, 260
From Sea to Shining Sea, 285
Prairie, The, 209
Sam Houston Story, The, 275
Thunder on the Plains, 239
Western Union, 171
**Frontier and Pioneer Life—1866-1899**
Buffalo Girls, 512
Cry of the Hawk, 493
Darlin' Bill, 456
Empire in the Dust, 479
Main Travelled Roads, 471
This Old Bill, 466
True Grit, 521
**Frontier and Pioneer Life—Alaska**
Alaska, 890
Ice Palace, 869
Magnetic North, 925
Rivers of Gold, 462
Sea Runners, 920
Silver Horde, 918
Sitka, 922
Smoke Bellew, 923
Stickeen, 924
Trail of the Gold Seekers, 921
**Frontier and Pioneer Life—Arizona**
Claws of the Eagle, 927
Cutting Stone, 926
Distant Trumpet, A, 489
Home Mountain, 530
Nevada, 476
Sing Down the Moon, 928
Warlock, 481
**Frontier and Pioneer Life—Arkansas**
Architecture of the Arkansas Ozarks, 931
Search for Temperance Moon, 498
This Savage Race, 882
Winding Stair, 499
**Frontier and Pioneer Life—California**
Authentic Death of Hendry Jones, The, 942

Bear Flag, The, 296
Fig Tree John, 935
Lonesome Gods, The, 940
Pinto and Sons, 938
Proud Breed, The, 936
Stampede, 304
Valley in Between, 937
**Frontier and Pioneer Life—Colorado**
Centennial, 891
Cherokee Trail, The, 504
Colorado Ransom, 945
High Trail to Danger, 516
Shortgrass Song, 859
**Frontier and Pioneer Life—Florida**
Maria, 188
Runaway, 169
**Frontier and Pioneer Life—Georgia**
Rascals Heaven, 59
**Frontier and Pioneer Life—Idaho**
Angle of Repose, 962
Indian Fighter's Return, The, 461
Thunder Mountain, 961
**Frontier and Pioneer Life—Illinois**
American Years, 226
Shaman, 875
**Frontier and Pioneer Life—Indiana**
Alice of Old Vincennes, 122
Bears of Blue River, 180
Massacre at Fall Creek, The, 230
Wilderness to Washington, 974
**Frontier and Pioneer Life—Iowa**
Amalie's Story, 221
Song of Years, A, 208
Vandemark's Folly, 222
**Frontier and Pioneer Life—Kansas**
Roman, 497
Sod and Stubble, 984
Turkey Red, 987
Wild Western Desire, 985
Woe to Live On, 988
**Frontier and Pioneer Life—Kentucky**
Circle of Gold, 997
Court Martial of Daniel Boone, The, 992
Eyes of the Woods, 110
Flowering of the Cumberland, 989
Forest Runners, 111
Free Rangers, 112
Great Meadow, 121
Green Centuries, 996

**Frontier and Pioneer Life—Kentucky**
(*continued*)
Hannah Fowler, 118
Keepers of the Trail, 113
Kentuckians, The, 119
Land Beyond the Mountains, 168
Oh Kentucky!, 120
Riflemen of the Ohio, 114
Young Trailers, 116
**Frontier and Pioneer Life—Louisiana**
Deep Summer, 143
**Frontier and Pioneer Life—Maine**
Come Spring, 107
**Frontier and Pioneer Life—Maryland**
Sot Weed Factor, The, 11
**Frontier and Pioneer Life—
    Massachusetts**
Winthrop Woman, The, 1012
**Frontier and Pioneer Life—Michigan**
Forest Life, 1022
Invasion, The, 885
Land of the Crooked Tree, 1019
New Home—Who'll Follow?, 219
Romance of Dollard, 1015
Young Voyageur, The, 1017
**Frontier and Pioneer Life—Minnesota**
White Indian Boy, 1025
Youngest Voyageur, 1026
**Frontier and Pioneer Life—Missouri**
Hannah's Mill, 1034
**Frontier and Pioneer Life—Montana**
Bone Wars, The, 1039
Dancing at the Rascal Fair, 1035
English Creek, 1036
For the Roses, 252
Heart of the West, 531
Justice, 543
Sand, 1038
Single Tree, 528
**Frontier and Pioneer Life—Nebraska**
Lantern in Her Hand, A, 231
Lieutenant's Lady, 433
Miss Morissa, Doctor of the Gold
    Trail, 525
My Antonia, 454
O Pioneers!, 455

Rim of the Prairie, 1041
Son of the Gamblin' Man, 526
Spring Came On Forever, 856
When the Tree Flowered, 1045
**Frontier and Pioneer Life—Nevada**
Breakheart Pass, 1052
**Frontier and Pioneer Life—New
    Hampshire**
Look to the Mountain, 14
**Frontier and Pioneer Life—New Mexico**
Death Comes for the Archbishop, 242
Eagle in the Sky, 1066
Heart's Desire, 490
Lady from Toledo, The, 1061
Lady, The, 522
Laughing Boy, 1065
No Life for a Lady, 1062
Of Arms I Sing, 1059
Sea of Grass, The, 1070
Wind Leaves No Shadow, The, 267
Wolf Song, 1063
**Frontier and Pioneer Life—New York**
Deerslayer, The, 18
Drums Along the Mohawk, 71
Eben Holden, 140
Firekeeper, The, 44
For Love of Two Eagles, 49
In the Time of the Wolves, 149
Last of the Mohicans, 19
Manitou's Daughter, 42
Pathfinder, The, 20
Pioneers, The, 158
Woman Who Fell from the Sky, The, 50
**Frontier and Pioneer Life—North
    Carolina**
Bennet's Welcome, 24
Lusty Wind for Carolina, 26
Men of Albemarle, 27
Roanoke Hundred, 28
**Frontier and Pioneer Life—North
    Dakota**
Bad Lands, 480
Dakotas: At the Wind's Edge, 1091
Dakotas: The Endless Sky, 1092
Emigrants, The, 441
Manifest Destiny, 469

**Frontier and Pioneer Life—Ohio**
Bad Man Ballad, 110
Bounty Lands, The, 217
Trees, The, 225
**Frontier and Pioneer Life—Oklahoma**
Cherokee Strip Fever, 1101
**Frontier and Pioneer Life—Oregon**
Across the Shining Mountains, 302
Earthbreakers, 295
Moontrap, 290
To Build a Ship, 291
Trask, 292
**Frontier and Pioneer Life—
Pennsylvania**
Bloody Country, The, 1105
Scouts of the Valley, 115
**Frontier and Pioneer Life—South
Carolina**
Yemassee, The, 56
**Frontier and Pioneer Life—South
Dakota**
Claim Jumpers, The, 1125
Conquest, 1120
Dakota Scouts, 463
Deadwood, 1115
Forgiving, 1126
Free Land, 506
Giants in the Earth, 523
Homesteader, The, 1121
In the Center of the Nation, 1124
King of Spades, 1118
Let the Hurricane Roar, 507
Life's Lure, 1123
Little Norsk, or Old Pap's Flaxen, A, 470
Only Earth and Sky Last Forever, 1113
Peder Victorious, 524
Scarlet Plume, 1119
Waterlily, 1114
Wind from Nowhere, The, 1122
**Frontier and Pioneer Life—Texas**
Dead Man's Walk, 270
Divine Average, 262
Edge of Time, The, 464
Empire of Bones, 268
Gone to Texas, 452
Lily, 442
Look to the River, 1138
Looking After Lily, 443
Love Is a Wild Assault, 263

North to Yesterday, 1133
Old Yeller, 474
Promised Land, 245
Road to San Jacinto, The, 1131
Sam Chance, 448
Searchers, The, 509
Sons of Texas, 248
Spanish Gold, 1139
Star of Empire, 278
Streets of Laredo, 514
Texan Scouts, 232
Texan Star, 233
Texan Triumph, 234
Texas, 895
Walk in My Soul, 1140
Wonderful Country, The, 508
**Frontier and Pioneer Life—Utah**
Ben Cooper, U.S. Marshal, 1143
Giant Joshua, 287
Riders of the Purple Sage, 477
**Frontier and Pioneer Life—Vermont**
Calico Captive, 1146
Not Without Peril, 137
**Frontier and Pioneer Life—Virginia**
Betty Zane, 82
Devil Water, 55
Durable Fire, A, 12
Pocahontas, 22
To Have and To Hold, 35
**Frontier and Pioneer Life—Washington**
Living, The, 1152
Many Horses, 1156
Mighty Mountain, 293
Sweetbriar, 1153
Sweetbriar Bride, 1154
Sweetbriar Spring, 1155
Swift Flows the River, 301
**Frontier and Pioneer Life—Wisconsin**
Come and Get It, 1161
Enemies, 1164
Hills Stand Watch, 212
Landlooker, The, 419
Tomorrow Is a River, 1160
**Frontier and Pioneer Life—Wyoming**
Bendigo Shafter, 1167
Grassman, The, 468
Riders of Judgment, 1168
Shane, 527
Tom Horn, 1166

**Fur Trappers and Trade**
Big Sky, The, 254
Bridger, 261
Bright Journey, 211
Carry the Wind, 300
Dance on the Wind, 260
Enemies, 1164
Long Rifle, 288
Lord Grizzley, 269
Mountain Man, 251
Splendid Wayfaring, 127
Wilderness, 289
With the Indians in the Rockies, 280
Young Voyageur, The, 1017
Youngest Voyageur, 1026

**Gabriel Insurrection**
Black Thunder, 141
**Georgia**
Before the Darkness Falls, 186
Beloved Invader, The, 417
Chiefs, 915
Cold Sassy Tree, 548
Color Purple, 681
Distant Lands, The, 170
Gone with the Wind, 357
Judas Flowering, 84
Lasso the Moon, 811
Legacies, 326
Legacy of Beulah Land, 390
Lighthouse, 187
New Moon Rising, 189
Proud and the Free, The, 160
Rascals Heaven, 59
Savannah Purchase, 957
Savannah, 190
Sherman's March, 315
Spite Fences, 785
Stranger in Savannah, 360
To See Your Face Again, 191
Where Shadows Go, 192
Year the Lights Came On, The, 783
Youngblood, 536

**German Americans**
Katy of Catoctin, 373
**Geronimo**
Apache Devil, 447
Claws of the Eagle, 927
Watch for Me on the Mountain, 453
**Gettysburg, Battle of**
Barefoot Brigade, 343
Killer Angels, The, 368
Look Away, 324
Slopes of War, 358
**Glass, Hugh**
Lord Grizzley, 269
Wilderness, 289
**Glover, John**
Trumpet to Arms, 91
**Gold Rush**
Pacific Street, 297
Pinto and Sons, 938
Thunder Mountain, 961
Travels of Jamie McPheeters, The, 283
**Gold Rush—Alaska**
Barrier, 435
Spoilers, 436
Yukon Queen, The, 515
**Goldman, Emma**
Pooles of Pismo Bay, The, 539
**Gompers, Samuel**
Giant Wakes, The, 880
**Grant, Ulysses S.**
Democracy, 381
1876, 427
Grant's War, 345
Tree of Appomattox, 313
**Greeley, Horace**
Big Freeze, The, 184
**Gunfighters**
Anything for Billy, 511
Assassination of Jesse James by
    the . . . , 482
Billy the Kid, 467
Bloody Season, 465
Dark Winter, 445
Gone to Texas, 452
Journal of the Gun Years, 510

**Hamilton, Alexander**
Burr, 134
Conqueror, The, 139
My Theodosia, 131
**Hardin, John Wesley**
Pistoleer, The, 438
Streets of Laredo, 514
**Harding, Warren**
Hollywood, 629
Revelry, 594
**Hawaii**
From Here to Eternity, 747
Hawaii Aloha, 958
Hawaii, 893
Let Us Go, 959
Under the Blood-Red Sun, 754
Wild Meat and the Bully Burgers, 855
**Hay, John**
Empire, 428
Lincoln, 374
**Hearst, William Randolph**
California Gold, 881
Empire, 428
Yellow, 410
**Heisman, John**
Let the Band Play Dixie, 1109
**Hemmings, Harriet**
President's Daughter, The, 151
Wolf by the Ears, 197
**Hemmings, Sally**
Sally Hemmings, 152
Wolf by the Ears, 197
**Hickok, James Butler**
Buffalo Girls, 512
Darlin' Bill, 456
Deadwood, 1115
Little Big Man, 437
This Old Bill, 466
**Hippies**
Peter Pan Bag, 830
**Hitler, Adolf**
Dragon's Teeth, 671
**Holliday, John H. (Doc)**
Bloody Season, 465
**Holmes, Oliver Wendell**
Shaman, 875
**Hoover Dam**
Boulder Dam, 1050

**Horn, Tom**
Claws of the Eagle, 927
Tom Horn, 1166
**Houdini, Harry**
Ragtime, 556
**Houston, Elizabeth Allen**
Raven's Bride, The, 246
**Houston, Sam**
Eagle and the Raven, The, 272
Empire of Bones, 268
Raven's Bride, The, 246
Road to San Jacinto, The, 1131
Sam Houston Story, The, 275
Star of Empire, 278
Walk in My Soul, 1140
**Howard, Oliver Otis**
Blood Brother, 235
**Howe, William**
Redcoat, 69
**Hutchinson, Anne**
Witnesses, 34

**Idaho**
Angle of Repose, 962
Indian Fighter's Return, The, 461
Stump Ranch Pioneer, 960
Thunder Mountain, 961
**Illegal Aliens**
Lasso the Moon, 811
**Illinois**
Across Five Aprils, 341
American Tragedy, An, 557
American Years, 226
Chosen Country, 965
Chute, The, 653
Dandelion Wine, 596
Dream Seekers, 412
Eighth Day, The, 972
Father and Son, 966
Folded Leaf, The, 614
Foundry, The, 606
Ghost Belonged to Me, The, 969
Grapple, The, 964
Graysons, The, 214
Homeland, 406
Hoopla, 574
Horse Shoe Bottoms, 425
Impresario, The, 564

**Illinois** (*continued*)
Jack Gance, 782
Jennie Gerhardt, 395
Jungle, The, 571
Landlooker, The, 419
Last Catholic in America, The, 970
Lincoln Hunters, The, 971
Little Caesar, 597
Love Is Eternal, 369
Maude Martha, 764
Native Son, 686
No Promises in the Wind, 657
Noah, Shaman, 875
O Canaan!, 542
Old Bunch, The, 610
Pit, The, 414
They Came Like Swallows, 967
Time Will Darken It, 968
Titan, The, 397
Tomorrow's Bread, 384
True Detective, 640
Yonnondio, 667
Your Blues Ain't Like Mine, 963
**Immigrants, Basque**
Shoshone Mike, 1049
**Immigrants, Cambodian**
Children of the River, 812
**Immigrants, Chinese**
Dragon's Gate, 533
Heart of the West, 531
Incorporation of Eric Chung, The, 1136
Joy Luck Club, 944
Typical American, 780
**Immigrants, Danish**
Amalie's Story, 221
**Immigrants, German**
Balance Wheel, 1104
House Divided, 338
**Immigrants, Hungarian**
Out of This Furnace, 858
**Immigrants, Indian**
Jasmine, 835
**Immigrants, Irish**
Captains and the Kings, The, 861
**Immigrants, Italian**
Fortunate Pilgrim, The, 538

1933 Was a Bad Year, 650
**Immigrants, Jewish**
Fathers, 873
Inside, Outside, 854
Island Within, The, 409
Laughter on a Weekday, 559
West to Eden, 535
**Immigrants, Korean**
Gathering of Pearls, 765
**Immigrants, Mexican**
Texas, 895
**Immigrants, Norwegian**
Giants in the Earth, 523
Peder Victorious, 524
**Immigrants, Polish**
Man's Courage, 680
**Immigrants, Russian**
In the House of My Pilgrimage, 570
Rivington Street, 540
Shukar Balan, 986
Union Square, 541
**Immigrants, Scottish**
Place Called Freedom, A, 29
**Immigrants, Swedish**
Emigrants, The, 1027
Papa's Wife, 385
Unto a Good Land, 1028
**Immigrants**
Midwife, The, 1082
**Indentured Servants.** (*See also* Apprentices)
Bennet's Welcome, 24
Spanish Bayonet, 64
Theory of War, 444
**Indian Americans.** Used for Americans whose ancestors were citizens of India
Jasmine, 835
**Indiana**
Alice of Old Vincennes, 122
Bears of Blue River, 180
For Us the Living, 220
Friendly Persuasion, The, 229
Gene, Freckles, 575
Gene, Laddie, 420
Gentleman from Indiana, The, 976

Girl of the Limberlost, 576
Harvester, The, 577
Hoosier School-Boy, The, 215
Hoosier School-Master, The, 216
In God We Trust, 975
Magnificent Ambersons, The, 422
Massacre at Fall Creek, The, 230
Pageant, 973
Peculiar People, The, 210
Penrod, 579
Raintree County, 886
Wilderness to Washington, 974
**Indians of North America**
Shadow Catcher, 560
Yellow Raft in Blue Water, A, 1037
**Indians of North America—Algonquin**
Pocahontas, 22
**Indians of North America—Apache**
Apache Autumn, 908
Apache Devil, 447
Apache, 243
Blood Brother, 235
Canyons, 520
Claws of the Eagle, 927
Distant Trumpet, A, 489
Eagle and the Iron Cross, The, 707
Fig Tree John, 935
Runs with Horses, 446
Spanish Gold, 1139
Watch for Me on the Mountain, 453
**Indians of North America—Athabaskan**
Ashana, 303
**Indians of North America—Blackfeet**
Fools Crow, 529
Quest of the Fish-Dog Skin, 279
With the Indians in the Rockies, 280
**Indians of North America—Blackhawk**
Shaman, 875
**Indians of North America—Captivities**
Circle Unbroken, A, 258
Follow the River, 57
I Am Regina, 37
Ride the Wind, 277
Where the Broken Heart Still Beats, 271
White Indian Boy, 1025
Wilderness, 289
Woman of the People, A, 241

**Indians of North America—Cherokee**
Legacies, 326
Mountain Windsong, 244
Ned Christie's War, 458
No Resting Place, 175
Proud and the Free, The, 160
Rifles for Watie, 349
This Savage Race, 882
**Indians of North America—Chickasaw**
Story of Deep Delight, A, 889
**Indians of North America—Chippewa**
Bingo Palace, 1094
Love Medicine, 865
Young Voyageur, The, 1017
**Indians of North America—Choctaw**
Okla Hannali, 883
**Indians of North America—Comanche**
Dances with Wolves, 439
Gone the Dreams and the Dancing, 496
Quanah Parker, 502
Ride the Wind, 277
Slaughter, 501
Walks Without a Soul, 276
Where the Broken Heart Still Beats, 271
White Man's Road, 450
Woman of the People, A, 241
**Indians of North America—Crow**
Ammahabas, 256
Follow the Free Wind, 240
Medicine Calf, 257
**Indians of North America—Delaware**
Light in the Forest, The, 48
**Indians of North America—Huron**
Romance of Dollard, 1015
This Widowed Land, 31
**Indians of North America—Inuit**
Longest Winter, The, 607
White Dawn, 491
**Indians of North America—Jumanos**
Indio, 7
**Indians of North America—Modoc**
Pinto and Sons, 938
**Indians of North America—Mohawk**
Firekeeper, The, 44
**Indians of North America—Narragansett**
Saturnalia, 1007

**Indians of North America—Navajo**
Ceremony, 795
Laughing Boy, 1065
Sing Down the Moon, 928
**Indians of North America—Nez Percé**
From Where the Sun Now Stands, 486
**Indians of North America—Ojibway**
Loon Feather, 218
**Indians of North America—Oneida**
For Love of Two Eagles, 49
Manitou's Daughter, 42
Woman Who Fell from the Sky, The, 50
**Indians of North America—Osage**
Cimmaron, 868
Mean Spirit, 609
This Savage Race, 882
**Indians of North America—Ottawa**
Land of the Crooked Tree, 1019
**Indians of North America—Paiute**
Ghost Dance Messiah, 1048
**Indians of North America—Paugussett**
Bloody Country, The, 1105
**Indians of North America—Pawnee**
Return of the Spanish, 16
**Indians of North America—Pawtucket**
Primrose Way, The, 38
**Indians of North America—Pueblo Nation**
Eagle in the Sky, 1066
House Made of Dawn, 1067
Man Who Killed the Deer, The, 1075
People of the Valley, 1076
Royal City, The, 1071
**Indians of North America—Seminole**
Forever Island, 956
Light a Distant Fire, 199
Say These Names (Remember Them), 159
Warrior, The, 201
**Indians of North America—Seneca**
Massacre at Fall Creek, The, 230
**Indians of North America—Shawnee**
Broken Days, 195
Panther in the Sky, 228
Shadow of the Long Knives, 117
Young Trailers, 116

**Indians of North America—Shoshone**
Sacajawea, 135
Shoshone Mike, 1049
Streams to the River, River to the Sea, 128
**Indians of North America—Sioux**
Bugles in the Afternoon, 484
Circle Unbroken, A, 258
Creek Called Wounded Knee, A, 495
Dakota Scouts, 463
Eyes of Darkness, The, 488
Grass Dancer, 900
No Survivors, 487
Only Earth and Sky Last Forever, 1113
Scarlet Plume, 1119
Stone Song, 440
Waterlily, 1114
When the Tree Flowered, 1045
**Indians of North America—Ute**
When the Legends Die, 544
**Indians of North America— Willamette Valley**
Bridge of the Gods, 1150
**Indians of North America— Wyandotte**
Riflemen of the Ohio, 114
**Indians of North America—Yana**
Beyond the Divide, 266
**Indians of North America—Yemassee**
Yemassee, The, 56
**Ingles, Mary**
Follow the River, 57
**International Brigade**
Hermanos!, 654
**Iowa**
Amalie's Story, 221
Main Travelled Roads, 471
Miss Bishop, 977
Night of Shadows, 475
Our Changing Lives, 979
Song of Years, A, 208
These Years of Promise, 978
This Rough New Land, 980
Vandemark's Folly, 222
**Irish Americans**
Answer As a Man, 550

Father and Son, 966
Last Hurrah, The, 1011
Our Own Kind, 616
**Italian Americans**
Fabulous Fifty, The, 604


**Jackson, Andrew**
President's Lady, The, 133
Sam Houston Story, The, 275
**Jackson, Rachel**
President's Lady, The, 133
**Jackson, Thomas J. (Stonewall)**
Bullet for Stonewall, 351
Scouts of Stonewall, 309
Star of Gettysburg, 311
Unwritten Chronicles of Robert E.
Lee, 339
**Jacobs, Harriet A.**
Letters from a Slave Girl, 179
**James, Jesse Woodson**
Assassination of Jesse James by the . . . ,
482
**Japan**
East and West, 741
Gods of War, 756
Occupation, 757
Unexpected Peace, The, 750
**Japanese Americans**
Kim/Kimi, 779
Talent Night, 839
Under the Blood-Red Sun, 754
Wild Meat and the Bully Burgers, 855
**Jefferson, Martha**
My Thomas, 83
**Jefferson, Thomas**
Burr, 134
Conqueror, The, 139
Fool of God, The, 156
Jefferson, 145
My Thomas, 83
President's Daughter, The, 151
Sally Hemmings, 152
Tree of Liberty, 899
Wolf by the Ears, 197
**Jeffords, Tom**
Blood Brother, 235
**Jennings, Ann Gilmore**
Wilderness to Washington, 974

**Jennings, Jonathan**
Wilderness to Washington, 974
**Jewish Americans**
Annie's Promise, 700
Changelings, The, 796
Chosen, The, 1086
Crescent City, 359
David and Jonathan, 801
Davita's Harp, 669
East River, 1080
Fathers, 873
Hate Crime, The, 827
In the Beginning, 1087
Inside, Outside, 854
Last Mission, The, 726
Midwife, The, 1082
Old Bunch, The, 610
Safe Harbors, 791
Summer of My German Soldier, 697
That Year of Our War, 696
Tunes for Bears to Dance To, 767
**Johnson, Lyndon B.**
Flying in to Love, 846
New Breed, The, 821
**Johnston Family**
Invasion, 885
**Jones, John Paul**
Israel Potter, 92
Raleigh's Eden, 75
Richard Carvel, 66
**Jones, Mary Harris (Mother)**
Scapegoat, The, 569
**Joseph, Chief**
From Where the Sun Now Stands, 486


**Kamehameha II**
Let Us Go, 959
**Kansas**
Desperadoes, 483
Last Cattle Drive, The, 982
Learning Tree, The, 620
Morning Glory Afternoon, 981
Not Without Laughter, 561
Persian Pickle Club, The, 644
Prairie Widow, 434
Raising Holy Hell, 274
Roman, 497
Shukar Balan, 986

**Kansas** (*continued*)
Sod and Stubble, 984
Story of a Country Town, The, 983
Theory of War, 444
Turkey Red, 987
Unplowed Sky, The, 632
While Angels Dance, 459
Wild Western Desire, 985
Woe to Live On, 988
**Kellogg, John H.**
Road to Wellville, The, 1014
**Kennedy, John F.**
Atomic Candy, 808
Flying in to Love, 846
Libra, 813
Till the End of Time, 689
**Kentucky**
Band of Angels, 913
Believers, The, 167
Bellsong for Sarah Raines, A, 990
Choices, 906
Circle of Gold, 997
Court Martial of Daniel Boone, The, 992
Dollmaker, The, 1013
Enduring Hills, 994
Eyes of the Woods, 110
Feather Crowns, 998
Flowering of the Cumberland, 989
For Us the Living, 220
Forest Runners, 111
Free Rangers, 112
Great Meadow, 121
Green Centuries, 996
Guns of Bull Run, 306
Hannah Fowler, 118
Hardcastle, 688
Hie to the Hunters, 999
In Country, 832
Jordon's Showdown, 676
Keepers of the Trail, 113
Kentuckians, The, 119
Kentucky Home, 193
Land Beyond the Mountains, 168
Little Shepherd of Kingdom Come, 335
Never No More, 54
Night Rider, 581

Oh Kentucky!, 120
Penhally, 874
Raccoon John Smith, 991
Rennie's Way, 627
Riflemen of the Ohio, 114
Taps for Private Tussie, 1000
Tara's Healing, 995
Trail of the Lonesome Pine, 993
Uncle Tom's Cabin, 204
World Enough and Time, 1001
Young Trailers, 116
**King's Mountain, Battle of**
Toil of the Brave, 77
**King, Martin Luther, Jr.**
Streets of Fire, 809
**Kissinger, Henry**
China Card, The, 817
**Korean War**
Bridges at Toko-Ri, 788
MASH, 778
Sword and Scalpel, 797
Useless Servants, The, 774
**Ku Klux Klan**
Children of the Dust, 451
Forge, The, 370
Morning Glory Afternoon, 981

**Laborers and Labor Unions.** (*See also*
Apprentices; Indentured Servants;
Miners and Mining)
Angel City, 955
Barefoot Man, The, 1157
Boulder Dam, 1050
Cannery Row, 672
Chute, The, 653
Clock, The, 947
Desert of Wheat, 590
Diana Stair, 163
Disinherited, The, 1033
Dream Seekers, 412
Edsel, 770
Executioner Waits, The, 608
Ferment, 663
Foundry, The, 606
Giant Wakes, The, 880

Grapes of Wrath, The, 673
Grapple, The, 964
Hardcastle, 688
Hazard of New Fortunes, A, 404
Homeland, 406
Horse Shoe Bottoms, 425
In Dubious Battle, 674
Industrial Valley, 1099
Jordon's Showdown, 676
Jungle, The, 571
King Coal, 572
Mark's Own, 857
Motor City, 1024
Never Victorious, Never Defeated, 862
Of Mice and Men, 675
Out of This Furnace, 858
Patch Boys, The, 621
Pooles of Pismo Bay, The, 539
Rivington Street, 540
Scapegoat, The, 569
Spanish Bayonet, 64
Time of Troubles, A, 679
To Have and Have Not, 951
Tomorrow's Bread, 384
Valley of Decision, The, 864
Waiting for the News, 662
Waterfront, 1088
Lee, Francis
  Tidewater Dynasty, 902
Lee, Henry (Light-Horse Harry)
  Tidewater Dynasty, 902
Lee, Richard Henry
  Tidewater Dynasty, 902
Lee, Robert E.
  Before the Darkness Falls, 186
  Grant's War, 345
  Killer Angels, The, 368
  Shades of the Wilderness, 310
  Star of Gettysburg, 311
  Sword of Antietam, 312
  Tidewater Dynasty, 902
  Traveller, 1147
  Tree of Appomattox, 313
  Unwritten Chronicles of Robert E.
    Lee, 339
Leininger, Regina
  I Am Regina, 37
LeMoyne Family
  High Towers, 2

Lewis, Meriwether
  Streams to the River, River to the Sea, 128
  Tale of Valor, 125
  Trail, 124
Liliuokalani, Lydia Kamekeha
  Hawaii Aloha, 958
Lincoln, Abraham
  American Years, 226
  Bullet for Lincoln, 350
  Court for Owls, A, 305
  For Us the Living, 220
  Graysons, The, 214
  Henry and Clara, 411
  Katy of Catoctin, 373
  Lincoln Hunters, The, 971
  Lincoln, 374
  Love Is Eternal, 369
  Perfect Tribute, 314
Lincoln, Mary Todd
  Love Is Eternal, 369
Little Big Horn, Battle of
  Last Stand, The, 492
  Little Big Man, 437
Longstreet, James
  Killer Angels, The, 368
  Let the Band Play Dixie, 1109
Louisiana
  Autobiography of Miss Jane Pittman,
    The, 871
  Band of Angels, 913
  Bayou Road, 328
  Crescent City, 359
  Deep Summer, 143
  Feast of All Saints, 194
  Five Smooth Stones, 866
  Foxes of Harrow, The, 207
  Gathering of Old Men, A, 818
  Handsome Road, 316
  In My Father's House, 1002
  Lesson Before Dying, A, 1003
  New Orleans Legacy, 1004
  Papa La-Bas, 146
  Royal Street, 198
  Saratoga Trunk, 399
  Serpent and the Staff, The, 583
  This Side of Glory, 547
  Vixens, The, 430
  Walk on the Wild Side, A, 635
  Wild Is the River, 317

**Luciano, Charles (Lucky)**
Luciano's Luck, 724
**Lumber and Lumbering**
Come and Get It, 1161
Roderick, Timber, 1102
Sometimes a Great Notion, 784


**MacArthur, Douglas A.**
Dear Ike, 728
Once an Eagle, 898
**MacDonald, Flora**
Scotswoman, The, 76
**Madison, Dolley**
Dolley, 144
**Madison, James**
Conqueror, The, 139
Dolley, 144
**Magoffin, Susan Shelby**
Turquoise Trail, The, 282
**Maine**
Arundel, 101
Colony, 1005
Come Spring, 107
Ebbing Tide, 701
Jennie Glenroy, 183
Lovely Ambition, The, 552
Spoonhandle, 665
Storm Tide, 702
Tree by Leaf, 593
Young Titan, The, 61
**Mangas Colorado**
Apache, 243
**Marines**
Battle Cry, 758
Battleground, 742
Call to Arms, 712
Counterattack, 743
**Marion, Francis**
Phantom Fortress, 89
Swamp Fox, Francis Marion, The, 80
**Marshall, George C.**
Dear Ike, 728
**Maryland**
Chesapeake, 892
Katy of Catoctin, 373

Lord's Oysters, The, 549
Mary's Land, 53
Miracles, 173
Miss Susie Slagle's, 580
Richard Carvel, 66
Sense of Honor, A, 851
Sot Weed Factor, The, 11
Swan's Chance, 161
This Child's Gonna Live, 687
**Massachusetts**
Ann of the Wild Rose Inn, 62
April Morning, 72
Atomic Candy, 808
Back Bay, 887
Bells of Freedom, 81
Beyond the Burning Time, 41
Blithedale Romance, The, 172
Boston, 579
Bostonians, The, 407
Break with Charity, A, 51
Broken Days, 195
Cape Cod, 888
David and Jonathan, 801
Devil and the Mathers, The, 23
Diana Stair, 163
Early Autumn, 1006
Face in My Mirror, The, 849
Fifth of March, The, 96
Gilman of Redford, 70
Green Desire, A, 897
Hate Crime, The, 827
Hester, 13
House of Seven Gables, The, 1008
I, Tituba, Black Witch of Salem, 17
Johnny Tremain, 78
Last Hurrah, The, 1011
Last Waltz, 431
Late George Apley, The, 1010
Massachusetts, 916
Mirror for Witches, A, 30
Nell's Quilt, 423
Oldtown Folks, 203
Peter Pan Bag, 830
Regulators, The, 162
Rise of Silas Lapham, The, 1009
Saturnalia, 1007

Entries 1-61: 1492-1775, Entries 62-122: 1776-1783, Entries 123-304: 1783-1860, Entries 305-380: 1861-1899, Entries 381-533: 1866-1899, Entries 534-688: 1900-1939, Entries 689-759: 1939-1945, Entries 760-855: 1945-1995, Entries 856-916: Epic Novels, Entries 917-1168: Additional Titles.

Scarlet Letter, The, 33
Secret of Sarah Revere, The, 99
Stitch in Time, A, 196
Those Who Love, 104
Tituba of Salem Village, 46
Trumpet to Arms, 91
Tunes for Bears to Dance To, 767
Ward Eight, 555
Wedding, The, 802
Winthrop Woman, The, 1012
Witches' Children, 15
Witnesses, 34
**Masterson, William Barclay**
Wild Western Desire, 985
**McClellan, George B.**
Sword of Antietam, 312
**Medicine**
Bless Me, Ultima, 1058
Canal Town, 136
Harvester, The, 577
Last Silk Dress, 362
Listen for Rachel, 348
MASH, 778
Midwife, The, 1082
Miss Morissa, Doctor of the Gold
    Trail, 525
Miss Susie Slagle's, 580
Over There, 588
Road Home, The, 852
Serpent and the Staff, The, 583
Shaman, 875
Testimony of Two Men, 551
**Mexican Americans**
Jesse, 845
Milagro Beanfield War, The, 1068
Riders to Cibola, 1078
Texas, 895
Thin Men of Haddam, 1141
Useless Servants, The, 774
**Mexican War**
North and South, 176
**Michigan**
Becca's Story, 333
Courage of Captain Plum, 1016
Dollmaker, The, 1013
Edsel, 770
Farmer, 1018
Forest Life, 1022

Gales of November, 1020
Good Negress, The, 800
Invasion, 885
Land of the Crooked Tree, 1019
Loon Feather, 218
Motor City, 1024
New Home—Who'll Follow?, 219
Northwest Passage, 10
Road to Wellville, The, 1014
Romance of Dollard, 1015
Ships Gone Missing, 1021
Small Bequest, A, 1023
Waiting for the News, 662
Whiskey River, 534
Young Voyageur, The, 1017
**Military History—1776-1783.** (*See also*
    Soldiers; Naval History; Naval
    Personnel; and similar headings)
Arundel, 101
Phantom Fortress, 89
Swamp Fox, Francis Marion, The, 80
**Military History—1783-1860.** (*See also*
    Soldiers; Naval History; Naval
    Personnel; and similar headings)
Immortal Wife, 132
Jessie, 123
**Military History—1861-1865.** (*See also*
    Soldiers; Naval History; Naval
    Personnel; and similar headings)
Andersonville, 347
Banners at Shenandoah, 319
Bull Run, 331
Farewell, My General, 367
Grant's War, 345
Guns of Bull Run, 306
Guns of Shiloh, 307
High Hearts, 318
Immortal Wife, 132
Jessie, 123
Killer Angels, The, 368
Rifles for Watie, 349
Sherman's March, 315
Shiloh, 332
Slopes of War, 358
Sword of Antietam, 312
Tamarack Tree, 320
Unwritten Chronicles of Robert E.
    Lee, 339

**Military History—1939-1945.** (*See also* Soldiers; Naval History; Naval Personnel; Aviators; and similar headings)
Woman at Otowi Crossing, 1077
**Mills and Mill Work**
Clock, The, 947
**Miners and Mining**
Angle of Repose, 962
Claim Jumpers, The, 1125
Colorado Ransom, 945
Comstock Lode, 265
Glory Enough for All, 365
Hardcastle, 688
Hills Stand Watch, 212
Jordon's Showdown, 676
King Coal, 572
Life's Lure, 1123
Mark's Own, 857
Pacific Street, 297
Remember the End, 1106
Spoilers, 436
Storming Heaven, 603
Wide Open Town, 546
**Minnesota**
Come in from the Cold, 842
Emigrants, The, 1027
Main Street, 537
November of the Heart, 1029
Unto a Good Land, 1028
White Indian Boy, 1025
Youngest Voyageur, 1026
**Mississippi**
'Sippi, 1031
Absalom, Absalom!, 867
Billy, 651
Children Bob Moses Led, The, 822
Choices, 906
Delta Wedding, 631
Intruder in the Dust, 1030
Losing Battles, 683
Mississippi Chariot, 670
Road to Memphis, The, 708
Rock of Chickamauga, 308
Roll of Thunder, Hear My Cry, 677
So Red the Rose, 379

Tamarack Tree, 320
Wolf Whistle, 1032
**Mississippi River**
Adventures of Huckleberry Finn, The, 153
At the Moon's Inn, 8
High Water, 762
No Bottom, 386
No Virtue, 387
Show Boat, 400
Stretch on the River, A, 763
**Missouri**
Adventures of Tom Sawyer, The, 154
Assassination of Jesse James by the . . . , 482
Betsy Brown, 792
Disinherited, The, 1033
Hannah's Mill, 1034
King of the Hill, 655
Pudd'nhead Wilson, 155
Three Lives of Elizabeth, 130
While Angels Dance, 459
**Montana**
Bone Wars, The, 1039
Dancing at the Rascal Fair, 1035
English Creek, 1036
For the Roses, 252
Heart of the West, 531
Justice, 543
Quest of the Fish-Dog Skin, 279
Sand, 1038
Single Tree, 528
Wide Open Town, 546
With the Indians in the Rockies, 280
Yellow Raft in Blue Water, A, 1037
**Morgan, John Hunt**
Little Shepherd of Kingdom Come, 335
**Morgan, John Pierpont, Sr.**
Alienist, The, 1081
Bullet for Lincoln, 350
1919, 586
Ragtime, 556
**Moses, Bob**
Children Bob Moses Led, The, 822
**Moss, Elizabeth**
Three Lives of Elizabeth, 130

**Motion Picture Industry**
Paloverde, 934
**Muir, John**
Stickeen, 924


**Naval History.** (*See also* Naval Personnel; Ships and Shipping)
Captain Caution, 129
Catherine, The, 355
Delilah, 589
Fragments of the Ark, 356
French Admiral, The, 85
Pilot, The, 67
Richard Carvel, 66
Sand Pebbles, The, 615
**Naval Personnel**
Bridges at Toko-Ri, 788
Caine Mutiny, The, 759
Captain Caution, 129
Catherine, The, 355
Clear for Action!, 337
Delilah, 589
Dust on the Sea, 734
French Admiral, The, 85
Good Shepherd, The, 720
King's Coat, The, 86
Last Lieutenant, The, 740
Mister Roberts, 744
O God of Battles, 691
Pilot, The, 67
Raditzer, 753
Raspberry One, 738
Red Rover, The, 21
Richard Carvel, 66
Run Silent, Run Deep, 735
Sand Pebbles, The, 615
Scuttlebutt, 853
Sense of Honor, A, 851
Silent Sea, 746
Till the End of Time, 689
Time and Tide, 739
**Nebraska**
Ceremony in Lonetree, 1043
Home Place, The, 1046
Lantern in Her Hand, A, 231
Lieutenant's Lady, 433
Ma Jeeter's Girls, 1047

Miss Morissa, Doctor of the Gold Trail, 525
My Antonia, 454
O Pioneers!, 455
One of Ours, 585
Plains Song, 1044
Red Menace, 761
Rim of the Prairie, 1041
Son of the Gamblin' Man, 526
Spring Came On Forever, 856
Strange Angels, 803
When the Tree Flowered, 1045
White Bird Flying, A, 1042
**Ness, Eliot**
Murder by the Numbers, 639
True Detective, 640
**Nevada**
Basque Hotel, The, 1051
Boulder Dam, 1050
Breakheart Pass, 1052
Comstock Lode, 265
Ghost Dance Messiah, 1048
Ox Bow Incident, 457
Shoshone Mike, 1049
**New Hampshire**
Boon Island, 52
Hue and Cry, 1057
Look to the Mountain, 14
Real Diary of a Real Boy, The, 1053
Second Growth, 1054
Separate Peace, A, 698
Sky Is Falling, The, 643
Town Burning, 1055
Whipple's Castle, 1056
**New Jersey**
Janice Meredith, 79
Look Away, 324
Ride into Morning, A, 98
Time Enough for Drums, 100
Trumpet to Arms, 91
**New Mexico**
Anything for Billy, 511
Apache, 243
Between Earth and Sky, 519
Billy the Kid, 467
Bless Me, Ultima, 1058
Blood Brother, 235
Ceremony, 795
Cross a Wide River, 1073

**New Mexico** (*continued*)
Dark Winter, 445
Death Comes for the Archbishop, 242
Eagle in the Sky, 1066
Far from Cibola, 1064
Fire on the Mountain, 760
Heart's Desire, 490
House Made of Dawn, 1067
In Time of Harvest, 1072
Lady from Toledo, The, 1061
Lady, The, 522
Land, The, 1074
Laughing Boy, 1065
Man Who Killed the Deer, The, 1075
Milagro Beanfield War, The, 1068
No Life for a Lady, 1062
Of Arms I Sing, 1059
People of the Valley, 1076
Red Sky at Morning, 1060
Riders to Cibola, 1078
Royal City, The, 1071
Sea of Grass, The, 1070
Spanish Bride, The, 1069
Time of the Gringo, 236
Turquoise Trail, The, 282
Wind Leaves No Shadow, The, 267
Wolf Song, 1063
Woman at Otowi Crossing, 1077
**New Orleans, Battle of, 1862**
Catherine, The, 355
**New York**
Age of Innocence, 429
Alienist, The, 1081
All This and Heaven Too, 165
And One for All, 838
Another World, 666
Arabian Jazz, 1079
Beautiful and the Damned, The, 601
Behind the Lines, 340
Big Freeze, The, 184
Billy Bathgate, 1083
Book of Daniel, 816
Boyds of Black River, The, 558
Canal Town, 136
Chosen, The, 1086
City Boy, 1089

Daddy Was a Numbers Runner, 664
Deerslayer, The, 18
Drowning Room, The, 47
Drums Along the Mohawk, 71
Dutchman, The, 43
East River, 1080
Eben Holden, 140
Fathers, 873
Firekeeper, The, 44
For Love of Two Eagles, 49
Fortunate Pilgrim, The, 538
Gathering of Pearls, 765
Gentleman's Agreement, 776
Go Tell It on the Mountain, 637
Golden Spur, The, 623
Great Gatsby, The, 602
Guns of Burgoyne, 88
Hazard of New Fortunes, A, 404
High Constable, The, 181
Home and Away, 772
In the Beginning, 1087
In the Time of the Wolves, 149
Inside, Outside, 854
Ironweed, 1085
Island Within, The, 409
Keeping the Good Light, 563
Kingsbridge Plot, The, 93
Last of the Mohicans, 19
Manitou's Daughter, 42
Measure of Time, 605
Midwife, The, 1082
Miracles, 173
Mrs. Parkington, 860
Northwest Passage, 10
Pathfinder, The, 20
Pay Day, 595
Pioneers, The, 158
Plot to Kill Jackie Robinson, The, 777
Quicksilver Pool, 375
Ragtime, 556
Rivington Street, 540
Safe Harbors, 791
Sarah Bishop, 94
Saratoga Trunk, 399
Scarlet Women, 389
Secret Road, 90

Seneca Falls Inheritance, 182
Sherwood Ring, 95
Sister Carrie, 396
Speak Softly, 383
Spoils of War, The, 401
Spy, The, 68
Step to the Music, 376
Tenderloin, 382
That Year of Our War, 696
Tomorrow Will Be Better, 628
Tree Grows in Brooklyn, A, 573
Union Square, 541
Washington Square, 177
Waterfront, 1088
Waterworks, The, 1084
Woman Who Fell from the Sky, The, 50
World's Fair, 646
You Can't Go Home Again, 685
**Nixon, Richard M.**
Atomic Candy, 808
China Card, The, 817
Inside, Outside, 854
**North Carolina**
Bennet's Welcome, 24
Cape Fear Rising, 402
Cormorant's Brood, 25
Fool's Errand, A, 426
Freedom Songs, 834
Holly, 695
Irregular Moon, An, 829
Letters from a Slave Girl, 179
Lusty Wind for Carolina, 26
Men of Albemarle, 27
Music from a Place Called Half Moon,
        790
Oldest Living Confederate Widow
        Tells All, The, 1090
Queen's Gift, The, 166
Raleigh's Eden, 75
Roanoke Hundred, 28
Scotswoman, The, 76
Sound the Jubilee, 334
Southern Exposure, A, 634
Tall Woman, The, 398
Thirteen Miles from Suncrest, 553
Toil of the Brave, 77
You Can't Go Home Again, 685
**North Dakota**
Bad Lands, 480

Beet Queen, The, 1093
Beyond the Bedroom Wall, 1096
Bingo Palace, 1094
Bones of Plenty, The, 656
Dakotas: At the Wind's Edge, 1091
Dakotas: The Endless Sky, 1092
Emigrants, The, 441
Grass Dancer, 900
Love Medicine, 865
Manifest Destiny, 469
Years, 1095
Yonnondio, 667
**Northwest Territory**
Bounty Lands, The, 217

**Oakley, Annie**
This Old Bill, 466
**Oglethorpe, James Edward**
Rascals Heaven, 59
**Ohio**
. . . And Ladies of the Club, 904
Bad Man Ballad, 110
Borning Room, The, 870
Bounty Lands, The, 217
Changelings, The, 796
Circuit Rider, The, 213
Fathers, 873
Fields, The, 223
Green Bay Tree, 1097
Industrial Valley, 1099
Light in the Forest, The, 48
Murder by the Numbers, 639
Quiet Shore, 1098
Shadow of the Long Knives, 117
Town, The, 224
Trees, The, 225
**Oil Workers and Oil Industry**
Black Gold, 1130
Fever in the Earth, 567
Mean Spirit, 609
Oil!, 626
Paloverde, 934
Texasville, 1137
**Oklahoma**
Cherokee Strip Fever, 1101
Children of the Dust, 451
Cimmaron, 868
Gone the Dreams and the Dancing, 496

**Oklahoma** (*continued*)
  Mean Spirit, 609
  Quanah Parker, 502
  White Man's Road, 450
**Old Northwest.** (*See* Northwest Territory)
**Onate, Juan de**
  Of Arms I Sing, 1059
**Oregon**
  Across the Shining Mountains, 302
  Children of the River, 812
  Earthbreakers, 295
  Honey in the Horn, 554
  Moontrap, 290
  Oregon Detour, 1103
  Sometimes a Great Notion, 784
  Timber, 1102
  To Build a Ship, 291
  Trask, 292
**Oregon Trail.** (*See* Overland Journeys)
**Oriskany, Battle of**
  Drums Along the Mohawk, 71
**Osceola**
  Light a Distant Fire, 199
  Warrior, The, 201
**Oswald, Lee Harvey**
  Flying in to Love, 846
  Libra, 813
**Overland Journeys**
  Bear Flag, The, 296
  Beyond the Divide, 266
  Blood Song, 281
  Covered Wagon, The, 259
  Land Is Bright, The, 238
  Mothers, The, 250
  On to Oregon, 273
  Turquoise Trail, The, 282
  Walking Up a Rainbow, 284
  Way West, The, 255
  When Lightning Strikes, 237

**Pacifists**
  And One for All, 838
  Come in from the Cold, 842
  Farewell to Arms, A, 591
  I Had Seen Castles, 691

  Linger, 828
  Long Time Passing, 826
**Paine, Thomas**
  Citizen Tom Paine, 73
**Pakistani Americans**
  American Brat, An, 843
**Paleontology**
  Bone Wars, The, 1039
**Parker, Cynthia Ann**
  Ride the Wind, 277
  Where the Broken Heart Still Beats, 271
**Parker, Isaac**
  Winding Stair, 499
**Parker, Quanah**
  Ride the Wind, 277
  Quanah Parker, 502
**Patton, George S., Jr.**
  Dear Ike, 728
**Pennsylvania**
  Answer As a Man, 550
  Balance Wheel, 1104
  Bloody Country, The, 1105
  Bread and Fire, 630
  Captains and the Kings, The, 861
  Chaneysville Incident, 142
  Citizen Tom Paine, 73
  Don't Ever Leave Me, 638
  Fabulous Fifty, The, 604
  Ferment, 663
  Financier, The, 394
  Finishing Becca, 97
  Heaven and Hell, 405
  Julie, 566
  Let the Band Play Dixie, 1109
  Light in the Forest, The, 48
  Linger, 828
  Mark's Own, 857
  Never Victorious, Never Defeated, 862
  North and South, 176
  One Red Rose Forever, 36
  Out of This Furnace, 858
  Patch Boys, The, 621
  Price of a Child, The, 147
  Proud and the Free, The, 74
  Redcoat, 69
  Remember the End, 1106

Richlands, The, 1107
Rolling Years, 1108
Scouts of the Valley, 115
Shades of the Wilderness, 310
Testimony of Two Men, 551
Valley of Decision, The, 864
**Perez, Albino**
Eagle in the Sky, 1066
**Pershing, John**
Once an Eagle, 898
Over There, 588
**Persian Gulf War, 1991**
Linger, 828
**Philippine Islands**
Empire, 428
Season for War, 503
**Piracy**
Red Rover, The, 21
**Pleasants, Henry**
Glory Enough for All, 365
**Pocahontas**
Pocahontas, 22
Serpent Never Sleeps, The, 45
Sot Weed Factor, The, 11
**Politics and Government—1492-1775**
Cormorant's Brood, 25
**Politics and Government—1776-1783**
Citizen Tom Paine, 73
Fifth of March, The, 96
Gilman of Redford, 70
Johnny Tremain, 78
My Thomas, 83
Those Who Love, 104
Traitor, The, 103
**Politics and Government—1783-1860**
Balisand, 174
Big Freeze, The, 184
Burr, 134
Conqueror, The, 139
Eagle and the Raven, The, 272
54-40 or Fight, 298
High Constable, The, 181
Immortal Wife, 132
Jefferson, 145
Jessie, 123
Kentucky Home, 193
Know Nothing, 200
Love Is a Wild Assault, 263

My Theodosia, 131
North and South, 176
President's Lady, The, 133
Queen's Gift, The, 166
Regulators, The, 162
Sally Hemmings, 152
**Politics and Government—1861-1865**
Freedom, 363
Lincoln, 374
Love and War, 342
**Politics and Government—1866-1899**
Come Winter, 494
Democracy, 381
1876, 427
Empire, 428
Playing the Mischief, 393
Tenderloin, 382
**Politics and Government—1900-1939**
All That Glitters, 660
All the King's Men, 682
Boston, 579
Grand Design, 647
Hollywood, 629
Murder by the Numbers, 639
Pay Day, 595
Revelry, 594
Sand Pebbles, The, 615
True Detective, 640
Ward Eight, 555
**Politics and Government—1939-1945**
Gods of War, 756
**Politics and Government—1946-1995**
Agents of Innocence, 825
Book of Daniel, 816
China Card, The, 817
Diamond's Compass, 831
Ethel, 789
Fire on the Mountain, 760
Home and Away, 772
I and My True Love, 787
Inside, Outside, 854
Jack Gance, 782
Lasso the Moon, 811
Linger, 828
Space, 833
Troubled Air, The, 793
Vida, 840
Way We Were, The, 786

**Politics and Government—Epic Novels**
Chiefs, 915
Five Smooth Stones, 866
Gentleman from Indiana, The, 976
Legacy, 894
Memorial Bridge, 863
Raintree County, 886
Tree of Liberty, 899
Washington, D.C., 911
**Politics and Government—Additional Titles**
Eagle in the Sky, 1066
Lady from Toledo, The, 1061
Land, The, 1074
Last Hurrah, The, 1011
Royal City, The, 1071
World Enough and Time, 1001
**Polk, James**
Before the Darkness Falls, 186
**Powell, Adam Clayton**
Daddy Was a Numbers Runner, 664
**Powell, Lewis**
Court for Owls, A, 305
**Prejudice.** (*See* Racism)
**Prisoners of War**
Andersonville, 347
Beloved Exiles, 749
Eagle and the Iron Cross, The, 707
Gods of War, 756
King Rat, 736
Last Mission, The, 726
Sea and Poison, The, 737
Summer of My German Soldier, 697
Whistle Punk, 704
**Prohibition**
Little Caesar, 597
True Detective, 640
Whiskey River, 534
**Pueblo Revolt of 1837**
Eagle in the Sky, 1066
**Pullman, George M.**
Dream Seekers, 412

**Quantrill, James**
While Angels Dance, 459

**Racism—1492-1775**
Sacred Hunger, 58
**Racism—1776-1783**
Bad Man Ballad, 110
**Racism—1783-1860**
Feast of All Saints, 194
President's Daughter, The, 151
Ramona, 299
**Racism—1861-1865**
Fragments of the Ark, 356
With Every Drop of Blood, 321
**Racism—1866-1899**
Cape Fear Rising, 402
Children of the Dust, 451
Season for War, 503
Sweetbitter, 472
**Racism—1900-1939**
Billy, 651
Color Purple, 681
Daddy Was a Numbers Runner, 664
Impresario, The, 564
Miss 4th of July, Goodbye, 562
Mississippi Chariot, 670
Native Son, 686
Place Called Sweet Shrub, A, 582
Roll of Thunder, Hear My Cry, 677
Star Fisher, The, 633
To Kill a Mockingbird, 661
Unplowed Sky, The, 632
West to Eden, 535
Youngblood, 536
**Racism—1939-1945**
And Then We Heard the Thunder, 751
Guard of Honor, 710
Road to Memphis, The, 708
Seven Six One, 715
**Racism—1946-1995**
Betsy Brown, 792
Ceremony, 795
Changelings, The, 796
Children Bob Moses Led, The, 822
Cry of Absence, 781
Face in My Mirror, The, 849
Gathering of Old Men, A, 818
Gentleman's Agreement, 776
Good Times Are Killing Me, The, 805

Entries 1-61: 1492-1775, Entries 62-122: 1776-1783, Entries 123-304: 1783-1860, Entries 305-380: 1861-1899, Entries 381-533: 1866-1899, Entries 534-688: 1900-1939, Entries 689-759: 1939-1945, Entries 760-855: 1945-1995, Entries 856-916: Epic Novels, Entries 917-1168: Additional Titles.

Hate Crime, The, 827
Heartbreak Hotel, 794
Invisible Man, 769
Irregular Moon, An, 829
Kim/Kimi, 779
Maude Martha, 764
Music from a Place Called Half Moon, 790
Nineteen Fifty Nine, 768
Plot to Kill Jackie Robinson, The, 777
Shadow of the Dragon, 819
Spite Fences, 785
Streets of Fire, 809
Talent Night, 839
Tobacco Sticks, 773
Tunes for Bears to Dance To, 767
Walk Through Fire, A, 766

**Racism—Epic Novels**
Autobiography of Miss Jane Pittman, The, 871
Band of Angels, 913
Chiefs, 915
David and Jonathan, 801
Five Smooth Stones, 866
Glory Field, The, 896
Jubilee, 912
Serpent's Gift, The, 884
Story of Deep Delight, A, 889
Texas, 895

**Racism—Additional Titles**
'Sippi, 1031
Arabian Jazz, 1079
Country of Strangers, A, 1148
In My Father's House, 1002
In the Fire of Spring, 949
Intruder in the Dust, 1030
Killing Mister Watson, 953
Lesson Before Dying, A, 1003
Lords of Discipline, The, 1110
Milagro Beanfield War, The, 1068
Montana 1948, 1040
Morning Glory Afternoon, 981
Riders to Cibola, 1078
Thin Men of Haddam, 1141
Time and Place, 1142
Wolf Whistle, 1032
Your Blues Ain't Like Mine, 963

**Radcliffe, Jenny**
Devil Water, 55

**Radicals and Radicalism**
Boston, 579
Pay Day, 595
Vida, 840

**Railroads**
Dragon's Gate, 533
Never Victorious, Never Defeated, 862
Thunder on the Plains, 239
U. P. Trail, The, 478

**Raleigh, Walter**
Roanoke Hundred, 28

**Rathbone, Clara**
Henry and Clara, 411

**Rathbone, Henry**
Henry and Clara, 411

**Reconstruction**
American Eden, 403
Charleston, 418
Fool's Errand, A, 426
Forge, The, 370
Heaven and Hell, 405
Legacy of Beulah Land, 390
Penhally, 874
Red Rock, 415
Sea Island Lady, 877
Store, The, 421
Vixens, The, 430

**Religion**
Answer As a Man, 550
Believers, The, 167
Beyond the Divide, 266
Children of God, 249
Circle of Gold, 997
Circuit Rider. The, 213
Courage of Captain Plum, 1016
Davita's Harp, 669
Death Comes for the Archbishop, 242
Elmer Gantry, 612
Fool of God, The, 156
Friendly Persuasion, The, 229
Giant Joshua, 287
Go Tell It on the Mountain, 637
Hawaii, 893
Lady from Toledo, The, 1061
Last Catholic in America, The, 970
Miracles, 173
Oldtown Folks, 203
Peculiar People, The, 210
Primrose Way, The, 38

**Religion** (*continued*)
Raccoon John Smith, 991
Spanish Bride, The, 1069
This Widowed Land, 31
Turkey Red, 987
Witnesses, 34
**Remington, Frederic**
Yellow, 410
**Revere, Paul**
Gilman of Redford, 70
Johnny Tremain, 78
Secret of Sarah Revere, The, 99
**Rhode Island**
Our Own Kind, 616
**Robinson, Jackie**
Plot to Kill Jackie Robinson, The, 777
**Rogers, Robert**
Northwest Passage, 10
**Roosevelt, Franklin Delano**
Dear Ike, 728
Gods of War, 756
Till the End of Time, 689
War and Remembrance, 692
Washington, D.C., 911
Winds of War, The, 693
**Roosevelt, Theodore**
Alienist, The, 1081
Empire, 428
Homeland, 406
Manifest Destiny, 469
1919, 586
Quanah Parker, 502
Remember Santiago, 408
Speak Softly, 383
**Rosenberg, Ethel**
Ethel, 789
**Rosenberg, Julius**
Ethel, 789
**Roussillon, Alice**
Alice of Old Vincennes, 122
**Russian Americans**
Dream Seekers, 412
Shukar Balan, 986

**Sacagawea**
Sacajawea, 135
Streams to the River, River to the Sea, 128
Tale of Valor, 125
Trail, 124
**Sacco, Nicola**
Boston, 579
Pay Day, 595
**Sailors.** (*See* Naval Personnel)
**Saint Clair, Arthur**
Proud and the Free, The, 74
**Santa Anna, Antonio Lopez de**
Eagle and the Raven, The, 272
Texan Scouts, 232
**Santa Fe Trail.** (*See* Overland Journeys)
**Sanutee**
Yemassee, The, 56
**Saratoga, Battle of**
Guns of Burgoyne, 88
**Sartwell, Jemima**
Not Without Peril, 137
**Schultz, Dutch**
Billy Bathgate, 1083
**Seminole War, 1835**
Light a Distant Fire, 199
Warrior, The, 201
**Seton, Elizabeth Ann**
Miracles, 173
**Seton, Margaret**
Margaret's Story, 901
**Seward, William H.**
Lincoln, 374
**Shays, Daniel**
Regulators, The, 162
**Shays' Rebellion**
Regulators, The, 162
**Sheridan, Philip H.**
Banners at Shenandoah, 319
Tree of Appomattox, 313
**Sherman, William Tecumseh**
Sherman's March, 315
**Shiloh, Battle of**
Guns of Shiloh, 307
Long Night, 354
Shiloh, 332

Entries 1-61: 1492-1775, Entries 62-122: 1776-1783, Entries 123-304: 1783-1860, Entries 305-380: 1861-1899, Entries 381-533: 1866-1899, Entries 534-688: 1900-1939, Entries 689-759: 1939-1945, Entries 760-855: 1945-1995, Entries 856-916: Epic Novels, Entries 917-1168: Additional Titles.

**Shippen, Peggy**
Finishing Becca, 97
Peggy, 65
**Ships and Shipping.** (*See also* Naval
History; Naval Personnel)
Blind Journey, 87
Boon Island, 52
Bride of a Thousand Cedars, 352
Clear for Action!, 337
French Admiral, The, 85
Gales of November, 1020
Good Shepherd, The, 720
High Water, 762
King's Coat, The, 86
Moby Dick, 126
Pilot, The, 67
Richard Carvel, 66
Sea Venture, The, 60
Ships Gone Missing, 1021
Stretch on the River, A, 763
To Build a Ship, 291
Two Years Before the Mast, 294
**Sickles, Daniel Edgar**
Let the Band Play Dixie, 1109
**Silsoose**
Apache Autumn, 908
**Slaves and Slavery**
Adventures of Huckleberry Finn, The,
153
Band of Angels, 913
Before the Darkness Falls, 186
Beloved, 413
Black Thunder, 141
Cezanne Pinto, 202
Chaneysville Incident, 142
Confessions of Nat Turner, The, 205
Cross a Wide River, 1073
Echo of Lions, 150
Family, 157
Grant's War, 345
I, Tituba, Black Witch of Salem, 17
Jubilee, 912
Legend of Storey County, The, 227
Letters from a Slave Girl, 179
Nightjohn, 185
President's Daughter, The, 151
Price of a Child, The, 147
Pudd'nhead Wilson, 155
Sacred Hunger, 58

Sally Hemmings, 152
Sapphira and the Slave Girl, 148
Sound the Jubilee, 334
Steal Away, 138
Story of Deep Delight, A, 889
Tituba of Salem Village, 46
Uncle Tom's Cabin, 204
Walks Without a Soul, 276
Wolf by the Ears, 197
**Smith, Jedediah**
Splendid Wayfaring, 127
**Smith, John (1580-1631)**
Sot Weed Factor, The, 11
**Smith, John (1784-1868)**
Raccoon John Smith, 991
**Smith, Joseph**
Children of God, 249

*Note: Novels of Social Life and Customs
that have a clear geographic setting are listed as Social Life and
Customs with the geographic
subdivision, e.g., Social Life and
Customs—Alaska. Others are
listed under Social Life and Customs with the time period as a
subdivision, e.g., Social Life and
Customs—1776-1783. See also
Women—Social Conditions*

**Social Life and Customs—1492-1776**
Remembrance Rock, 903
Strife Before Dawn, 905
**Social Life and Customs—1776-1783**
Remembrance Rock, 903
Strife Before Dawn, 905
**Social Life and Customs—1783-1860**
Adventures of Huckleberry Finn, The,
153
Historian, 872
President's Lady, The, 133
Remembrance Rock, 903
**Social Life and Customs—1861-1865**
Remembrance Rock, 903
**Social Life and Customs—1866-1899**
Both Sides of Time, 392
Historian, 872
If I Never Get Back, 388
No Bottom, 386
No Virtue, 387

**Social Life and Customs—1900-1939**
Babbitt, 611
Big Money, The, 600
Dragon's Teeth, 671
Elmer Gantry, 612
Executioner Waits, The, 608
Huge Season, The, 617
Hungry Men, 636
Kings in Disguise, 678
Least One, The, 645
Longest Road, The, 684
Mr. Bridge, 641
Mrs. Bridge, 642
Plastic Age, 613
**Social Life and Customs—Alabama**
American Eden, 403
Forge, The, 370
Foundation Stone, 206
Heartbreak Hotel, 794
Store, The, 421
To Kill a Mockingbird, 661
Train Whistle Guitar, 619
Unfinished Cathedral, The, 917
Walk Through Fire, A, 766
**Social Life and Customs—Alaska**
Big Rock Candy Mountain, 909
Inside Passage, The, 919
White Dawn, 491
**Social Life and Customs—Arizona**
Foxfire, 929
West to Eden, 535
**Social Life and Customs—Arkansas**
Architecture of the Arkansas Ozarks,
        The, 931
Big Doc's Girl, 932
Come Winter, 494
Hunter's Heart, 933
Idols and Axle-Grease, 652
Place Called Sweet Shrub, A, 582
Plum Thicket, The, 473
Weedy Rough, 658
**Social Life and Customs—California**
California Gold, 881
Californios, The, 939
Cannery Row, 672
East of Eden, 910

Ella Price's Journal, 806
Establishment, The, 771
Flower Drum Song, The, 941
Glitter and the Gold, The, 943
Hollywood, 629
How Far Would You Have Gotten If . . . ,
        775
Human Comedy, The, 706
Jesse, 845
Joy Luck Club, The, 944
Kim/Kimi, 779
Long Time Passing, 826
Lost and Found, 878
Lotus Land, 879
McTeague, 517
Melvin, Panther, 848
Oil!, 626
Ramona, 299
Rumors of Peace, 699
Time Too Swift, A, 703
Toward What Bright Glory?, 648
Wars of the Heart, 709
Way We Were, The, 786
**Social Life and Customs—Colorado**
American Brat, An, 843
Monte Walsh, 568
1933 Was a Bad Year, 650
No Reck'ning Made, 876
Tie That Binds, 946
**Social Life and Customs—Connecticut**
Bound Girl of Cobble Hill, 178
Tory Hole, 948
Wings of the Morning, The, 950
**Social Life and Customs—Florida**
Angel City, 955
Forever Island, 956
Hallapoosa, 954
Killing Mister Watson, 953
Margaret's Story, 901
Their Eyes Were Watching God, 952
To Have and Have Not, 951
**Social Life and Customs—Georgia**
Before the Darkness Falls, 186
Beloved Invader, The, 417
Chiefs, 915
Cold Sassy Tree, 548

Color Purple, 681
Distant Lands, The, 170
Gone with the Wind, 357
Legacy of Beulah Land, 390
Lighthouse, 187
New Moon Rising, 189
Savannah Purchase, 957
Savannah, 190
Spite Fences, 785
Stranger in Savannah, 360
To See Your Face Again, 191
Where Shadows Go, 192
Year the Lights Came On, The, 783
Youngblood, 536
**Social Life and Customs—Hawaii**
Hawaii Aloha, 958
Hawaii, 893
Let Us Go, 959
Wild Meat and the Bully Burgers, 855
**Social Life and Customs—Idaho**
Stump Ranch Pioneer, 960
**Social Life and Customs—Illinois**
Across Five Aprils, 341
American Tragedy, An, 557
Chosen Country, 965
Chute, The, 653
Dandelion Wine, 596
Dream Seekers, 412
Eighth Day, The, 972
Father and Son, 966
Folded Leaf, The, 614
Foundry, The, 606
Ghost Belonged to Me, The, 969
Grapple, The, 964
Graysons, The, 214
Impresario, The, 564
Jack Gance, 782
Jennie Gerhardt, 395
Jungle, The, 571
Last Catholic in America, The, 970
Lincoln Hunters, The, 971
Maude Martha, 764
No Promises in the Wind, 657
O Canaan!, 542
Old Bunch, The, 610
They Came Like Swallows, 967
Time Will Darken It, 968
Yonnondio, 667
Your Blues Ain't Like Mine, 963

**Social Life and Customs—Indiana**
For Us the Living, 220
Freckles, 575
Gentleman from Indiana, The, 976
Girl of the Limberlost, 576
Harvester, The, 577
Hoosier School-Boy, The, 215
Hoosier School-Master, The, 216
In God We Trust, 975
Laddie, 420
Magnificent Ambersons, The, 422
Pageant, 973
Penrod, 579
Raintree County, 886
**Social Life and Customs—Iowa**
Miss Bishop, 977
Our Changing Lives, 979
These Years of Promise, 978
This Rough New Land, 980
**Social Life and Customs—Japan**
East and West, 741
Occupation, 757
Unexpected Peace, The, 750
**Social Life and Customs—Kansas**
Learning Tree, The, 620
Morning Glory Afternoon, 981
Not Without Laughter, 561
Persian Pickle Club, The, 644
Prairie Widow, 434
Shukar Balan, 986
Story of a Country Town, The, 983
Unplowed Sky, The, 632
**Social Life and Customs—Kentucky**
Believers, The, 167
Bellsong for Sarah Raines, A, 990
Choices, 906
Dollmaker, The, 1013
Enduring Hills, 994
Feather Crowns, 998
For Us the Living, 220
Hardcastle, 688
Hie to the Hunters, 999
In Country, 832
Kentucky Home, 193
Night Rider, 581
Penhally, 874
Raccoon John Smith, 991
Rennie's Way, 627
Taps for Private Tussie, 1000

**Social Life and Customs—Kentucky**
  (*continued*)
  Tara's Healing, 995
  Trail of the Lonesome Pine, 993
  Uncle Tom's Cabin, 204
  World Enough and Time, 1001
**Social Life and Customs—Louisiana**
  Autobiography of Miss Jane Pittman,
    The, 871
  Bayou Road, 328
  Crescent City, 359
  Feast of All Saints, 194
  Five Smooth Stones, 866
  Foxes of Harrow, The, 207
  Gathering of Old Men, A, 818
  In My Father's House, 1002
  Lesson Before Dying, A, 1003
  New Orleans Legacy, 1004
  Papa La-Bas, 146
  Royal Street, 198
  Saratoga Trunk, 399
  Serpent and the Staff, The, 583
  Show Boat, 400
  This Side of Glory, 547
  Vixens, The, 430
  Walk on the Wild Side, A, 635
  Wild Is the River, 317
**Social Life and Customs—Maine**
  Colony, 1005
  Ebbing Tide, 701
  Jennie Glenroy, 183
  Lovely Ambition, The, 552
  Spoonhandle, 665
  Storm Tide, 702
  Tree by Leaf, 593
**Social Life and Customs—Maryland**
  Chesapeake, 892
  Katy of Catoctin, 373
  Lord's Oysters, The, 549
  Mary's Land, 53
  Miss Susie Slagle's, 580
  Swan's Chance, 161
  This Child's Gonna Live, 687
**Social Life and Customs—Massachusetts**
  Ann of the Wild Rose Inn, 62
  Atomic Candy, 808

Back Bay, 887
Blithedale Romance, The, 172
Broken Days, 195
Cape Cod, 888
David and Jonathan, 801
Devil and the Mathers, The, 23
Early Autumn, 1006
Green Desire, A, 897
Hate Crime, The, 827
Hester, 13
House of Seven Gables, The, 1008
Last Hurrah, The, 1011
Last Waltz, 431
Late George Apley, The, 1010
Massachusetts, 916
Nell's Quilt, 423
Oldtown Folks, 203
Peter Pan Bag, 830
Rise of Silas Lapham, The, 1009
Saturnalia, 1007
Scarlet Letter, The, 33
Secret of Sarah Revere, The, 99
Stitch in Time, A, 196
Tunes for Bears to Dance To, 767
Ward Eight, 555
Wedding, The, 802
Witnesses, 34
**Social Life and Customs—Michigan**
  Dollmaker, The, 1013
  Edsel, 770
  Farmer, 1018
  Gales of November, 1020
  Good Negress, The, 800
  Motor City, 1024
  Road to Wellville, The, 1014
  Ships Gone Missing, 1021
  Small Bequest, A, 1023
  Waiting for the News, 662
  Whiskey River, 534
**Social Life and Customs—Minnesota**
  Come in from the Cold, 842
  Emigrants, The, 1027
  Main Street, 537
  November of the Heart, 1029
  Unto a Good Land, 1028

Entries 1-61: 1492-1775, Entries 62-122: 1776-1783, Entries 123-304: 1783-1860, Entries 305-380: 1861-1899, Entries 381-533: 1866-1899, Entries 534-688: 1900-1939, Entries 689-759: 1939-1945, Entries 760-855: 1945-1995, Entries 856-916: Epic Novels, Entries 917-1168: Additional Titles.

**Social Life and Customs—Mississippi**
Absalom, Absalom!, 867
Billy, 651
Children Bob Moses Led, The, 822
Choices, 906
Delta Wedding, 631
Intruder in the Dust, 1030
Losing Battles, 683
Mississippi Chariot, 670
Road to Memphis, The, 708
Roll of Thunder, Hear My Cry, 677
'Sippi, 1031
So Red the Rose, 379
Wolf Whistle, 1032
**Social Life and Customs—Missouri**
Adventures of Tom Sawyer, The, 154
Betsy Brown, 792
Disinherited, The, 1033
King of the Hill, 655
Pudd'nhead Wilson, 155
Three Lives of Elizabeth, 130
**Social Life and Customs—Montana**
Montana 1948, 1040
Yellow Raft in Blue Water, A, 1037
**Social Life and Customs—Nebraska**
Ceremony in Lonetree, 1043
Home Place, The, 1046
Ma Jeeter's Girls, 1047
One of Ours, 585
Plains Song, 1044
Red Menace, 761
Spring Came On Forever, 856
Strange Angels, 803
White Bird Flying, A, 1042
**Social Life and Customs—Nevada**
Basque Hotel, The, 1051
Boulder Dam, 1050
Ghost Dance Messiah, 1048
Shoshone Mike, 1049
**Social Life and Customs—New Hampshire**
Hue and Cry, 1057
Real Diary of a Real Boy, The, 1053
Second Growth, 1054
Separate Peace, A, 698
Sky Is Falling, The, 643
Town Burning, 1055
Whipple's Castle, 1056

**Social Life and Customs—New Jersey**
Look Away, 324
Time Enough for Drums, 100
**Social Life and Customs—New Mexico**
Between Earth and Sky, 519
Bless Me, Ultima, 1058
Cross a Wide River, 1073
Far from Cibola, 1064
Fire on the Mountain, 760
House Made of Dawn, 1067
In Time of Harvest, 1072
Land, The, 1074
Man Who Killed the Deer, The, 1075
Milagro Beanfield War, The, 1068
People of the Valley, 1076
Red Sky at Morning, 1060
Riders to Cibola, 1078
Royal City, The, 1071
Spanish Bride, The, 1069
Time of the Gringo, 236
Woman at Otowi Crossing, 1077
**Social Life and Customs—New York**
Age of Innocence, 429
Alienist, The, 1081
All This and Heaven Too, 165
Another World, 666
Arabian Jazz, 1079
Beautiful and the Damned, The, 601
Behind the Lines, 340
Billy Bathgate, 1083
Book of Daniel, 816
Boyds of Black River, The, 558
Chosen, The, 1086
City Boy, 1089
Daddy Was a Numbers Runner, 664
Drowning Room, The, 47
Dutchman, The, 43
East River, 1080
Fathers, 873
Fortunate Pilgrim, The, 538
Gathering of Pearls, 765
Gentleman's Agreement, 776
Go Tell It on the Mountain, 637
Golden Spur, The, 623
Great Gatsby, The, 602
High Constable, The, 181
Home and Away, 772
In the Beginning, 1087
Inside, Outside, 854

**Social Life and Customs—New York**
(*continued*)
Ironweed, 1085
Keeping the Good Light, 563
Midwife, The, 1082
Mrs. Parkington, 860
Plot to Kill Jackie Robinson, The, 777
Quicksilver Pool, 375
Ragtime, 556
Rivington Street, 540
Safe Harbors, 791
Saratoga Trunk, 399
Scarlet Women, 389
Seneca Falls Inheritance, 182
Sister Carrie, 396
Speak Softly, 383
Spoils of War, The, 401
Step to the Music, 376
Tomorrow Will Be Better, 628
Tree Grows in Brooklyn, A, 573
Union Square, 541
Washington Square, 177
Waterfront, 1088
Waterworks, The, 1084
World's Fair, 646
You Can't Go Home Again, 685
**Social Life and Customs—North Carolina**
Cormorant's Brood, 25
Fool's Errand, A, 426
Freedom Songs, 834
Holly, 695
Irregular Moon, An, 829
Music from a Place Called Half Moon, 790
Oldest Living Confederate Widow Tells All, The, 1090
Queen's Gift, The, 166
Southern Exposure, A, 634
Tall Woman, The, 398
Thirteen Miles from Suncrest, 553
You Can't Go Home Again, 685
**Social Life and Customs—North Dakota**
Beet Queen, The, 1093
Beyond the Bedroom Wall, 1096

Bingo Palace, 1094
Bones of Plenty, The, 656
Years, 1095
Yonnondio, 667
**Social Life and Customs—Ohio**
. . . And Ladies of the Club, 904
Borning Room, The, 870
Changelings, The, 796
Circuit Rider, The, 213
Fathers, 873
Fields, The, 223
Green Bay Tree, 1097
Industrial Valley, 1099
Quiet Shore, 1098
Town, The, 224
**Social Life and Customs—Oklahoma**
Cimmaron, 868
**Social Life and Customs—Oregon**
Children of the River, 812
Honey in the Horn, 554
Oregon Detour, 1103
Sometimes a Great Notion, 784
Timber, 1102
**Social Life and Customs—Pennsylvania**
Answer As a Man, 550
Captains and the Kings, The, 861
Don't Ever Leave Me, 638
Ferment, 663
Heaven and Hell, 405
Julie, 566
Let the Band Play Dixie, 1109
Linger, 828
Mark's Own, 857
Never Victorious, Never Defeated, 862
One Red Rose Forever, 36
Out of This Furnace, 858
Patch Boys, The, 621
Price of a Child, The, 147
Remember the End, 1106
Richlands, The, 1107
Rolling Years, 1108
Testimony of Two Men, 551
Valley of Decision, The, 864
**Social Life and Customs—South Carolina**
Alice Flagg, 1111

Charleston, 418
Glory Field, The, 896
Hearts Divided, 380
Heaven and Hell, 405
Her Own Place, 705
Lords of Discipline, The, 1110
Sea Island Lady, 877
**Social Life and Customs—South
Dakota**
Golden Bowl, The, 1117
Leaving the Land, 799
Man Who Was Taller Than God, The,
1112
Skinny Angel, 1116
**Social Life and Customs—Tennessee**
Christy, 565
Cry of Absence, 781
Listen for Rachel, 348
Newfound, 1128
Original Sins, 1127
Story of Deep Delight, A, 889
Summons to Memphis, 1129
**Social Life and Customs—Texas**
Another Part of the House, 649
Black Gold, 1130
Fast Copy, 1135
Fever in the Earth, 567
Giant, 1132
Incorporation of Eric Chung, The, 1136
Lost and Found, 878
Ordways, The, 1134
Shadow of the Dragon, 819
Texas, 895
Texasville, 1137
Thin Men of Haddam, 1141
Time and Place, 1142
Wandering Star, 584
Whistle Punk, 704
**Social Life and Customs—Vermont**
Day No Pigs Would Die, A, 622
Part of the Sky, A, 668
**Social Life and Customs—Virginia**
Balisand, 174
Bugles Blow No More, 327
Country of Strangers, A, 1148
Fair and Tender Ladies, 1149
Fathers, 371
In My Father's House, 361
Last Silk Dress, 362

Nineteen Fifty Nine, 768
Red Rock, 415
Sally Hemmings, 152
Serpent Never Sleeps, The, 45
Steal Away, 138
Tidewater Dynasty, 902
Tobacco Sticks, 773
Traveller, 1147
Yankee Stranger, 372
**Social Life and Customs—Washington**
April and the Dragon Lady, 837
Good Times Are Killing Me, The, 805
Living, The, 1152
Talent Night, 839
Walk Gently This Good Earth, 1151
Winds of Morning, 599
**Social Life and Customs—Washington,
D.C.**
All That Glitters, 660
China Card, The, 817
Henry and Clara, 411
Hollywood, 629
I and My True Love, 787
Inside, Outside, 854
Jack Gance, 782
Memorial Bridge, 863
My Theodosia, 131
Refinements of Love, 391
Three Lives of Elizabeth, 130
Washington, D.C., 911
**Social Life and Customs—West
Virginia**
Barefoot Man, The, 1157
Family Fortune, 329
Killing Ground, 1159
Know Nothing, 200
Machine Dreams, 1158
Miss 4th of July, Goodbye, 562
Scapegoat, The, 569
Storming Heaven, 603
**Social Life and Customs—Wisconsin**
Empty Meadow, The, 1162
Fisherman's Beach, 1165
Glory from the Earth, A, 624
Land Remembers, The, 1163
Spring Harvest, 578
**Social Life and Customs—Wyoming**
Yonnondio, 667

Soldiers. (*See also* headings such as
    Military History; Naval Personnel;
    Aviators; etc.)
Soldiers—1776-1783
    April Morning, 72
    Arundel, 101
    Guns of Burgoyne, 88
    Israel Potter, 92
    Jordan Freeman Was My Friend, 106
    Oliver Wiswell, 102
    Phantom Fortress, 89
    Proud and the Free, The, 74
    Redcoat, 69
    Swamp Fox, Francis Marion, The, 80
    Trumpet to Arms, 91
Soldiers—1861-1865
    Banners at Shenandoah, 319
    Barefoot Brigade, 343
    Becca's Story, 333
    Bull Run, 331
    Company of Cowards, 364
    Copperhead, 322
    Fightin' with Forrest, 378
    Glory Enough for All, 365
    Hard Road to Gettysburg, 346
    Lincoln's Dreams, 377
    Little Shepherd of Kingdom Come, 335
    Long Night, 354
    Look Away, 324
    Perfect Tribute, 314
    Rebel, 323
    Red Badge of Courage, 325
    Rifles for Watie, 349
    Scarlet Patch, 353
    Shiloh, 332
    Slopes of War, 358
    Star of Gettysburg, 311
    Trail-Makers of the Middle Border, 336
    Wave, The, 366
    With Every Drop of Blood, 321
Soldiers—1866-1899
    Deserter Troop, The, 460
    Season for War, 503
Soldiers—1900-1939
    Desert of Wheat, 590
    Johnny Got His Gun, 592

1919, 586
Over There, 588
Three Soldiers, 587
Soldiers—1939-1945
    And Then We Heard the Thunder, 751
    Bell for Adano, A, 723
    Castle Keep, 719
    Commandos, The, 714
    End of It, The, 721
    From Here to Eternity, 747
    Gone to Soldiers, 690
    I Had Seen Castles, 691
    Midnight Clear, 733
    Naked and the Dead, The, 752
    Seven Six One, 715
    Stronger Than Fear, 732
    Thin Red Line, The, 748
    Till the End of Time, 689
    Unexpected Peace, The, 750
    Walk in the Sun, A, 716
    Whistle, 713
    Young Lions, The, 729
Soldiers—1946-1995
    American Boys, 844
    And One for All, 838
    Army Blue, 847
    Body Count, 824
    Fallen Angels, 836
    Fields of Fire, 850
    Gardens of Stone, 841
    In Country, 832
    Lionheads, The, 807
    Long March, The, 798
    MASH, 778
    Memorial, The, 804
    New Breed, The, 821
    Sword and Scalpel, 797
    Thirteenth Valley, The, 814
    Useless Servants, The, 774
    Word of Honor, 815
Soldiers—Epic Novels
    Raintree County, 886
    Once an Eagle, 898
    Woe to Live On, 988
Soldiers—Additional Titles
    Brothers in Arms, 1144

Entries 1-61: 1492-1775, Entries 62-122: 1776-1783, Entries 123-304: 1783-1860, Entries 305-380:
1861-1899, Entries 381-533: 1866-1899, Entries 534-688: 1900-1939, Entries 689-759: 1939-1945,
Entries 760-855: 1945-1995, Entries 856-916: Epic Novels, Entries 917-1168: Additional Titles.

Green Mountain Hero, 1145
Lords of Discipline, The, 1110
Oldest Living Confederate Widow Tells
    All, The, 1090
Traveller, 1147
**South Carolina**
Alice Flagg, 1111
Charleston, 418
Glory Field, The, 896
Hearts Divided, 380
Heaven and Hell, 405
Her Own Place, 705
Lords of Discipline, The, 1110
North and South, 176
Phantom Fortress, 89
Sea Island Lady, 877
Swamp Fox, Francis Marion, The, 80
Yemassee, The, 56
**South Dakota**
Bugles in the Afternoon, 484
Claim Jumpers, The, 1125
Conquest, 1120
Creek Called Wounded Knee, A, 495
Dakota Scouts, 463
Deadwood, 1115
Eyes of Darkness, The, 488
Forgiving, 1126
Free Land, 506
Giants in the Earth, 523
Golden Bowl, The, 1117
Homesteader, The, 1121
In the Center of the Nation, 1124
King of Spades, 1118
Last Stand, The, 492
Leaving the Land, 799
Let the Hurricane Roar, 507
Life's Lure, 1123
Little Big Man, 437
Little Norsk, or Old Pap's Flaxen, A, 470
Main Travelled Roads, 471
Man Who Was Taller Than God, The,
    1112
No Survivors, 487
Only Earth and Sky Last Forever, 1113
Peder Victorious, 524
Scarlet Plume, 1119
Skinny Angel, 1116
Stone Song, 440
Waterlily, 1114

Wind from Nowhere, The, 1122
**Space Program**
Space, 833
**Spanish American War, 1898**
Empire, 428
Ever After, 424
Homeland, 406
Remember Santiago, 408
Yellow, 410
**Spanish Civil War.** (*See* International
    Brigade)
**Spies.** (*See* Espionage)
**St. Denis, Juchereau de**
Soldier of Good Fortune, 3
**Stagg, Alonzo**
Let the Band Play Dixie, 1109
**Stanford, Leland**
California Gold, 881
Streets of Laredo, 514
**Stanton, Elizabeth Cady**
Seneca Falls Inheritance, 182
**Steel Industry and Trade**
Bread and Fire, 630
Julie, 566
Valley of Decision, The, 864
**Stiegel, Henry William**
One Red Rose Forever, 36
**Story, Ann**
Green Mountain Hero, 1145
**Story, Solomon**
Green Mountain Hero, 1145
**Stuart, J. E. B.**
Farewell, My General, 367

**Tanner, John**
White Indian Boy, 1025
**Tecumseh**
Loon Feather, 218
Panther in the Sky, 228
**Telegraph**
Western Union, 171
**Tennessee**
Christy, 565
Cry of Absence, 781
Guns of Shiloh, 307
Listen for Rachel, 348
Newfound, 1128
Original Sins, 1127

**Tennessee** (*continued*)
President's Lady, The, 133
Raven's Bride, The, 246
Southern Woman, 330
Story of Deep Delight, A, 889
Summons to Memphis, 1129
**Texas**
Another Part of the House, 649
Black Gold, 1130
Canyons, 520
Day the Cowboys Quit, The, 500
Dead Man's Walk, 270
Divine Average, 262
Eagle and the Raven, The, 272
Edge of Time, The, 464
Empire in the Dust, 479
Empire of Bones, 268
Fast Copy, 1135
Fever in the Earth, 567
Flying in to Love, 846
Giant, 1132
Gone to Texas, 452
House Divided, 338
Incorporation of Eric Chung, The, 1136
Indio, 7
Lily, 442
Lonesome Dove, 513
Look to the River, 1138
Looking After Lily, 443
Lost and Found, 878
Love Is a Wild Assault, 263
North to Yesterday, 1133
Old Yeller, 474
Ordways, The, 1134
Pistoleer, The, 438
Promised Land, 245
Ride the Wind, 277
Road to San Jacinto, The, 1131
Rockspring, 286
Sam Bass, 532
Sam Chance, 448
Sam Houston Story, The, 275
Searchers, The, 509
Shadow of the Dragon, 819
Sons of Texas, 248
Spanish Gold, 1139

Star of Empire, 278
Streets of Laredo, 514
Sweetbitter, 472
Texan Scouts, 232
Texan Star, 233
Texan Triumph, 234
Texas, 895
Texasville, 1137
Thin Men of Haddam, 1141
Time and Place, 1142
True Women, 914
Walk in My Soul, 1140
Walks Without a Soul, 276
Wandering Star, 584
Where the Broken Heart Still Beats, 271
Whistle Punk, 704
Wonderful Country, The, 508
**Tituba**
I, Tituba, Black Witch of Salem, 17
Tituba of Salem Village, 46
**Tobacco Industry and Trade**
Night Rider, 581
**Townsend, Robert**
Secret Road, 90
**Trail of Tears.** (*See* Indians of North America—Cherokee)
**Trask, Elbridge**
Trask, 292
**Trenton, Battle of**
Trumpet to Arms, 91
**Tules, Maria**
Wind Leaves No Shadow, The, 267
**Turner, Nat**
Confessions of Nat Turner, The, 205
**Turner's Rebellion**
Confessions of Nat Turner, The, 205
**Tyler, John**
Before the Darkness Falls, 186
54-40 or Fight, 298

**Underground Railroad**
Cezanne Pinto, 202
Chaneysville Incident, 142
Peculiar People, The, 210
Vandemark's Folly, 222

Entries 1-61: 1492-1775, Entries 62-122: 1776-1783, Entries 123-304: 1783-1860, Entries 305-380: 1861-1899, Entries 381-533: 1866-1899, Entries 534-688: 1900-1939, Entries 689-759: 1939-1945, Entries 760-855: 1945-1995, Entries 856-916: Epic Novels, Entries 917-1168: Additional Titles.

**Utah**
Alias Butch Cassidy, 485
Ben Cooper, U.S. Marshal, 1143
Children of God, 249
Giant Joshua, 287
Powderkeg, 253
Riders of the Purple Sage, 477

**Vanzetti, Bartolomeo**
Boston, 579
Pay Day, 595
**Vermont**
Brothers in Arms, 1144
Calico Captive, 1146
Day No Pigs Would Die, A, 622
Green Mountain Hero, 1145
Not Without Peril, 137
Part of the Sky, A, 668
**Vicksburg, Battle of**
Rock of Chickamauga, 308
Tamarack Tree, 320
**Vietnamese Americans**
Face in My Mirror, The, 849
Shadow of the Dragon, 819
**Vietnam War**
American Boys, 844
And One for All, 838
Army Blue, 847
Aviators, The, 820
Body Count, 824
Come in from the Cold, 842
Fallen Angels, 836
Fields of Fire, 850
Finding Moon, 823
Flight of the Intruder, 810
Gardens of Stone, 841
In Country, 832
Lionheads, The, 807
Long Time Passing, 826
Memorial Bridge, 863
Memorial, The, 804
Road Home, The, 852
Sense of Honor, A, 851
Thirteenth Valley, The, 814
Word of Honor, 815
**Villa, Francisco (Pancho)**
Cutting Stone, 926

**Virginia**
Balisand, 174
Betty Zane, 82
Black Thunder, 141
Bugles Blow No More, 327
Confessions of Nat Turner, The, 205
Country of Strangers, A, 1148
Dawn's Early Light, 105
Devil Water, 55
Durable Fire, A, 12
Ever After, 424
Fair and Tender Ladies, 1149
Fathers, 371
In My Father's House, 361
Last Silk Dress, 362
My Thomas, 83
Never No More, 54
Nineteen Fifty Nine, 768
Pocahontas, 22
President's Daughter, The, 151
Red Rock, 415
Sally Hemmings, 152
Sapphira and the Slave Girl, 148
Scouts of Stonewall, 309
Serpent Never Sleeps, The, 45
Shades of the Wilderness, 310
Steal Away, 138
Tidewater Dynasty, 902
To Have and To Hold, 35
To the Far Blue Mountains, 40
Tobacco Sticks, 773
Traveller, 1147
Wolf by the Ears, 197
Yankee Stranger, 372
**Von Braun, Werner**
Space, 833

**War of 1812**
Bright Journey, 211
Captain Caution, 129
Clear for Action!, 337
Dolley, 144
Savannah, 190
**Washington**
April and the Dragon Lady, 837
Bridge of the Gods, 1150
Good Times Are Killing Me, The, 805
Living, The, 1152

**Washington** (*continued*)
Many Horses, 1156
Mighty Mountain, 293
Sweetbriar, 1153
Sweetbriar Bride, 1154
Sweetbriar Spring, 1155
Swift Flows the River, 301
Talent Night, 839
Walk Gently This Good Earth, 1151
Winds of Morning, 599
**Washington, D.C.**
All That Glitters, 660
Burr, 134
China Card, The, 817
Democracy, 381
Dolley, 144
1876, 427
Empire, 428
Gods of War, 756
Henry and Clara, 411
Hollywood, 629
I and My True Love, 787
Inside, Outside, 854
Jack Gance, 782
Lincoln, 374
Memorial Bridge, 863
My Theodosia, 131
New Breed, The, 821
Refinements of Love, 391
Revelry, 594
Three Lives of Elizabeth, 130
Washington, D.C., 911
**Washington, George**
Conqueror, The, 139
Janice Meredith, 79
Kingsbridge Plot, The, 93
**WASP.** (*See* Women Airforce Service Pilots)
**Water Supply**
Big Freeze, The, 184
Boulder Dam, 1050
Milagro Beanfield War, The, 1068
People of the Valley, 1076
**Watie, Stand**
Rifles for Watie, 349

**Watson, Edgar J.**
Killing Mister Watson, 953
**Wayne, Anthony**
Ride into Morning, A, 98
**Weaver, Buck**
Hoopla, 574
**West Virginia**
Barefoot Man, The, 1157
Family Fortune, 329
Fool of God, The, 156
Killing Ground, 1159
Know Nothing, 200
Machine Dreams, 1158
Miss 4th of July, Goodbye, 562
Scapegoat, The, 569
Star Fisher, The, 633
Storming Heaven, 603
**Wick, Tempe**
Ride into Morning, A, 98
**Wilkinson, James**
Land Beyond the Mountains, 168
**Wilson, Woodrow**
Hollywood, 629
**Winthrop, Elizabeth**
Winthrop Woman, The, 1012
**Wisconsin**
Bright Journey, 211
Come and Get It, 1161
Empty Meadow, The, 1162
Enemies, 1164
Fisherman's Beach, 1165
Glory from the Earth, A, 624
Hills Stand Watch, 212
Land Remembers, The, 1163
Landlooker, The, 419
Main Travelled Roads, 471
Spring Harvest, 578
Tomorrow Is a River, 1160
Trail-Makers of the Middle Border, 336
**Witchcraft**
Beyond the Burning Time, 41
Break with Charity, A, 51
Devil and the Mathers, The, 23
I, Tituba, Black Witch of Salem, 17
Mirror for Witches, A, 30

Tituba of Salem Village, 46
Witches' Children, 15
**Women Airforce Service Pilots (WASP)**
Silver Wings, Santiago Blue, 711
**Women—Biography**
Alice Flagg, 1111
Alice of Old Vincennes, 122
All This and Heaven Too, 165
Devil Water, 55
Finishing Becca, 97
Follow the River, 57
Hawaii Aloha, 958
I Am Regina, 37
I, Tituba, Black Witch of Salem, 17
Immortal Wife, 132
Jessie, 123
Love Is a Wild Assault, 263
Love Is Eternal, 369
Margaret's Story, 901
Miracles, 173
My Theodosia, 131
My Thomas, 83
Never No More, 54
Not Without Peril, 137
Peggy, 65
Pocahontas, 22
President's Daughter, The, 151
President's Lady, The, 133
Refinements of Love, 391
Ride into Morning, A, 98
Ride the Wind, 277
Sacajawea, 135
Sally Hemmings, 152
Sarah Bishop, 94
Scotswoman, The, 76
Those Who Love, 104
Three Lives of Elizabeth, 130
Tituba of Salem Village, 46
Turquoise Trail, The, 282
Where the Broken Heart Still Beats, 271
Winthrop Woman, The, 1012
Witnesses, 34
Wolf by the Ears, 197
**Women Indians of North America.**
(*See* Indians of North America)
**Women Slaves.** (*See* Slaves and Slavery)

**Women—Social Conditions**
True Women, 914
**Women—Social Conditions—1492-1775**
Beyond the Burning Time, 41
Break with Charity, A, 51
Cormorant's Brood, 25
Durable Fire, A, 12
Girl in Buckskin, 32
Hester, 13
Mirror for Witches, A, 30
Primrose Way, The, 38
Scarlet Letter, The, 33
To Have and To Hold, 35
Winthrop Woman, The, 1012
**Women—Social Conditions—1776-1783**
Great Meadow, 121
**Women—Social Conditions—1783-1860**
Ashana, 303
Clock, The, 947
Diana Stair, 163
Giant Joshua, 287
Kentucky Home, 193
Miracles, 173
Pacific Street, 297
Price of a Child, The, 147
Rockspring, 286
Sapphira and the Slave Girl, 148
Savanna, 930
Seneca Falls Inheritance, 182
Steal Away, 138
Wings of the Morning, The, 950
**Women—Social Conditions—1861-1865**
Crescent City, 359
Handsome Road, 316
Hearts Divided, 380
High Hearts, 318
House Divided, 338
Southern Woman, 330
**Women—Social Conditions—1866-1899**
Between Earth and Sky, 519
Bostonians, The, 407
Both Sides of Time, 392
Cherokee Trail, The, 504
Forgiving, 1126
Heart of the West, 531
Homeland, 406
Last Waltz, 431
Nell's Quilt, 423

**Women—Social Conditions—1866-1899**
(*continued*)
Night of Shadows, 475
Refinements of Love, 391
Rivers of Gold, 462
Season for War, 503
Tall Woman, The, 398
These Years of Promise, 978
**Women—Social Conditions—1900-1939**
Daughters of the New World, 907
Davita's Harp, 669
Plains Song, 1044
Rivington Street, 540
Their Eyes Were Watching God, 952
Tie That Binds, 946
Union Square, 541
**Women—Social Conditions—1939-1945**
Her Own Place, 705
Silver Wings, Santiago Blue, 711
**Women—Social Conditions—1946-1995**
Daughters of the New World, 907

Ella Price's Journal, 806
Scuttlebutt, 853
Yellow Raft in Blue Water, A, 1037
**Wyeth, Nathaniel J.**
Across the Shining Mountains, 302
**Wyoming**
Bendigo Shafter, 1167
Grassman, The, 468
I, Tom Horn, 1166
Riders of Judgment, 1168
Shane, 527
Yonnondio, 667

**Yemassee War**
Yemassee, The, 56
**Yorktown, Battle of**
Blind Journey, 87
**Young, Brigham**
Children of God, 249
Powderkeg, 253